T0213655

Communications
in Computer and Information Science 755

Commenced Publication in 2007
Founding and Former Series Editors:
Alfredo Cuzzocrea, Xiaoyong Du, Orhun Kara, Ting Liu, Dominik Ślęzak,
and Xiaokang Yang

More information about this series at http://www.springer.com/series/7899

Emmanouel Garoufallou · Sirje Virkus
Rania Siatri · Damiana Koutsomiha (Eds.)

Metadata and Semantic Research

11th International Conference, MTSR 2017
Tallinn, Estonia, November 28 – December 1, 2017
Proceedings

 Springer

Editors

Emmanouel Garoufallou
Department of Library Science
  and Information Systems
Alexander Technological Educational
  Institute of Thessaloniki
Macedonia
Greece

Rania Siatri
Department of Library Science
  and Information Systems
Alexander Technological Educational
  Institute of Thessaloniki
Macedonia
Greece

Sirje Virkus
School of Digital Technologies
Tallinn University
Tallinn
Estonia

Damiana Koutsomiha
American Farm School
Thessanloniki
Greece

ISSN 1865-0929   ISSN 1865-0937   (electronic)
Communications in Computer and Information Science
ISBN 978-3-319-70862-1   ISBN 978-3-319-70863-8   (eBook)
https://doi.org/10.1007/978-3-319-70863-8

Library of Congress Control Number: 2017959601

Printed on acid-free paper

This Springer imprint is published by Springer Nature
The registered company is Springer International Publishing AG
The registered company address is: Gewerbestrasse 11, 6330 Cham, Switzerland

Preface

Since 2005, the International Metadata and Semantics Research Conference (MTSR) has served as a significant venue for the dissemination and sharing of metadata and semantic-driven research and practices. This year, 2017, marked the 11th MTSR, drawing scholars, researchers and practitioners who are investigating and advancing our knowledge on a wide range of metadata and semantic-driven topics. The 11th International Conference on Metadata and Semantics Research (MTSR 2017) was held at Tallinn University (Estonia) from November 28 to December 1, 2017.

Metadata and semantics are integral to any information system and important to the sphere of Web data. Research and development addressing metadata and semantics is crucial to advancing how we effectively discover, use, archive, and repurpose information. In response to this need, researchers are actively examining methods for generating, reusing, and interchanging metadata. Integrated with these developments is research on the application of computational methods, linked data, and data analytics. A growing body of literature also targets conceptual and theoretical designs providing foundational frameworks for metadata and semantic applications. There is no doubt that metadata weaves its way through nearly every aspect of our information ecosystem, and there is great motivation for advancing the current state of understanding in the fields of metadata and semantics. To this end, it is vital that scholars and practitioners convene and share their work.

MTSR 2017 focused on an emerging theme of "Internet of Things (IoT) in Library and Information Science Research" and the practical implementation of ontologies and linked data in various applications. The conference focuses on: theoretical and foundational principles of metadata, ontologies and information organization; the emergence and application of the Internet of Things (IoT) in libraries and cultural heritage institutions (such as RFID technologies, smart libraries, and virtual museums); the applications of linked data, open data, big data and user-generated metadata; digital interconnectedness – the what, why, and how of linked open data and the Semantic Web; metadata standardization, authority control, and interoperability in digital libraries and research data repositories; emerging issues in RDF, OWL, SKOS, schema. org, BIBFRAME, metadata and ontology design; linked data applications for e-books, digital publishing, and content management systems (CMSs); content discovery services, search, information retrieval, and data visualization applications.

MTSR conferences have grown in number of participants and paper submission rates over the last decade, marking it as a leading, international research conference. Continuing in the successful legacy of previous MTSR conferences (MTSR 2005, MTSR 2007, MTSR 2009, MTSR 2010, MTSR 2011, MTSR 2012, MTSR 2013, MTSR 2014, MTSR 2015, and MTSR 2016), MTSR 2017 brought together scholars and practitioners who share a common interest in the interdisciplinary field of metadata, linked data, and ontologies.

The MTSR 2017 program and the following proceedings show the rich diversity of research and practices from metadata and semantically focused tools and technologies, linked data, cross language semantics, ontologies, metadata models, semantic systems, and metadata standards. The general session of the conference included nine papers covering a broad spectrum of topics, proving the interdisciplinary view of metadata. Metadata as a research topic is maturing, and the conference supported the following seven tracks: Digital Libraries, Information Retrieval, Big, Linked, Social, and Open Data; Metadata and Semantics for Cultural Collections and Applications; Track on European and National Projects; Metadata and Semantics for Open Repositories, Research Information Systems and Data Infrastructures; Track on Digital Humanities and Digital Curation; Metadata and Semantics for Agriculture, Food, and Environment; Track on Knowledge IT Artifacts in Professional Communities and Aggregations. Each of these tracks had a rich selection of short and full research papers, in total 22, giving broader diversity to MTSR, and enabling deeper exploration of significant topics.

All the papers underwent a thorough and rigorous peer-review process. The review and selection for this year were highly competitive and only papers containing significant research results, innovative methods, or novel and best practices were accepted for publication. From the general session, only five submissions were accepted as full research papers, representing 33.3% of the total number of submissions, and four as short papers. An additional 13 contributions from tracks covering noteworthy and important results were accepted as full research papers representing 30.2% of the total number of submissions, and nine as short papers, making up 31 contributions for this year's MTSR conference. The acceptance rate of full research papers for both the general session and tracks was 31% of the total number of submissions.

Tallinn University is the third largest public university in Estonia, focusing primarily on the fields of humanities and the social and natural sciences. In its activities, the university adheres to the following basic values: openness, quality, professionalism, and unity. The study area of information sciences of the School of Digital Technologies is the co-organizer of the MTSR 2017. The School of Digital Technologies aims to integrate the study areas of digital learning ecosystems, information sciences, human–computer interaction, mathematics and didactics of mathematics, and applied informatics in order to develop interdisciplinary competencies related to the digital information and learning environment and information and digital competencies.

This year the MTSR conference was pleased to host one remarkable keynote presentation by Dr. Trond Aalberg, Associate Professor in the Department of Computer Science, Data and Artificial Intelligence Group at NTNU (Norwegian University of Science and Technology). In his presentation "The Path Toward Bibliographic Ontologies and Linked Data," Professor Aalberg shared his extensive experience and insights about the various models of bibliographic data, transformation of existing data, quality issues, reuse, and use of such data in search systems.

We conclude this preface by thanking the many people who contributed their time and efforts to MTSR 2017 and made this year's conference possible. We also thank all the organizations that supported this conference. We extend a sincere gratitude to members of the Program Committees of both main and special tracks, the Steering Committee, and the Organizing Committees (both general and local), and the conference reviewers who invested their time generously to ensure the timely review of the submitted manuscripts. A special thanks to Program Chair Dr. Getaneh Alemu from Southampton Solent University, UK; to Anxhela Dani and Pirje Jürgens for supporting us throughout this event and to Iro Sotiriadou and Anxhela Dani, who assisted us with the preparation of proceedings; and to Stavroula, Nikoleta, and Vasiliki for their endless support and patience. Our thanks go to all participants of MTSR 2017 for making the event a great success.

September 2017   Emmanouel Garoufallou
                                                        Sirje Virkus
                                                        Rania Siatri
                                                  Damiana Koutsomiha

Organization

General Chairs

Emmanouel Garoufallou   Alexander Technological Educational Institute
     (ATEI) of Thessaloniki, Greece
Sirje Virkus   Tallinn University, Estonia

Program Chair

Getaneh Alemu   Southampton Solent University, UK

Special Track Chairs

Ernesto William De Luca   Georg Eckert Institute – Leibniz Institute
     for International Textbook Research, Germany
Paolo Bianchini   Università degli Studi di Torino, Italy
Miguel-Ángel Sicilia   University of Alcalá, Spain
Armando Stellato   University of Rome Tor Vergata, Italy
Juliette Dibie   AgroParisTech and INRA, France
Liliana Ibanescu   AgroParisTech and INRA, France
Michalis Sfakakis   Ionian University, Greece
Lina Bountouri   Ionian University and EU Publications Office,
     Luxembourg
Emmanouel Garoufallou   Alexander Technological Educational Institute
     (ATEI) of Thessaloniki, Greece
Sirje Virkus   Tallinn University, Estonia
R.J. Hartley   Manchester Metropolitan University, UK
Rania Siatri   Alexander Technological Educational Institute
     (ATEI) of Thessaloniki, Greece
Stavroula Antonopoulou   Perrotis College, Greece
Georgia Zafeiriou   University of Macedonia, Greece
Fabio Sartori   University of Milano-Bicocca, Italy
Angela Locoro   University of Milano-Bicocca, Italy
Arlindo Flavio da Conceição   Federal University of São Paulo (UNIFESP), Brazil

Steering Committee

Juan Manuel Dodero   University of Cádiz, Spain
Emmanouel Garoufallou   Alexander Technological Educational Institute
     (ATEI) of Thessaloniki, Greece

Nikos Manouselis	AgroKnow, Greece
Fabio Sartori	University of Milano-Bicocca, Italy
Miguel-Ángel Sicilia	University of Alcalá, Spain

Organizing Committee

Aile Möldre	Tallinn University, Estonia
Elviine Uverskaja	Tallinn University, Estonia
Silvi Metsar	Tallinn University, Estonia
Sigrid Mandre	Tallinn University, Estonia
Sirli Peda	Tallinn University, Estonia
Hans Põldoja	Tallinn University, Estonia
Pirje Jürgens	Tallinn University, Estonia
Damiana Koutsomiha	American Farm School, Greece
Anxhela Dani	Alexander Technological Educational Institute (ATEI) of Thessaloniki, Greece
Chrysanthi Chatzopoulou	Alexander Technological Educational Institute (ATEI) of Thessaloniki, Greece
Iro Sotiriadou	American Farm School, Greece
Panorea Gaitanou	Ionian University, Greece
Ioanna Andreou	Hellenic-American Educational Foundation, Greece

Technical Support Staff

Ilias Nitsos	Alexander Technological Educational Institute (ATEI) of Thessaloniki, Greece

Program Committee

Rajendra Akerkar	Western Norway Research Institute, Norway
Arif Altun	Hacettepe University, Turkey
Ioannis N. Athanasiadis	Democritus University of Thrace, Greece
Panos Balatsoukas	University of Manchester, UK
Tomaz Bartol	University of Ljubljana, Slovenia
Ina Bluemel	German National Library of Science and Technology TIBm, Germany
Derek Bousfield	Manchester Metropolitan University, UK
Gerhard Budin	University of Vienna, Austria
Özgü Can	Ege University, Turkey
Caterina Caracciolo	Food and Agriculture Organization (FAO) of the United Nations, Italy
Christian Cechinel	Federal University of Pampa, Brazil
Artem Chebotko	University of Texas - Pan American, USA
Philip Cimiano	Bielefeld University, Germany
Sissi Closs	Karlsruhe University of Applied Sciences, Germany
Ricardo Colomo-Palacios	Universidad Carlos III, Spain

Rania Siatri	Alexander Technological Educational Institute (ATEI) of Thessaloniki, Greece
Miguel-Ángel Sicilia	University of Alcalá, Spain
Armando Stellato	University of Rome Tor Vergata, Italy
Imma Subirats	Food and Agriculture Organization (FAO) of the United Nations, Italy
Shigeo Sugimoto	University of Tsukuba, Japan
Stefaan Ternier	Open University of the Netherlands, The Netherlands
Giannis Tsakonas	University of Patras, Greece
Andrea Turbati	University of Rome Tor Vergata, Italy
Fabio Massimo Zanzotto	University of Rome Tor Vergata, Italy
Thomas Zschocke	World Agroforestry Centre (ICRAF), Kenya

Track on Digital Libraries, Information Retrieval, Big, Linked, Social, and Open Data

Special Track Chairs

Emmanouel Garoufallou	Alexander Technological Educational Institute (ATEI) of Thessaloniki, Greece
Rania Siatri	Alexander Technological Educational Institute (ATEI) of Thessaloniki, Greece
Sirje Virkus	Tallinn University, Estonia

Program Committee

Panos Balatsoukas	University of Manchester, UK
Özgü Can	Ege University, Turkey
Sissi Closs	Karlsruhe University of Applied Sciences, Germany
Mike Conway	University of North Carolina at Chapel Hill, USA
Phil Couch	University of Manchester, UK
Milena Dobreva	University of Malta, Malta
Ali Emrouznejad	Aston University, UK
Panorea Gaitanou	Ionian University, Greece
Jane Greenberg	Drexel University, USA
Jill Griffiths	Manchester Metropolitan University, UK
R.J. Hartley	Manchester Metropolitan University, UK
Nikos Korfiatis	University of East Anglia, UK
Rebecca Koskela	University of New Mexico, USA
Valentini Moniarou-Papaconstantinou	Technological Educational Institute of Athens, Greece
Dimitris Rousidis	University of Alcalá, Spain
Athena Salaba	Kent State University, USA

Rania Siatri   Alexander Technological Educational Institute
                                   (ATEI) of Thessaloniki, Greece
Miguel-Ángel Sicilia   University of Alcalá, Spain
Christine Urquhart   Aberystwyth University, UK
Evgenia Vassilakaki   Technological Educational Institute of Athens,
                                   Greece
Sirje Virkus   Tallinn University, Estonia
Georgia Zafeiriou   University of Macedonia, Greece

Track on Metadata and Semantics for Cultural Collections and Applications

Special Track Chairs

Michalis Sfakakis   Ionian University, Greece
Lina Bountouri   Ionian University, Greece and EU Publications
                                   Office, Luxembourg

Program Committee

Trond Aalberg   Norwegian University of Science and Technology
                                   (NTNU), Norway
Karin Bredenberg   The National Archives of Sweden, Sweden
Enrico Francesconi   EU Publications Office, Luxembourg,
                                   and Consiglio Nazionale delle Ricerche,
                                   Firenze, Italy
Manolis Gergatsoulis   Ionian University, Greece
Antoine Isaac   Vrije Universiteit Amsterdam, The Netherlands
Sarantos Kapidakis   Ionian University, Greece
Peter McKinney   National Library of New Zealand, New Zealand
Christos Papatheodorou   Ionian University and Digital Curation Unit, IMIS,
                                   Athena RC, Greece
Chrisa Tsinaraki   Joint Research Centre, European Commission, Italy
Andreas Vlachidis   University of South Wales, UK
Katherine Wisser   Simmons College, USA
Maja Žumer   University of Ljubljana, Slovenia

Track on European and National Projects

Special Track Chairs

Stavroula Antonopoulou   Perrotis College, Greece
R.J. Hartley   Manchester Metropolitan University, UK

| Georgia Zafeiriou | University of Macedonia, Greece |
| Rania Siatri | Alexander Technological Educational Institute (ATEI) of Thessaloniki, Greece |

Program Committee

Stavroula Antonopoulou	Perrotis College, Greece
Panos Balatsoukas	University of Manchester, UK
Mike Conway	University of North Carolina at Chapel Hill, USA
Jane Greenberg	Drexel University, USA
R.J. Hartley	Manchester Metropolitan University, UK
Nikos Houssos	RedLink, Greece
Nikos Korfiatis	University of East Anglia, UK
Damiana Koutsomiha	American Farm School, Greece
Paolo Manghi	Institute of Information Science and Technologies (ISTI), National Research Council (CNR), Italy
Dimitris Rousidis	University of Alcalá, Spain
Rania Siatri	Alexander Technological Educational Institute (ATEI) of Thessaloniki, Greece
Miguel-Ángel Sicilia	University of Alcalá, Spain
Armando Stellato	University of Rome Tor Vergata, Italy
Sirje Virkus	Tallinn University, Estonia
Georgia Zafeiriou	University of Macedonia, Greece

Track on Metadata and Semantics for Open Repositories, Research Information Systems, and Data Infrastructures

Special Track Chairs

| Miguel-Ángel Sicilia | University of Alcalá, Spain |
| Armando Stellato | University of Rome Tor Vergata, Italy |

Honorary Track Chairs

| Imma Subirats | Food and Agriculture Organization (FAO) of the United Nations, Italy |
| Nikos Houssos | RedLink, Greece |

Program Committee

Sophie Aubin	Institut National de la Recherche Agronomique, France
Thomas Baker	Sungkyunkwan University, Korea
Hugo Besemer	Wageningen UR Library, The Netherlands
Gordon Dunshire	University of Strathclyde, UK

Jan Dvorak	Charles University of Prague, Czech Republic
Jane Greenberg	Drexel University, USA
Siddeswara Guru	University of Queensland, Australia
Keith Jeffery	Keith G. Jeffery Consultants, UK
Nikolaos Konstantinou	University of Manchester, UK
Rebecca Koskela	University of New Mexico, USA
Jessica Lindholm	Malmö University, Sweden
Paolo Manghi	Institute of Information Science and Technologies - Italian National Research Council (ISTI-CNR), Italy
Brian Matthews	Science and Technology Facilities Council, UK
Eva Mendez Rodriguez	Universidad Carlos III, Spain
Jochen Schirrwagen	University of Bielefeld, Germany
Birgit Schmidt	University of Göttingen, Germany
Joachim Schöpfel	University of Lille, France
Kathleen Shearer	Confederation of Open Access Repositories (COAR), Germany
Chrisa Tsinaraki	European Commission, Joint Research Centre, Italy
Yannis Tzitzikas	University of Crete and ICS-FORTH, Greece
Zhong Wang	Sun-Yat-Sen University, China
Marcia Zeng	Kent State University, USA

Track on Digital Humanities and Digital Curation (DHC)

Special Track Chairs

Ernesto William De Luca	Georg Eckert Institute – Leibniz Institute for International Textbook Research, Germany
Paolo Bianchini	Università degli Studi di Torino, Italy

Program Committee

Wolf-Tilo Balke	TU Braunschweig, Germany
Elena Gonzalez-Blanco	Universidad Nacional de Educación a Distancia, Spain
Francesca Fallucchi	Guglielmo Marconi University, Italy
Ana Garcia-Serrano	ETSI Informatica - UNED, Spain
Steffen Hennicke	Georg Eckert Institute for International Textbook Research, Germany
Ivo Keller	TH Brandenburg, Germany
Maret Keller	Georg Eckert Institute for International Textbook Research, Germany
Andreas Lommatzsch	TU Berlin, Germany
Philipp Mayr	GESIS, Germany
Gabriela Ossenbach	UNED, Spain

Alessandra Pieroni	Guglielmo Marconi University, Italy
Christian Scheel	Georg Eckert Institute for International Textbook Research, Germany
Lena-Luise Stahn	Georg Eckert Institute for International Textbook Research, Germany
Armando Stellato	University of Rome Tor Vergata, Italy
Andrea Turbati	University of Rome Tor Vergata, Italy
Andreas Weiß	Georg Eckert Institute for International Textbook Research, Germany

Track on Metadata and Semantics for Agriculture, Food, and Environment (AgroSEM 2017)

Special Track Chairs

Juliette Dibie	AgroParisTech and INRA, France
Liliana Ibanescu	AgroParisTech and INRA, France

Program Committee

Ioannis Athanasiadis	Wageningen University, The Netherlands
Patrice Buche	INRA (Institut National de Recherche Agronomique), France
Caterina Caracciolo	Food and Agriculture Organization (FAO) of the United Nations, Italy
Johannes Keizer	Food and Agriculture Organization (FAO) of the United Nations, Italy
Stasinos Konstantopoulos	NCSR Demokritos, Greece
Claire Nédellec	INRA (Institut National de Recherche Agronomique), France
Ivo Jr. Pierozzi	Embrapa Agricultural Informatics, Brazil
Armando Stellato	University of Rome Tor Vergata, Italy
Maguelonne Teisseire	Irstea Montpellier, France
Jan Top	Wageningen Food and Biobased Research, The Netherlands
Robert Trypuz	John Paul II Catholic University of Lublin, Poland

Track on Knowledge IT Artifacts (KITA) in Professional Communities and Aggregations (KITA 2017)

Special Track Chairs

Fabio Sartori	University of Milano-Bicocca, Italy
Angela Locoro	University of Milano-Bicocca, Italy
Arlindo Flavio da Conceição	Federal University of São Paulo (UNIFESP), Brazil

Program Committee

Federico Cabitza	University of Milano-Bicocca, Italy
Luca Grazioli	ICteam SpA, Italy
Riccardo Melen	University of Milano-Bicocca, Italy
Aurelio Ravarini	Università Carlo Cattaneo - LIUC, Castellanza, Italy
Carla Simone	University of Siegen, Germany
Flávio Soares Corrêa da Silva	University of São Paulo, Brazil
Cecilia Zanni-Merk	Insa Rouen Normandie, France

Contents

Track on European and National Projects

Track on Open Repositories, Research Information Systems and Data Infrastructures

Track on Digital Humanities and Digital Curation (DHC)

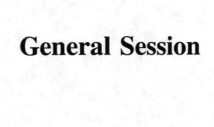

General Session

Version Control and Change Validation for RDF Datasets

Manuel Fiorelli[✉], Maria Teresa Pazienza, Armando Stellato, and Andrea Turbati

Department of Enterprise Engineering, University of Rome Tor Vergata,
Via del Politecnico, 1, 00133 Rome, Italy
{fiorelli,pazienza,turbati}@info.uniroma2.it,
stellato@uniroma2.it

Abstract. The dynamic and distributed nature of the Semantic Web demands for methodologies and systems fostering collective participation to the evolution of datasets. In collaborative and iterative processes for dataset development, it is important to keep track of individual changes for provenance. Different scenarios may require mechanisms to foster consensus, resolve conflicts between competing changes, reversing or ignoring changes etc. In this paper, we perform a landscape analysis of version control for RDF datasets, emphasizing the importance of change reversion to support validation. Firstly, we discuss different representations of changes in RDF datasets and introduce higher-level perspectives on change. Secondly, we analyze diverse approaches to version control. We conclude by focusing on validation, characterizing it as a separate need from the mere preservation of different versions of a dataset.

Keywords: Change management · Version control · Change validation · Collaborative editing · RDF · Knowledge bases · Metadata

1 Introduction

In the context of collaborative and iterative development processes for dataset development, there is a clear need for methodologies and systems to manage changes in datasets. Users and developers of a dataset have different perspectives: from the users' viewpoint, changes are always associated with published versions of a dataset. On the other hand, developers look at the evolution of a dataset from the inside, therefore they are interested in changes associated with different contributions, irrespectively of whether they will be part of a new version. Developers certainly benefit from the possibility to record individual changes, discuss them and, depending on the scenario, get a formal acceptance workflow. Conversely, a continuously evolving dataset may be more difficult to use, as resources can be deleted and, in general, their semantic description can be changed in a backward incompatible manner (e.g. an individual is turned into a class). Versioning may isolate consumers from change by recording and providing access to different versions of a dataset. OWL 2 [1] achieves that goal by distinguishing the notion of an ontology IRI from the concept of version IRI, which can be used to locate and, then, import a specific version of an ontology in a series.

© Springer International Publishing AG 2017
E. Garoufallou et al. (Eds.): MTSR 2017, CCIS 755, pp. 3–14, 2017.
https://doi.org/10.1007/978-3-319-70863-8_1

Datasets on the Semantic Web encompass both factual and conceptual knowledge, as they can be classified as ontologies, thesauri and other Knowledge Organization Systems [2], other than mere data. In general, this variability is coped with a layered approach: at the structural level, these different sources are seen as RDF [3] datasets, while higher levels may deal with the semantics of specific modeling languages and applications.

In this paper, we have performed a landscape analysis of the field of version control for RDF, discussing it in the context of collaborative processes for dataset development.

2   Understanding Change

From the perspective of the users of an editing environment, a change in an RDF dataset might be associated with any of the operations provided by the environment used for its maintenance. The result is an ever-evolving language of changes, which should grow as new operations are added to the editor. Moreover, it is difficult to reason upon that language, as for instance it is impossible to tell in general whether two changes conflict. Furthermore, selective reversion of a change requires the definition of the inverse of the operation originating the change. These difficulties can be avoided through the adoption of a more general approach, based on the observation that a change in a dataset boils down to the addition or deletion of triples. Accordingly, the authors of [4] claim that the triple is the "smallest directly manageable piece of knowledge". Furthermore, they claim that a triple can only be added or removed, but not modified, because there is nothing to the identity of a triple beyond the identity of its parts. For example, let us assume that the triple :s   :p   :o1   is removed, while the triple :s   :p   :o2 is added. The RDF data model does not give us any instrument to relate the two edits, and perhaps to state that a property of a resource has been modified. Similarly, it is not easy to determine that a resource has been renamed. This is a higher-level determination, which can be based on the interactions within an editor, the human judgement or, as observed in [5], some matcher.

At the semantic level, the change of an ontology is similarly determined primarily as the addition or deletion of axioms [6].

2.1   Blank Nodes

If we equate two datasets d_1, d_2 to their associated sets of triples $d_1, d_2 \subseteq (IRI \cup BNODE) \times IRI \times (IRI \cup BNODE \cup LITERAL)$, their difference can be computed by subtracting them as sets. By assuming that d_1 and d_2 are two subsequent versions of the same dataset, we shall define the added triples $\Delta_{add} = d_2 \backslash d_1$ and the removed triples $\Delta_{del} = d_1 \backslash d_2$.

Blank nodes complicate the matter significantly, especially for what concerns the representation of a change [7]: blank nodes in fact behave like existentially quantified variables, and as such do not have a stable identifier. Concrete syntaxes and programmatic APIs for RDF usually provide blank nodes with a local identifier, which can be changed each time the dataset is loaded into memory or serialized back to a file.

Let us consider the following dataset consisting of a single triple:

```
_:b1 rdf:first "hello" .
```

If a triple is added to the previous dataset, a new serialization is produced. Since blank nodes have only local scope, new local identifiers are generated:

```
_:b2 rdf:first "hello" .
_:b2 rdf:last  "world" .
```

According to [8], a conservative algorithm for comparing RDF datasets never assumes that two blank nodes from different files are equal: in our case the resulting difference would consist of a triple deletion and two triple additions. If we want to replace a serialized dataset with another, blank nodes hurt us mainly when we want to compare two versions, since we obtain larger than necessary differences. However, the biggest problems occur when we want to represent the changes themselves, for communicating them, and eventually applying them to another copy of the dataset. Indeed, the assertion «remove triple `_:b1 rdf:first   "world"` » is not well-defined, unless we assume that `_:b1` will be the local identifier of the blank node at the time the change is applied.

If changes are stored together with the data (e.g. in a separate named graph), then there is really no problem, since the coreference of blank nodes will be always preserved. Otherwise, we need to identify blank nodes by relying or even introducing some identifying information [9]. For example, we may rely on the semantics of an ontology, in order to uniquely identify a blank node through a chain of properties (inverse functional or functional). In the Delta [7] ontology, this is accomplished by replacing blank nodes with variables that have to be matched against the target graph. Similarly, the authors of [8] suggest to enrich blank nodes with an inverse functional property holding a unique identifier (e.g. a UUID). Another possibility is to avoid the use of blank nodes altogether, by replacing them with globally unique IRIs (i.e. Skolem IRIs).

In [10], Auer & Herre introduce the notion of atomic change, which may be larger than necessary, since it may include some unchanged statements, in order to provide a syntactic context for the identification of blank nodes. A negative atomic change (deleted triples) should include every triple that affects a given blank node, and this must hold for any other blank node introduced transitively. A positive atomic change (added triples) shall never mention blank nodes already in the dataset.

2.2 Representing Changes in RDF

There are several compelling reasons for the representation of changes in RDF. Firstly, RDF is very flexible in the use of a vocabulary for the description of changes. Indeed, one can adopt widespread vocabularies to represent metadata such as the creator of a change, the date-time it was issued, the affected resources or the motivation. Moreover, RDF allows the simultaneous adoption of different vocabularies, to represent different facets of a change. Secondly, syntactic interoperability implies the possibility to reuse the same tools and methodologies applied to data, while also allowing interesting scenarios in which the description of a change references another resource on the Semantic Web. It is thus possible to select changes based on complex criteria, such as changes affecting resources of a given type created by people working for a given department of a company (based on the background knowledge about people and their works).

We might be interested in representing the content of a change, as well. In the previous section, we have shown that a change can be conveniently reduced to the addition and removal of triples. We follow [9] in the review of different representation strategies, concluding that reification is generally inefficient and that there is a need for some construct to explicitly represent graphs.

The Delta [7] ontology supports a compact representation of changes, by leveraging the mechanism found in N3 [11] (a superset of RDF) for quoting graphs. The example below (from [7]) shows the selection of a resource based on an identification property:

```
{ ?x  bank:accountNo "1234578"}
    diff:deletion  { ?x  bank:balance 4000};
    diff:insertion { ?x  bank:balance 3575}.
```

The change above can be represented similarly through a SPARQL 1.1 update:

```
DELETE { ?x  bank:balance 4000 }
INSERT { ?x  bank:balance 3575}
WHERE { ?x  bank:accountNo "1234578". }
```

The widespread support of named graphs by major triple stores and concrete syntaxes offers a pure RDF solution: added and removed triples are asserted in two different named graphs, which are then related to a resource representing the specific change.

Unfortunately, named graphs are quite weak as an isolation mechanism, since inference and SPARQL queries (by default) are computed over all graphs. Moreover, there could be interoperability problems with general-purpose RDF management systems, which often rely on named graphs for other purposes (e.g. to store imported ontologies). A solution to these problems may be found in a hybrid approach [12] combining named graphs with reification (which notoriously does not entail the assertion of a triple). Another option is to save changes in a separate triple store, so that inference/querying problems can be simply ignored. Another opportunity is an explicit support from triple stores, which should implement quintuples including a component for tracking the lifecycle of the associated quadruple (i.e. a triple plus a graph name).

2.3 Higher-Level Changes

So far, we have characterized a change to a dataset in terms of the triples it adds or removes. Additions and deletions of triples can be understood as part of the same change, or they can be modeled as a pair of positive and negative changes, which can be composed into a single complex change. In a certain sense, we are adopting a higher-level perspective that is more specifically bound to the modeling vocabulary at hand. Thus, not only we group together changes by differentiating between levels of granularity, but we also recognize different types of changes. For instance, if a dataset encodes an OWL ontology, we may recognize changes such as "addition of a class", "merging of two classes", and so on. In [10], Auer & Herre suggest the classification of composite changes with respect to ontology evolution patterns. These patterns are associated with data migration algorithms, which serve two purposes. On the one hand, they precise the intention of a change to an ontology in terms of the desired changes to the facts. On the other hand, downstream users of an ontology are facilitated in the adoption of a newer version, since they can use the migration algorithms to change the instance they have already described. The CHAO ontology [13] is similarly based on the classification of changes to an ontology, but it does not register the affected triples. In [14], Klein et al. use a set of rules to translate low-level triple changes to higher-level changes specific for ontology versioning. In [5], Papavassiliou et al. are similarly concerned with higher-level changes, although their focus is limited to RDF/S knowledge bases. These authors define a language of changes, which should be concise, intuitive and support the unambiguous interpretation of low-level triple changes. They also define an efficient algorithm to recognize such changes starting from the low-level changes. Both Klein et al. and Papavassiliou et al. propose a divisive approach, somehow symmetric to the aggregative one of Auer & Herre. An interesting observation reported in [5] is that a high-level change may have a condition, consisting of unchanged triples that must be asserted in order for the change to be defined. For instance, changing the domain of a property :p from :Male to :Person, can be understood as the higher level change Generalize_Domain(p, Male, Person), only if the original dataset entails that :Male is a subclass of :Person.

3   RDF Version Control

In the previous section, we discussed the notion of change in an RDF dataset, and how changes can be represented in an economical, robust and intuitive way. However, manual sharing and application of changes require much diligence and are impractical at scale, especially if it is desirable to guarantee a globally consistent history of a dataset.

There is thus a need for methodologies and tools that support the proper management of changes and versions of a dataset. Most works in this area are clearly inspired by version control systems in the software development domain. Unsurprisingly, we observed a change in the referenced systems, from (nowadays) legacy systems such as CVS (http://www.nongnu.org/cvs/) and those losing hype, as in the case of Subversion (https://subversion.apache.org/), to current ones such as GIT (https://git-scm.com/). We also observed an approach [12] inspired by Darcs (http://darcs.net/), the distinguished feature of which is the focus on changes rather than snapshots. These systems transitioned from centralized architectures to decentralized ones, a trend that is only marginally reflected in the relevant works in the area of Semantic Web. In fact, even in the software development world, distribution is exploited to a limited extent, since most development workflows depend on centralized repository as the single source of truth about the history of a project.

3.1 Analysis of Existing RDF Version Control Systems

We have surveyed some works on version control for RDF datasets, analyzing their approaches and, when appropriate, establishing connections or drawing comparisons.

In [14], Kiryakov & Ognyanov propose a unified framework encompassing change-tracking, access-control and metadata management. These authors are often acknowledged for having established the idea that triples are the unit of management. Each edit of the data is individually registered, and specific states of the dataset can be tagged as versions. Individual versions, resources and statements can be described via metadata, at least ideally represented in RDF.

For performance reasons, metadata about triples is recorded via a relational representation possibly constructed as an extension to the representation of the dataset itself. The dataset is associated with an update counter that is incremented monotonically (establishing a logical clock) upon each edit. This counter is then used to annotate the creation and deletion time of each triple, making it possible to identify the triples that were valid during a given interval. Since no triple is ever really deleted, the repository grows monotonically. Purging the history prior to a certain state actually limits the growth of the repository. The system manages automatically the versioning of imported (read-only) data, as well as inferred triples, by applying techniques of truth maintenance to decide their validity interval. The system, implemented over the Sesame (http://rdf4j.org/) middleware for RDF, is intended to support anything that can be encoded in RDF, from factual data to ontologies. It is possible to branch a dataset, but this is quite an onerous operation based on cloning the entire repository.

In [8], Völkel et al. present a full version control system for RDF, implemented as a standalone server exposing its functionalities via a restful HTTP interface. The implementation supports all operations commonly found in a version control system, such as checking out, branching, merging and computing differences between states. They represent a change via the `TripleSet` ontology, representing each added/removed triple by means of reification. A change contains a link to the preceding one in the branch, and the sequence of changes leading to a given state can be seen as a delta-compressed representation of that state. This representation is used to compute the difference between two arbitrary states, and to merge two branches. Merging can fail, because of a conflict between a change adding a triple and another removing the same triple.

Blank nodes are explicitly supported through the enrichment mechanism described in Sect. 2.1. Similarly to [4], Völkel et al. focus on RDF at the structural level, on top of which another semantic level can be defined. This further level is characterized by a semantic difference function, which compares two states accounting for inferences enabled by an ontology language. Different notions of semantic conflict can be defined, in addition to the structural level conflict between additions and deletions.

In [12], Cassidy & Ballantine describe a version control system for RDF based on the theory of patches. Starting from an empty dataset, a given version of the dataset can be obtained by applying a sequence of patches (the authors' name for change):

$c_1 \cdot c_2 \cdot \ldots \cdot c_n = V_n$. Each patch adds or removes triples, and may be conditioned on unchanged triples. The implementation instruments the Redland (http://librdf.org/) RDF API to intercept any editing operation over the triple store containing the working graph. The patches are stored in a dedicated quad-store, in which each patch is stored in a separate named graph, while individual triples are represented as reified triples. The use of a separate dataset for patches means that the performance of read-only operations over the working dataset are completely unaffected by the tracking system. There is no specific support for blank nodes, nor is there for inference.

To restore the previous version (V_{n-1}), it is sufficient to forget the last change, and replay the full history from the empty dataset. However, the longer the sequence of patches, the more computational demanding this operation is. An alternative is to start from the working state (V_n) and undo the effect of the last change (c_n), by applying its inverse (c_n^{-1}), obtained by swapping additions and deletions.

The theory of patches also supports the undo of intermediate changes in the history. To achieve that, adjacent patches can be commuted, so that the relevant change is moved to the last position, where it can be reversed by applying its inverse. The key observation is that two patches can be commuted freely, unless they conflict. A conflict occurs between patches A and B, when A depends on a triple added by B, or either deletes a triple added by the other. Clearly, if two patches conflict, they cannot be reordered, unless some conflict resolution strategy is employed. By applying the same operations, it is possible to support branching and then merging of different branches.

In [15], Im et al. describe a version management system for RDF based on a relational representation. The system only stores the latest version of graph, plus the delta for reconstructing the previous one. A query against a previous version is rewritten so that it utilizes the current graph and all deltas up to the right version. To reduce the response time, Im et al. introduce the notion of aggregated delta, which can be computed in advance between each pair of versions. In this manner, the query should be rewritten using the current graph and only one aggregated delta. Obviously, this approach trades space occupation for response time.

In [16], Sande et al. develop a versioned RDF store on top of an arbitrary quad store, by relying on the mechanism of named graphs to store individual changes. Each change consists of two named graphs (one for the additions and one for the deletions), as well as some metadata describing the change itself. The identifier of a change is externally unique, since it is based on the hash of the change content. That enables a push/pull mechanism similar to one found in distributed version control systems for source code. There is no specific provisioning for blank nodes. The system also supports branching and merging, and conflicts are only determined at the structural level as addition/deletion conflicts. The history can be purged and deltas be rebased to shorten the history. A change is linked to its parent, so that the state of the dataset after each change can be easily reconstructed. Differently from [15], queries against an arbitrary version first require that the relevant version is materialized beforehand.

In [17], Graube et al. describe a system similar to the one presented in [16]. Both use named graphs to efficiently store deltas, and use RDF to describe individual changes. However, this new work avoids the use of hashmaps and other non-RDF structures. The system is again a standalone versioning system, supporting branching and merging. Its interface is based on an extension of SPARQL with keywords added to reference specific versions. While [16] uses a quad store to version an individual graph, this work uses a quad store to version a collection of graphs (although each graph is versioned independently). Differently from [15], queries against an arbitrary version first require that it is materialized in a temporary named graph. To speed-up common scenarios, the latest version of each graph is stored in the respective named graph. Additionally, tagged versions are materialized as well.

In [18], Halilaj et al. observe that some community-driven datasets have already adopted GIT for their version management needs. The perspective of these authors is on vocabulary development, thus they propose a set of best practices to extend (when necessary) GIT to meet the requirements of collaborative vocabulary development.

In fact, they observe that GIT already meets some of them, including flexible workflow support, branching and tagging of versions. Text-based version control systems are based on textual diff algorithms, which are known to have problems with non-linear data such as RDF [7]. In particular, Halilaj et al. commit on the use of the Turtle syntax to sidestep the fact that editing tools may produce arbitrary different representations of the same graph because of differences in their writing algorithms.

Other requirements are met by other systems integrated in the GIT ecosystem, such as JIRA (https://www.atlassian.com/software/jira) and other issue tracking systems to support communication and coordination. Halilaj et al. introduce OWL2VCS [6] as a means to compare two versions on a higher level than raw triples. Other requirements can be met by a combination of native functionality and purpose-built hook, i.e. scripts triggered upon certain events, such as before and after a commit.

4   Change Validation

In curated datasets, change validation is an activity whose purpose is to review individual changes to a dataset, so that unwanted ones can be rejected. Differently, versioning is primarily about the ability to store and access the different states of an evolving dataset. Nonetheless, the two activities are related in various ways, since validation can be defined on top of the concepts and even the systems we described for version control.

We first observe that in a sense any version control system supporting branches allows a form of change validation. As shown in [8], each contribution is allocated to a separate branch, while accepting the contribution requires integrating it into the main development branch. More generally, we can consider an asynchronous workflow, in which proposed changes are represented explicitly, so that they can be validated and in case of acceptance be incorporated into the main copy of the dataset. Obviously, rejected changes do not affect the history of the main development copy, as it is updated only by accepted changes. However, this asynchronous workflow delays the identification of conflicts between contributors working on independent copies of the dataset.

The second point of contact between versioning and validation is thus the notion of conflicting changes. In literature, there are slightly different notions of conflict, but at the structural level there is an agreement about the idea of addition/deletion conflict. For instance, while performing a three-way merging of two branches, it should not be possible for a branch to remove a triple that is added by the other. Other forms of conflict occur at the semantic level. For instance, a contribution merged into an ontology should preserve the consistency and coherency of the ontology.

In addition to structural and consistency/coherency conflicts, there is a range of conflicts that sit somehow in the middle, as they depend in part on the specific modeling vocabularies and in part on the applications. Let us consider an ontology concept, say C, for which a label is suggested. Before that suggestion is revised, the concept is removed from the ontology. Intuitively, it should not be possible anymore to accept the label contribution, since the labeled class no longer exists. Unfortunately, from a structural perspective there is no conflict at all, since the contributed triple is not explicitly deleted by the deletion of the concept C. This problem can be solved by relying on the possibility (e.g. [12]) to add a condition to a change. Indeed, we may express that the addition of a label depends on the fact that the subject resource exists in the dataset. In our example, the simplest way to assert the existence of concept C is to assert the triple C rdf:type rdfs:Resource (assuming that a reasoner is able to infer that anything that is locally defined is at least a resource).

We observe that change validation does not necessarily require the use of branches, and that it can be implemented in synchronous workflows as well, when all contributors work simultaneously on the same working copy of the dataset. This is a form of continuous integration that reduces the risk of subsequent conflicts, although they are not completely removed. In this synchronous workflow, we are no longer interested in maintaining separate versions for each contribution, but rather we are interested in managing the applied changes so that they can be evaluated and, if necessary, reversed.

Most version control systems for RDF use a delta-compressed representation of the history of a branch, so it is relatively easy to determine what has changed because of a committed change. In [10], Auer & Herre suggest to implement arbitrary change rollback, by checking the compatibility of a change with a version of a graph different from the one the change was originally created.

By swapping additions and deletions of the triples, it is easy to create a change that reverses a given change, as long as subsequent changes are not conflicting. In a continuous integration scenario, a conflict is due to the fact that subsequent changes somehow overwrite the previous one. Therefore, it is right that the change can no longer be rejected. In fact, it may be the case that a change is not atomic (e.g. it adds two classes), and it may be the case that the conflict arises only because of a part of the change. In such cases, we can exploit the ability (previously discussed) of decomposing a change into cohesive changes, which can be independently rejected.

In this scenario, the reversal of a change is in fact another change that is registered by the version control system. In a sense, a change and its reversal share the same nature, and thus we could even undo the undo of a change, and so on. In fact, we advise in favor of adding some metadata to tell the difference between the two types of change.

As discussed in the previous section, the authors of [12] shift the focus from version management to change management, by adopting the theory of patches. The system manages a sequence of patches that lead to the current working state of a dataset. As long as the changes are not conflicting, the sequence can actually be seen as a set of changes, which can be independently rejected.

A similar interest in change management can be recognized in many collaborative editors, such as VocBench [19], PoolParty (https://www.poolparty.biz/) and Protégé [13]. The additions of collaboration features [20] to Protégé have eventually led to its web-based incarnation [21].

The management of changes clearly presupposes these to be identified in the first place. To this end, there are two main strategies: monitored vs non monitored. Protégé supports both approaches [13], while VocBench and PoolParty mainly support the monitored approach. The monitoring of changes consists in recording the changes as they are produced. Usually, it requires the instrumentation of the editing environment or a low-level middleware to intercept and record individual editing actions. Without monitoring, there are only two versions (before and after the modification), and then a comparison function is used to compute the difference. If the second version of the dataset contains numerous modifications, we must break down the triple-based difference into numerous more cohesive changes, so that they can be analyzed independently.

A general argument in favor of a monitored solution is its higher efficiency, since comparing two large RDF graphs can be computationally expensive (no wonder that among the above cited tools, the one supporting non monitored changes is meant to support ontology development, while the other two deal with large thesauri). Moreover, the transactional boundaries of an application offer a natural criterion for defining atomicity of changes. In fact, it may be useful to further decompose changes into hierarchies, so that it is possible to analyze the changes at different levels of detail. Another advantage of the monitored approach is that individual changes are identified early on, so that it is possible to annotate them and, in some cases, start discussions about them.

One disadvantage of the monitored scenario is that changes naturally occur in a temporal sequence, and it may happen that subsequent changes are redundant, possibly conflicting. As an example, let us consider a team of maintainers working simultaneously on the same ontology. If the maintainers are in disagreement, a same class might happen to be repeatedly added and deleted. These changes are both conflicting and redundant, and would pollute the list of changes pending for acceptance. It is a matter of policy, whether the system should react to these problematic cases or the application should prevent such cases to occur in the first place.

VocBench, PoolParty and Protégé (in the monitored configuration) share a similar architecture. All users work simultaneously on the same data, while changes are tracked and stored. All of the systems record high-level changes. VocBench models changes as a Java class hierarchy, and stores the objects representing individual changes into a separate relational database. PoolParty represents the changes in RDF together with the data in a dedicated named graph, by relying on the ChangeSet [22] ontology. As already discussed, Protégé stores the changes in RDF using the CHAO ontology (like PoolParty), but separately from the data (like VocBench). The change tracking capability of these tools is valuable in its own, but it is interesting mostly because it allows a form of validation. Protégé has followed the path to integrate many communication and coordination facilities, aimed at forming consensus. For instance, it is possible to annotate changes, discuss them and even vote on a change. VocBench, on the other hand, follows a different approach, because communication is performed externally by means of Wikis, issue management systems, etc.

5   Conclusions

We have performed a landscape analysis of RDF version control systems and approaches, focusing on the demands of collaborative and iterative development processes. Under this perspective, the controlled rejection of individual changes is very important, especially in the context of curated datasets, in which proposed changes must undergo an explicit acceptance process.

We observed that change validation is complementary to the need for discrete snapshots of a dataset, and that it can be realized on top of different strategies for version control. We first remarked that in asynchronous workflows validation can be implemented in terms of selective merging of changes into the main development copy of a dataset. Differently, in synchronous workflows changes are already applied to the dataset, therefore validation should be based on an explicit undo mechanism. By shifting the focus of the management from versions to changes, we observed that it is possible to implement this synchronous workflow in a clearer manner. Finally, we observed that this is the path that many collaborative editing environments for RDF have followed.

Acknowledgments. This work has been funded by the European Commission ISA^2 programme, supporting development of the collaborative RDF editing platform Vocbench 3 [23].

References

1. W3C: OWL 2 Web Ontology Language. In: World Wide Web Consortium (W3C). http://www.w3.org/TR/2009/REC-owl2-overview-20091027/. Accessed 27 Oct 2009
2. Hodge, G.: Systems of Knowledge Organization for Digital Libraries: Beyond Traditional Authority Files. Council on Library and Information Resources, Washington, DC (2000)
3. W3C: Resource Description Framework (RDF). http://www.w3.org/RDF/. Accessed 2004
4. Ognyanov, D., Kiryakov, A.: Tracking changes in RDF(S) repositories. In: Gómez-Pérez, A., Benjamins, V.R. (eds.) EKAW 2002. LNCS, vol. 2473, pp. 373–378. Springer, Heidelberg (2002). http://doi.org/10.1007/3-540-45810-7_33
5. Papavassiliou, V., Flouris, G., Fundulaki, I., Kotzinos, D., Christophides, V.: On detecting high-level changes in RDF/S KBs. In: Bernstein, A., Karger, D.R., Heath, T., Feigenbaum, L., Maynard, D., Motta, E., Thirunarayan, K. (eds.) ISWC 2009. LNCS, vol. 5823, pp. 473–488. Springer, Heidelberg (2009). http://doi.org/10.1007/978-3-642-04930-9_30
6. Zaikin, I., Tuzovsky, A.: Owl2vcs: tools for distributed ontology development. In : Proceedings of the 10th International Workshop on OWL: Experiences and Directions (OWLED 2013) Co-located with 10th Extended Semantic Web Conference (ESWC 2013), Montpellier, France, May 26–27, 2013 (2013)
7. Berners-Lee, T., Connolly, D.: Delta: an ontology for the distribution of differences between RDF graphs. In: World Wide Web Consortium (W3C). https://www.w3.org/DesignIssues/Diff. Accessed 2001
8. Völkel, M., Enguix, C.F., Kruk, S.R., Zhdanova, A.V., Stevens, R., Sure, Y.: SemVersion - versioning RDF and ontologies. In: KnowledgeWeb Deliverable D2.3.3.v1, Institute AIFB, University of Karlsruhe, June 2005
9. Seaborne, A., Davis, I.: Supporting change propagation in RDF. In: Proceedings of the W3C Workshop - RDF Next Steps, June 26–27, 2010, Stanford, Palo Alto, CA, USA (2010)

10. Auer, S., Herre, H.: A versioning and evolution framework for RDF knowledge bases. In: Virbitskaite, I., Voronkov, A. (eds.) PSI 2006. LNCS, vol. 4378, pp. 55–69. Springer, Heidelberg (2007). http://doi.org/10.1007/978-3-540-70881-0_8

11. Berners-Lee, T., Connolly, D.: Notation3 (N3): a readable RDF syntax. In: World Wide Web Consortium - Team Submission. https://www.w3.org/TeamSubmission/n3/. Accessed 28 Mar 2011

12. Cassidy, S., Ballantine, J.: Version control for RDF triple stores. In: ICSOFT 2007, Proceedings of the Second International Conference on Software and Data Technologies, Volume ISDM/EHST/DC, Barcelona, Spain, July 22–25, 2007, pp. 5–12 (2007). http://doi.org/10.5220/0001340100050012

13. Noy, N.F., Chugh, A., Liu, W., Musen, M.A.: A framework for ontology evolution in collaborative environments. In: Cruz, I., Decker, S., Allemang, D., Preist, C., Schwabe, D., Mika, P., Uschold, M., Aroyo, L.M. (eds.) ISWC 2006. LNCS, vol. 4273, pp. 544–558. Springer, Heidelberg (2006). http://doi.org/10.1007/11926078_39

14. Klein, M., Fensel, D., Kiryakov, A., Ognyanov, D.: Ontology versioning and change detection on the web. In: Gómez-Pérez, A., Benjamins, V.R. (eds.) EKAW 2002. LNCS, vol. 2473, pp. 197–212. Springer, Heidelberg (2002). http://doi.org/10.1007/3-540-45810-7_20

15. Im, D.-H., Lee, S.-W., Kim, H.-J.: A version management framework for RDF triple stores. Int. J. Softw. Eng. Knowl. Eng. 22(01), 85–106 (2012). http://doi.org/10.1142/S0218194012500040

16. Sande, M.V., Colpaert, P., Verborgh, R., Coppens, S., Mannens, E., Van de Walle, R.: R&Wbase: Git for triples. In: Proceedings of the WWW 2013 Workshop on Linked Data on the Web, Rio de Janeiro, Brazil, 14 May, 2013 (2013)

17. Graube, M., Hensel, S., Urbas, L.: R43ples: revisions for triples - an approach for version control in the semantic web. In: Proceedings of the 1st Workshop on Linked Data Quality Co-located with 10th International Conference on Semantic Systems, LDQ@SEMANTiCS 2014, Leipzig, Germany, 2nd September, 2014 (2014)

18. Halilaj, L., Grangel-González, I., Coskun, G., Lohmann, S., Auer, S.: Git4Voc: collaborative vocabulary development based on git. Int. J. Semant. Comput. 10(2), 167–191 (2016). http://doi.org/10.1142/S1793351X16400067

19. Stellato, A., Rajbhandari, S., Turbati, A., Fiorelli, M., Caracciolo, C., Lorenzetti, T., Keizer, J., Pazienza, M.T.: VocBench: a web application for collaborative development of multilingual thesauri. In: Gandon, F., Sabou, M., Sack, H., d'Amato, C., Cudré-Mauroux, P., Zimmermann, A. (eds.) ESWC 2015. LNCS, vol. 9088, pp. 38–53. Springer, Cham (2015). http://doi.org/10.1007/978-3-319-18818-8_3

20. Tudorache, T., Noy, N.F., Tu, S., Musen, M.A.: Supporting collaborative ontology development in protégé. In: Sheth, A., Staab, S., Dean, M., Paolucci, M., Maynard, D., Finin, T., Thirunarayan, K. (eds.) ISWC 2008. LNCS, vol. 5318, pp. 17–32. Springer, Heidelberg (2008). http://doi.org/10.1007/978-3-540-88564-1_2

21. Tudorache, T., Nyulas, C., Noy, N.F., Musen, M.A.: WebProtégé: a collaborative ontology editor and knowledge acquisition tool for the Web. Semant. Web 4(1), 89–99 (2013). http://doi.org/10.3233/SW-2012-0057

22. Tunnicliffe, S., Davis, I.: Changeset. http://vocab.org/changeset/. Accessed 2005

23. Stellato, A., Turbati, A., Fiorelli, M., Lorenzetti, T., Costetchi, E., Laaboudi, C., Van Gemert, W., Keizer, J.: Towards VocBench 3: pushing collaborative development of thesauri and ontologies further beyond. In: 17th European Networked Knowledge Organization Systems (NKOS) Workshop, Thessaloniki, Greece, 21st September 2017

Effect of Enriched Ontology Structures on RDF Embedding-Based Entity Linking

Emrah Inan[(✉)] and Oguz Dikenelli

Department of Computer Engineering, Ege University,
35100 Bornova, Izmir, Turkey
emrah.inan@ege.edu.tr

Abstract. RDF embeddings are recently used in Entity Linking systems for disambiguation of candidate entities to match the best mention and entity pairs. In this study, we evaluate the effect of enriched ontology structures for disambiguation task when RDF embeddings are used to identify semantic relatedness between knowledge base concepts. We generate a domain-specific core ontology and put new components upon previous ontology structures. In this way, we obtain four different enriched structures and transform them into RDF embeddings. Then, we observe which enriched structure has more importance to enhance the overall performance of RDF embeddings-based Entity Linking approaches. We select two well-known knowledge-base-agnostic approaches, including AGDISTIS and DoSeR and adapt them into RDF embeddings-based entity disambiguation. Finally, a domain-specific evaluation dataset is generated from Wikipedia to observe the effect of enriched structures on these adapted approaches.

Keywords: RDF embeddings · RDF2Vec · HITS · PageRank

1 Introduction

Entity Linking systems map mentions of a text with their referent entities in a given knowledge base. These systems involve mention detection and entity disambiguation tasks. After detecting mentions, Entity Linking systems choose the highest ranked entity over all identified candidates for each mention. Ranking of candidate entities is the most critical step of the disambiguation task and independent (local) and collective (global) rankings are two main approaches became prominent in the literature [1]. While independent ranking only considers the relatedness between a candidate entity and a mention, collective ranking approaches focus on the relatedness of candidate entities identified for mentions surrounded by other entities in the referent knowledge base. To compute this relatedness, Milne and Witten [2] propose the semantic relatedness that is one of the primary methods and highly depends on the Wikipedia link structure. Most of the studies such as [3,4] exploit this measurement in the global coherence based disambiguation task. The main drawback of this measurement is that whether

© Springer International Publishing AG 2017
E. Garoufallou et al. (Eds.): MTSR 2017, CCIS 755, pp. 15–24, 2017.
https://doi.org/10.1007/978-3-319-70863-8_2

the background knowledge is not based on the Wikipedia link structure, it is impossible to compute the semantic relatedness of candidate entities.

To avoid the dependency for the Wikipedia link structure, knowledge agnostic approaches have appeared in recent years. Hence we need a knowledge base independent semantic relatedness measure to apply Entity Linking with other knowledge bases than Wikipedia. In recent Entity Linking systems such as AGDISTIS [5] and DoSeR [6] being knowledge agnostic is one of their main focus and they can use any ontology like knowledge bases for Entity Linking. Most recent work DoSeR has achieved higher precision and recall values than AGDISTIS using a transformation Word2Vec [7] model into RDF embeddings to compute semantic similarities. These similarities are leveraged in PageRank algorithm to find out global coherence. Based on successful results of DoSeR, we mainly investigate which joined component of ontology structure has the most impact to the RDF embeddings-based semantic relatedness computation. The different levels of components are added to the core ontology structure and observed which ontology component has more importance than others to increase the performance for knowledge-agnostic Entity Linking approaches depends on RDF embeddings. We adapt HITS algorithm to RDF embeddings in AGDISTIS and PageRank algorithm in DoSeR. Finally, we evaluate them in the entity disambiguation task built from RDF embeddings of domain-specific ontology structures over a domain-specific dataset generated from Wikipedia.

The rest of this paper is organized as follows: In Sect. 2, it gives an overview of related work. In Sect. 3, the selected knowledge agnostic approaches and adaptations of these approaches to RDF embeddings are explained in detail. We present results of the selected approaches on the domain-specific evaluation set in Sect. 4. We conclude our study and highlight the research questions in Sect. 5.

2   Related Work

Global coherence approaches for open domain Entity Linking systems such as DBpedia Spotlight [8], Babelfy [9] and WAT [10] have achieved remarkable results in recent years. However, open domain resources are not sharp enough to model domain-specific knowledge bases. Navigli [11] emphasizes the importance of domain specific knowledge bases in Entity Linking task. There are domain specific knowledge bases such as KnowLife [12] and LinkedMDB [13] which can be used in Entity Linking. But these knowledge bases are not depending on a powerful link structure. As a result, knowledge agnostic approaches are one of the directions of this domain-specific Entity Linking because these approaches are independent of the Wikipedia link structure.

The majority of Entity Linking studies mainly depend on Wikipedia link structure in the entity disambiguation step. For instance, TAGME [4] exploits Wikipedia anchor link texts for the mention detection and aims on-the-fly annotation of short texts using agreement approach based on Wikipedia link structure. Also, these approaches focus on global coherence approaches that emphasize the consistency of all mention-entity pairs in the given text. AIDA-light [14] considers global coherence to disambiguate the entities and exploits YAGO2 [15] and Wikipedia domain hierarchy to annotate "easy tags" first.

In recent years, knowledge agnostic approaches without having a dependency of Wikipedia link structure have become reveal. Further, these approaches can be executed with any knowledge bases. AGDISTIS [5] has a method that is independent of Wikipedia link structure. It uses a Named Entity Recognition tool for detection mentions in the web pages and performs Named Entity Disambiguation into the web-scale. Then, it chooses candidate entities for the detected mentions from surface forms and generates a disambiguation graph for these candidates. The generated disambiguation graph is used in graph-based HITS algorithm to match the best mention-entity pairs in the disambiguation step. RDF embedding-based entity disambiguation approaches achieve remarkable results. One of the prior studies in these approaches is DoSeR [6] and it exploits semantic embeddings generated by given knowledge bases to compute semantic similarities between entities thanks to the personalized PageRank algorithm. In this perspective, this study mainly examines the impact of the semantic embeddings gathered by different ontology structures as explained in the following section.

3 Disambiguation Using Enriched Ontology Structures

The enrichment of ontology structure can be defined as adding new ontology elements such as class, property and instances to a given ontology. To obtain the enriched structure, we select an ordinary domain ontology that is independent of DBpedia and Wikipedia link structure to meet the requirement for the knowledge-agnostic environment. Then we add extra categorized components to generate different enriched structures. In this study, Movie Ontology (MO)[1] is selected as the core ontology and categorized components such as financial and locational properties of movies are added to enrich the core ontology. After obtaining different enriched structures, they are transformed into RDF embeddings to disambiguate the best mention-entity pair in Entity Linking task. The main purpose of this study is to observe the impact of these structures in RDF embedding-based Entity Linking approaches.

3.1 Categorization of MO and Quality Metrics

The MO ontology is divided into personal (MO-Per), financial (MO-Fin) and locational (MO-Loc) levels of ontology structures. The selected properties of each ontology structure are enriched by relevant classes, relations and instances from LinkedMDB [13] and DBpedia [16] for the movie domain. MO-Per structure involves enriched director and cast information, whereas MO-Fin structure has enriched budget, distributor and producer properties and MO-Loc has extended location and language properties. After obtaining the core ontology as MO-Per, quality metrics are measured for combinations of financial and locational structures with the core ontology.

---

[1] http://www.movieontology.org/.

To measure ontology quality, OntoQA [17] and OntoMetrics [18] are reviewed in terms of schema, base and knowledge base metrics. Schema metrics focus on the design of the ontology such as attribute, relationship and inheritance richness. Base metrics address the distribution of data on the knowledge base and class categories. Knowledge base metrics deals with class richness, average population and cohesion parameters. As denoted in Table 1, attribute richness (AR) is the average number of attributes for each class and indicates the knowledge density of classes in the given schema. If AR has a higher value, it shows that each class has more comprehensive information.

Relationship richness (RR) describes the diversity of relations in the schema and its score reflects the size of connections between classes. If it has low value, it may have only class-subclass relationships. OntoMetrics [18] explains extra metrics such as axiom, class and relation ratio. Axiom/class ratio (ACR) demonstrates the average numbers of axioms for each class and class/relation ratio (CRR) is the average amount of classes per relationship.

Enriched ontology structures in schema metrics clearly indicate that if an ontology structure is added up categorized elements, it increases measures of schema metrics. MO-Per is selected as the core ontology and is not covered by any other enriched structure, so it has the lowest schema metrics. MO-PerFin is covered by financial features in addition to personal elements. For this reason, RR and CRR values are increased, but AR and ACR values almost remain as the same. MO-PerLoc has greater values than previous structures for all schema metrics and MO-PerFinLoc has the largest covered structure having the highest scores.

Table 1. Schema and class metrics for enriched ontology structures.

Schema metrics	MO-Per	MO-PerFin	MO-PerLoc	MO-PerFinLoc
AR	0.054	0.056	0.12	0.248
RR	0.414	0.53	0.642	0.759
ACR	10.865	10.882	11.487	11.98
CRR	0.702	0.785	0.836	0.878

Table 2. Base and knowledge base metrics for enriched ontology structures.

Base and KB metrics	MO-Per	MO-PerFin	MO-PerLoc	MO-PerFinLoc
Axioms	891	1062	1287	1521
Class count	82	95	112	127
Properties count	48	65	84	96
Individual count	298	372	468	565
Average population	3.634	3.92	4.185	4.456
Class richness	0.67	0.762	0.834	0.912

In Table 2, Base Metrics comprises axioms, classes and property counts. Axioms are fundamental statements of an ontology and show what is true in a domain. Classes are concepts and involve other classes or individuals. Property counts are the total number of links of classes to individuals or other classes. Individuals are the class instances and describe the actual object of the domain.

Knowledge base metrics is important to measure the effectiveness of the ontology design and observe the number of real-world knowledge representations. The average population is the ratio of individuals per class defined in the given schema. Class richness (CR) states the distribution of instances across classes and is the ratio between classes including instances and the total number of classes. Thus, if a knowledge base contains a high CR value it demonstrates most of the knowledge in the schema is represented by comprehensive data. MO-Per is the core ontology and especially involves classes, properties and individuals from personal features such as director or cast information. Table 2 shows that every combination of categorized structures with MO-Per enlarges the overall metrics in terms of class, property and individual counts. For instance, MO-PerFin is the combination of MO-Per with financial features such as budget and publisher of movies. Therefore, average population and class richness scores are increased after each combination and finally MO-PerFinLoc involves all enriched elements and has the highest scores.

3.2   Entity Disambiguation

Entity linking approaches comprise mention detection and entity disambiguation tasks. To detect mentions, we follow mention parsing method of TAGME. This method receives input text and split it into words that are sequenced up to 6 words and queried in the mention dictionary. To build this dictionary, we exploit instances of movie ontology instead of generating mentions from Wikipedia. If a mention of the dictionary is a substring of another mention or any other overlapped strings problem, we use the boundary detection approach of TAGME for overlapped strings. This approach handles two mentions m_1, m_2 and m_1 can be assumed as a substring of m_2 for this condition. If link-probability (lp) of m_2 is greater than $lp(m_1)$, then m_1 is removed from the mention dictionary. So, $lp(m_i)$ is computed as the division of the number of mention m_i links to the frequency of all occurrences of m_i.

In this study, we focus on the entity disambiguation task and transform disambiguation methods of AGDISTIS and DoSeR approaches into RDF embedding-based entity relatedness computation to map the best possible mention and entity pair among candidates. In disambiguation step, the entity relatedness measures how candidate entities for each mention are related to each other in the given knowledge base and it is computed with each adapted algorithm from AGDISTIS and DoSeR approaches exploiting the RDF2Vec [19] model. RDF2Vec is an adaptation of Word2Vec model to the RDF embeddings to obtain a neural language model. The main assumption of this model, closer words in texts have high relatedness scores. Instead of using words, RDF embeddings are generated by entities and relations from the given RDF model. Before the neural language model is trained, RDF model is transformed into the form of RDF embeddings. Consequently, each embedding can be represented as a numerical vector in Latent Feature Space. We use graph walks to transform RDF model into entity-relation sequences. Then, we built Neural Language Model with Skip-gram from generated entity-relation sequences. Ristoski et al. [19] demonstrates that Skip-gram model with negative sampling gives the best performance on computations of relatedness scores. The computation of entity relatedness with Softmax function and has a range between 0 and 1. If the relatedness score of entity pairs are closer to 1, it demonstrates these two entities are more related to each other. Equation 1 denotes the computation of the entity relatedness from the trained model.

$$p(e_0|e_i) = \frac{exp(v_e0'^T v_{ei})}{\sum_{e=1}^{V} exp(v_e'^T v_{ei})} \quad (1)$$

where the entity e has v_e as the input vector and v_e' as the output vector, and V indicates all entities vocabulary. Iterations and graph depth remain same as optimal values having the best evaluation performance as stated in the RDF2Vec study.

To constitute fair and objective experiments of disambiguation step we detect mentions with the proposed method of TAGME rather than using mention detection steps of AGDISTIS and DoSeR approaches. After obtaining mentions, we transform the similarity function of AGDISTIS into the relatedness function (1) and use HITS algorithm to compute global coherence between entities. The formal model of AGDISTIS aims to find the assignment μ^*:

$$\mu^* = arg_\mu max(p(e_C|e_N)) + \phi(\mu(C,N),K)) \quad (2)$$

where ϕ is the coherence function implemented by the HITS algorithm involving an assignment $\mu(C,N)$ between the matrix of candidate-entity mappings (C) and the vector of named entities (N) in the given knowledge base (K). The similarity function of AGDISTIS is adapted to the entity relatedness method (2) among candidate and named entities.

DoSeR is the last adapted approach and currently adaptable semantic embeddings. Based on semantic embeddings, it applies PageRank algorithm as the global coherence computation to map the best possible mention-entity pair in the entity disambiguation step. For this reason, Entity Transaction Probability (ETP) is computed to identify edge weights between entity nodes in the given knowledge base:

$$ETP(e_u^i, e_v^j) = \frac{cos(vec(e_u^i), vec(e_v^j))}{\sum_{k \in (V \setminus V_i)} cos(vec(e_u^i), vec(k))} \quad (3)$$

where transaction probability is calculated for vectors e_u^i and e_v^j as a cosine similarity. ETP measurement indicates edge weights for PageRank algorithm and a transaction possibility from one entity node to another node. In this study, we compute this transaction possibility using Eq. 1 instead of ETP function (3).

4   Evaluation

In the evaluation, we serve a domain-specific dataset and compare knowledge agnostic Entity Linking approaches depend on different enriched ontology structures. The main focus of this section is to observe the effect of enriched ontology structures on knowledge-agnostic approaches.

4.1   Domain-Specific Evaluation Set

Domain-specific evaluation dataset is generated from Wikipedia articles and is publicly available at the following link[2]. WeDGeM generates automatically an evaluation set for specific domains using Wikipedia categories and DBpedia. Wikipedia category pages and DBpedia taxonomy are used for adjusting domain-specific annotated text generation. Wikipedia disambiguation (Category: Disambiguation) pages are used for adjusting the ambiguity level of the generated texts. This dataset contains many annotated documents represented as NLP Interchange Format(NIF)[3] that is an RDF/OWL-based format providing interoperability between entity annotator tools. Annotated documents include entities for the movie domain and their features such as director, cast and genre. Mentions of the annotated texts are extracted from anchor texts of Wikipedia articles. Each mention is connected to its MO ontology links that are stored as annotated entity list.

English Wikipedia dump[4] is used to generate annotated texts in movie domain. To propose an ambiguous environment, Wikipedia disambiguation pages are used for movies and their properties such as actors, directors and cast. For instance, a sample mention *Wicker Park* has a Wikipedia disambiguation page [5] involving disambiguation pages such as *WickerPark_(film)*, *WickerPark_ (soundtrack)* and *WickerPark_(ChicagoPark)*. Thanks to these disambiguation pages, we can increase the number of candidate entities for the selected movie domain. The movie evaluation dataset involves 945 annotated texts in English (EN). The number of entities such as movies, directors and starring is 3648 and these are extracted from Wikipedia infoboxes and mapped with referent entities by DBpedia.

To generate an ambiguous evaluation set, the strategy of preparing evaluation test for open domain datasets of Entity Linking task in TAC[6] conference is emulated into the domain specific dataset generation. The generated dataset has entities including their offsets in the annotated text and other entity annotated documents from different domains such as music, books and location to provide a more ambiguous environment for Entity Linking systems. This dataset involves 945 annotated documents and 3648 entities. Whereas Ellis et al. [20]

---

[2] https://github.com/einan/WeDGeM.
[3] http://persistence.uni-leipzig.org/nlp2rdf/.
[4] https://dumps.wikimedia.org/enwiki/20170420/.
[5] https://en.wikipedia.org/wiki/Wicker_Park.
[6] http://nlp.cs.rpi.edu/kbp/2016/.

Table 3. Performance of approaches on enriched ontology structures

Ontology structure	AGDISTIS			DoSeR		
	P	R	F1	P	R	F1
MO-Per	0.65	0.463	0.54	0.704	0.47	0.573
MO-PerFin	0.724	0.59	0.65	0.738	0.616	0.672
MO-PerLoc	0.709	0.572	0.633	0.729	0.574	0.642
MO-PerFinLoc	0.781	0.728	0.753	0.819	0.77	0.793

study demonstrates 13% ambiguity and the reference open domain evaluation dataset of [21] study contains 18% ambiguity, the generated dataset has 28.51% ambiguity of entities.

4.2   Results

After the preparation of the evaluation set, precision (P), recall (R) and F1 scores are measured for the selected Entity Linking approaches in order to observe the impact of ontology quality on the RDF2Vec model which involves different enriched ontology structures as background knowledge in Table 3.

The evaluation dataset covers 68% of personal, 20% of locational and 12% financial elements in terms of class, property and individual counts. Mo-Per is built by almost personal features but it has also a few fundamental elements in financial and locational components smaller than 5%. MO-PerFin involves 70% personal and 25% financial features whereas MO-PerLoc has 75% personal and 20% locational elements. Both ontology structures involve almost 5% out of enriched elements. The last ontology is MO-PerFinLoc has the most similar coverage as the testbed. In these circumstances, the core ontology MO-Per has the lowest F1 scores for all approaches due to its class, relation and instance count. The coverage of locational features is smaller than financial features and this slightly leads to falling in the overall performance. One of the reasons in this fall is that location names increase the ambiguity between movie names. For example, Wicker Park is a public urban park in Chicago, but it has also a link to the movie as indicated in Wikipedia disambiguation page[7]. In this context, the disambiguation method of DoSeR outperforms AGDISTIS for all ontology structures as denoted in Table 3.

5   Conclusion

In this study, Entity Linking approaches based on knowledge-agnostic methods are examined under different enriched ontology structures. Each ontology structure produces RDF embeddings as an input for the RDF2Vec model to evaluate the impact of ontology structure in the Entity Linking task. The evaluation data

---

[7] https://en.wikipedia.org/wiki/Wicker_Park.

set is gathered from Wikipedia and RDF embeddings for these structures and RDF2Vec model compared with four ontology structures. Hence, the evaluation scores prove that if the ontology has an instance and class rich structure RDF2Vec method can perform better on the domain-specific environment.

The main aim of the proposed study is to observe the effect of enriched features of ontology structures in a small sample set rather than comparing AGDISTIS and DoSeR approaches and exploiting huge amounts of instances. So, instance counts will be increased and different semantic similarity measurements will be inserted into the global coherence computation to improve the overall performance of Entity Linking approaches in the future work. As an another future direction, semantic embedding algorithms are analyzed for different domains besides movie domain. Furthermore, a novel hybrid method will be presented depends on the RDF and document embeddings and compared with knowledge-agnostic Entity Linking systems.

References

1. Shen, W., Wang, J., Han, J.: Entity linking with a knowledge base: issues, techniques, and solutions. IEEE Trans. Knowl. Data Eng. **27**(2), 443–460 (2015)
2. Milne, D., Witten, I.H.: Learning to link with wikipedia. In: Proceedings of the 17th ACM Conference on Information and Knowledge Management, CIKM 2008, New York, pp. 509–518. ACM (2008)
3. Cucerzan, S.: Large-scale named entity disambiguation based on wikipedia data. In: EMNLP-CoNLL 2007, Proceedings of the 2007 Joint Conference on Empirical Methods in Natural Language Processing and Computational Natural Language Learning, June 28–30, 2007, Prague, Czech Republic, pp. 708–716 (2007)
4. Ferragina, P., Scaiella, U.: Tagme: on-the-fly annotation of short text fragments (by wikipedia entities). In: Proceedings of the 19th ACM International Conference on Information and Knowledge Management, CIKM 2010, New York, pp. 1625–1628. ACM (2010)
5. Usbeck, R., Ngonga Ngomo, A.-C., Röder, M., Gerber, D., Coelho, S.A., Auer, S., Both, A.: AGDISTIS - graph-based disambiguation of named entities using linked data. In: Mika, P., Tudorache, T., Bernstein, A., Welty, C., Knoblock, C., Vrandečić, D., Groth, P., Noy, N., Janowicz, K., Goble, C. (eds.) ISWC 2014. LNCS, vol. 8796, pp. 457–471. Springer, Cham (2014). https://doi.org/10.1007/978-3-319-11964-9_29
6. Zwicklbauer, S., Seifert, C., Granitzer, M.: DoSeR - a knowledge-base-agnostic framework for entity disambiguation using semantic embeddings. In: Sack, H., Blomqvist, E., d'Aquin, M., Ghidini, C., Ponzetto, S.P., Lange, C. (eds.) ESWC 2016. LNCS, vol. 9678, pp. 182–198. Springer, Cham (2016). https://doi.org/10.1007/978-3-319-34129-3_12
7. Mikolov, T., Chen, K., Corrado, G., Dean, J.: Efficient estimation of word representations in vector space. CoRR abs/1301.3781 (2013)
8. Mendes, P.N., Jakob, M., García-Silva, A., Bizer, C.: Dbpedia spotlight: shedding light on the web of documents. In: Proceedings of the 7th International Conference on Semantic Systems. I-Semantics 2011, New York, pp. 1–8. ACM (2011)
9. Moro, A., Raganato, A., Navigli, R.: Entity linking meets word sense disambiguation: a unified approach. Trans. Assoc. Comput. Linguist. (TACL) **2**, 231–244 (2014)

10. Piccinno, F., Ferragina, P.: From tagme to WAT: a new entity annotator. In: ERD 2014, Proceedings of the First ACM International Workshop on Entity Recognition & Disambiguation, July 11, 2014, Gold Coast, Queensland, Australia, pp. 55–62 (2014)
11. Navigli, R.: Babelnet and friends: a manifesto for multilingual semantic processing. Intelligenza Artificiale **7**(2), 165–181 (2013)
12. Ernst, P., Siu, A., Weikum, G.: Knowlife: a versatile approach for constructing a large knowledge graph for biomedical sciences. BMC Bioinform. **16**, 157–15713 (2015)
13. Hassanzadeh, O., Consens, M.P.: Linked movie data base. In: Proceedings of the WWW 2009 Workshop on Linked Data on the Web, LDOW 2009, Madrid, Spain, April 20, 2009 (2009)
14. Nguyen, D.B., Hoffart, J., Theobald, M., Weikum, G.: Aida-light: high-throughput named-entity disambiguation. In: Bizer, C., Heath, T., Auer, S., Berners-Lee, T. (eds.) LDOW, vol. 1184. CEUR Workshop Proceedings, CEUR-WS.org (2014)
15. Hoffart, J., Suchanek, F.M., Berberich, K., Weikum, G.: Yago2: a spatially and temporally enhanced knowledge base from wikipedia. Artif. Intell. **194**, 28–61 (2013)
16. Lehmann, J., Isele, R., Jakob, M., Jentzsch, A., Kontokostas, D., Mendes, P.N., Hellmann, S., Morsey, M., van Kleef, P., Auer, S., Bizer, C.: Dbpedia - a large-scale, multilingual knowledge base extracted from wikipedia. Semant. Web **6**(2), 167–195 (2015)
17. Tartir, S., Arpinar, I.B., Moore, M., Sheth, A.P., Aleman-meza, B.: OntoQA: metric-based ontology quality analysis. In: IEEE Workshop on Knowledge Acquisition from Distributed, Autonomous, Semantically Heterogeneous Data and Knowledge Sources (2005)
18. Lantow, B.: Ontometrics: application of on-line ontology metric calculation. In: Joint Proceedings of the BIR 2016 Workshops and Doctoral Consortium Co-located with 15th International Conference on Perspectives in Business Informatics Research (BIR 2016), Prague, Czech Republic, September 14–16, 2016 (2016)
19. Ristoski, P., Paulheim, H.: RDF2Vec: RDF graph embeddings for data mining. In: Groth, P., Simperl, E., Gray, A., Sabou, M., Krötzsch, M., Lecue, F., Flöck, F., Gil, Y. (eds.) ISWC 2016. LNCS, vol. 9981, pp. 498–514. Springer, Cham (2016). https://doi.org/10.1007/978-3-319-46523-4_30
20. Ellis, J., Getman, J., Mott, J., Li, X., Griffitt, K., Strassel, S., Wright, J.: Linguistic resources for 2013 knowledge base population evaluations. In: Proceedings of the Sixth Text Analysis Conference, TAC 2013, Gaithersburg, Maryland, USA, November 18–19, 2013 (2013)
21. Li, X., Strassel, S., Ji, H., Griffitt, K., Ellis, J.: Linguistic resources for entity linking evaluation: from monolingual to cross-lingual. In: Proceedings of the Eighth International Conference on Language Resources and Evaluation, LREC 2012, Istanbul, Turkey, May 23–25, 2012, pp. 3098–3105 (2012)

Cross-Querying LOD Datasets Using Complex Alignments: An Application to Agronomic Taxa

Elodie Thiéblin[1]([✉]), Fabien Amarger[1], Nathalie Hernandez[1],
Catherine Roussey[2], and Cassia Trojahn Dos Santos[1]

[1] IRIT UMR 5505, 118 Route de Narbonne, 31062 Toulouse Cedex 9, France
{elodie.thieblin,fabien.amarger,nathalie.hernandez,
cassia.trojahn}@irit.fr
[2] Irstea, 9 avenue Blaise Pascal CS 20085, 63178 Aubière, France
catherine.roussey@irstea.fr

Abstract. Farmers have new information needs to change their agricultural practices. The Linked Open Data is a considerable source of knowledge, separated into several heterogeneous and complementary datasets. This paper presents a process to query LOD datasets from a known ontology using complex alignments. The approach was applied on AgronomicTaxon, a taxonomic classification ontology, to query Agrovoc and DBpedia.

Keywords: Query rewriting · Complex alignments · Agronomic sources · Linked Open Data

1 Introduction

The Linked Open Data (LOD) is a considerable source of knowledge, divided into several heterogeneous and complementary datasets. Following LOD principles, a dataset should be linked to others datasets. There exist two different kinds of links. Direct links between two datasets using properties like *owl:sameAs* or *rdfs:seeAlso*. These properties establish correspondences between entities of distinct datasets [19]. Indirect links when two datasets reuse some existing ontologies[1]. That means that the two dataset schemas share some common entity types. These kinds of links are mainly used to browse the different sources or to retrieve corresponding entities. A retrieval system should consider that the query is based on predefined ontology: either all datasets share the same ontology either a selected ontology is used as a reference and all dataset schemas are linked to it. With existing approaches, end-users interactions with the system are needed.

Hence, the LOD has become a needful source of knowledge in many domains, such as in the agriculture domain. For example, due to climatic change and their willingness to improve environmental impacts, farmers and agronomists must rethink agricultural practices. To do so, farmers need to find information about

---

[1] Ontologies are defined as semantic web data schema.

© Springer International Publishing AG 2017
E. Garoufallou et al. (Eds.): MTSR 2017, CCIS 755, pp. 25–37, 2017.
https://doi.org/10.1007/978-3-319-70863-8_3

plant or any living organism. They can be looking for new crops that are able to better support their pedoclimatic conditions. Farmers can also find in their plots unknown insects and may want to know if they are pests of their crops. Furthermore, they can find in their plots some unknown plants and want to know if they are weed plants or auxiliary plants for their crops. These kind of informations can be extracted from scientific sources as presented in [10]. To answer to these information needs, farmers needs to query several datasets that describe living organisms. In such a domain, users are becoming more and more familiar with particular LOD datasets and are able to query them with SPARQL[2]. However, as many domain datasets are nowadays published on the LOD, complementary information may be relevant in other sources. Reformulating the information need according to other ontologies is time consuming. Ontology represents a specific point of view on the domain often influenced by the application needs. Exploiting available ontologies implies taking into account the different modelling issues of the same domain. We propose to take into account this aspect by considering complex correspondences between ontologies [22].

In this paper, we propose a method for helping end-users query the LOD when they have a specific need and have expressed it on a first dataset that can satisfy it. The main idea is to automatically reformulate their SPARQL query by using correspondences established between the different ontologies to find complementary information in the other datasets. The originality of our proposition is to take into account complex correspondences which define expressive correspondences between the ontologies. A first experiment has been carried out with agriculture domain experts that have specific needs dealing with agronomic taxa.

The paper is organised as follows. First we present the context of this work by describing available sources in the agronomic domains and existing Semantic Web approaches dealing with query reformulation. Then we give an overview on our approach. Finally we detail the results we obtained when applying our approach on agronomic taxa.

2   Context

2.1   Agricultural Sources

For information needs related to living organisms, farmers may query several type of information sources available on the Web; For example NCBI[3], TaxRef[4] or Encyclopedia of life[5]. Unfortunatelly these sources are not represented in the Semantic Web formalisms which makes them difficult to query automatically. For that reason these sources are out of scope of this paper, we will focus only on sources available on the LOD.

---

[2] The W3C recommandationhttps://www.w3.org/TR/sparql11-query/ for a query and update language for the Semantic Web.
[3] http://www.ncbi.nlm.nih.gov/taxonomy.
[4] https://inpn.mnhn.fr/programme/referentiel-taxonomique-taxref.
[5] http://eol.org/.

AgronomicTaxon. [6]When searching for information related to plants, Agro-nomicTaxon [18] can be considered as it is, as far as we know, the well formalised ontology available on the domain. This ontology has been developed using the NeOn methodology and reuses several sources and ontology design patterns.

As described in [18] this ontology models the taxonomy thanks to a central class which is *agro:Taxon*. This class is specialised in several sub-classes to model the different levels in the taxonomy. This specialisation, from *agro:VarietyRank* to *agro:KingdomRank*, uses the *agro:hasHigherRank* property to link the different levels. Each *agro:Taxon* is described with vernacular and/or scientific names.

To populate this ontology we used the Muskca system described in [1]. The Muskca system output has been validated manually. The final output deals with the wheat taxonomic classification. We chose this sub-domain to avoid a large number of concepts and allow the manual validation.

DBPedia. [7][2] is a dataset based on the Wikipedia[8] data export.

This dataset covers a lot of domains and is populated with several millions of individuals. For this reason, it is largely used as an instance alignment reference: its instances are linked with other datasets' instances. DBpedia can be seen as a hub between different sources on the LOD. Nevertheless, the Wikipedia policy such as community participation and correction, brings some errors and approximation in its model. The part that deals with agronomic classification contains a large number of taxa but the model is unclear. For example the resource *dbo:Eukaryote* is defined as a *owl:Class*. The resource *dbr:Eukaryote* is defined as an individual. The redundancy here brings some ambiguities because some taxa have the relation *dbo:domain* with the individual *dbr:Eukaryote* and others are typed with the class *dbo:Eukaryote*.

Agrovoc. [9][4] is maintained by experts all over the world thanks to the VocBench platform and overviewed by the Food and Agriculture Organization of the United Nations (FAO). Agrovoc covers all the FAO's areas of interest, such as agriculture, forestry, fisheries, food and related domains. It is available in 20 languages, with an average of 40,000 terms per language. AGROVOC is available in SKOS-XL[10] (with close to 32,000 concepts), and published as Linked Open Data.

The strength of this thesaurus is the lexical coverage with a large number of concepts. The second strength is that this source is used as a reference by experts who wants to manage agricultural data. These strength especially concern the agronomic taxonomic part. Nevertheless, this source cannot be manipulate easily because of its update policy. It is updated manually by some experts, then we can found some erroneous information and information lack [20]. Concerning the agronomic classification we can encounter some ambiguities because of

---

[6] We will use the prefix *agro* for the reference of this ontology.

[7] http://dbpedia.org/prefixes: *dbo* (*Tbox*), *dbr* (*Abox*).

[8] https://fr.wikipedia.org/.

[9] http://aims.fao.org/aos/agrovoc/, prefixes: *agronto* (*Tbox*), *agrovoc* (*Abox*).

[10] http://www.w3.org/TR/skos-reference/skos-xl.html.

the thesaurus model. The hierarchical relation (skos:broader/skos:narrower) can represent several kind of relation (subsumption, partOf, domain specific specialisation). For example, the skos:Concepts link by the skos:narrower property to the skos:Concept "Triticum" are "Winter wheat" and "Summer wheat". They are not known to be scientific agronomic rank.

Figure 1 presents fragments of the 3 sources in [21]'s visualisation format.

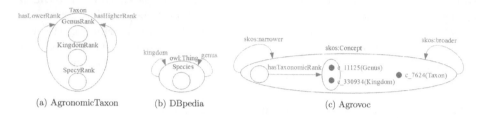

(a) AgronomicTaxon   (b) DBpedia   (c) Agrovoc

Fig. 1. Fragments of the three ontologies in [21]'s visualisation format

2.2   Alignment Definition and Applications

As can be observed for the 3 fragments of the sources presented in the Fig. 1, the ontologies describing the datasets are heterogeneous. The purpose of ontology matching is to reduce the heterogeneity between ontologies [9]. Ontology matching is the process of generating an ontology alignment A between two ontologies [9]: a source ontology o and a target ontology o'. A is a set of correspondences. Each correspondence is a triple $\langle e_o, e_{o'}, r \rangle$

- if the correspondence c_i is **simple**, both e_o and $e_{o'}$ are atomic entities (e.g. class, object property, data property or instance). One IRI is matched with another IRI (1:1), e.g. $\forall x$, *agro:Taxon(x)* $\equiv$ *dbo:Species(x)* is a simple correspondence.
- if the correspondence is **complex**, at least one of e_o or $e_{o'}$ involves one or more atomic entities in a logical construction. The correspondence is therefore (1:n), (m:1) or (m:n) according to the number of entities, constructors or functions involved on each side of the correspondence.
  $\forall x$, *agro:GenusRank(x)* $\equiv$ *agronto:hasTaxonomicRank(x,agrovoc:c_11125)* is a (1:n) complex correspondence with more than one entity.
- r is a relation: equivalence ($\equiv$) or subsumption ($\geq$, $\leq$) between e_o and $e_{o'}$;

An alignment is called a *complex alignment* if at least one of its correspondences is complex. Approach that automatically generate complex alignments between ontologies are emerging [14,16,17]. Ontology alignments can be used for various applications such as ontology merging [15,24] and query mediation [9].

In this paper, the purpose is to query the agronomic sources on the LOD without transforming the ontologies or the data they contain. We consider this hypothesis because we want to preserve the different point of view available in each source. This is especially true for the agronomic classification domain because the domain experts do not agree on which classification they should use. This is why query mediation is the most adapted solution. These methods use correspondences to rewrite queries to adapt to the second ontology. We need here to consider rewriting queries using complex correspondences because AgronomicTaxon/Agrovoc and AgronomicTaxon/DBpedia correspondences cannot be expressed with only simple correspondences. Some complex correspondence examples are presented in the Sect. 4.1.

3 Related Work

A SPARQL query is intrinsically related to the ontological model that describes the RDF source. To federate information from different sources described by various ontologies, a SPARQL query must be adapted to each of them.

A naive approach for rewriting SPARQL queries consists in replacing the IRI of an entity of the initial query by the corresponding IRI in the alignment, using simple correspondences. This approach is integrated in the Alignment API [7]. However, it does not take into account the specific kind of relation expressed in the correspondence (e.g., generalisation or specialisation). Makris *et al.* [12,13] present the SPARQL-RW rewriting framework that applies a set of predefined rules for (complex) correspondences. They define a set of correspondence types on which the rewriting process is based (i.e., *Class Expression, Object Property Expression, Datatype Property,* and *Individual*). Zheng *et al.* [25] propose a rewriting algorithm that serves the purpose of context (i.e., units of measure) interchange for interoperability. Correndo *et al.* [5] apply a declarative formalism for expressing alignments between RDF graphs to rewrite SPARQL queries. In [6], a subset of EDOAL expressions are transformed into a set of rewriting rules. The expressions involving the restrictions on classes and properties and the restrictions on property occurrences and values are not featured in the rewriting rules. Thiéblin *et al.* [22] propose a set of rewriting rules from EDOAL expression. In comparison with Correndo *et al.*'s [6] approach, it can deal with expressions such as Class by Attribute Occurrence. The approach is based on the assumption that the queries to be transformed aim at retrieving new instances to meet a given need. This is why only *Tbox* elements are taken into account.

Some approaches have also been proposed in order to query several LOD datasets, thus helping the users to adapt the expression of their need to several sources. [23], for example, relies on explicit correspondences expressed within the dataset (with *owl:sameAs, owl:equivalentClass,* or *owl:equivalentProperty* properties) to automatically reformulate queries. Another example come from the SemaGrow [11] project. One use case is about querying multiple bibliographic datasets related to agricultural domain. All the dataset schemas share the same ontology. Some simple alignment between individuals are used to translate the query into the targetted dataset. The performance of this kind of methods depends on how datasets are explicitly linked. Most of the time, only simple correspondences between instances (expressed with *owl:sameAs* property) are expressed which limits the possibility of reformulation. Instances typed by classes or linked by properties for which no correspondences have been established will not be retrieved. The approach presented in [3] helps end-users express their query by means of a graphical interface that automatically adapts to a specific selected LOD dataset. An overview of the ontology used to describe the data is presented and the interface assists the formulation of the query according to it. More intuitive, SimplePARQL [8] proposes a way for formulating SPARQL queries by using terms for designating resources instead of their IRI. The users do not need to know the underlying ontology but this approach implies that the ontology is exhaustively annotated with all the *rdfs:label* that can be associated with the resources. The aim of our work is to reformulate queries automatically by using the expressiveness of complex correspondences.

4   An Approach for Querying LOD Datasets

Figure 2 presents the global work-flow of the approach. The users knows an ontology (e.g. AgronomicTaxon) and can write a SPARQL query expressing their needs using this ontology. An ontology alignment exists between the known ontology and ontologies from the LOD (e.g. DBpedia, Agrovoc). The SPARQL rewriting system rewrites the query to query the LOD dataset. The users get the information fitting their needs from various sources. The SPARQL rewriting system as well as the alignments are publicly available[11].

The approach is illustrated by the use case with the known ontology being AgronomicTaxon, and two LOD datasets being Agrovoc and DBpedia.

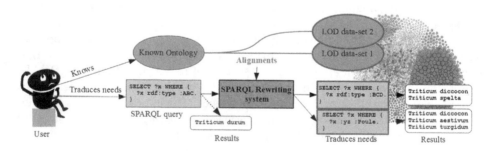

Fig. 2. Global work-flow of the approach

4.1   Ontology Alignments

Our SPARQL rewriting system needs alignments between the known ontology and the LOD ontologies. Alignments between ontologies are not always available. In this case, some approaches may be able to generate them [14,16,17]. If the approaches are not exhaustive enough, the alignments can be manually written.

---

[11] https://framagit.org/IRIT_UT2J/sparql-translator-complex-alignment.

Table 1. Extract of correspondences of the AgronomicTaxon-DBpedia and AgronomicTaxon-Agrovoc alignments

AgronomicTaxon entity	Rel	Right member	Ref
$\forall x$, agro:Taxon(x)	$\equiv$	dbo:Species(x)	(1)
	$\equiv$	$\exists y$, agronto:hasTaxonomicRank(x,y) $\wedge$ skos:broader(y,agrovoc:c_7624)	(2)
$\forall x,y$, agro:hasHigherRank(x,y)	$\geq$	dbo:Species(x) $\wedge$ dbo:Species(y)$\wedge$ (dbo:genus(x,y) $\vee$ dbo:family(x,y) $\vee$ dbo:order(x,y) $\vee$ dbo:classis(x,y) $\vee$ dbo:phylum(x,y) $\vee$ dbo:kingdom(x,y))	(3)
	$\leq$	skos:broader+(x,y)	(4)
$\forall x,y$, agro:hasLowerRank(x,y)	$\geq$	dbo:Species(x) $\wedge$ dbo:Species(y)$\wedge$ (dbo:genus(y,x) $\vee$ dbo:family(y,x) $\vee$ dbo:order(y,x) $\vee$ dbo:classis(y,x) $\vee$ dbo:phylum(y,x) $\vee$ dbo:kingdom(y,x))	(5)
	$\leq$	skos:narrower+(x,y)	(6)
$\forall x,y$, agro:prefScientificName(x,y)	$\leq$	rdfs:label(x,y)	(7)
	$\leq$	$\exists z$, skos:prefLabel(x,y) $\vee$ (skosxl:prefLabel(x,z) $\wedge$ skosxl:literalForm(z,y))	(8)
$\forall x$, agro:SpecyRank(x)	$\leq$	$\exists y$, dbo:Species(x) $\wedge$ dbo:genus(x,y) $\wedge$ dbo:Species(y)	(9)
	$\equiv$	agronto:hasTaxonomicRank(x, agrovoc: c_331243)	(10)

Table 2. Original (AgronomicTaxon) and automatically rewritten SPARQL queries (Agrovoc and DBpedia) to retrieve sub-taxa of Triticum. The numbers are the correspondences references from Table 1 used to translate each triple.

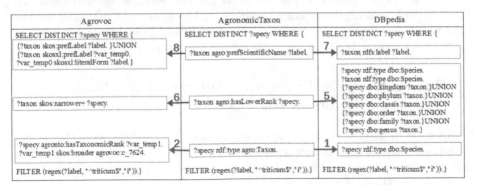

For our use case considering AgronomicTaxon, DBpedia and Agrovoc, these approaches did not generate any correspondence. For this reason, the alignments between the chosen ontologies were manually written in EDOAL[12] to apply the approach. AgronomicTaxon being the known ontology, it is the source ontology of the alignments. Each entity of AgronomicTaxon was put in correspondence when possible. During the alignment establishment phase, (1:n) correspondences were sought, equivalence correspondences were favoured over subsumption correspondences, simple equivalence correspondences were favoured over complex. This way, the correspondences are as simple and correct as possible. Table 1 presents a few correspondences of the alignment. The AgronomicTaxon-Agrovoc alignment contains 31 correspondences and the AgronomicTaxon-DBpedia alignment contains only 29 as 2 properties could not be translated. The granularity heterogeneity of the ontologies made it impossible for some entities (classes, object properties, data properties) to be put in an equivalence relation. For this reason, some correspondences have a subsumption relation. In correspondences (4) and (6), the + symbol stands for the transitivity of the object property.

4.2   SPARQL Query Rewriting from Complex Alignments

We use the rewriting SPARQL approach from [22] because it deals with complex alignments expressed in the EDOAL format and can process expressions such as *ClassByAttributeOccurrence* not processed by other systems. This system translates the triples of a SPARQL query one after the other. It can only translate two kinds of triples: Class Triples of the form `?x rdf:type o:SomeClass.` and Predicate Triples `?x o:predicate ?y.`. The subject of the triples of the query to be rewritten must always be a variable, the object is either a Class URI (in a class triple), a variable or a literal (in a predicate triple).

The following example presents the rewriting process of a SPARQL query on AgronomicTaxon for retrieving every subtaxa of Triticum. Table 2 presents the initial SPARQL query on AgronomicTaxon. The query is rewritten for Agrovoc and DBpedia using the alignments.

The first triple of the query is rewritten using the correspondences (8) for Agrovoc and (7) for DBpedia. The second triple was rewritten using (6) and (5). The last triple was rewritten using (2) and (1). The filter and the header are the same for all the queries. The query results on their respective dataset are shown in Fig. 3. The analysis of the results is detailed in the next section.

5   Result Analysis: Extracting Information About AgronomicTaxon on the LOD

In this section, we present the information needs defined and we detail the results of the approach for each information need. The information needs considered in this experiment have been defined with domain experts when designing AgronomicTaxon. They are presented in Table 3.

---

[12] http://alignapi.gforge.inria.fr/edoal.html.

Table 3. Information needs in natural language

Question	Description
IN1	What is the rank of the taxon Triticum?
IN2	What is the kingdom of the Triticum taxon?
IN3	What are the common names of Triticum taxon in French?
IN4	What are the common names of Triticum taxon in English?
IN5	What are the different wheat species?

Each information need was express with a SPARQL query for Agronomic-Taxon. The results of the approach are presented below. Every SPARQL query and its results are available on the Framagit repository[13].

IN1: the rank of Triticum: Genus Rank. The concept "Genus" is represented as a class in AgronomicTaxon and as an instance in Agrovoc and DBpedia. The SPARQL query on AgronomicTaxon specifies that the expected answer is a class with a *rdf:type* relation and uses the structure of the ontology through a *rdfs:subClassOf* relation. No answer is provided for the Agrovoc dataset as the rewriting approach can not properly translate the `?rank rdfs:subClassOf agro:Taxon` triple from the initial query using a complex correspondence. As correspondence (2) from Table 1 is a complex correspondence and should be used in the rewriting process, the triple is not well translated. For DBpedia, the (1) correspondence is a simple correspondence. Therefore, the triple can be translated. However, the structure of DBpedia is different from Agronomic-Taxon's. The *dbo:Eukaryote* class is returned because Triticum is an instance of *dbo:Eukaryote* and *dbo:Eukaryote* is a subclass of *dbo:Species*. This answer is wrong and comes from the fact that some taxa in DBpedia are defined as classes (*dbo:Eukaryote*) and instances (*dbr:Eukaryote*).

This query used the structure of the source ontology which is very different from the target ontologies'. Therefore, the given results are poor.

IN2: the kingdom of Triticum: Plantae. Plantae is an instance in Agronomic-Taxon. Both rewritten queries are semantically correct. The query on Agrovoc retrieves the *agrovoc:c_330074* instance which is the Plantae taxon. The filter for the "wheat" label was changed to "triticum" because Agrovoc contains few vernacular names. The query on DBpedia does not retrieve anything because even though the *dbo:kingdom* property holds between *dbr:Triticum* and *dbr:Plantae*, *dbr:Plantae* was not specified as a taxon (*dbo:Species*).

This query was successfully rewritten for both target ontologies but DBpedia could not give an answer as some information is missing in the dataset.

---

[13] https://framagit.org/IRIT_UT2J/sparql-translator-complex-alignment/tree/master/mtsr2017/.

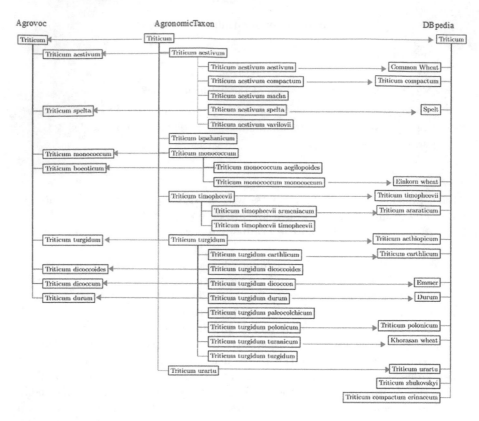

Fig. 3. Correspondences between the taxa under the Triticum genus in Agrovoc (left), AgronomicTaxon (center) and DBpedia (right). The red arrows are *rdfs:seeAlso* relations. (Color figure online)

IN3-4: vernacular names of Triticum in French and English: Blé and Wheat. In AgronomicTaxon, the French vernacular name of Triticum is not specified while the English is. The AgronomicTaxon ontology distinguishes vernacular names from scientific names. In Agrovoc and DBpedia, no such distinction is made. Agrovoc uses *skos:prefLabel, skosxl:prefLabel ∘ skosxl:literalForm* properties to label its instances. The dataset mostly contains scientific labels. DBpedia uses the *rdfs:label* property and was populated with common names. In the alignments, the label properties of AgronomicTaxon could not find equivalents. The results of the queries are therefore more general than what is expected. Agrovoc returns "Triticum" as French common name and "Triticum" as English common name. DBpedia returns "Blé" for French and "Wheat" for English.

As there was no equivalence relation for the properties used in these queries but only more general properties, the results given by the queries is more general. The outcome of the query depends on the way the datasets were populated. The outcome of these queries shows the complementarity of the sources on the LOD. The "Blé" information was only present in DBpedia.

IN5: the species of Triticum genus. Figure 3 presents the manual instance mappings made between the sub-taxa of Triticum in AgronomicTaxon and the instances in Agrovoc and DBpedia.

In the Agrovoc tree (left) a child relation between two nodes stands for a *skos:narrower* relation, in the AgronomicTaxon tree (left), it stands for a direct *agro:hasLowerRank* relation. In the DBpedia tree (right), a child has a *dbo:genus* relation with the *dbr:Triticum* taxon. In AgronomicTaxon (center), the species are the direct children of Triticum and the subspecies are the children of the species. In Agrovoc, all subtaxa of Triticum have a specie rank. There are no subspecies. In DBpedia, there is no rank distinction between the sub-taxa of a genus. DBpedia is not as fine-grained as AgronomicTaxon so the class *agro:SpecyRank* has no equivalence in DBpedia. In the alignment, it is subsumed in correspondence (9) of Table 1. Therefore the rewritten query will return all taxa below Triticum.

The result of this query emphasises the granularity heterogeneity between datasets. It also shows the complementarity of the sources as some sub-taxa of Triticum only appear in DBpedia and some only in AgronomicTaxon.

6   Conclusion

We presented the use of complex alignments for a SPARQL rewriting approach applied to agronomic LOD sources. This evaluation of this approach highlights a few points. First of all, the agronomic ontologies of the LOD are heterogeneous and simple alignments are not always expressive enough to provide interoperability between them. Secondly, LOD datasets contain complementary information based on how they are populated (IN3-4, Fig. 3). A SPARQL rewriting approach based on complex alignments can show good results in information crossing depending on the nature of the query. Queries expecting a part of ontology as a result or using the structure of the query itself will not give good results with complex alignments (IN1). The granularity heterogeneity between ontologies will affect the semantic equivalence between two queries (IN5). This should be in mind when using the rewriting approach. Because of the scope heterogeneity between ontologies, some queries cannot be rewritten. The missing information of a dataset can affect the results of a query (e.g. DBpedia in IN2).

A few downsides can be stressed and shall be addressed in future works. First of all, the automatically obtained queries are not optimised for performance because of the triple by triple rewriting approach. This is an issue when querying large-scale datasets such as DBPedia. (m:n) correspondences are not processed by SPARQL query rewriting systems yet. A global interpretation of the SPARQL query, instead of a triple-by-triple process could be a solution to both problems. Another issue pointed out in IN1, is that the expected answer to a query can be a class in a dataset (*agro:GenusRank*) or an instance in another one (*agovoc:c_11125*). There still is no formalisation of this kind of correspondence (class-instance).

Acknowledgements. This work is partially supported by the French FUI Sparkin-Data project.

References

1. Amarger, F., Chanet, J.-P., Haemmerlé, O., Hernandez, N., Roussey, C.: Knowledge engineering method based on consensual knowledge and trust computation: the MUSCKA system. In: Haemmerlé, O., Stapleton, G., Faron Zucker, C. (eds.) ICCS 2016. LNCS (LNAI), vol. 9717, pp. 177–190. Springer, Cham (2016). https://doi.org/10.1007/978-3-319-40985-6_14
2. Auer, S., Bizer, C., Kobilarov, G., Lehmann, J., Cyganiak, R., Ives, Z.: DBpedia: a nucleus for a web of open data. In: Aberer, K., et al. (eds.) ASWC/ISWC -2007. LNCS, vol. 4825, pp. 722–735. Springer, Heidelberg (2007). https://doi.org/10.1007/978-3-540-76298-0_52
3. Benedetti, F., Bergamaschi, S., Po, L.: Lodex: a tool for visual querying linked open data. In: ISWC (2015)
4. Caracciolo, C., Stellato, A., Morshed, A., Johannsen, G., Rajbhandari, S., Jaques, Y., Keizer, J.: The agrovoc linked dataset. Semant. Web 4(3), 341–348 (2013)
5. Correndo, G., Salvadores, M., Millard, I., Glaser, H., Shadbolt, N.: SPARQL query rewriting for implementing data integration over linked data. In: 1st International Workshop on Data Semantics (DataSem 2010) (2010)
6. Correndo, G., Shadbolt, N.: Translating expressive ontology mappings into rewriting rules to implement query rewriting. In: 6th Workshop on Ontology Matching (2011)
7. David, J., Euzenat, J., Scharffe, F., Trojahn, C.: The alignment API 4.0. Semant. Web 2(1), 3–10 (2011)
8. Djebali, S., Raimbault, T.: Simpleparql: a new approach using keywords over sparql to query the web of data. In: Proceedings of the 11th International Conference on Semantic Systems. ACM (2015)
9. Euzenat, J., Shvaiko, P.: Ontology Matching. Springer, Berlin (2013)
10. Kulicki, P., Trypuz, R., Trójczak, R., Wierzbicki, J., Woźniak, A.: Ontology-based representation of scientific laws on beef production and consumption. In: Garoufallou, E., Greenberg, J. (eds.) MTSR 2013. CCIS, vol. 390, pp. 430–439. Springer, Cham (2013). https://doi.org/10.1007/978-3-319-03437-9_42
11. Lokers, R., Konstantopoulos, S., Stellato, A., Knapen, R., Janssen, S.: Designing innovative linked open data and semantic technologies in agro-environmental modelling (2014)
12. Makris, K., Bikakis, N., Gioldasis, N., Christodoulakis, S.: SPARQL-RW: transparent query access over mapped RDF data sources. In: 15th International Conference on Extending Database Technology. ACM (2012)
13. Makris, K., Gioldasis, N., Bikakis, N., Christodoulakis, S.: Ontology mapping and SPARQL rewriting for querying federated RDF data sources. In: Meersman, R., Dillon, T., Herrero, P. (eds.) OTM 2010. LNCS, vol. 6427, pp. 1108–1117. Springer, Heidelberg (2010). https://doi.org/10.1007/978-3-642-16949-6_32
14. Parundekar, R., Knoblock, C.A., Ambite, J.L.: Discovering concept coverings in ontologies of linked data sources. In: Cudré-Mauroux, P., et al. (eds.) ISWC 2012. LNCS, vol. 7649, pp. 427–443. Springer, Heidelberg (2012). https://doi.org/10.1007/978-3-642-35176-1_27
15. Pokharel, S., Sherif, M.A., Lehmann, J.: Ontology based data access and integration for improving the effectiveness of farming in Nepal. IEEE (2014)

16. Qin, H., Dou, D., LePendu, P.: Discovering executable semantic mappings between ontologies. In: Meersman, R., Tari, Z. (eds.) OTM 2007. LNCS, vol. 4803, pp. 832–849. Springer, Heidelberg (2007). https://doi.org/10.1007/978-3-540-76848-7_56
17. Ritze, D., Völker, J., Meilicke, C., Sváb-Zamazal, O.: Linguistic analysis for complex ontology matching. In: 5th Workshop on Ontology Matching (2010)
18. Roussey, C., Chanet, J.P., Cellier, V., Amarger, F.: Agronomic taxon. In: Proceedings of the 2nd International Workshop on Open Data, p. 5. ACM (2013)
19. Schmachtenberg, M., Bizer, C., Paulheim, H.: Adoption of the linked data best practices in different topical domains. In: Mika, P., et al. (eds.) ISWC 2014. LNCS, vol. 8796, pp. 245–260. Springer, Cham (2014). https://doi.org/10.1007/978-3-319-11964-9_16
20. Soergel, D., Lauser, B., Liang, A., Fisseha, F., Keizer, J., Katz, S.: Reengineering thesauri for new applications: the AGROVOC example. J. Digit. Inf. 4, 1–23 (2004)
21. Stapleton, G., Howse, J., Bonnington, A., Burton, J.: A vision for diagrammatic ontology engineering. In: International Workshop on Visualizations and User Interfaces for Knowledge Engineering and Linked Data Analytics (2014)
22. Thiéblin, É., Amarger, F., Haemmerlé, O., Hernandez, N., Trojahn, C.: Rewriting select sparql queries from 1: n complex correspondences. In: 11th Workshop on Ontology Matching (2016)
23. Torre-Bastida, A.I., Bermúdez, J., Illarramendi, A., Mena, E., González, M.: Query rewriting for an incremental search in heterogeneous linked data sources. In: Larsen, H.L., Martin-Bautista, M.J., Vila, M.A., Andreasen, T., Christiansen, H. (eds.) FQAS 2013. LNCS (LNAI), vol. 8132, pp. 13–24. Springer, Heidelberg (2013). https://doi.org/10.1007/978-3-642-40769-7_2
24. Wang, Y., Wang, Y., Wang, J., Yuan, Y., Zhang, Z.: An ontology-based approach to integration of hilly citrus production knowledge. Comput. Electron. Agric. 113, 24–43 (2015)
25. Zheng, X., Madnick, S.E., Li, X.: SPARQL query mediation over RDF data sources with disparate contexts. In: WWW Workshop on Linked Data on the Web (2012)

Deploying Metadata on Blockchain Technologies

Elena García-Barriocanal, Salvador Sánchez-Alonso,
and Miguel-Angel Sicilia(✉)

Computer Science Department, University of Alcalá, Polytechnic building,
Ctra. Barcelona km. 33.6, 28871 Alcalá de Henares, Madrid, Spain
{elena.garciab,salvador.sanchez,msicilia}@uah.es

Abstract. Metadata repositories and services support the key functions required by the curation of digital resources, including description,
management and provenance. They typically use conventional databases
owned and managed by different kinds of organizations that are trusted
by their users. Blockchains have emerged as a means to deploy decentralized databases secured from tampering and revision, opening the doors
for a new way of deploying that kind of digital archival systems. In this
paper we review and evaluate the functions of metadata in that new
light and propose an approach in which a blockchain combined with
other related technologies can be arranged in a particular way to obtain
a decentralized solution for metadata supporting key functions. We discuss how the approach overcomes some weaknesses of current digital
archives, along with its important implications for the management and
sustainability of digital archives.

Keywords: Blockchain · Metadata · Decentralization · Provenance ·
Trust · Ethereum · IPFS · BlockchainDB

1   Introduction

Blockchain technologies have emerged as a means to deploy applications that
provide decentralized database functions secured from tampering and revision
and that are able to operate on open networks in a completely decentralized way.
Complementary technologies as decentralized file systems (as the *Interplanetary
File System*, IPFS [1]) and blockchain layers for databases has also been developed to fill particular gaps that are currently not provided currently by public
blockchain system implementations in an efficient way. The first successful application of blockchain technology has been the Bitcoin crypto-currency, but the
applicability of the underlying distributed ledger technology spans many other
areas beyond [15], that are currently being explored.

Digital repositories and systems serve different functions, notably the permanent archival of digital resources and the provision of descriptions that ease their
retrieval, encoding provenance and descriptive information as metadata. There
exist a number of software solutions supporting various forms of management
of metadata and digital resource preservation. Concretely, open source ones as

E. Garoufallou et al. (Eds.): MTSR 2017, CCIS 755, pp. 38–49, 2017.
https://doi.org/10.1007/978-3-319-70863-8_4

DSpace, EPrints or Fedora [10] are widespread, and they fundamentally serve the role of institutional repositories. The actual usage of these systems nowadays assume trust in the repository owner, and rely on the institution or network of institutions for its sustainability along time. This is not without problems, as some of them might fail in funding the costs of their running activity [2,12] or they may be exposed to other risks concerning the concern for sustainability [3].

Blockchain and associated technologies provide a new type of platform to overcome some of the problems of current repository technology and are thus promising candidates to build a decentralized approach to the archival of digital resources. However, reformulating the current system of digital archives, aggregators and services requires a careful consideration of the functions of metadata, its desirable properties, and the extent to which different technologies are able to support them. Further, blockchain-based decentralized systems are not without risks, especially as they are built around systems of incentives for the participants in the network, so sustainability should be incorporated in their design.

In this paper, we report on the analysis and early proof-of-concept implementation of a decentralized metadata system that considers the different functions of metadata as point of departure. We start from an account of these functions and then assess the fit of different kind of technologies. Then, the fundamental data models, interfaces and processes are described and contrasted with current practice. We only address the base mechanisms for deploying metadata on blockchains and not the required systems of incentives and end-user systems needed for a complete solution, as those should be subject to separate inquiry and research.

The rest of this paper is structured as follows. Section 2 provides the rationale and requirements for the approach presented. Then, the proposed approach is described in Sect. 3. Section 4 describes a proof-of-concept implementation using concrete technologies. Finally, conclusions and outlook are provided in Sect. 5.

2   Background and Rationale

2.1   Blockchains as Shared, Immutable Repositories

The term "blockchain" refers to the core data structure of a category of decentralized database architectures that rely on cryptographic techniques and distributed consensus to provide tamper-proof distributed ledgers. The first widespread blockchain application was that of Bitcoin [15], that used that technology to implement the possibility of interchanging a token (a digital currency) among non-trusted parties without the need of a central authority and preventing double spending.

The application of blockchains have since Bitcoin inception be extended to the notion of "smart contracts" (first proposed by Szabo [14]) in which non-trusted parties can interact with the blockchain for different kinds of transactions including some logic that can be implemented in Turing-complete programming languages. This supports the implementation of token interchange systems as Bitcoin, but also many other applications as voting, registries or future markets to name a few. The main current exponent of such technology is Ethereum [19], that we consider here as the foundation for the analysis.

Here we are interested fundamentally in blockchains as immutable archives that do not rely on a trusted party, in contrast with current repository systems. While this is discussed here essentially from its practical, technological implications, it has the potential to impact the economics of current archival institutions, their funding models, and eventually, their archival cycles and responsibilities. There are a few recent proposals for digital repository architectures based on blockchains [9,18], but the core underlying representational commitments of metadata have not been discussed to date.

2.2   Metadata Functions and Requirements

Metadata schemas are the specifications of how metadata descriptions should be interpreted, syntactically and semantically. While different schemas developed and evolved by different communities may differ in their objectives (e.g. an schema for museum collections differs in its aims from one devised for environmental data), their resulting metadata serves a number of functions in all cases. Here we use the classification in [5] that in turn consolidates classifications from other authors. The departure point for the approach presented here is thus mapping those functions to required core architectural properties, which are summarized in Table 1.

Table 1. Types, functions and architectural requirements for metadata

Type	Function facilitated	Architectural req.
Identification/Description	Resource discovery Information retrieval	Decentralized identification Dereferencing Indexing
Administrative	Resource management	Pricing, interchange
Terms and conditions	Resource usage	Rights management
Content rating	Resource use by appropriate audiences	Labelling
Provenance	Authentication and related	Proof of statement
Linkage/relationship	Linking with related resources	Referencing
Structural	Software and hardware needs	Media typing

Among the requirements in Table 1, a first analysis results in three categories[1] depending on how they are influenced by blockchain and related decentralized technology:

– Requirements not directly supported by the blockchain network. This includes *media typing*, as these is related to the long-term capability to understand,

---

[1] It should be noted that we are considered concretely Ethereum as the reference model for public blockchain technology combined with a decentralized P2P storage model as IPFS. The analysis reported here may be different considering other emerging blockchain technologies.

process and render digital objects. Decentralized storage can only refer in the metadata to the software of specifications needed, but this remains a matter of preserving the capability of processing that has been addressed before typically via emulation or migration [16]. Also *labeling* is out of the core blockchain implementation, as this entails interpreting the needs of different audiences, which is an interpretive assessment by nature.

– Requirements that are impacted by decentralized solutions. *Indexing* is not a capability directly supported by current public blockchains and thus requires some additional infrastructure, but is dependent on referencing the blockchain for tamper-proof provenance. The same occurs with referencing (linking) that takes a different form if referencing resources in decentralized systems [13], but it is not fully resolved with it and requires additional conventions. *Pricing*, *rights management* and *interchange* are not granted as a direct consequence of using a blockchain, but the blockchain enables the creation of new mechanisms for such applications. The music industry is the focus of inquiry on the application of rights management, but there are still not clear, comprehensive and widespread blockchain solutions for it but only some experimental work [4].

– Requirements that are directly supported by the blockchain network. These include *identification*, *dereferencing* and *proof of statement* as functions that are directly supported by a combination of a blockchain and a decentralized file system as described below.

One additional key issue in metadata is that of interoperability. While interoperability at a syntactic or data transfer level is tackled by mappings or transformations, semantic interoperability poses different challenges [6] requiring model mapping at different levels. Decentralization entails the exposure of a heterogeneity of autonomous, incompatible media repositories and it is unlikely that there will ever exist a single agreed-upon metadata schema (if it ever exists it should be based on a system of incentives that is still to be conceived). This entails that the interpretation of the metadata also requires that the schemas and ontologies or terminologies used by them are also deployed in immutable decentralized systems, but this has been focus of previous research [13] and is not considered in further detail here.

3 Proposed Approach

3.1 Resources and Identifiers

At a very basic level, metadata can be considered an statement about a *resource*. Digital resources[2] are usually identified by different means, as URIs or DOIs. However, these have two problems associated: (a) they rely on some trusted party

---

[2] Here we limit our discussion to digital resources, but they could be surrogates of physical entities, provided that these surrogates can be unambiguously linked to its corresponding physical counterpart.

or authority, as in the case of the DOI and (b) some of them (as URIs) cannot be guaranteed (and are not intended to) retrieve the same resource over time.

In a context of untrusted parties, digital resources should be identified via mechanisms that uniquely identify them from their content. As we are dealing with resources that are coded and represented by different media types and conventions, using hashes of their byte content appears as a universally applicable approach. An example of this is the addressing used in IPFS, that relies on a P2P architecture to store (almost) permanently digital resources in decentralized storage. Existing or future identification systems may eventually link other identifiers to the actual hashes, serving thus as effective aliases. This brings the decentralized file system as the first component of the approach.

It should be noted that metadata records are themselves digital resources, so that they can also be identified by content.

An additional desirable requirement is that identifiers are dereferenceable, i.e. that they can be used to resolve the actual resource. This is a basic principle in the Web of Linked Data, for example. In consequence, a basic model for identifiers is that of introducing a notion of decentralized *handlers*, defined as follows (using Solidity, from here on we use Ethereum as the smart contract technology):

```
struct Handler {
    bytes   hash;       // identifier
    string service;     // location
    string meta;        // processing info
}
```

The field `meta` is a placeholder for additional information required for dereferencing the item from the given `service`. The requirement on the service is that it provides decentralized, tamper resistant permanent storage, thus avoiding the problems of availability that hamper the usefulness of approaches as that of Linked Data [11]. An example service that could be used is IPFS. The `hash` will be an IPFS hash, service will be some conventional reference to IPFS and no additional information would be required in this case. Note that meta could be used for supporting *media typing* functions (requiring some new or existing conventions), a simple case is providing the MIME type, or some reference to the metadata schema if the resource is actually a piece of metadata. For example, a simple handler representation may be:

```
Handler h = Handler({hash:"QmYwAPJzv5CZsnA625s3Xf2nemtYgPpHd...",
                    service:"ipfs-base58", meta:"audio/mpeg3"});
```

Note that this does not resolve the problem of the different representations of intellectual works which remains a matter of modeling and ontology, as addressed for example in the FRBR model [17]. This simple representation also allows both for public schemes or private ones, as the underlying representation is just a stream of bytes which may be encrypted itself or require some special non-public software for processing. However, we limit ourselves here on public descriptions and open access resources.

3.2 Statements and Provenance

Once we have an account by which resources and their metadata can be identified, the next important feature is that of provenance. This has two levels: (a) allowing for metadata authors (individuals but also institutions as libraries or archives) to proof that a given metadata is provided by them, and (b) describing the provenance that the metadata author claims to be associated to the object. The former is in some schemas as IEEE LOM known as "meta-metadata". Once (a) can be established, then (b) becomes a matter of trust in the issuer of the metadata.

We are here concerned with (a), which is the basic problem of authenticity of metadata. A blockchain can be the appropriate solution here as it allows for metadata authors to add transactions to the blockchain in which they can cryptographically proof their provenance, and that cannot be removed, so services relying on them are not dependant on their availability. It should be noted that blockchains can also be used to claim authorship priority just by depositing hashes to files in transactions, but this is not our focus here.

The relation of a metadata record to a resource then becomes a claim with a core data model sketched as follows.

```
enum Verb {Add, Retract, Replace}
struct Claim {
   Handler resource;
   Handler metadata;
   Verb OP;
   uint256 timestamp;
}
```

Then, different operations can be implemented using a smart contract in a straightforward way:

```
contract MetadataRepository {
  // ...
  mapping(address => mapping(bytes => Claim[])) statements;

  function claim(bytes rhash, string rservice, string rmeta,
                 bytes mhash, string mservice, string mmeta){
     var resource = Handler(rhash, rservice, rmeta);
     var meta = Handler(mhash, mservice, mmeta);
     oraclize(resource); oraclize(meta);
     var claim = Claim(resource, meta, Verb.Add, block.timestamp);
     statements[msg.sender][resource.hash].push(claim);
  }
function retract(...){
    // ...
  }
function check(address curator, bytes rhash)
               constant public returns (bool){
    //...
}
```

The key here is that the transactions need to check that the resource is really available using an external oracle. A possible solution is for example that of using *Oraclize*[3], that provides proof for different external sources using in turn *TLSNotary*. This provides the basic functionality of registering claims (that may be a retraction of a previous one) of dereferenceable resources and metadata records. However, given the characteristics of public blockchains as Ethereum this cannot be used to implement indexing functions.

Metadata then becomes a set of series of immutable claims, that reflect the current description of the digital object by a network participant, where claims may be revised, so that there is some non-monotonicity entailed that require some handling of fact retraction (as in e.g. [8]) if metadata is used in reasoning systems. Each series comes from an address, which is in the blockchain a pseudonym. However, institutions or individuals may disclose their physical world identity via means as digital certificates.

3.3 Search and Discovery

Resource search and discovery is currently done in archives by using search technology on top of conventional databases, and using typically harvesting protocols as OAI-PMH for mirroring, sub-setting or aggregating archives. Real-time queries using rich syntaxes require an additional layer on top of the blockchain and decentralized storage of resources. Using conventional indexing and retrieval engines as Apache Lucene is an option, but it requires a copy of the resources to be indexed, thus becoming a trusted party. An option that brings some of the benefits of blockchains is using blockchain databases, that add functionalities to conventional scalable database systems. BigchainDB adds a layer on top of RethinkDB or MongoDB featuring a number of query facilities.

Deploying databases as BigchainDB as front-ends should attempt to bring decentralization and tamper resistance to the query layer, which in that case is facilitated by *node diversity*.

BigchainDB is optimized to the transfer of assets in high loading cases, so it would become an ideal candidate to resource usage and management functions of metadata. While this can also be done using platforms as Ethereum that support arbitrarily complex contracts, it brings scalability.

While BigchainDB is not currently featuring a full-fledged search language, its asset consensus model can be used to implement mirrors. There are two use cases here:

(a) The creators of metadata records submit CREATE transactions for each of their records in the blockchain.
(b) The owner of the aggregator or surrogate submit the CREATE transactions and include a back-reference to the transaction and block in the original blockchain.

---

[3] http://www.oraclize.it/.

Case (a) has the interesting feature of supporting cryptographic transfer of the metadata (asset in BigchainDB jargon). Case (b) has the benefit of allowing third parties build their systems independently while still providing a way by which the records can be trusted by inspecting the original blockchain transaction. In this second case, the consensus protocol of the blockchain database could be augmented to reject transactions not consistent with the original blockchain, which can be verified by using the `check` operation described above.

In both cases, as BigchainDB is a front-end for a NoSQL engine, the query facilities of that engine can be used for trusted records.

3.4   Semantics

Semantics is introduced by the use of vocabularies, terminologies or ontologies (we can collectively refer to all of them as Knowledge Organization Systems, KOS) in particular metadata elements. The implications is that terminologies can be considered another resource that must be subject to decentralized storage and attestation of authenticity via blockchain transactions. In [13] the distributed storage part is discussed, and the proof of authenticity could be achieved by similar means to that of the metadata, but in this case, just registering the different versions of the KOS.

The problem is that current metadata is now using typically URIs or other codes for the referencing. This has many problems, as in many cases these codes do not refer to a concrete version, or in some cases are not dereferenceable or are at risk of becoming unavailable. However, converting all those references is not trivial and changes the contents (and thus the handlers) of metadata records, which makes this seldom viable in the short-term.

3.5   Other Functions

Media typing in the approach presented is maintained as an informative function of the metadata elements, but it is not dealt with specifically. The field `meta` in handlers may be used for that purpose, but a more complex approach would be that of using a similar architecture for storing media type declarations associated to media type descriptions, converters or even software artifacts that can be used to process them, supporting different preservation strategies [7].

Content rating allows for the real-time selective dissemination of resources depending on the user or audience. We have not found any blockchain-specific advantage for this kind of functionality, as it is typically deployed by players. Those players may use the information on the blockchain to retrieve trusted information on ratings, but this is not different from the retrieval of any other kind of description.

Linkage is also not dealt here. The common use of linkage in metadata uses URIs or other conventional identifiers along with predicate vocabularies. Making these links first-class in a blockchain solution would require the use of handlers inside the metadata or as separate link metadata records (to avoid the problem of circular references). This, as mentioned in the section about semantics, has been discussed elsewhere in the context of linked data over IPFS [13].

4 Example Implementation

A proof of concept design prototype was built using a combination of the Ethereum blockchain, the IPFS decentralized file system, and the BigchainDB database.

4.1 Metadata Repositories on Ethereum and IPFS

The registration of metadata claims and its eventual update is realized using the `MetadataRepository` contract discussed before, devised and deployed over a Ethereum test net. One or several instances of the contract may be deployed in the network, and as they become autonomous from the original creator, their number is not a problem.

Preservation of metadata requires the availability of the schemas that are used for the expression of metadata. This is usually achieved in metadata registries. A metadata registry could be implemented in Ethereum with a similar `MetadataRegistry` contract in which schema curators or communities could deploy the different versions of their schemas. Then, a higher level of preservation integrity could be achieved by extending the `Claim` model with a mandatory additional handler to the metadata schema used. This would enable checking the validity of metadata records before they are registered as claims, and guarantee that the specifications are also preserved. However, this may be considered unpractical for the registering of legacy metadata in the blockchain architecture, which is often not free of errors.

This entails that the preservation of the claims is supported by the sustainability of the blockchain, so it rests on a global incentive system. The cost for curators is then that of registering the claims, which have a cost (used by the Ethereum's *gas* required to execute the transactions). This is in a sense inverting the cost, from maintaining the database to registering or updating new elements which was before with no inherent cost.

4.2 Indexing and Search on BigchainDB

The model for registering metadata claims as a collection of series supports metadata curation, but contracts are not currently devised to perform iterations over mappings or return large collections. One option may be that of using external blockchain *explorers*, that read the database directly and scan it. However, explorers are not adequate as query systems, and this is where other solutions may have a place, concretely databases that use an additional consensus layer. Essentially, these provide a middle ground so that it is possible to copy fragments of the claims of the blockchain to a database dedicated for query, while retaining a degree of security and providing a way to check provenance referring to the original blockchain record.

BigchainDB[4] stores digital *assets*, which are essentially JSON documents with some optional metadata. In our case, we would want to include metadata records as assets. The basic functionality is then that of storing metadata records using `CREATE` transactions, and eventually using `TRANSFER` transactions to change their ownership. As transactions are digitally signed by its owner, this guarantees provenance and enables a degree of administration. The `metadata` part of the asset refers to the handler and the location of the claim (the transaction hash of the claim in this case):

```
{"hash": "QmYwAPJzv5CZsnA625s...",
"service": "ipfs",
"meta":"",
"claim":"0xbd53b39f64ce9a96d..."}
```

It should be noted that the transaction hash provides sufficient reference, but the rest of the information is used for convenience and ease of retrieval in queries.

Then, the `data` element of the asset would be a representation of the metadata part of the handler. This entails the need for transforming records in other metadata language bindings as XML or RDF into JSON. However, this is a limitation of the database backend of the solution, and not an inherent constraint of the overall architecture.

The adaptation required a modification in the consensus rules of BigchainBD by writing and including a simple plugin. This was limited to a change in the `validate_transaction()` method on a subclass of `BaseConsensusRules`. The method then could do the checking that the document to be included is in the Ethereum component, by using `check`[5]. As the registration of the metadata in that part used the `oraclize()` calls in the Ethereum contracts, then we guarantee that the metadata can be retrieved via its handler and it is a legitimate claim.

Once a metadata record is in the database, we are able to know: (a) its owner, i.e. the signer of the transaction or a subsequent recipient, (b) that the metadata record is legitimate and current up to the given timestamp, and (c) that we can at any moment query in the Ethereum component if the record is updated or retracted.

Then, it is possible to use the underlying query mechanisms of the storage component (in our case, a *MongoDB* backend) to query or build search systems on top of it.

---

[4] https://www.bigchaindb.com/.
[5] Or alternatively exploring the blockchain, but that would be inefficient.

5   Conclusions and Outlook

Blockchain technologies considered as immutable decentralized databases have the potential to change the practices and systems used for archival functions, both for the storage of the digital resources and of the metadata describing them.

In this paper, we have sketched a possible architecture that fulfills with three different components several of the key functions of metadata: decentralized identification, deferencing, proof of statement and (separately) indexing. The discussion has stayed at a generic level, but it could be extended to cover domain-specific cases that may require additional processing before the claims are included in the blockchain or that may include additional information.

It is still too early to value if a blockchain architecture as the one presented here is acceptable as an alternative to current centralized systems. But in any case, it represents an option to achieve higher levels of availability, transparency and tamper resistance, which would solve some of the problems of current metadata systems built on conventional databases.

References

1. Benet, J.: IPFS-Content Addressed, Versioned, P2P File System. arXiv preprint arXiv:1407.3561 (2014)
2. Burns, C.S., Lana, A., Budd, J.M.: Institutional repositories: exploration of costs and value. D-Lib Mag. **19**(1/2), 1–17 (2013)
3. Eschenfelder, K.R., Shankar, K., Williams, R., Lanham, A., Salo, D., Zhang, M.: What are we talking about when we talk about sustainability of digital archives, repositories and libraries? Proc. Assoc. Inf. Sci. Technol. **53**(1), 1–6 (2016)
4. Fujimura, S., Watanabe, H., Nakadaira, A., Yamada, T., Akutsu, A., Kishigami, J.J.: BRIGHT: a concept for a decentralized rights management system based on blockchain. In: Proceedings of the IEEE 5th International Conference on Consumer Electronics, pp. 345–346 (2015)
5. Greenberg, J.: Understanding metadata and metadata schemes. Cat. Classif. Q. **40**(3–4), 17–36 (2005)
6. Haslhofer, B., Klas, W.: A survey of techniques for achieving metadata interoperability. ACM Comput. Surv. (CSUR) **42**(2), 7 (2010)
7. Hunter, J., Choudhury, S.: Implementing preservation strategies for complex multimedia objects. In: Koch, T., Sølvberg, I.T. (eds.) ECDL 2003. LNCS, vol. 2769, pp. 473–486. Springer, Heidelberg (2003). https://doi.org/10.1007/978-3-540-45175-4_43
8. Lam, E.S.L., Cervesato, I.: Modeling datalog fact assertion and retraction in linear logic. In: Proceedings of the 14th Symposium on Principles and Practice of Declarative Programming, pp. 67–78. ACM (2012)
9. Liang, X., Shetty, S., Tosh, D., Kamhoua, C., Kwiat, K., Njilla, L.: Provchain: a blockchain-based data provenance architecture in cloud environment with enhanced privacy and availability. In: Proceedings of the 17th IEEE/ACM International Symposium on Cluster, Cloud and Grid Computing, pp. 468–477. IEEE Press (2017)
10. Pyrounakis, G., Nikolaidou, M., Hatzopoulos, M.: Building digital collections using open source digital repository software: a comparative study. Int. J. Digit. Libr. Syst. (IJDLS) **4**(1), 10–24 (2014)

11. Rajabi, E., Sanchez-Alonso, S., Sicilia, M.A.: Analyzing broken links on the web of data: an experiment with DBpedia. J. Assoc. Inf. Sci. Technol. **65**(8), 1721–1727 (2014)
12. Rinehart, K., Prud'homme, P.A., Reid Huot, A.: Overwhelmed to action: digital preservation challenges at the under-resourced institution. OCLC Syst. Serv. **30**(1), 28–42 (2014)
13. Sicilia, M.-A., Sánchez-Alonso, S., García-Barriocanal, E.: Sharing linked open data over peer-to-peer distributed file systems: the case of IPFS. In: Garoufallou, E., Subirats Coll, I., Stellato, A., Greenberg, J. (eds.) MTSR 2016. CCIS, vol. 672, pp. 3–14. Springer, Cham (2016). https://doi.org/10.1007/978-3-319-49157-8_1
14. Szabo, N.: Formalizing and securing relationships on public networks. First Monday **2**(9) (1997)
15. Tapscott, D., Tapscott, A.: Blockchain Revolution: How the Technology Behind Bitcoin is Changing Money, Business, and the World. Penguin, New York (2016)
16. Thibodeau, K.: Overview of technological approaches to digital preservation and challenges in coming years. CLIR Reports 107, The state of digital preservation: an international perspective, pp. 4–31 (2002). https://www.clir.org/pubs/reports/pub107
17. Tillett, B.: What is FRBR? A conceptual model for the bibliographic universe. Aust. Libr. J. **54**(1), 24–30 (2005)
18. Tran, A.B., Weber, X.X., Staples, M., Rimba, P.: Regerator: a registry generator for blockchain. In: Proceedings of the CAiSE-Forum-DC 2017, pp. 81–88 (2017)
19. Wood, G.: Ethereum: a secure decentralised generalised transaction ledger. Ethereum Project Yellow Paper, 151 (2014). http://www.cryptopapers.net/papers/ethereum-yellowpaper.pdf

Creative Knowledge Environments Promotion Through Case-Based Knowledge Artifacts

Fabio Sartori[✉]

Department of Computer Science, Systems and Communication (DISCo),
University of Milan - Bicocca, viale Sarca 336, 20126 Milan, Italy
sartori@disco.unimib.it

Abstract. The adoption of case-based reasoning could be useful in the development of creative knowledge environments. In fact, it is one of the most suitable to reproduce decision making processes according to the reasoning by analogy paradigm. Given that analogies, and distant analogies in particular, are strictly connected to human creativity, case-based reasoning would result a good approach to provide knowledge artifacts with the capability to solve intrinsically creative problems. This is an important research topic in knowledge artifacts research: to this aim the paper will introduce CKS-Net, a conceptual and computational framework to manage with creative problems and domains, from both the theoretical and practical perspective.

1 Introduction

The *creative knowledge environment* (CKE) notion was introduced to identify those environments, contexts and surroundings exerting a positive influence on human beings engaged in creative work aiming to produce new knowledge or innovations, whether they work individually or in collaboration with others.

A first question emerging from the definition above is if and how Computer Science, and knowledge engineering in particular, can support the promotion and management of CKEs. According to [1, p. 396], creativity is the tendency to generate or recognize ideas, alternatives, or possibilities that may be useful in solving problems, communicating with others, and entertaining ourselves and others.

Another definition [2] associates the word *creative* to both novel products and the person(s) working on it, pointing out that the product novelty is condition necessary but not sufficient to be creative, since it must be *valuable* or *appropriate* to the *cognitive demands of the situation.*

A possible approach to represent creativity in computer systems is *analogical reasoning* that is typical of human beings. As pointed out in [3] analogy involves the comparison of two structured representations. These representations typically include labeled relationships between entities, given that people are sensitive to relational structure in processing analogy. Moreover, the authors point out that analogy is capable to suggest new inferences: the most familiar type of analogy is mapped onto the less familiar target domain, with the consequence

© Springer International Publishing AG 2017
E. Garoufallou et al. (Eds.): MTSR 2017, CCIS 755, pp. 50–61, 2017.
https://doi.org/10.1007/978-3-319-70863-8_5

to discover new predictions or explanations. As reported in many papers [4,5], reasoning by analogy is one of most suitable paradigms to manage creativity, also from the computational perspectives. The relationship existing between creativity and analogy in human physiology was highlighted by [6], focusing *distant analogies* as the conceptual mean to improve creativity in human beings.

Case-Based Reasoning (CBR) is one of the most important computational models based on reasoning by analogy. It allows solving new problems by comparison with similar ones solved in the past. The development of CBR systems is typically divided into four steps, as stated by the well-known 4Rs' cycle [7]: *Retrieve*: the current case C_c is compared with the case base (possibly indexed to increase efficiency) in order to find the most similar past case, namely the *retrieved case C_r*; *Reuse*: the C_r solution is associated to C_c; *Revise*: since C_r is the most similar past problem to C_c, but it is not equal to C_c, the reused solution is modified in order to transform it in the real C_c solution; *Retain*: finally, the current case is solved and added to the case base together with its solution. Doing so, the CBR system learns new problem solving experiences that can be exploited in the future.

In this paper we present CKS-Net, a CBR framework whose main characteristic is the capability to manage *complex knowledge structures* (CKS) rather than cases. Doing so, CKS-Net allows retrieving, reusing and revising solutions to problems from heterogeneous domains, being able to develop innovative and creative decision making processes. For this reason, CKS-Net could be profitably exploited to develop (virtual) creative knowledge environments.

The rest of the paper is organized as follows. Section 2 introduces the CKS-Net framework from the theoretical point of view, defining complex knowledge structures and the 4R's cycle to manage them. Section 3 presents a practical application of CKS-Net in a creative domain, the configuration of a menu for a lunch or dinner at home. The same case study is exploited in Sect. 4 to make considerations about the effectiveness of CKS-Net in dealing with creative tasks, thanks to the collaboration of a young chef employed in a restaurant of Milan. Finally, conclusion and future works are briefly pointed out in Sect. 5.

2   The CKS-Net Framework

As introduced above, creativity is closely related to analogy: the more a person makes distant analogies, the more creative he/she will be. This definition seems to be in contrast with CBR principles, stating that similar problems have similar solutions. To be similar, problems should have the same (or slightly different) structures and similar values for attributes. In other words, problems should be homogeneous from the description perspective.

Thus, how can a CBR system be creative? A creative CBR system should be capable to compare problems characterized by distant analogies; this means that retrieval and revise algorithms should be able to analyze heterogeneous case structures, that are not comparable in traditional case based reasoning approaches, to find similarities among them, reusing and revising solutions being sure they are compatible with the current problem.

In the following, the CKS-Net framework is presented, to show how this research topic can be tackled. The framework introduces a similarity metric based on the *equivalence of critical nodes* notion. The targets of this metric are complex knowledge structures, sort of cases characterized by the integration into a unique conceptual framework of their description, solution and outcome components. The similarity metric is used to develop both retrieval and revise algorithms.

2.1 Complex Knowledge Structures

A complex knowledge structure is a conceptual and computational tool to acquire, represent and use episodic knowledge involved in complex decision-making processes. Figure 1 shows the main architectural elements of CKS-Net. In order to capture the variability of CKSs, they are represented in CKS-Net by means of *graphs*, whose *nodes* are bounded by *direct* and *labeled arcs*, where an arc is an instance of relationships between two entities:

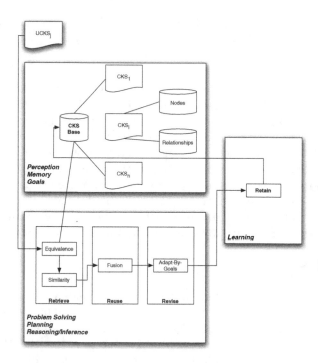

Fig. 1. A sketch of the CKS-Net architecture

Definition 1 (Complex Knowledge Structure). *A Complex Knowledge Structure is a labelled and direct graph $CKS = \langle N, R \rangle$ where $N = N_{wt} \cup N_{wy} \cup N_{hw}$ is a set of nodes and $R = R_{wt} \cup R_{wy} \cup R_{hw}$ is a set of relationships among nodes.*

In the definition above, N_{wt}, N_{wy}, N_{hw} (R_{wt}, R_{wy}, R_{hw}) are the sets of nodes (relationships) for the description of the problem, called *WHAT-Nodes* (*WHAT-Relationships*), for the specification of the solution to it, called *HOW-Nodes* (*HOW-Relationships*) and for the definition of benefits/drawbacks, called *WHY-Nodes* (*WHY-Relationships*), respectively. Different from case structure definition in traditional CBR systems, the three components of the case are linked. Doing so, it is possible to understand which nodes of the problem description are involved in the solution, as well as to clearly indicate the benefits/drawbacks associated to a specific solution part.

Syntactic rules of CKS design are: WHAT-Relationships start from a WHAT-Node and enter a WHAT-Node, being HOW-Nodes and WHY-Nodes not involved in them; HOW-Relationships start from a WHAT-Node or a How-Node and terminate into a HOW-Node; WHY-Relationships start from a HOW-Node or a WHY-Node to end with a WHY-Node.

Up to now, a Complex Knowledge Structure has been considered as the representation of a solved problem. But a Complex Knowledge Structure can be profitably used to describe *unsolved problems* too:

Definition 2 (Unsolved Complex Knowledge Structure). *A Complex Knowledge Structure is said to be Unsolved (UCKS) if N_{hw} and R_{hw} are empty sets.*

An UCKS is the representation of a new problem to be solved in the CKS-Net framework. It is important to highlight that both the description (i.e. the N_{wt} and R_{wt} sets) and the goals (i.e. N_{wy} and R_{wy} sets) must be described in the UCKS definition. Both parts will be exploited in the reasoning process, as presented in the following.

2.2   Retrieve, Reuse and Revise Steps

Different from the typical approaches emerging by literature review, these phases in CKS-Net manage heterogeneous and highly variable case structures. For this reason, the algorithms proposed are designed and implemented to reduce the problem descriptions, solutions and outcomes to well-defined, atomic patterns, namely *critical structures*, and compare them by means of opportune similarity functions.

The critical structure of a CKS is obtained from the identification of *critical nodes*. The algorithm was inspired by the *node centrality metrics* in *social network analysis* [8], according to which a node in a diagram (typically representing the social relationships of a person) is said *central* if it is crucial to preserve the diagram structure. The centrality depends on metrics like the number of relationships ingoing/outgoing the node, the possibility to reach another node from it, and so on.

In CKS-Net, the centrality definition has been converted into the criticality one, taking care of the peculiarity of the CBR paradigm, that is solving a new problem, represented by an UCKS, by comparison with solved ones, represented by one or more CKSs. For this reason, a criticality measure for nodes of a Complex Knowledge Structure has been introduced taking care of HOW-Nodes, while a second criterium has been followed to establish whether a node of a UCKS is critical or not:

Definition 3 (Critical Nodes for CKSs). *A node* $n \in N$ *of a Complex Knowledge Structure is said critical if one of the following conditions is satisfied:* $n \in N_{hw}$; $n \in N_{wy}$; $n \in N_{wt} \wedge \exists m \in N_{hw}, R \in R_{hw} \mid nRm$.

Definition 4 (Critical Nodes for Unsolved CKSs). *A node* $n \in N$ *of an Unsolved Complex Knowledge Structure is conditions is satisfied:* $n \in N_{wy}$; $n \in N_{wt} \wedge \forall m \in N \mid nRm \nexists p \in N \mid pRm$; $n \in N_{wt} \wedge \exists R \in R_{wt} \mid nRn$; $n \in N_{wt} \wedge R_{IN}(n) = \varnothing \wedge R_{OUT}(n) = \varnothing$.

The introduction of Unsolved Complex Knowledge Structures allows to adopt a case-based strategy to find a possible solution to the problem represented by them on the basis of their comparison with past Complex Knowledge Structures: a retrieval algorithm has been designed based on the comparison of critical nodes, that is the subject of the next section. A last important notion must be introduced in order to understand how it works, that is the *equivalence of critical nodes*:

Definition 5 (Equivalent Critical Nodes). *Given two Complex Knowledge Structures* CKS_1 *and* CKS_2 *and two critical nodes* $A \in N_{CKS_1}$ *and* $B \in N_{CKS_2}$. *A and B are said to be equivalent if one of the following conditions is verified: (1) A and B are the same node, i.e.* $A = B$; *(2) A and B are different nodes (i.e. they have different labels) but the intersection between their sets of ingoing relationships is not empty, i.e.* $A \neq B \wedge R_{IN}(A) \cap R_{IN}(B) \neq \varnothing$; *(3) A and B are different nodes (i.e. they have different labels), but A is a How-Node and B is an isolated WHAT-Node, i.e.* $A \neq B \wedge a \in N_{hw}(CKS_1) \wedge b \in N_{wt}(CKS_2) \wedge R_{IN}(b) = \varnothing \wedge R_{OUT}(b) = \varnothing$ *or viceversa.*

The similarity function $SIM(UCKS, CKS_i)$ is defined by the Eq. 1.

$$SIM = \frac{SIM_{CRIT} + SIM_{GOAL}}{2} = \left(\frac{(\frac{Card(EN)}{N_{cc} + N_{cp}} * 100) + (\frac{n_{wy}}{max(N_{wc}, N_{wp})} * 100)}{2} \right)$$
(1)

where $Card(EN)$ is the cardinality of the equivalent node set; N_{cc} is the number of critical nodes of the current UCKS; N_{cp} is the number of critical nodes of the CKS; n_{wy} is the number of WHY-Nodes that the current UCKS shares with the CKS; N_{wc} is the number of WHY-Nodes of the current UCKS; N_{wp} is the number of WHY-Nodes of the CKS.

The similarity function is divided into two parts, namely SIM_{CRIT}, devoted to calculate how many critical nodes the current UCKS shares with the current CKS, and SIM_{GOAL}, devoted to determine how many objectives of the current UCKS were achieved in the reasoning process represented by the current CKS.

The two parts are equally weighted in the formula, that is used in the following CKS-Net retrieval algorithm.

The CKS is evaluated for the *Fusion* step if and only if the total similarity degree reaches a value of 50%. This value is a first attempt to find a good threshold for considering similar a past CKS to a UCKS. Since the similarity function is splat into two parts, the one devoted to capture all the features of the structure (i.e. description, solution and outcome), the latter focused only on outcome issues, it is reasonable to suppose that each of them can contribute at most for the 50% of the total similarity degree.

The Fusion operation allows to reproduce HOW-Relationships and WHY-Relationsips of retrieved CKS on the current UCKS. Fusion is an instance of the *reuse* phase of CBR 4'Rs cycle, designed as an iterative algorithm that takes care of all CKSs overcoming the similarity threshold. In this way, more than one HOW-Relationships can be shown that allow to reach the same goal. Moreover, it is possible that all the aims of current UCKS are achieved by a fusion of all the solutions adopted in the past: in fact, by reusing only the HOW-Relationships concerning the most similar past CKS it is possible that some new goals don't find a corresponding outcome in the retrieved CKS representation. To take care of all the possible candidates in the retrieved CKSs set increases the probability to cover all the requirements specified by the UCKS representation.

Building a solution for the current UCKS starts with the comparison of its critical nodes with the ones of the retrieved CKS. This is accomplished in the first part of the Fusion function, where each critical node n belonging to the WHAT-Node set of the CKS in input is tested for equivalence with any critical node m of UCKS. In case of success, the process of building a solution starting from the node m begins.

For this reason, the initially empty $R_{hw}(UCKS)$ and $N_{hw}(UCKS)$ sets are added with all HOW-Relationships having n as the outgoing node and all the nodes belonging to $N_{hw}(CKS)$ which are linked to n by a HOW-Relationship. Then, WHY-Nodes and WHY-Relationships are considered: if there are two equivalent WHY-Nodes w and y in the representation of current CKS and UCKS respectively, the link between w and a node of $N_{hw}(CKS)$ is reproduced in UKCS.

As introduced in Eq. 1, the CKS-Net similarity metric is made of two parts, SIM_{CRIT} and SIM_{GOAL}. The retrieval algorithm considers both of them in the identification of CKSs similar to the current UCKS. Although their weights in the overall calculus are the same, the retrieval step introduces a strong constraint to select only the CKSs whose WHY-Node set contains the UCKS WHY-Node set. As a consequence, CKSs characterized by higher values in case descriptions similarity evaluation could be not considered given that their outcomes do not fully match the goals of the UCKS. The revise step in CKS-Net relaxes this constraint, looking for the CKSs with highest SIM_{CRIT} values that satisfy a subset of UCKS goals. In this way, the revise algorithm in CKS-Net is able to build up solutions for the current UCKS through a goal by goal comparison with the most similar CKSs in the case base, realizing a Fusion operation for each of them.

3 Case Study

The case study to discuss the behavior of CKS-Net is a typical configuration problem in the CBR domain, about the definition of lunch or dinner. This problem can be tackled from different points of view, ranging from the meal preparation to the disposition of invited people around the table. This section presents some samples of how possible problems can be managed by the different steps CKS-Net is composed of. As a first example, let's suppose the dinner menu starts with an appetizer, that is an asparagus flan. The goals to be obtained by its preparation are *pleasant* and *little spicy* taste. During the recipe preparation, we realize that asparagus lack and we have no time to go to buy them. Figure 2 show the UCKS describing the problem, with three WHAT-Nodes and three WHAT-Relationships and two WHY-Nodes, together with the XML code representing it in the CKS-Net framework.

Each node is characterized by an identifier, a name and a type, each relationships by a name, a type and the identifiers of the source and target nodes. The first step to solve the problem is the application of the retrieval algorithm. As described above, the retrieval algorithm looks for the most similar CKS in the CKS-Base to allow meeting the same goals as the UCKS.

It is interesting to point out how the problem represented by the CKS seems to be completely different from the UCKS, given that it describes the preparation of a *potatoes' focaccia*, where potatoes are substituted by onions. Moreover, it looks more complex than the current problem. Anyway, it is possible to highlight some points of contact with the UCKS: the crucial ingredient (i.e. potatoes) lacks and the two goals of the UCKS are present in the CKS as outcomes. Thus, the retrieval algorithm is able to extract a reduced CKS structure, based on the equivalence notion that is very similar to the UCKS one, as shown in Fig. 3.

The similarity function $SIM(UCKS, CKS_i)$ is defined by the Eq. 1.

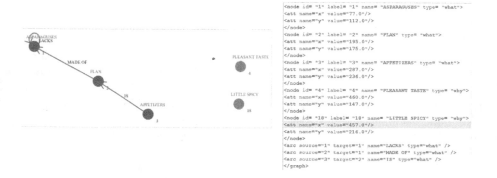

Fig. 2. The graphical and XML descriptions of case study UCKS

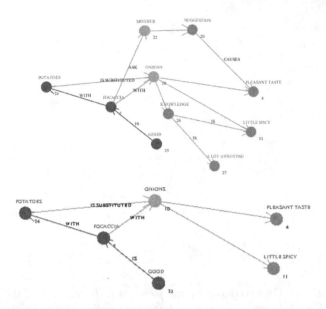

Fig. 3. On the top, the graphical representation of the retrieved CKS; on the bottom, its reduction according to the equivalence notion.

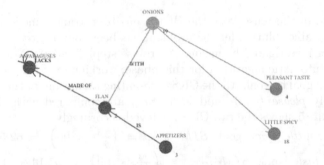

Fig. 4. The graphical representation of the Fusion algorithm result

$$SIM = \frac{SIM_{CRIT} + SIM_{GOAL}}{2} = \left(\frac{(\frac{8}{4+9} * 100) + (\frac{2}{5} * 100)}{2} \right) = 50.05\% \quad (2)$$

The Fusion operation can be then applied, reusing the CKS solution to UCKS. The effect is shown in Fig. 4, where a bridge between the UCKS case description and outcome parts has been created: the *onions* HOW-Node, together with its relationships has been attached to the *flan* WHAT-Node in the UCKS, that is *equivalent* to the *focaccia* WHAT-Node in the retrieved CKS.

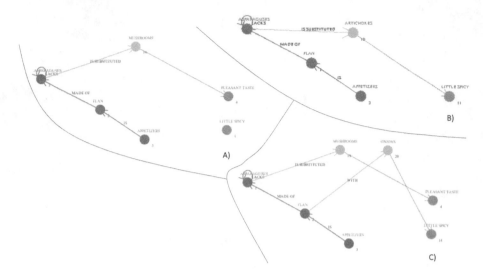

Fig. 5. Part (A): the CKS retrieved for the *pleasant taste* goal during the revise step; Part (B): the CKS retrieved for the *little spicy* goal during the revise step; Part (C): the final solution for the initial problem

At the end of the reuse step, the UCKS has been transformed into a CKS, since an acceptable solution for the problem has been found. Now, this solution can be further investigated by means of a revise step. The CKS-Net framework proposes an automatic algorithm for this phase, working on SIM_{CRIT} calculus and evaluation goal by goal. All the CKSs presenting a solution for the two WHY-Nodes, namely *pleasant taste* and *little spicy* are compared with the current problem. Figure 5 shows the two CKS retrieved accordingly.

About the *little spicy* goal, $SIM_{CRIT_1} = \left(\frac{5}{4+4} * 100\right) = 62.5\%$. About the *pleasant taste* goal, $SIM_{CRIT_2} = \left(\frac{4}{4+3} * 100\right) = 57.14\%$. Thus, since $SIM_{CRIT_1} > SIM_{CRIT}$ and $SIM_{CRIT_2} < SIM_{CRIT}$, the solution of our problem is adapted to substitute *onions* with *mushrooms* to obtain *pleasant taste*, while *artichokes* instead of *onions* possibility to get *little spicy* goal is discarded. Part (C) of Fig. 5 shows the final CKS to be retained at the end of CBR cycle in CKS-Net.

4   Results and Discussion

In the previous sections, the CKS-Net framework has been described from both the conceptual and practical point of view. With respect to traditional case-based reasoning approaches, the most innovative characteristics introduced by CKS-Net are the inclusion of outcomes (i.e. the WHY-Nodes) in the retrieval algorithm, the possibility for the method to compare heterogeneous case structures and to revise reused solutions exploiting multiple past experiences, as briefly presented in the case study.

CKS-Net allows reproducing reasoning by analogy decision making processes, trying to solve complex problems by looking at solutions adopted in the past in similar situations. As introduced at the beginning of the paper, this way of thinking is typical of human beings and other forms of intelligence, and increases significantly the possibility of finding solutions to problems too difficult to model. In this sense, CBR is suitable for creative knowledge environments, given that it provides conceptual and computational methods to deal with domains where creativity, memory and practical experience are crucial.

This last point is well depicted by the case study analyzed above. Creativity is really important in the cuisine domain, where the capability to mix properly (or not) ingredients can bring to excellent (or not) results. CKS-Net allows describing recipes in a very easy way, focusing on the goals to reach. Moreover, CKS-Net is capable to memorize both positive and negative experiences. To test the framework effectiveness, we have asked a young (male) chef to build up an archive of CKSs about various problems he could encounter in the menu preparation. Our request was only to indicate problems related to ingredients, not about the relationships with his colleagues (we are still working on this topic). The chef produced a case base of both *traditional* and *not traditional* recipes: the first set was composed of 370 recipes, the second one contained 220 cases, for a total of 590 recipes. Then, he tried to implement a collection of possible problems, like the lack of one or more ingredients, the presence of the wrong type of a given ingredient (e.g. white onions instead of red onions), and so on. He was able to generate 160 unsolved complex knowledge structures. Then it applied the retrieval and revise algorithms obtaining the generation of new CKSs from the UCKSs.

Table 1. Summarization of results obtained applying CKS-Net in the menu configuration problem

	CKS set cardinality	UCKS set cardinality
At the beginning	590	160
After retrieval	715	35
After revise	738	12

As reported in Table 1, 125 of the 160 initial UCKSs became CKSs at the end of the retrieval-reuse steps, for a total of 715 CKSs. This means that for 35 of them no previous CKS was able to cover completely the whole set of goals. After the revise step, this number was reduced to 12 cases. The revise step allowed modifying 87 reused solutions: 25 of them were totally modified. The remaining 38 new CKSs were left unchanged: this means that the revise algorithm threshold was not overcome (13 cases of 38) or the expert refused the results of revise step (25 cases of 38). About the last option, 14 cases were manually revised by the expert, while the reused solutions were recovered in the remaining 11 ones. About the capability of CKS-Net to solve the 160 initial problems the following considerations can be made: CKS-Net was able to create 134 new CKSs from the initial set of 160 UCKSs. Each of them proposed a solution considered acceptable by the expert. The percentage of success in solving the case study problems is 83.75%; CKS-Net failed in 26 cases (the 12 unsolved UCKSs plus the 14 CKSs manually revised by the expert), with an error percentage of 16.25%. Indeed, these results are encouraging, given the nature of the case study proposed, characterized by high level of creativity. From the CKEs support perspective, the proposed approach was able to generate and memorize 134 acceptable solutions to the initial set of 160 problems. In twelve cases it declared its inability to tackle the situation, failing completely in 14 attempts. Creative Knowledge Environments are still an important research topic. As suggested by [9], eight components must be taken into account to stimulate CKEs. Table 2 shows how the proposed approach supports the foundational characteristics of CKEs.

The main aim of CKS-Net was creating a sort of *virtual creative knowledge environment*, where users can exploit knowledge of colleagues (i.e. the cases in the CKS-Base) to find innovative solutions to their problems, as pointed out in the case study. The only point not covered by the CKS-Net steps is the last one, that is typical of concrete, not virtual working environments.

Table 2. Summarization of results obtained applying CKS-Net in the menu configuration problem

CKE feature	Description	CKS-Net step
Task characteristics	Repetitive tasks are not intrinsically creative	Reuse
Discipline-field	The type of knowledge and skills relevant for the problem solving strategy are important	Retrieve-Reuse-Revise
Individuals	Creativity may be enhanced by contact with researchers in neighbouring research areas	Reuse-Revise
Group characteristics	Groups including members from different cultural or disciplinary backgrounds tend to be more creative	Reuse-Revise
General work situation for individuals	Each individual has a number of tasks and experiences from one domain can exert positive influence on another	Reuse-Revise
Physical environment	Individuals needs facilities that offer solitude	Retrieve-Reuse-Revise
Organisation	Organisation leadership provides rules enabling people to behave creatively	Retrieve-Reuse-Revise
Extra-organis. environment	Creative potential of an organisation is linked to external events	/

5   Conclusion

This paper has presented CKS-Net, a CBR framework to support creative decision making processes. Different from many similar tools, CKS-Net implements the whole 4R's cycle, allowing not only to retrieve similar cases from the memory, but also to revise solutions in order to make them better fit the current problem. Another difference from previous works is the development of *equivalence* metric to compare heterogeneous case structures, exploiting the critical node identification as well as the inclusion of goals in the similarity evaluation. Doing so, it is possible to exploit the proposed method to compare case structures over different (or, better, *equivalent*) domains, generating creative solutions to complex problem. The CKS-Net framework can be exploited to develop distributed applications. In this sense, one of the most promising research field is the design and implementation of agent-based systems: in particular, one of the planned future works is the integration of CKS-Net into KAFKA, a knowledge engineering methodology devoted to design and implement time-evolving expert systems, based on the higher-level knowledge artifact notion [10].

References

1. Franken, R.E.: Human Motivation, 3rd edn. Thomson Wadsworth, Belmont (1998)
2. Weisberg, R.: The study of creativity: from genius to cognitive science. Int. J. Cult. Policy **16**(3), 235–253 (2010)
3. Gentner, D., Forbus, K.D.: Computational models of analogy. Wiley Interdisc. Rev. Cogn. Sci. **2**(3), 266–276 (2011)
4. Goel, A.K.: Design, analogy, and creativity. IEEE Expert **12**(3), 62–70 (1997)
5. Hummel, J.E., Holyoak, K.J.: Analogy and creativity: schema induction in a structure-sensitive connectionist model (2002)
6. Green, A.E., Kraemer, D.J., Fugelsang, J.A., Gray, J.R., Dunbar, K.N.: Neural correlates of creativity in analogical reasoning. J. Exp. Psychol. Learn. Memory Cogn. **38**(2), 264 (2012)
7. Aamodt, A., Plaza, E.: Case-based reasoning: foundational issues, methodological variations, and system approaches. AI Commun. **7**(1), 39–59 (1994)
8. Everett, M.G., Borgatti, S.P.: Extending centrality. Models Methods Soc. Netw. Anal. **35**(1), 57–76 (2005)
9. Hemlin, S., Allwood, C.M., Martin, B.R.: Creative knowledge environments. Creat. Res. J. **20**(2), 196–210 (2008)
10. Sartori, F., Melen, R.: Time evolving expert systems design and implementation: The KAFKA approach. In: KEOD 2015 - Proceedings of the International Conference on Knowledge Engineering and Ontology Development, Part of the 7th International Joint Conference on Knowledge Discovery, Knowledge Engineering and Knowledge Management (IC3K 2015), vol. 2, Lisbon, Portugal, November 12–14, 2015, pp. 84–95 (2015)

Representation of Tensed Relations in OWL

A Survey of Philosophically-Motivated Patterns

Paweł Garbacz[1](✉) and Robert Trypuz[2]

[1] Tadeusz Manteuffel Institute of History,
Polish Academy of Sciences, Warsaw, Poland
garbacz@kul.pl
[2] Faculty of Philosophy Poland,
John Paul II Catholic University of Lublin, Lublin, Poland
trypuz@kul.pl

Abstract. The topic of this paper are the so-called tensed relations, i.e., those relations that hold between objects with respect to time. As tensed relations are not, almost by definition, binary relations, they need a special treatment in the case of such formal languages as OWL where only binary relations are explicitly expressible. We study in this paper a number of ways in which this expressivity constraint can be worked around focusing only on the solutions that seek their rationale in a philosophical argument of some sort. Besides fleshing out the details of those patterns we compare them to one another to show their strengths and limitations in various usage scenarios.

1 Introduction

Except for mathematical knowledge and the like, most of the facts we know involve some kind of temporal references. Take a simple example. Anna was married to Paul from 2010 to 2014, but they divorced in January 2014. If we are to represent such facts in a formal language and if we have at our disposal the full power of, say, first-order logic, then our task is trivial. For example, using Common Logic's CLIF language we could grasp this change in the marital status of Anna by: "*and (married Anna Paul 2014) not (married Anna Paul 2015)*". The task becomes more demanding if the symbolic formalism of our choice is more restricted, e.g., when we are restricted to a DL language, say a language from the OWL family, where we do not have access to ternary and higher-arity relations.

This paper focuses on one specific sub-case of that problem, namely how to express tensed binary relations (see: [4]) in OWL. By *tensed binary relation* we mean any ternary relation of the form $R(x, y, t)$, where one of its arguments, say the third one, refers to times (i.e., moments or periods). More generally speaking,

The research presented in this paper was supported by the *Ontological Foundations for Building Historical Geoinformation Systems* (2bH 15 0216 83) grant funded by National Programme for the Development of Humanities (http://nprh.org/).

© Springer International Publishing AG 2017
E. Garoufallou et al. (Eds.): MTSR 2017, CCIS 755, pp. 62–73, 2017.
https://doi.org/10.1007/978-3-319-70863-8_6

we are interested in OWL representations of *tensed relation*, i.e. $(n + 1)$-ary relations $(n > 2)$ of the form $R(x_1, x_2, \ldots, x_n, t)$.

Section 2 provides ample evidence that this issue has recently attracted some attention in the Semantic Web community. Still, this research seems to be more focussed on the formal structures than on their justification. In this paper we want to fill this gap and collect and compare those solutions that seek their rationale in a philosophical argument of some sort. In addition, we ignore those approaches whose expressivity go beyond OWL, e.g., the so-called temporal description logics.

The solutions discussed here are partially determined by the context of this study, which is a research project on the historical geoinformation systems. One of the main conceptual issues we came across within this project is the problem of variability of human settlements (e.g., hamlets, villages, towns, etc.) and their identity through time. Human settlements change their types, names, even locations in time, so use of tensed relations is unavoidable.

To make the issue more palatable we will use in this paper the following running example. The contemporary city of Nieszawa was first mentioned in historical records around 1425 as located at N52°59.48′ E18°30.28′ – we will call this location "location 1". Around 1460 Nieszawa was relocated to N52°50.12′ E18°54.05′ – we will call this location "location 2". In short:

1. Nieszawa is located at location 1 from 1425 to 1459.
2. Nieszawa is located at location 2 from 1460 to the present day.

In each solution Nieszawa is represented as the OWL individual :`settlement1` and the two locations as :`location1` and `location2`. Using this minimal dataset each pattern was implemented as an OWL ontology for the running example – all ontologies can be accessed from http://onto.kul.pl/change/.

2   Related Works

Most of the research relevant for this paper can be traced back either to the W3C recommendation on n-triple reification [14] or to the 4DFluents ontology [17], where Welty and Fikes recommend, with certain caveats, the perdurantist approach. The basic idea of the former is that each n-ary relation between individuals be represented as a separate OWL class and each instance of the relation—an n-tuple—be represented as an instance of the class plus n additional binary relations providing links to each argument of the n-tuple. Perdurantism, which is a *par excellence* philosophical position assumed in [17], is explained here in the next section. [18] compare these two trends with an eye for reconciliation.

[15] presents a lightweight reification-based ontology extended with a temporal ontology and [1] investigates the types of queries that can be formulated to the pattern. [7] proposes the NdFluents ontology that extends 4DFluents ontology [17] to an arbitrary number of context dimensions. [10] proposes "4D reinterpretation" of [17]. [3] offers two representations – the first one based on 4DFluents ontology and the second one on n-triple reification. Each of them is

extended with qualitative descriptions of temporal relations, such as "before" or "overlaps", and reasoning support. Finally, starting from the logical analysis reported in [6,9] define seven formal patterns to represent tensed relations in RDF.

3   Philosopically-Motivated Patterns

The question of how things exist in time haunts philosophy from its very beginning. In order to scope the debate to a manageable body of "philosophical data". One needs to apply some conceptual filter – in this case we focus on the so-called analytic philosophy. In contemporary analytic philosophy *locus classicus* to look up is the debate between endurantism (aka: 3D view) and perdurantism (aka: 4D view).

Very roughly speaking (and significantly simplifying), an endurantist believes that things that exist in time occur at different moments as wholly present, i.e. each such thing has a kind of an ontological core that remains its identity throughout its life – despite a number of changes the thing undergoes. So Nieszawa existed both in 1425 and 1460 because there was something, which existed as one and the same object at both times – despite the fact that Nieszawa in 1425 had a different street plan, building density, population, location, etc., as compared to Nieszawa at 1460. Note that endurantism is, usually, interpreted in the weak sense: there are entities that occur at different moments as wholly present, but there might exists other entities that exist in time in a different way. So endurantists usually allow for such entities like processes or events, which are sometimes called perdurants, due to their specific mode of temporal existence.

Opposing to this view a perdurantist claims that *all* things that exists in time do not last (or endure) in time, so there is no such a thing as Nieszawa that exists at two different moments in time. All things that exist in time are believed to have special kind of parts, called temporal parts, due to which they exist at different moments. So Nieszawa existed in 1425 because it has a temporal part that was present at 1425. And it existed in 1460 because it has another temporal part, which was present at 1460.

Among all the patterns related in Sect. 2 we selected those that search for their validity by referring to one of these two main philosophical positions. In addition, we extended this set with two new patterns of our own: State-Based and History-Based Patterns.

3.1   Endurantist Patterns

All endurantist solutions sketched below accept endurants, i.e., things that exist in time by being wholly present at every moment they exist. The first two solution we discuss are, so to speak, purely endurantistic as they do not require perdurants. The temporal references are assigned here directly to endurants. The other three solutions require processes and/or events and the last two of these three assign temporal references to the latter.

Manifestation-Based Endurantist Pattern. Manifestation-based endurantist pattern is based on the seminal Kit Fine's work [5] and has been introduced to the Semantic Web community during FOIS 2016 [16] by Makolab's R&D Group. The basic idea of this approach is that all entities are divided into *variable entities*, i.e. the entities exist and change in time and have different manifestations at different times, and *non-variable entities*, which do not change in time – the latter include *manifestations of variable entities*. The following assumptions introduced by Kit Fine and generalized by F. Moltmann in [13] have been adopted in [16]. Each variable entity (e.g. Nieszawa) has at least one manifestation. If a variable entity is manifested at a certain time by some manifestation m, then the entity exists at t, takes the location and all other properties of the manifestation at that time. In our example we will say that Nieszawa, i.e. : settlement1, has two manifestations: : settlement1_manifestation1 – for the interval from 1425 to 1459 – and : settlement1_manifestation2 – for the interval from 1460 to this day. Given these assumptions, our temporal story can be expressed by means of the following graph (Fig. 1):

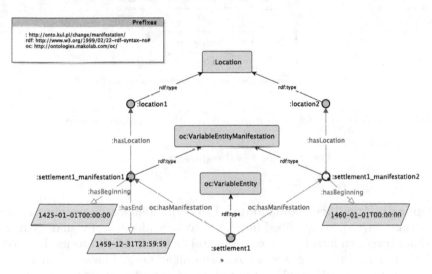

Fig. 1. Manifestation-based endurantist pattern

Trope-Based Endurantist Pattern. This pattern is defined in [18,19] as an ontologically-motivated version of the standard reification pattern. The main idea here has to do with the notion of trope (aka: moment) or property instance. As construed in these papers tropes are individual properties with the unique values fixed to certain times (or intervals). Beware that these properties may be binary relations, so, for instance, the particular geographical location of a human settlement and the settlement itself are related by a third individual, a reified relator (a kind of trope), which mediates its bearers. All tropes, including all relators, have their time extents. If the settlement changes its location at some later time, there is another relator, specified by different time extent, that mediates the settlement and the new location.

In our running example there will be (i) three objects: Nieszawa (settlement1), location1 and location2; (ii) two tropes (or relators): settlement1_position1 and settlement1_position2; and (iii) two time extents: settlement1_position1_te and settlement1_position2_te (see Fig. 2) of these tropes.

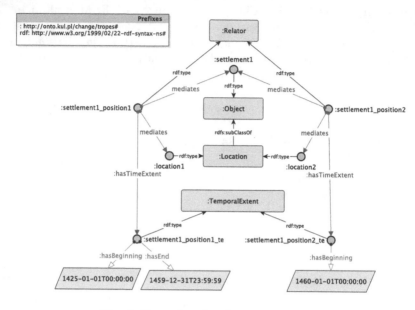

Fig. 2. Trope-based endurantist pattern

Temporally Qualified Continuants Pattern. Temporally qualified continuants (aka: TQCs), as described in [8], are to be understood by analogy to the relation between endurants (aka: continuants) and their (life) histories. Each continuant has its unique history, which contains all events and processes in which it takes part. (Technically speaking the history of an endurant is the mereological fusion of all such perdurants – see [2, pp. 122–123].) And if we are interested in a particular period in its life, we can take a proper part of this history – a *phase*. Then each such phase delimits, so to speak, the endurant restricted to the phase – also known as temporally qualified continuant. Then the relations in which the original continuant is involved in time can be directly and unambiguously attached to this TQC (see Fig. 3).

State-Based Endurantist Pattern. This pattern needs a special kind of perdurants called states. A state is understood here in the same way as in the DOLCE ontology [12], i.e., as a perdurant that is cumulative and homeomoeric. The most common example of states are such perdurants as: being connected,

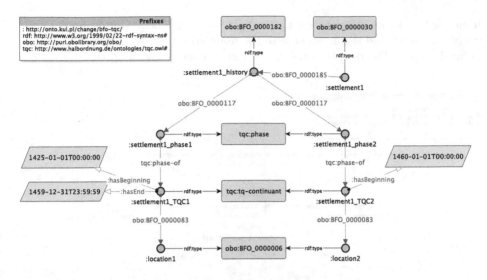

Fig. 3. Temporally qualified continuants pattern

sitting, etc. We also need the concept of participation, by means of which we can say that an endurant participates in a perdurant, e.g., when a football player participates in a football match.

In order to express that a certain object has a certain property at a certain time (be it a point in time or an interval) we take the state such that (i) its temporal boundaries are determined by the time and (ii) both the object and the property participate in it. For instance, to represent the fact that Nieszawa is located at location 1 from 1425 to 1459, we need, besides Nieszawa and location 1, also the state of Nieszawa being located at location 1 in 1425, (i) whose boundaries are determined by the beginning of 1425 and the end of year 1459 and (ii) such that Nieszawa and location 1 participate in this state. Obviously, a similar structure is needed for Nieszawa's location 2.

To implement this idea in an OWL ontology we will use DOLCE-Lite OWL version[1] despite the fact that it introduces some extra complexity due to the way DOLCE handles properties and their values. The reason for this design decision is based on the pattern's conceptual requirements: the concept of cumulative and homeomeric perdurants and the relation of participation, which get their intended meanings within the context of DOLCE. In other words, the pattern at stake is not just a formal hack to handle ternary relations within the binary constraints, but it requires some background ontology whose role is to provide the proper meanings for certain terms and predicates. We do not, however, either claim or assume that the state-based pattern we implement in DOLCE is the only one congruent with the philosophical presuppositions of this ontology. That is to say, we admit that one can implement other pattern(s) within this ontology, some of which may better harmonise with those presuppositions. On the other

---

[1] See: http://www.loa.istc.cnr.it/ontologies/DOLCE-Lite.owl.

hand, we took the effort to guarantee that our implementation is both internally consistent and is consistent with the main specification of this ontology, as defined in [12]. The details of the pattern are shown below (Fig. 4):

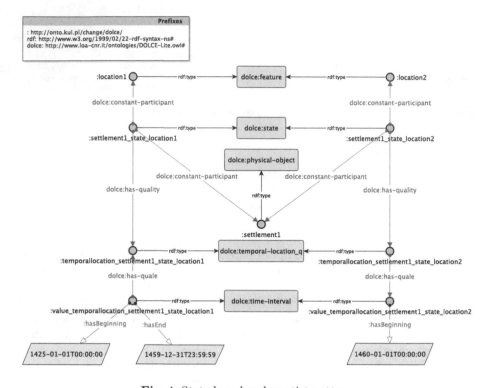

Fig. 4. State-based endurantist pattern

History-Based Endurantist Pattern. The history-based pattern requires the notion of endurant history, which we know from Sect. 3.1, and the conception of mereology, i.e., formal theory of parthood relation. This time we need to signify three histories:(i) history of Nieszawa (`:settlement1_history`), (ii) history of location 1 (`:location1_history`), and (iii) history of location 2 (`:location2_history`). Then we will consider an individual that is the mereological intersection (or greatest common part) of the history of Nieszawa and the history of location 1, say `:product_histories_settlement_1_location_1`, and we identify the temporal boundaries of this intersection by years 1425 and 1459. Obviously, a similar structure is needed for Nieszawa's location 2.

The implementation of this pattern is embedded in BFO 2.0 ontology[2]. Again this adds some conceptual overhead to the pattern, which we are ready to accept

---

[2] http://ifomis.uni-saarland.de/bfo/.

for the same reason as in the previous case. And as before we flesh out this pattern only by means of the Fig. 5.

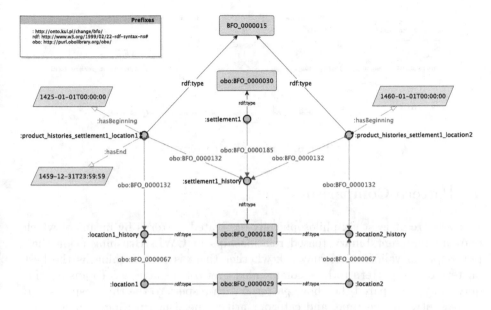

Fig. 5. History-based endurantist pattern

3.2 Perdurantist Pattern

Let us repeat that perdurantism represents all objects that exist in time as if they were processes. So the perdurantist solution splits, so to speak, Nieszawa, which is considered here as a process, into two temporal parts (or sub-processes): (i) temporal part of Nieszawa that existed from 1425 until 1459 – we will represent it as :temporalpart1_settlementunit1; and (ii) temporal part of Nieszawa that existed from 1460 onwards – we will represent it as :temporalpart2_settlementunit1. Then instead of positing Nieszawa being located in location 1 from 1425 until 1459, which would require a ternary relationship, we simply state that :temporalpart1_settlementunit1 is located in :location1. And similarly for the other location of Nieszawa – use :temporalpart2_settlementunit1.

To make this pattern more palatable we will express it in GFO ontology[3] with the same caveats as before. Then we can express the relocation of Nieszawa as shown in the Fig. 6.

As mentioned above the perdurantist pattern was first discussed (in the context of OWL ontologies) in [17]. Let us briefly note that [18, Sect. III] extends this pattern with the notion of individual concepts.

---

[3] See: http://www.onto-med.de/ontologies/gfo/.

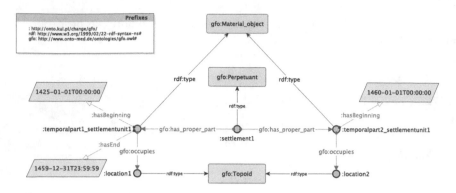

Fig. 6. Perdurantist pattern

4 Pattern Comparison

So there are at least six philosophically-motivated patterns by means of which one can represent binary tensed relationships in OWL. Brushing aside their philosophical validity, one may ask whether there is such a thing as the best pattern or the pattern to be recommended over other patterns? To answer this question we compared the above patterns with respect to the three aspects: DL expressivity, change type, and category arity type. Unsurprisingly enough, we get slightly different answers in each case.

4.1 DL Expressivity

Table 1 shows the DL expressivity of the respective patterns. From this perspective of computational complexity the most efficient pattern is the Trope-Based Endurantist Pattern and the worst efficient is the History-Based Endurantist Pattern. On the other hand, from the perspective of applied ontology more expressive theories are preferable to less expressive ones since the former are capable of providing more precise and accurate models.

Table 1. Patterns' DL expressivity

Pattern	DL expressivity
TQC pattern	SRIQ(D)
Manifestation-based endurantist pattern	SHIQ(D)
State-based endurantist pattern	SHOIF(D)
History-based endurantist pattern	SROIQ(D)
Trope-based pattern	ALCHIQ(D)
Perdurantist pattern	SHIQ(D)

4.2   Pattern Usage Scenario Comparisons

The second comparison may be drawn with respect to usage scenarios, which take into account some specific types of changes one may need to represent. This comparison is multi-facetted, i.e., we classify the usage scenarios with respect to two facets:

1. change type cardinality facet, which takes into account a number of simultaneous change types one needs to track down, e.g., whether one needs to represent only settlement location changes or location changes together with changes in settlement names, settlement types, etc. ;
2. arity facet, which takes into account change "arities", i.e., whether one represents changes within (monadic) categories, binary relations, ternary relations, etc.

Change Type Cardinality Facet. We consider here two types of usage scenarios: (i) mono-change scenarios, where only one type of change is recorded and (ii) multi-change scenarios, where we need to record multiple types of changes.

So in order to estimate their "performance" in this respect we calculated (cf. Tables 2 and 3) the sizes of their TBoxes and ABoxes in a multi-change scenario with the following parameters:

- we track one changing individual;
- we track its n tensed relations;

Table 2. Patterns' TBox size comparison in multi-change scenarios

Pattern	Classes	Object properties	Datatype properties	Annotation properties
TQC pattern	4	$n + 1$	2	0
Manifestation-based pattern	3	$n + 1$	2	0
State-based pattern	4	$n + 3$	2	0
History-based pattern	2	$\dot{n} + 2$	2	0
Trope-based pattern	$n + 2$	2	2	0
Perdurantist pattern	3	$n + 1$	2	0

Table 3. Patterns' ABox size comparison in multi-change scenarios

Pattern	Triples	Individuals
TQC pattern	$8 \cdot n \cdot t + 3$	$3 \cdot n \cdot t + 2$
Manifestation-based endurantist pattern	$(n + 5) \cdot t + 1$	$(n + 1) \cdot 5 + 1$
State-based endurantist pattern	$10 \cdot n \cdot t + 1$	$4 \cdot n \cdot t + 1$
History-based endurantist pattern	$8 \cdot n \cdot t + 2$	$3 \cdot n \cdot t + 2$
Trope-based pattern	$7 \cdot n \cdot t + n + 1$	$2 \cdot n \cdot t + n + 1$
Perdurantist pattern	$(n + 5) \cdot t + 1$	$(n + 1) \cdot 5 + 1$

– we record its status both at the beginnings and at the ends of t intervals;
– in each case we assume "the worst-case scenario": at each interval the individual is related to different objects.

So, given that the smaller RDF graphs are preferred over bigger ones, the Manifestation-Based and Perdurantist Patterns are the most efficient provided that the number of change aspects is greater than 1 (i.e., that $n > 1$). On the other hand, for those unusual cases when one needs to trace only one temporal aspect the most efficient is the Trope-Based Pattern.

Arity Facet. Here we consider three types of usage scenarios: (i) monadic scenarios, where change concerns (monadic) categories, i.e. we record changes with respect to (monadic) categories; (ii) binary scenarios, where change concerns binary relations, i.e. we record changes with respect to binary relations; and finally (iii) higher-arity scenarios, where change concerns ternary, quaternary, etc. relations, i.e. we record changes with respect to higher arity relations.

First note that all patterns do not handle higher-arity scenarios and in order to manage the latter one needs to resort to other resources, e.g., to the standard reification pattern [14]. In other words, all patterns discussed in this paper are defective in this respect. Secondly note that TQC Pattern, Manifestation-Based Pattern, and Perdurantist Pattern are capable of representing changes with respect to (monadic) categories in the same way as they represent changes with respect to binary relations. The situation is different with respect to other patterns. Neither Trope-Based, State-Based Endurantist, nor History-Based Endurantist Pattern can handle such changes unless they are extended with some suitable modifications.

5   Future Work

As mentioned in Sect. 1 the main rationale for this research is the need to represent time and change in a historical geoinformation system. Consequently, we see this paper as a preparatory work to provide for the crucial design choice concerning the logical schema of the database component of this system and its triple store component where the data will be made available as a LOD dataset. Then, when the choice is made, we will be able to implement the selected pattern and validate its applicability not on a single, simplified example but in large scale. This validation will concern not only the technical aspects discussed in this paper but also how the selected pattern is to facilitate the data management for the laymen users of the system.

References

1. Andronikos, T., Stefanidakis, M., Papadakis, I.: Adding temporal dimension to ontologies via owl reification. In: 2009 13th Panhellenic Conference on Informatics, pp. 19–22 (2009)
2. Arp, R., Smith, B., Spear, A.D.: Building Ontologies with Basic Formal Ontology. The MIT Press, Cambridge (2015)

3. Batsakis, S., Petrakis, E., Tachmazidis, I., Antoniou, G.: Temporal representation and reasoning in OWL 2. Semant. Web J. **8**, 981–1000 (2016)
4. Brogaard, B.: Tensed relations. Analysis **66**, 194–202 (2006)
5. Fine, K.: Things and their parts. Midwest Stud. Philos. **23**(1), 61–74 (1999)
6. Gangemi, A., Presutti, V.: A multi-dimensional comparison of ontology design patterns for representing n-ary relations. In: van Emde Boas, P., Groen, F.C.A., Italiano, G.F., Nawrocki, J., Sack, H. (eds.) SOFSEM 2013. LNCS, vol. 7741, pp. 86–105. Springer, Heidelberg (2013). https://doi.org/10.1007/978-3-642-35843-2_8
7. Giménez-García, J.M., Zimmermann, A., Maret, P.: NdFluents: an ontology for annotated statements with inference preservation. In: Blomqvist, E., Maynard, D., Gangemi, A., Hoekstra, R., Hitzler, P., Hartig, O. (eds.) ESWC 2017. LNCS, vol. 10249, pp. 638–654. Springer, Cham (2017). https://doi.org/10.1007/978-3-319-58068-5_39
8. Grewe, N., Jansen, L., Smith, B.: Permanent generic relatedness and silent change. In: Kutz, et al. [11]. http://ceur-ws.org/Vol-1660
9. Hayes, P.: Formal Unifying Standards for the Representation of Spatiotemporal Knowledge. Technical report, Advanced Decision Architectures Alliance (2004). https://www.ihmc.us/users/phayes/arlada2004final.pdf
10. Krieger, H.-U.: Where temporal description logics fail: representing temporally-changing relationships. In: Dengel, A.R., Berns, K., Breuel, T.M., Bomarius, F., Roth-Berghofer, T.R. (eds.) KI 2008. LNCS (LNAI), vol. 5243, pp. 249–257. Springer, Heidelberg (2008). https://doi.org/10.1007/978-3-540-85845-4_31
11. Grewe, N., Jansen, L., Smith, B.: Permanent generic relatedness and silent change. In: Kutz, O., et al. (eds.) Proceedings of the Joint Ontology Workshops 2016, CEUR Workshop Proceedings, vol. 1660. CEUR-WS.org (2016). http://ceur-ws.org/Vol-1660
12. Masolo, C., Borgo, S., Gangemi, A., Guarino, N., Oltramari, A.: Wonder-Web Deliverable D18. The WonderWeb Library of Foundational Ontologies and the DOLCE ontology (2003). http://wonderweb.semanticweb.org/deliverables/documents/D18.pdf
13. Moltmann, F.: Variable objects and truth-making. In: Dumitru, M. (ed.) Metaphysics, Meaning, and Modality. Themes from Kit Fine, vol. (forthcoming). Oxford Univerity Press (2016)
14. Noy, N., Rector, A.: Defining N-ary Relations on the Semantic Web. W3C Working Group Note, World Wide Web Consortium, April 2006. http://www.w3.org/TR/swbp-n-aryRelations/
15. O'Connor, M.J., Das, A.K.: A method for representing and querying temporal information in OWL. In: Fred, A., Filipe, J., Gamboa, H. (eds.) BIOSTEC 2010. CCIS, vol. 127, pp. 97–110. Springer, Heidelberg (2011). https://doi.org/10.1007/978-3-642-18472-7_8
16. Trypuz, R., Kuzinski, D., Sopek, M.: General legal entity identifier ontology. In: Kutz, et al. [11]. http://ceur-ws.org/Vol-1660
17. Welty, C.A., Fikes, R.: A reusable ontology for fluents in OWL. In: Bennett, B., Fellbaum, C. (eds.) FOIS. Frontiers in Artificial Intelligence and Applications, vol. 150, pp. 226–236. IOS Press (2006)
18. Zamborlini, V., Guizzardi, G.: On the representation of temporally changing information in OWL. In: EDOCW, pp. 283–292. IEEE Computer Society (2010)
19. Zamborlini, V.C., Guizzardi, G.: An ontologically-founded reification approach for representing temporally changing information in OWL. In: 11th International Symposium on Logical Formalizations of Commonsense Reasoning (COMMONSENSE 2013) (2013)

A Data Exchange Tool Based on Ontology for Emergency Response Systems

Félix Simas[1,4], Rebeca Barros[1,2], Laís Salvador[1,2], Marian Weber[3(✉)], and Simone Amorim[4]

[1] Fraunhofer Project Center for Software and Systems Engineering at UFBA, Salvador, Brazil
`felixneto@ifba.edu.br, rebecasbarros@dcc.ufba.br, laisns@ufba.br`
[2] Federal University of Bahia (UFBA), Salvador, Brazil
[3] Karlsruhe Institute of Technology (KIT), Karlsruhe, Germany
`marian.weber@student.kit.edu`
[4] Federal Institute of Bahia (IFBA), Salvador, Brazil
`simone.amorim@ifba.edu.br`

Abstract. Considering the potential of Emergency Response Systems (ERS) in combination with crowd-based information, this article presents a data integration solution within the scope of the RESCUER project: an ontology based data exchange solution to allow semantic interoperability between ERS of Command and Control Centers, referred to as Legacy Systems, and RESCUER. The solution is implemented by the Data Integration with Legacy Systems (DILS) component which can be used for the exchange of incident information by any ERS. As a result, we evaluated simulated emergency cases by sending RESCUER emergency reports to another ERS with the DILS.

Keywords: Emergency Response System · Data integration · Data exchange · EDXL-RESCUER

1 Introduction

Crowdsourcing information is becoming widely used as a source of knowledge and solutions for different problems [1]. The "Reliable and Smart Crowdsourcing Solution for Emergency and Crisis Management" (RESCUER)[1] project aims to develop a solution for managing emergencies and crises. It uses crowd sourced information from different origins: people affected by the incident, eyewitnesses, security forces and others. Handling an emergency requires the coordination and cooperation of people and systems from external organizations, as well as other initiatives on the part of government and society in general.

RESCUER is considered an example of Emergency Response Systems (ERS). One of its tasks is to supply an infrastructure for exchanging information with

---

[1] http://www.rescuer-project.org/.

© Springer International Publishing AG 2017
E. Garoufallou et al. (Eds.): MTSR 2017, CCIS 755, pp. 74–79, 2017.
https://doi.org/10.1007/978-3-319-70863-8_7

other ERS that belong to the Command and Control Centers (C&CC), hereafter referred to as Legacy Systems[2]. The core of this infrastructure is a conceptual model for information exchange, the EDXL-RESCUER ontology [2], abbreviated to EDXL-R, defined on the basis of the Emergency Data Exchange Language (EDXL)[3]. In addition to EDXL-R, we propose the integration of RESCUER with Legacy Systems during an emergency response situation based on two motivation scenarios: **RESCUER**'s access to incident information from a Legacy System can provide a novel and more reliable source of emergency information; the **Legacy System**'s access to information related to a confirmed incident from RESCUER can provide a more detailed source of information including analyzed crowd sourced data.

Therefore this paper presents a data integration approach used to provide semantic interoperability between RESCUER and Legacy Systems. This approach is realized by the Data Integration with Legacy Systems (DILS) component, an ongoing work on data exchange based on EDXL-R, that provides mechanisms for semantic data integration to support the coexistence of multiple ERS, including RESCUER.

The remainder of this document is structured as follows: Sect. 2 presents the data exchange model based on ontology; followed by the DILS component specification and its application in RESCUER in Sect. 3. In Sects. 4 and 5 related work, the conclusion and future works are discussed.

2   Ontology Based Data Exchange

Data exchange is the task of finding an instance of a target schema with a given instance of a source schema and a specification of the relationship between these schemas. In other words, there is a conversion process between source and target schema based on mappings [3]. In an ontology based data exchange, the data sources (source schema) are transformed into the vocabulary of an ontology (target schema) [4].

For the implementation of this model, we used Karma[4], a data integration tool based on ontology. Karma enables data integration from a variety of data sources including databases, spreadsheets, delimited text files and CSV, XML, JSON and Web API files. Furthermore, it supports data exchange for the target ontology in RDF or JSON-LD format. In Karma, the data exchange process comprises two phases. The first phase (at design time) is responsible for mapping the data source schema to the schema of a preselected ontology. In the second phase (at execution time), the mapping file is used to convert the data source into the ontology. The **Karma web service** is responsible for translating the input data to the predefined ontology vocabulary.

---

[2] The term "Legacy Systems" was used in the context of the RESCUER project to refer to pre-existent ERS which could interact with RESCUER.

[3] https://www.oasis-open.org/committees/emergency/.

[4] http://usc-isi-i2.github.io/karma/.

3   Component for Data Integration with Legacy Systems

The Data Integration with Legacy Systems (DILS) component aims to provide a solution for integrating ERS during an emergency. The proposed integration follows the approach of a data exchange based on ontology, where the ERS data sources are converted to EDXL-R, as the target schema. The idea is to use EDXL-R as a common exchange vocabulary. The main goal of DILS is to support the exchange of information related to an incident (during an emergency situation) which is simultaneously monitored by the ERS.

The DILS component uses RabbitMQ[5], a message broker, to send and receive messages to/from other components or systems. RabbitMQ works with queues, where the sender (a component/system) posts a message and the receiver (a component/system) gets the posted message.

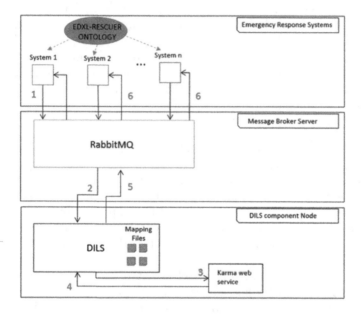

Fig. 1. DILS workflow

In general, the data exchange process based on the EDXL-R ontology requires that an ERS sends the information about an incident to other ERS or waits until it receives the information about an incident in the ontology vocabulary from other ERS. Figure 1 shows the building blocks of the proposed data exchange solution:

(i) **Emergency Response Systems:** an ERS sends incident information in its own data source format and *n-1* ERS receive incident information

---
[5] http://www.rabbitmq.com.

translated into the ontology vocabulary in RDF or JSON-LD format. For this reason all ERS need to have access to the EDXL-R ontology.

(ii) **Rabbit MQ Message Server:** the message broker where an ERS publishes incident information or is notified when a new incident information is published by another ERS. In this implementation two (2) queues were defined for each ERS, one for exchange of messages in the direction from ERS to DILS and another for the direction from DILS to ERS.

(iii) **DILS Node:** translates the incident information from an ERS into the EDXL-R vocabulary (RDF or JSON-LD) and consists of two modules:

  (a) **DILS component:** responsible for gathering the incident from an ERS and finding the correct mapping file according to the ERS data source. In addition, it is responsible for delivering the incident to all other ERS.

  (b) **Karma web service:** a module from the Karma integration tool that receives data and the mapping file from the DILS component, and translates the input data into EDXL-R.

3.1 The DILS Component and RESCUER

In the architecture of RESCUER, DILS interacts with the Emergency State Builder (ESB) component, which is responsible for creating and updating the emergency state. In this sense, ESB is also responsible for updating the status of an incident to the confirmed status. When the DILS component gets a confirmed incident from ESB, it converts the consumed data to EDXL-R and sends a confirmed incident in the EDXL-R format to the Legacy Systems.

Figure 1 also shows the workflow for a specific ERS (System 1) sending incident information to all other systems. Here we exemplify the case of RESCUER(ESB) sending incident information to all other systems (Legacy Systems) according to the DILS workflow (as indicated by the numbered arrows in Fig. 1):

1. RESCUER (System 1) publishes the incident information within RabbitMQ; the following code excerpt shows a confirmed incident with the id 1_b99e995d from RESCUER in JSON:

```
"keyword": "FIRE", #Incident is classified as Fire
"position": {
  "latitude": -12.9232658, #Location latitude
  "longitude": -38.3883258, #Location longitude
  "altitude": 0.0
},
"reliability": "high", #Incident has a high reliability
"incidentIdentifier": "1_b99e995d", #Incident's id
```

2. RabbitMQ notifies the DILS component that acquires this incident information;

3. DILS sends the incident information and the associated mapping file to the Karma web service via HTTP request;

4. The Karma web service sends the incident information in accordance with the EDXL-R vocabulary back to the DILS component;
5. DILS publishes the incident information (in the EDXL-R format) within RabbitMQ; the same confirmed incident from RESCUER with the id 1_b99e995d translated to the EDXL-R schema can be seen in the following excerpt:

```
[{ "hasConfidence": {
"a": "http://fpc.ufba.br/ontologies/edxl_sitrep#Unsure" },
"a": "http://fpc.ufba.br/ontologies/edxl_sitrep#Incident",
"fromDateTime": "2016-06-14T12:48:15.143Z",
"hasLocation": { #relates to the location of an Incident
    "a": "http://fpc.ufba.br/ontologies/edxl_rm#Location",
    "locationLatitude": "-12.9232658", #Location latitude
    "locationLongitude": "-38.3883258", #Location longitude
    "iri": "http://fpc.ufba.br/ontologies/edxl_sitrep#location/
    1_b99e995d"},
"incidentID": "1_b99e995d", #Incident id
"iri": "http://fpc.ufba.br/ontologies/edxl_sitrep#incident/
        1_b99e995d",
"hasIncidentType": { #Incident classified as Fire
    "a": "http://fpc.ufba.br/ontologies/edxl_cap#Fire"}]
```

6. RabbitMQ notifies all other ERS (Legacy Systems) to acquire the incident information (in EDXL-R format) from RESCUER (System 1).

The above mentioned codes contain a confirmed incident with id, type, position and reliability from the RESCUER base and its respective translation into the EDXL-R vocabulary.

4   Related Work

SoKNOS support system [5] is a prototype for emergency management systems using semantic technologies. In SoKNOS, information sources and services are annotated using ontologies to improve the prediction of the right information at the right time. The implementation uses OntoBroker[6] which converts data stored in relational databases or accessed via web services into the facts of an ontology.

In [6] a SPARQL endpoint is proposed to implement the Ontology Based Data Access (OBDA) approach. In this work, the databases used for interoperability are made available over a single JDBC interface through a virtual database. Mappings are designed to bind domain ontologies to this virtual database by allowing SPARQL queries, which are performed at the endpoint to retrieve the data stored in the connected databases. This solution has been used in the context of emergency management with the support of the EDXL' ontology.

---

[6] http://www.semafora-systems.com/en/products/ontobroker/.

Both works present solutions based on ontologies for emergency management systems in the same way as DILS. In turn, the DILS component focuses on data exchange which is more suitable for communication during an emergency situation.

5   Conclusions

This paper presented an experience report about the mechanisms for data integration between RESCUER and Legacy Systems. The proposal is a component that applies a data exchange model based on the EDXL-R ontology. We developed a simulator of Legacy Systems and used emergency response reports (the dataset from the Public Safety & Security Department of the State of Bahia) to evaluate our data exchange approach. The data sources were mapped to the EDXL-R ontology and we were able to show that the Data Integration with Legacy Systems (DILS) component works in a test scenario. In addition, the mappings of the ERS data sources with EDXL-R showed that the ontology works as a common vocabulary, promoting semantic interoperability between Emergency Response Systems. Finally, in certain data exchange tools, such as the tool Karma, the resulting mapping files can also be used by a data integration platform that provides a method to expose and populate the ontology and further execute queries to retrieve information. A future work is to populate the EDXL-R ontology with the ERS reports and to publish the ontology on the Web of Data.

As this paper describes a work in progress, the baseline for future exploitation of the project's results will be the constituency of a strong user community. The exploitation of the results may include application and performance evaluation of the DILS component in real life emergency management scenarios.

References

1. Besaleva, L.I., Weaver, A.C.: Applications of social networks and crowdsourcing for disaster management improvement. In: 2013 International Conference on Social Computing (SocialCom), pp. 213–219. IEEE (2013)
2. Barros, R., Kislansky, P., Salvador, L., Almeida, R., Breyer, M., Gasparin, L.: EDXL-RESCUER ontology: conceptual model for semantic integration (2015)
3. Arenas, M., Libkin, L.: XML data exchange: consistency and query answering. J. ACM **55**, 7 (2008)
4. Peng, L., Man, Y.: A novel data exchange model based on P2P and ontology. In: Proceedings 2013 International Conference on Mechatronic Sciences, Electric Engineering and Computer, MEC 2013, pp. 1693–1696 (2013)
5. Babitski, G., Bergweiler, S., Grebner, O., Oberle, D., Paulheim, H., Probst, F.: SoKNOS – Using Semantic Technologies in Disaster Management Software. In: Antoniou, G., Grobelnik, M., Simperl, E., Parsia, B., Plexousakis, D., Leenheer, P., Pan, J. (eds.) ESWC 2011. LNCS, vol. 6644, pp. 183–197. Springer, Heidelberg (2011). https://doi.org/10.1007/978-3-642-21064-8_13
6. Barros, R., Vieira, V., Salvador, L., Almeida, R.: Semantic interoperability between emergency response systems. In: Proceedings of the 31st Brazilian Symposium on Databases, pp. 199–204 (2016). (In Portuguese)

An Ontology Based Approach for Host Intrusion Detection Systems

Ozgu Can[(✉)], Murat Osman Unalir, Emine Sezer,
Okan Bursa, and Batuhan Erdogdu

Department of Computer Engineering, Ege University, 35100 Bornova-Izmir, Turkey
{ozgu.can,murat.osman.unalir,emine.sezer,okan.bursa}@ege.edu.tr,
batuhanerdogdu@gmail.com

Abstract. In recent years, cyber-attacks have emerged and these attacks result
in serious consequences. In order to overcome these consequences, a fully-func-
tioning and performance-improved intrusion detections systems are required. For
this purpose, we used ontologies to provide semantic expressiveness and knowledge description for an intrusion detection system. In this work, a host intrusion
detection system is implemented by using ontologies. The proposed system scans
for malwares running on the operating system. Also, services and processes that
are working on the system are scanned, and results are compared with the malware
database. If any match occurs, the proposed system displays a malware list that
matches with the information of that malware and where it is running. The
proposed ontology based intrusion detection system aims to reduce the search
time for malware scanning and to improve the performance of intrusion detection
systems.

Keywords: Intrusion detection system · Host intrusion detection · Ontology ·
Semantic web

1 Introduction

Today, there are many types of computer security threats and these threats increase
everyday. As a result of this increase, cyber-attacks have become a part of our daily
lives. Cyber-attacks cause personal, financial, professional and also emotional damages.
Unfortunately, most of the losses still can not be prevented. Thus, computer security has
a significant importance in today's world and it is at the top of the international agendas.
As there are several approaches to ensure security, Intrusion Detection System (IDS) is
one of the critical detection approaches to protect computer systems. IDS, monitors the
events in the computer or the network, analyzes them in order to detect the unauthorized
or malicious activities within the computer or the network, and generates alerts when it
observes potentially malicious activities. There are two types of IDS: Host IDS (HIDS)
and Network IDS (NIDS). HIDS is an intrusion detection that monitors and analyzes
the computer system, detects malicious activity and malwares on the host system, logs
the activity and notifies the user. On the other hand, NIDS monitors and analyzes all the
data passing through the network. The most effective protection is provided by a

© Springer International Publishing AG 2017
E. Garoufallou et al. (Eds.): MTSR 2017, CCIS 755, pp. 80–86, 2017.
https://doi.org/10.1007/978-3-319-70863-8_8

combination of both NIDS and HIDS. Our proposed IDS model aims to provide both of these technologies in a single ontology-based IDS system.

In this work, an IDS ontology is developed and implemented by using Semantic Web technologies. As this is an ongoing work, the presented work is part of an HIDS. Therefore, the aim of the proposed system is to detect intrusions that may violate the security aspects of a computer system and to increase the performance of intrusion detection systems. For this purpose, we used ontologies as a database for the rule-based intrusion detection system. First, we created an IDS ontology. Later, all the processes and services that work on a computer system are added as individuals to the IDS ontology by using Facebook's osquery [1]. Also, we parsed malwares from Symantec's website [2] and added these malwares to the IDS ontology in order to compare with the processes and services that are working within the existing computer system. Finally, if any threat listed in the IDS ontology occurs in the working system, the proposed ontology based IDS system lists the malicious activities and malwares, and notifies the user. The paper is organized as follows: Sect. 2 presents the related work. Section 3 explains the IDS ontology. Section 4 presents the first implementation of the relevant ontology. Finally, Sect. 5 concludes and summarizes the future work.

2 Background

The purpose of our entire work is to implement a rule-based intrusion detection system by using Semantic Web technologies. Since IDS needs to monitor and analyze all the data passing through the network (NIDS) and processes in a single computer system (HIDS), the IDS needs to be very fast for this analysis in order to detect the malwares or malicious activities. Therefore, we used ontologies in order to use a semantic reasoner and a rule engine to detect intrusions and to improve performance of IDS. Also, the aim of the proposed model is to support both HIDS and NIDS for a better security. So far, as a result of our research, we have not found an ontology based IDS system that supports both HIDS and NIDS. And also, there is not much published research based on ontology use in IDS. In [3], an ontology is specified to model attacks. While the proposed attack ontology is based on DAML + OIL [4], our IDS ontology is based on OWL2 [5]. Also, our model and IDS ontology focus on IDS as a whole system, however the attack ontology just models attacks. An IDS based on ontology for web attacks is proposed in [6]. However, the proposed ontology and its concepts are inadequate to model an IDS system and just deals with web attacks. A rule status monitoring algorithm is given in [7]. The algorithm searches through the rules and reports whether they are enabled or disabled, and then reports it. This work does not use ontologies and Semantic Web technologies. In [8], a rule and a cluster based intrusion detection system for wireless sensor networks (WSN) is presented. The proposed system uses a relational database to store and manipulate data, and focuses on attacks in WSN. In our work, we focus on both HIDS and NIDS and use ontologies instead of relational database and osquery results instead of log-audit data.

3   IDS Ontology

An ontology is an explicit formal specifications of a conceptualization [9]. As a consequence, ontologies are used to share a common understanding among users or agents, to enable reuse of the domain knowledge, to analyze the domain knowledge, to make explicit domain assumptions and to separate the domain knowledge from the operational knowledge [10]. While developing the Intrusion Detection System (IDS) Ontology, we used the ontology development steps defined in [10].

The IDS ontology has been developed to implement an intrusion detection system that examines the processes and services of a device and the devices connected to the network, and also the packets on the network to which these devices are connected. As this is an ongoing work, IDS ontology is still being developed.

In the IDS ontology, the enumerated IDS terms are listed as: Device, DatabaseServer, ManagedDevice, NetworkManagementSystem, Packet, SignaturedPacket, Process, Service, Software, Malware, destination, destinationMac, destinationPort, information, ack, fin, payload, syn, win, name, os, protocol, source, sourcePort, sourceMac, type. The classes, object and data type properties defined in the IDS ontology are shown in Figs. 1, 2 and 3, respectively.

Fig. 1.   The class hierarchy of IDS ontology.

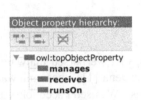

Fig. 2. The object property hierarchy of IDS ontology.

Fig. 3. The data property hierarchy of IDS ontology.

The classes are defined according to the following purposes: Device is used to store the devices in the network, DatabaseServer is used to store the list of malwares and harmful packets. The list will be taken from Symantec's [2] website, ManagedDevice is used to store devices that are controlled in the network, NetworkManagement-System is used to store devices that in which the intrusion detection system is executed, Packet is used to store the packets that come from internet, SignaturedPacket is a subclass of Packet and used to store harmful or malicious packets, Process is used to store processes that work in the device. Service is used to store services that work in the device, Software is used to store software, Malware is a subclass of Software and used to store malwares that are detected in the device.

The object properties are defined according to the following purposes: manages is the action of a NetworkManagementSystem (Network Management System) to manage other ManagedDevices on the network, receives is the action of receiving a Packet from a Device, runsOn is the action of the Software in a Device. Table 1 shows the domain and range information for the defined object properties.

Table 1. Domain and Range information of the object properties.

Name	Range	Domain
manages	ManagedDevice	NetworkManagementSystem
receives	Packet	Device
runsOn	Device	Software

The data properties are defined according to the following purposes: destination is the final device that the Packet arrives, destinationMAC is the MAC address of the Packet's destination, destinationPort is the port number of the Packet's destination, information is the data in the Packet, ack is the signal to acknowledge the receipt of the `Packet`, `fin` is used to give information about whether the `Packet` transfer is finished or not, `payload` is the essential data that is being carried within a `Packet`, `syn` is used for synchronization with the `Packet` source, `win` is used for the window size, `os` is the operating system of the `Device`, `source` indicates the `Device` where the `Packet` comes from, `sourceMAC` is the MAC address of the `Packet`'s source, `sourcePort` is the port number of the `Packet`'s source, `type` is the type of the malware (for example: Virus, Trojan, etc.).

4　Implementation

In order to detect intrusions by using IDS ontology, first we parsed malwares from Symantec's website [2] to a `csv` file. Then, by using Jena [11], these malwares are written as individuals to IDS ontology's `Malware` class. We used Facebook's osquery [1] to create the individuals of `Process` and `Service` classes. These individuals belong to the working computer system. The automatically added individuals of `Process` and `Service` classes, and `Malware` classes are given in Fig. 4.

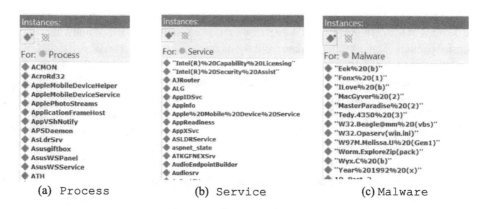

Fig. 4. Individuals of `Process`, `Service` and `Malware` classes.

The implementation compares the individuals of `Malware` class with the individuals of `Process` and `Service` classes to detect intrusions. If it finds a match between individuals in these classes of the IDS ontology, then an intrusion is detected and a warning message is shown as seen in Fig. 5.

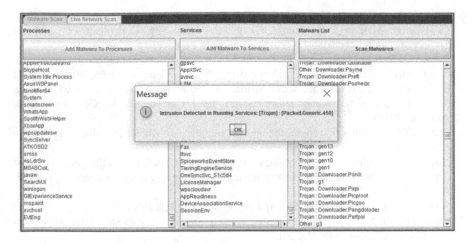

Fig. 5. Detecting intrusion in a computer system.

5 Conclusion

As information technology has become a key component for critical infrastructures, intrusion detection systems also become increasingly important due to the increased cyber-attacks in recent years. Our project aims to develop an ontology based IDS including both NIDS and HIDS for an effective security. As this is an ongoing project, in this work, we developed an IDS ontology and implemented this ontology to detect intrusions in a computer system. The proposed work is a part of HIDS. As a future work, IDS ontology will be extended according to provide NIDS. For this purpose, Live Network Scan tab seen in Fig. 5 will be activated and pcap4j [12] library will be used for the implementation. Besides, log analysis, event correlation and policy enforcement will be added to the intended ontology-based IDS model. New rules will be added in order to detect which devices are affected by interprocess dependencies and which processes are affected from which malwares.

References

1. Facebook Osquery, SQL powered operating system instrumentation, monitoring, and analytics. https://github.com/facebook/osquery. Accessed 08 July 2017
2. Symantec: Security Response. https://www.symantec.com/security_response/landing/azlisting.jsp. Accessed 08 July 2017
3. Undercoffer, J., Joshi, A., Pinkston, J.: Modeling computer attacks: an ontology for intrusion detection. In: Vigna, G., Kruegel, C., Jonsson, E. (eds.) RAID 2003. LNCS, vol. 2820, pp. 113–135. Springer, Heidelberg (2003). doi:10.1007/978-3-540-45248-5_7
4. DAML + OIL Reference Description Homepage. https://www.w3.org/TR/daml+oil-reference. Accessed 08 July 2017
5. OWL2 Homepage. https://www.w3.org/TR/owl2-overview/. Accessed 08 July 2017

6. Khairkar, A.D.: Intrusion Detection System based on Ontology for Web Applications. Dissertation, Master of Technology, Computer Engineering, Department of Computer Engineering and Information Technology College of Engineering, Pune (2013)
7. Turner, C., Rolston, J., Richards, D., Joseph, A.: A rule status monitoring algorithm for rule-based intrusion detection and prevention systems. Procedia Comput. Sci. **95**, 361–368 (2016)
8. Deshmukh, R., Deshmukh, R., Manoj Sharma, M.: Rule-based and cluster-based intrusion detection technique for wireless sensor network. Int. J. Comput. Sci. Mobile Comput. **2**(6), 200–208 (2013)
9. Gruber, T.R.: A translation approach to portable ontologies. Knowl. Acquisition **5**(2), 199–220 (1993)
10. Noy, N.F., McGuinness, D.L.: Ontology Development 101: A Guide to Creating Your First Ontology. http://protege.stanford.edu/publications/ontology_development/ontology101.pdf. Accessed 08 July 2017
11. Apache Jena Homepage. https://jena.apache.org. Accessed 08 July 2017
12. Kaitoy Pcap4J: A Java library for capturing, crafting, and sending packets. https://github.com/kaitoy/pcap4j. Accessed 08 July 2017

An Approach for Systematic Definitions Construction Based on Ontological Analysis

Patricia Merlim Lima Scheidegger[1], Maria Luiza Machado Campos[1]([✉]),
and Maria Cláudia Cavalcanti[2]

[1] Federal University of Rio de Janeiro, Rio de Janeiro, Brazil
{patricia.merlim,mluiza}@ufrj.br
[2] Military Institute of Engineering, Rio de Janeiro, Brazil
yoko@ime.eb.br

Abstract. This research motivation is to find a way to minimize the distance between business concepts and their respective representations in Information Technology artifacts, specially conceptual models. This distance leads to inconsistencies, ambiguities and implementation issues. Our approach is based on ontological analysis, which considers each concept according to its nature, capturing more precisely its essence and generally improving semantic richness and precision. Our main goal is to help in the process of systematic concepts definitions construction, contributing to generate more consistent definitions and associated conceptual modeling artifacts. The foundational ontology used as a theoretical reference is the Unified Foundational Ontology (UFO) which has been, in the last decade, successfully used to evaluate conceptual modeling languages and representations.

Keywords: Conceptualization · Definitions · Conceptual modeling

1 Introduction

The alignment between IT (Information Technology) and business is considered of fundamental importance and constitutes an essential factor to achieve the strategic goals of an organization. IT teams make great effort to construct technology deliverables to satisfy business requirements. There is a need to identify and correctly understand the main concepts associated to the business domain. Despite these efforts, there are still many challenges to shorten the gap between reality and the corresponding concepts represented in information systems.

Nowadays, most of business knowledge is still tacit, as people often have difficulty to externalize it. The development of terminological artifacts like glossaries and thesauri, is one of the main tasks to support knowledge capture and sharing. This task is far from trivial, considering the difficulties of representing the real world that is, in its essence, full of subjectiveness and ambiguity [6]. Domain specialists, although capable of understanding the domain, are not usually able to identify its essential elements, characteristics and relationships between them.

© Springer International Publishing AG 2017
E. Garoufallou et al. (Eds.): MTSR 2017, CCIS 755, pp. 87–99, 2017.
https://doi.org/10.1007/978-3-319-70863-8_9

Also, most often, when creating terminological artifacts, developers do not follow a systematic approach to construct definitions. This is usually a manual task that demands expertise not always available in the organizations or still focus too much on syntactic and linguistic guidelines.

From another perspective, during the system development cycle, there seems to be not enough effort in collecting and formalizing the main concepts of the domain. The vision is usually focused in the way computational artifacts will capture, provide and maintain data associated to the concept. Besides, these artifacts usually are not maintained consistently aligned with the resources that were initially their references. For example when conceptual models exist they sometimes fail to properly reflect the business point of view. They are commonly influenced by implementation considerations from IT professionals, whose real world perspective may differ from those who deal directly with the domain. Besides, concepts that are not directly represented in IT artifacts may be excluded or hidden, although they can be meaningful and relevant for business.

In this work we propose an approach to construct more consistent definitions to preserve semantics throughout different phases of the system development cycle, more specifically during the conceptual modeling phase. We intend to contribute to reduce the distance between IT and business, proposing mechanisms that can consistently support concepts identification and definition so that they can be aligned and properly used to add expressivity to conceptual models.

In the next section we discuss in more detail some issues related to concepts definitions construction and conceptual modeling. In Sect. 3 we present the main ideas behind ontological analysis and introduce the main elements of a foundational ontology that is the basis of our approach. In Sects. 4 and 5, the approach is described and an application example is presented, respectively. Finally, we discuss related work, then we conclude with general considerations and future work.

2   Concepts Definitions and Conceptual Modeling

Humans have great capabilities in terms of capturing implicit meaning in communications as well as solving ambiguities using contextual information. Computers, on the other hand, have strong limitations to determine the intended meaning associated to the representations they have to deal and manipulate. The success of computer systems interoperability and data integration greatly depends on precisely capturing the conceptualizations and human interpretations of the reality being represented. In this section we present a review of two areas that constitute the basis of our work. In Sect. 2 we include a brief review of principles for building definitions that can also be adopted for the organization of concepts and their relationships, as discussed in Sect. 2, where conceptualizations are presented as the basis of a system development cycle, in the form of conceptual models.

Information Science studies include a series of principles and canons for knowledge organization, which allow concepts of a domain to be structured in a systematic way, constituting a so called concepts system [7]. Thus, the content and structure of a definition must clearly reflect the place of a concept in a certain concepts system [13]. In this sense, a definition must include the essential characteristics needed to identify and delimit a concept, and, in the same way, a term must reflect the intension of the corresponding concept as well as possible.

In the case of terminological artifacts, glossaries are an important instrument to reflect a vocabulary and associated definitions. But very often, it is difficult to perceive a concepts system underlying a glossary, either because there are incipient definitions or because there are inconsistencies between terms definitions.

Among several approaches concerning the structure of definitions in Information Science, definitions by *genus* and *differentia* are an interesting and useful strategy. In [11], the Aristotelian way to define a thing is defined by the formula:

S = def. a G which Ds, where G is the genus, and the parent term of S; D is the differentia and tells us about certain Gs in virtue of which they are Ss.

Genus is the set of elements that have a common origin. It brings the notion of class as a set of distinct objects with common characteristics. *Differentia* is the description of the specific features of the object being defined, which distinguish it from the other objects of the same class.

When the *genus* is selected some features are automatically associated without the need of showing them in the definition. The *genus* selection is very important in order to categorize the concept as part of a contextual domain. The *genus* role is to establish the term type through the relation is-a. [9] states that the definition portion that plays the role of genus can express other types of relations like part-whole.

The initial phases of the system development cycle involve understanding the concepts associated to the business domain. The development cycle is in fact a transformation from a human-oriented view of reality to a machine-representation of a relevant part of this reality. Conceptual modeling is a fundamental activity to capture the domain perspective and to conciliate perspectives from both the developer and the domain expert. According to [1] the conceptual modeling process includes perceptions inherently human and very subjective. This process involves 2 main activities: getting the concepts related to the universe of discourse and representing these concepts according to the grammar of a modeling language. It is similar to the translation process as it identifies concepts in natural language and represents them in another language, the modeling one.

A semantic rich conceptual model needs to provide the necessary elements to represent reality as accurate as it can be in a way that turns to be understandable and implementation independent. For this reason, the modeling language must provide the essential modeling constructs to precisely represent the intended conceptualization. If the language is poor in expressiveness, a good part of the concepts will not be represented. "A modeling language is said to be complete if every concept in a domain conceptualization is covered by at least one modeling construct of the language" [3]. Taking advantage of a well grounded conceptualization and representing it using an adequate language increases the chances to implement computational systems that are consistent and reality compatible.

Getting an accurate representation is even more important and critical when we need to integrate different models that share the same domain.

3   Ontological Analysis

In the last decades, there has been significant advances on using ontological analysis to provide a sound foundation for conceptual models development, in order to reach better representations of computational artifacts, specially conceptual schemas [4]. Ontological analysis can be defined as "the process of eliciting and discovering relevant distinctions and relationships bound to the very nature of the entities involved in a certain domain"[2].

Ontological Analysis is based on the use of foundational ontologies (also called top-level ontologies), which provide a set of principles and basic categories [2], such as space, time, matter, object, event, action, etc., which are independent of any particular domain. Examples of popular foundational ontologies are BFO [12] and UFO [3]. In this work UFO (Unified Foundational Ontology) was adopted, because it has been successfully used in recent years to evaluate conceptual model languages and representations, applying more real world semantics to modeling elements.

UFO categories are organized in three segments: UFO-A, UFO-B and UFO-C. UFO-A focuses on *Endurants*. Endurants and their parts are always present during existence and their identities are preserved. UFO-B focuses on *Perdurants*, which differ from *Endurants* specially because of their relation with time. UFO-B richly characterizes events, as entities that are composed by one or more temporal parts and occur in time. Finally, UFO-C focuses on social elements. Figure 1 shows a fragment of UFO-A.

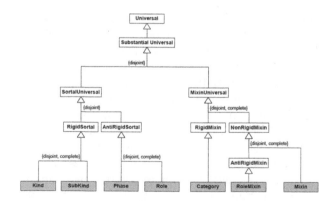

Fig. 1. UFO-A fragment [3]

Each UFO-A basic category (represented in gray in Fig. 1) has distinct aspects depending on its nature. These aspects are organized in metaproperties: identity, rigidity, dependence and unity, which are described in detail in [3] and summarized in Table 1.

In Table 1 we have the presence or absence of metaproperties in each category. The positive signal indicates presence and the negative signal indicates absence. The tilde indicates the possibility of presence.

Table 1. Categories x Metaproperties. Adapted from [3]

Category	Provide identity	Identity	Rigidity	Dependence
kind	+O	+I	+R	−D
subkind	−O	+I	+R	−D
role	−O	+I	$^-$R	+D
phase	−O	+I	$^-$R	−D
category	−O	−I	+R	−D
roleMixin	−O	−I	$^-$R	+D
mixin	−O	−I	$^-$R	−D

Therefore, in the light of these categories, it is possible for us to perform an ontological analysis of a specific domain, and find out, for each concept, to which UFO category it belongs. For instance, a person, since it provides identity, and for its rigid characteristic and for its independent existence, it may be categorized as a KIND. A ROLE, on the other hand, emerges from an intrinsic dependency, which is expressed by a relation with other concepts [1]. For instance, a student may be categorized as a ROLE. If there are essential elements for each category, these elements need to be explicitly represented in the conceptual models.

According to UFO-B, Event, by its turn, exists as long as its temporal parts exist. Every event has a start, a duration and an end. An Event can be either an AtomicEvent or a ComplexEvent. Atomic events are those who have only one temporal part. Complex events are those who have two or more temporal parts.

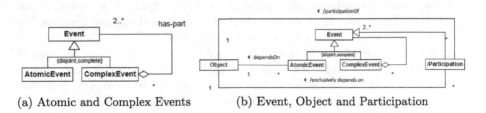

(a) Atomic and Complex Events   (b) Event, Object and Participation

Fig. 2. UFO-B Fragments [5]

In Fig. 2(a) we can see that Atomic Events and Complex Events specialize Event with the restrictions *disjoint, complete*. *Disjoint* means that event can be Atomic or Complex, but can not be both. *Complete* means that Event can only be an AtomicEvent or a ComplexEvent, and nothing else.

Events are ontologically dependent entities because they need participants in order to exist. Figure 2(b) shows the participation of *Objects* in *Events*. An AtomicEvent is directly dependent on one Object participation. ComplexEvents are dependent on all Objects that their temporal parts also depends on.

For each temporal part of an Event, no matter ComplexEvent or AtomicEvent, there are two time points: begin-point and end-point. There is a precedence relation between the time points of temporal parts.

Events can change reality characteristics, turning one situation into another. A situation is one specific configuration of reality. Situation is the "state of affairs" in philosophy [5]. Two situations, with the same characteristics, are different if they occur in distinct moments. Events have two kind of relation with situations. "Situation triggers Event" and "Event brings-about Situation".

- When "Situation triggers Event", the event occurs because of that situation. Situation is the start-point of the Event. This is called pre-state.
- When "Event brings-about Situation", the event provokes one situation and this situation is the end-point. This is called pos-state.
- If one Situation X is provoked by the Event Y and the same situation triggers the Event Z we can say that Event Y is directly related to Event Z.

4   Building Consistent Definitions

In our approach, to guide the construction of a definition we identified four macro activities, which are described as follows:

a - Select relevant concepts. First, it is necessary to identify a glossary that contains real business definitions, and avoid definitions that are created and maintained by IT. In other words, try to identify business or corporative glossaries. Once identified the glossary, we then select the concepts that are part of the analysis scope, usually supervised by a domain specialist.

b - Analyze the selected concepts. In this activity we analyze each selected concept through an ontological point of view, classifying it according to an ontological category. Here we use UFO categories and meta-properties. To do this, we should interact with domain specialists.

c - Apply the guidelines. Here we recommend the use of guidelines also based on UFO categories and meta-properties that we propose in this work. These guidelines work as a support to the construction of definitions in terminological control artifacts, used in corporate environments. We identify the meta-properties associated to the concept, like identity, rigidity and dependency (mentioned in Sect. 3), and we try to describe the concept by making these meta-properties explicit through the elements of UFO.

d - Refine the analysis. In this activity we verify the consistency between related concepts, refining the respective definitions. We identify incomplete definitions and point to the inconsistencies that must be treated, and also possible improvements on the definitions.

In order to construct definitions it is also necessary to take into account the theoretical base from the Information Science to address terminological aspects, like properties, context and gender. As mentioned in Sect. 2, we consider that a definition is formed by *genus* (determining the class of the concept) and *differentia* (determining the specific characteristics of the concept being defined).

The main contributions of our work are the approach and the guidelines proposed to construct a definition, which involve the ontological analysis. Many categories of the ontological analysis (UFO categories) are covered by these guidelines, and are fully described in [8]. For this article we focused on the guidelines to construct the definition of concepts that are categorized as an Event, in order to show their applicability in a real example.

In addition, we developed a mapping framework, which, for each foundation ontology category, lists its relation to other categories and recommends them to be mandatory, optional or desirable in the definition of the concept. This mapping framework will be described in the following subsection. Then, another subsection describes the guidelines for the Event category.

4.1 Mapping Framework

Table 2 shows the mapping framework. For each category we indicate the markers that represent the functions that this category has in relation to another category. In meronimic relations the markers indicate the function hat relates the parts to their whole. This framework also helps to identify relationships that reflect on conceptual models like generalization, specialization and dependence. For example, if one class is identified by another, we have a specialization. Similarly, if one class depends on another, we have a dependence.

Table 2. Concepts correlation mapping

Category	Function	Related to	Mention related concept in the definition
kind	owns identity	N/A	N/A
kind	generalizes	Subkind	Desirable
kind	generalizes	Role	Optional
kind	generalizes	Phase	Optional
Subkind	is_identified_by	Kind	Mandatory
Role	is_identified_by	Kind	Mandatory
Role	depends_on	Relator	Mandatory
Phase	is_identified_by	Kind	Mandatory
Phase	depends_on	Kind.intrinsicProperty	Mandatory
Event	is_composed_by	Event	Optional
Event	depends_on	participants	Mandatory
Event	can_bring_about	Situation	Mandatory if exists
Event	can_be_trigged_by	Situation	Mandatory if exists

The markers are described as follows:

owns_identity - Indicates that one category is able to provide identity to its individuals

is_identified_by - Indicates that the identity is provided by another category

depends_on - Indicates existential dependence. The existential dependence can occur not only from one category to another but also from one category to an intrinsic property of another category. In meronimic relationships, this marker indicates the dependence from the whole to the part, in the case of essentiality. It also indicates the dependence from the part to the whole, in the case of inseparability.

generalizes - indicates that this category generalizes other(s) category(ies) and provides identity to these categories.

is_composed_by - indicates meronimic relationship between categories

can_bring_about - indicates that this category brings other category to existence.

can_be_trigged_by - indicates that this category can emerge from the existence of another category. It is not an existential dependency because in this case one category does not depend on another to exist.

The last column in Table 2 indicates if it is mandatory that a concept must be mentioned in a related concept definition. This is important to provide consistence between definitions of related concepts. This mapping board is a summary that leads to the guidelines proposed for each type of category considered in the scope of this work.

Observing the markers identified in each category in Table 2, we highlight two markers that have a direct influence in a definition: the markers *is_identified_by* and *depends_on*.

The marker *is_identified_by* indicates that the category identity is provided by another category. The meta-property identity is relevant in a definition because it determines to which class the concept belongs. It determines the *genus*. Therefore, all the definitions classified in categories that have the marker *is_identified_by* need to make reference to the concept that provides its identity.

The marker *depends_on* indicates the meta-property dependence. This meta-property is also relevant in a definition because it shows that a concept needs another concept in order to be well defined.

4.2   Guidelines to Construct a Definition of an *Event*

The guidelines proposed in our approach cover the construction of definitions of concepts classified in categories like Kind, Subkind, Role, Relator, Phase and Event which, as mentioned before, are fully described in [8]. For this article, due to space limitations and aiming to apply the guidelines in a real example, we only describe the guidelines to construct an Event definition.

In Sect. 3 we saw that an Event can be Atomic or Complex. In Sect. 2 we also saw that a definition must contain only the necessary elements to make the concept understandable. A Complex Event can have several temporal parts. If we mention all its temporal parts it will turn the definition much longer than needed. Instead, if among these several temporal parts, there is one (or more) that is relevant to the concept comprehension, and its begin and end points are under the limits of the event being defined, we recommend mentioning this relevant temporal part. We also saw in Sect. 3 that Events are existentially dependent on participants, so the definition of an event must mention its participants. Considering the aspects highlighted in the ontological analysis of an event and using our framework as a reference, we proposed the following guidelines to construct an Event definition:

G1.1 Identify the temporal parts that compose the Event. Mention in the definition only temporal parts that are relevant for the concept's comprehension.
G1.2 For each temporal part, identify the participants
G1.3 (desirable) Mention what determines the event to start
G1.4 (desirable) Mention what determines the event to end
G1.5 (desirable) Identify the situation that triggers the event
G1.6 (desirable) Identify the situation that is provoked by the event

These guidelines indicate which other concepts must be naturally included in a definition, as they are directly related to the concept being defined.To provide consistence between concepts, it is important to verify not only one definition but, of course, the related ones, making an analysis throughout all the glossary. As an example we can mention that for an Event, the G1.1 guideline recommends to mention in the definition only the temporal part that is relevant for the comprehension of the complex event. Then it is recommended that in the same concepts system those relevant temporal parts must also be defined.

5   Application Example

We based the application example in corporative artifacts. In order to get definitions that were not influenced by a computational view, we chose to use a business glossary related to Health, Safety and Environment. The access to domain specialists was also relevant.

The analysis was held according to the activities described in Sect. 4:

a - Select relevant terms

In this glossary, we noticed that 63% of the definitions were related to events. On the other hand, there were definitions from Health that had nothing to do with Safety. For our example here the scope was reduced to seven concepts related to ACCIDENTS, which are listed as follows.

ACCIDENT - Unwanted and unforeseen event, instantaneous or not, that has resulted in damage to person, patrimony or environment; ACCIDENT WITH LESION AND WITHDRAWAL - Accident that causes personal lesion that prevent the injured one to get back to work the day immediately after the accident; ACCIDENT WITH LESION AND WITHOUT WITHDRAWAL - Accident that causes personal lesion and do not prevent the injured one to get back to work the day immediately after the accident; ON ROUTE ACCIDENT - Accident that the employee suffers in his way from home to work or from work to home, no matter the mean of transportation; FATAL ACCIDENT - Accident, instantaneous or not, that resulted in death; WORK ACCIDENT - Accident that occurs in the course of work causing corporal lesion or functional damage that can lead to death or loss of work capacity; ROAD TRAFFIC ACCIDENT - Every non premeditated event that results in damage to patrimony, environment or person, and where at least one of the parts is in movement through a route or the air.

b - Analyze the selected terms

The definition of ACCIDENT already classifies the term as an event. As we have seen through UFO categories we also can classify ACCIDENT as an event. It is a perdurant, which means that it can happen in time and have a well defined beginning and an end. To understand the ACCIDENT concept and its specializations (FATAL, WITH LESION, OF ROUTE, and so on) it is important to identify the criteria that specialize the ACCIDENT. As we have seen, *differentia* brings the specificities of what is being defined in relation to the other individuals of the same class. We identified the following criteria for the selected definitions: (i) the type of damage caused by the accident; and (ii) the circumstances in the moment of the accident (place, time).

We noticed that the specificities of ACCIDENT can emerge from only one criterion or from two at the same time. The accidents that are classified only by the type of damage are: ACCIDENT WITH LESION AND WITHDRAWAL, ACCIDENT WITH LESION AND WITHOUT WITHDRAWAL and FATAL ACCIDENT. The accident that is classified only by the circumstances in the moment of the accident is ON ROUTE ACCIDENT. The ACCIDENTs that occur both for the circumstances and type of damage is WORK ACCIDENT and ROAD TRAFFIC ACCIDENT.

c - Apply Guidelines and d - Refine Analysis

The proposed guidelines can be applied in the construction of definitions or in the analysis of existent definitions. As We are working in a real example of existent definitions we will apply the guidelines and refine the analysis in the same subsection. Considering the guidelines proposed for an event definition we can highlight some aspects in the ACCIDENT definition and in related concepts.

In guideline G1.1 we identify the temporal parts of the event. ACCIDENT is an event, instantaneous or not. All the specializations of ACCIDENT that we found seem to be instantaneous, which means they have only one temporal part. So ACCIDENT and its specializations defined here are all atomic events. All the definitions include the type ACCIDENT, so the temporal part is explicit. This guideline is accomplished.

In guideline G1.2 we emphasize the importance of identifying the participants of each temporal part. In ACCIDENT the definition mentions person, patrimony or environment as participants involved in accidents. When it is not explicit, the other definitions mention a damage that is related to a kind of participant, like "personal lesion" and "corporal lesion". This guideline is accomplished.

The guidelines G1.3 and G1.4 are related to what determines the beginning and end moments of an event. The ACCIDENT is an "unforeseen event" where we can not determine the beginning and the end. These are (desirable) guidelines and do not apply in this specific example.

In guideline G1.5 we consider desirable to identify the *Situation* that triggers the event (pre-state). At the ACCIDENT definition there is not pre-state situation. But, considering other definitions in the same glossary, we could find terms that are related to the pre-state situation of an accident:

CAUSE - Fact or circumstance that contributes for an event to occur, in the case of accidents and incidents; RISK FACTOR - Situation or potential damage that can lead to personal accident, disease, material damage, environment damage or their combination; INSECURE BEHAVIOR - Tasks executed without following Health, Safety and Environment (HSE) patterns by an individual or by a group of persons causing accident risk situations; SERIOUS and IMINENT RISK - Environmental conditions of work that can cause work accident or professional disease with serious lesion to the worker physical integrity. In these definitions we can notice that all the definitions mention ACCIDENT as a consequent event and they must be examined and consistently checked as well (the discussion is also not included here for space limitations).

In guideline G1.6 we consider desirable to mention the situation that is caused by the event. In the case of ACCIDENT, the definition mentions *damage* as a consequence of the event. We did not find the definition of *damage* in the glossary. It is important to include this definition in the same glossary to improve consistency between definitions in a context.

6   Related Work

In [9], the author created domain independent models based on top level ontological categories. These generic models had the function to predict the features selection and so the definition content in any domain. This work proposes an analysis methodology to compare the internal structure of definitions with the internal structure of the generic model related to each type. The top level ontology used to construct the generic models was BFO. This top-level ontology was originally conceived focusing in natural science, specially the biomedical domain. At our work it was more adequate to use a top level ontology conceived to improve domain independent conceptual models.

In [10], the author also proposes the use of an ontological analysis of business concepts. She proposed guidelines to revise a database schema with the intention to generate richer and more consistent representations in the logical level. It starts with the computational artifacts and applies the method to rescue essential concepts from the specific domain. Differently, the present work starts from the concepts before they might be used by computational artifacts. Common to both works is the ontological analysis of the concepts, verifying the associated meta-properties and then classifying them according to UFO categories.

7   Conclusion and Future Work

Concepts come to existence in the business area of an organization and are represented in IT artifacts. The alignment between business and IT is a critical success factor in organizations. Besides, consistent definitions can provide characteristics that are essential to be represented in the conceptual modeling phase. These characteristics, that are turned evident after an ontological analysis, can add semantics to the concept definition before it can be used by IT artifacts through the system development cycle.

In this work, from an Information Science point of view, we saw the relevance of classifying correctly one concept by identifying features that distinguish one concept from another. From the ontological analysis point of view we can identify relevant aspects associated to the nature of a concept that must be present at its definition. Then we can identify restrictions that some categories have in relation to others, that must be considered when constructing a definition. We proposed a systematic approach, based on guidelines, to be applied in the construction of definitions. In addition the guidelines also help to identify consistence between definitions of related concepts.

We are currently extending the guidelines to other categories and evaluating their use applying them to other domains, revising both glossary definitions and associated conceptual models also involving domain specialists and modelers in this evaluation. On another experiment in the environmental domain, we are building definitions and the conceptual model in parallel and the ontological analysis approach is proving to be very effective.

References

1. Castro, L., Baião, F.A., Guizzardi, G.: A linguistic approach to conceptual modeling with semantic types and ontoUML. In: Workshops Proceedings of 14th IEEE International Enterprise Distributed Object Computing Conference, EDOCW, Vitória, Brazil, pp. 215–224 (2010)
2. Guarino, N.: Formal Ontology in Information Systems: Proceedings of the 1st International Conference 1998, Trento, Italy, 1st edn. IOS Press, Amsterdam (1998)
3. Guizzardi, G.: Ontological Foundations for Structural Conceptual Models. Telematica Institut Fundamental Research Series (2005)
4. Guizzardi, G.: Ontological meta-properties of derived object types. In: Ralyté, J., Franch, X., Brinkkemper, S., Wrycza, S. (eds.) CAiSE 2012. LNCS, vol. 7328, pp. 318–333. Springer, Heidelberg (2012). https://doi.org/10.1007/978-3-642-31095-9_21
5. Guizzardi, G., Wagner, G., Almeida Falbo, R., Guizzardi, R.S.S., Almeida, J.P.A.: Towards ontological foundations for the conceptual modeling of events. In: Ng, W., Storey, V.C., Trujillo, J.C. (eds.) ER 2013. LNCS, vol. 8217, pp. 327–341. Springer, Heidelberg (2013). https://doi.org/10.1007/978-3-642-41924-9_27
6. Kent, W.: Data and Reality. Technics Publications, LLC (2012)
7. Ranganathan, S.R.: Hidden roots of classification. Inf. Storage Retrieval **3**, 399–410 (1967). Pergamon

8. Scheidegger, P.M.L.: Análise Ontológica na Construcao de Definicoes: Diretrizes baseadas em Ontologia de Fundamentacao (in Portuguese). M.sc. dissertation, Universidade Federal do Rio de Janeiro (UFRJ) (2016)
9. Seppälä, S.: Contraintes sur la sélection des informations dans les définitions terminographiques: vers des modèles relationnels génériques pertinents (In French). Ph.D. thesis, Université de Genève, Faculté de traduction et d'interprétation, Département de traitement informatique multilingue (2012)
10. Silva, A.M.F.R.d.: Diretrizes para o Resgate do Esquema Conceitual e seu Compromisso Ontológico a partir de um Banco de Dados: Um Estudo de Caso no Domínio da Litoestratigrafia (in Portuguese). M.sc. dissert., IME (2012)
11. Smith, B.: Introduction to the logic of definitions. In: Proceedings of the ICBO2013, Montreal, Canada (2013)
12. Smith, B., Grennon, P., Goldberg, L.: Biodynamic ontology: Applying BFO in the biomedical domain. Stud. Health Technol. Inform. **102**, 20–38 (2004)
13. Walton, D., Macagno, F.: Classification and ambiguity: The role of definition in a conceptual system, vol. 16, pp. 245–264. Bialystok University Press (2009)

Track on Digital Libraries, Information Retrieval, Big, Linked, Social and Open Data

The Representation of Agents as Resources for the Purpose of Professional Regulation and Global Health Workforce Planning

Amy Opalek[1,2(✉)] and Jane Greenberg[1]

[1] Metadata Research Center <MRC>, College of Computing and Informatics (CCI),
Drexel University, Philadelphia, PA, USA
{ao58,jg3243}@drexel.edu

[2] Foundation for Advancement of International Medical Education and Research (FAIMER),
Philadelphia, PA, USA

Abstract. International migration of health professionals has been increasing in our globalized world, compounding a pressing need to improve information systems that confirm their qualifications and track health workforce volume. This paper reports on research to help address this need by introducing a framework for defining health professionals as agents. A case study and a categorical analysis of 11 metadata schemes was conducted. The results report and discuss three approaches to the representation of agents as either Access Point, Information Object, or Resource. The schemas that describe agents as resources best align with the representation of health professionals for the purpose of health workforce research.

Keywords: Metadata · Agent metadata · Health workforce · HRIS for health

1 Introduction

The international migration of health professionals has long been a concern for regulatory authorities and health workforce researchers [1, 2]. Recipient countries struggle to interpret the qualifications of foreign trained professionals [3], and all countries struggle to maintain an adequate supply and distribution of practitioners to serve their communities [4]. The health of populations is dependent, in part, upon an adequate supply and distribution of health professionals, but health workforce monitoring and planning for the future is hampered by a lack of timely, uniform collection of data about individual practitioners internationally [5]. Researchers in many domains, including library science, education, and health informatics, have developed schemas and standards to address comparable challenges in their own fields, and their work could inform similar efforts in health professions regulation. The development of an international standard for the representation of skilled professionals and their qualifications could promote streamlined collection of interoperable agent data, advancing the accuracy of health workforce research and allowing policy-makers to more quickly respond to community health needs.

E. Garoufallou et al. (Eds.): MTSR 2017, CCIS 755, pp. 103–111, 2017.
https://doi.org/10.1007/978-3-319-70863-8_10

This paper reports on the results of content analysis of metadata schemes from a variety of disciplines as potential frameworks for the representation of health professionals in support of their regulation and of health workforce planning. The following sections provide background information, identify research objectives, and report our method and results in context. The conclusion summarizes results and suggests future research directions.

2   Background

2.1   Data Needs of Regulators and Workforce Researchers

Though there is no consensus on an ideal methodology for health workforce planning [6], the relative success of any methods is dependent upon accurate data. Health workforce planning at the international level is complicated by national variations in data collection practices and data availability [1]. However, there are fundamental individual characteristics relevant to health workforce research that should be obtainable by the regulatory authorities that permit practice. An individual's current employment status, location, and area of specialization serve as indicators of present health workforce participation, but additional factors are also used to project future supply and distribution. Studies have shown that system determinants such as medical school characteristics and individual factors such as ethnicity, age, and gender can affect geographical distribution of health professionals [4]. From an information science perspective, all of these attributes can be seen as metadata elements which describe agents, and there are many metadata schemas which could potentially encompass the data needs of those who monitor the health workforce.

Research in the area of health informatics has made considerable contributions to healthcare practice, but most person metadata efforts have been directed as the patient as agent rather than the health professional [7]. More recently, human resource information systems (HRIS) for health has emerged as a focus of study [8–10], but most research in this area is conducted at an institutional level rather than a national level, and most examine system implementations rather than data structures or interoperability [11]. Research in this area could be advanced through an exploration of agent-level data needs and their standardization.

2.2   Research Objective

The objective of this research is to assess metadata schemes which contain representations of agents, specifically persons in this case. This assessment was conducted in furtherance of the longer-term goal of recommending a metadata scheme for the regulatory community to represent data about health professionals. Considering the volume and diversity of metadata schemas and standards already in use, it is likely that the information needs of workforce researchers and regulators with respect to agent metadata are addressed by one or more existing standards. This research considers existing schemas and their applicability to the health workforce as a step toward establishing a standard for the representation of health professionals.

3   Methods and Procedures

This study is a content analysis of the standards documents of agent-focused metadata schemes across a number of disciplines. To begin, researchers conducted a literature review and consulted key informants to create a list of metadata standards including representations of agents, particularly persons. The initial sample of 15 standards included those created for the sole purpose of representing agent data as well as those that defined agent elements as part of a larger scheme. These are listed in Table 1.

Table 1. Schemas including representations of agents

Schema type	Schemas identified
Schema primarily for agent data	EAC-CPF, ISAAR (CPF), FOAF, hCard, MedBiquitous Healthcare Professional Profile, Library of Congress Name Authority File, MADS, ULAN, vCard
Agent data included in a larger schema	CASS, CTDL, Europass, HR Open Standard CandidateProfile, PESC Academic ePortfolio, schema.org

Several of the schemas in Table 1 were excluded from subsequent analysis for different reasons. The Union List of Artist Names (ULAN) and other name authority files and thesauri were excluded because they did not publish standards as a basis for their resources or they were operationalizations of another reviewed schema, such as the Metadata Authority Description Standard (MADS). The Credential Transparency Description Language (CTDL) – a recently developed standard for the description of qualifications, their requirements, and their accreditation – was excluded because subclasses of its Agent class are used predominantly for the representation of organizations and "do not include people to whom credentials have been awarded" [12]. The CASS schema – an open source effort to represent competencies and competency frameworks – was excluded because it was developed as an extension of schema.org with no additional agent elements defined [13].

Once the final study sample of 11 standards was determined, each schema's documentation was reviewed, and their characteristics were tabulated. Agent metadata sets from each schema were compared and classified into three groups based on number, focus, granularity, and extensibility of metadata elements describing agents. The following section presents our results in context by categorical grouping.

4   Results: Review and Categorization of Agent Schemas

The representation of agents, specifically individuals in this case, has been a feature common to many metadata schemas developed over the past several decades. However, the relative level of detail among different areas of agent characteristics (e.g., demographic data or employment information) has varied according to the underlying purpose of the schema and the field or context in which it was developed. This paper describes three broad groups of schemas categorized by their context and associated focus and level of detail. A summary of the reviewed schemas is presented in Table 2, and a categorization of these schemas is presented in Table 3.

Table 2. Schema sample for analysis

Schemes	Domain	Published encoding	Number of metadata elements
PESC Academic ePortfolio	Education	XML	12 metadata element sets
HR Open Standard CandidateProfile	Human resources	XML or JSON	24 attribute sets
EAC-CPF	Archiving	XML	90 elements; 30 attributes
Europass	Human resources	XML	> 25 schemata + 3 adjusted ISO standards
FOAF	Web-based information about people, networking	RDF	19 core classes + 25 social web classes
hCard	Web-based information about people, networking	HTML	38 properties
ISAAR (CPF)	Archiving	(multiple)	31 elements
MADS	Cataloging	XML	3 main elements, 8 descriptor elements, 9 minor elements
MedBiquitous Healthcare Professional Profile	Health professions education	XML	8 element sets; ~ 150 elements
schema.org	Web-based information	(multiple)	571 types; 832 properties; 114 enumeration values
vCard	Business card information, networking	Proprietary file format	~25 properties

4.1 Schema Group 1: Agent as Access Point

The earliest standards that provide frameworks for the description of agents were developed in the field of library science and archiving. Some of these standards guided the development of name authority files, including those that catalog agent names. For example, the Metadata Authority Description Standard (MADS) was developed for the presentation of authority data, specifically the type of data that would be included in the MARC Authority element [14]. Other standards were developed specifically for the representation of agents related to archival objects. Examples include the Encoded Archival Context for Corporate Bodies, Persons, and Families (EAC-CPF) [15] and

Table 3. Categorization of schemas incorporating agents

Category	Schemes	Characteristics
Agent as access point	EAC-CPF, ISAAR(CPF), MADS	• Context: information science, archiving • Lean structure for describing agents • Emphasis on identity and relationships
Agent as information object	hCard, vCard, FOAF, schema.org	• Context: web-based linked data, self-documentation • Lean but extensible structure for describing agents • Emphasis on contact information and web interoperability
Agent as resource	Europass, HR Open Standard CandidateProfile, MedBiquitous Healthcare Professional Profile, PESC Academic ePortfolio	• Context: multiple domains (education, human resources, health) • Granular structure specific to domain • Emphasis on detailed representation of agent characteristics, qualifications

International Standard Archival Authority Record for Corporate Bodies, Persons and Families [ISAAR (CPF)] [16]. A major strength of these schemas is that they were constructed with international use in mind, providing mechanisms for representing multiple variations of agent names in multiple languages and formats.

In each of these schemas, representations of agents are designed primarily to serve in the context of their relationship to information objects, hence their categorization under the Agent as Access Point heading. Agent representations in these schemas emphasize factors crucial to identifying and differentiating among agents (e.g., current and former names), capturing an agent's relationships with other agents (e.g., an individual's membership in an organization), and finding the information objects with which those agents are associated. While these schemas excel at capturing identifying characteristics of agents irrespective of national origin, they do not have the level of detail required by regulators in the area of professional qualifications.

4.2 Schema Group 2: Agent as Information Object

The second category of schemas can be associated with the rise of linked data on the web. These schemas are designed to capture formatted information about agents as independent objects, not as metadata describing related information objects. These schemas are more likely than others to be used for the purpose of self-documentation by agents themselves. Early examples of this type of schema are hCard and vCard [17], both developed for the purpose of sharing personal contact information as a kind of electronic business card. While agents are described in these schemas as the point of interest, rather than as an access point to other resources, they are limited in the scope of agent characteristics captured.

More recently developed schemas under the heading of Agent as Information Object have defined a greater number of detailed elements to represent other agent characteristics. The FOAF (friend of a friend) ontology is widely used to represent individuals and their relationships on the web, particularly within social networks [18]. While some researchers have explored using FOAF as a method for describing the demographic and dynamic properties of patients [19], this schema's application to the health workforce has not been investigated. Agents are also represented in detail in schema.org, a standard that was designed to represent any kind of object on the web [20]. In this schema, the Person entity type is a child entity of the Thing entity type, and it has approximately 50 allowable properties defined in addition to those inherited from the Thing type. Only one subtype of Person is defined in an extension to schema.org: the Patient type.

The Agent as Information Object schemas are more amenable to extension than those that represent agents primarily as an access point, which would theoretically allow for the incorporation of additional agent characteristics necessary for health workforce analysis. On the other hand, the only healthcare-related elements so far proposed by the communities that author extensions to these schemas are those related to patient data.

4.3   Schema Group 3: Agent as Resource

The third category of schemas includes those schemas with the most detailed representations of agents. In this group, schemas represent agents as the information object or resource of interest. Metadata in these schemas are created within specific use contexts and contain element definitions for a variety of characteristics relevant to those contexts. The domains of education and human resources are both home to metadata schemas where detailed individual characteristics, particularly those that are of use to regulators and workforce researchers, are represented.

In the field of human resources, metadata schemas have been developed to capture agent characteristics relevant to employers. The HR Open Standards group provides several XML schema standards used to support human resources activities such as recruiting, payroll, and performance evaluation. The CandidateProfile metadata element group of the Recruiting Specification [21] includes element sets for employment history, education history, licenses, certifications, publications, affiliations, references, and other topic areas used evaluating job candidates. The European Centre for the Development of Vocational Training (CEDEFOP) has developed a similar standard, the Europass schema, which supports the Curriculum Vitae and the Language Passport, standardized documents that are designed to assist educators, learners, and employers in communicating skills and qualifications in a uniform manner across Europe [22]. CEDEFOP emphasizes internationality and interoperability by supporting multiple languages, referencing ISO standards for languages and occupations, and making available APIs for use with their schema. The elements represented in these human resource schemas overlap strongly with the types of data elements needed in the assessment of individual fitness to practice and in health workforce analysis and projection.

Similarly, in the field of education, a number of schemas have developed to capture an individual's competencies and educational achievements. As the education community has turned its attention to competency-based and workplace-based education, their data standards have evolved to capture these more diverse activities. The Academic ePortfolio is an XML standard approved by the PK20W Education Standards Council (PESC) for the representation of an individual's educational activities and achievements, including those outside the classroom [23]. Included are elements to describe competencies, employment history, military history, licenses, and other credentials. Finally, the MedBiqitous organization has developed a number of XML standards for the exchange of data in the specific area of health professions education [24]. Their Healthcare Professional Profile (HPP) schema provides a framework for describing this particular group of agents. In addition to the educational characteristics found in the Academic ePortfolio, the HPP schema includes elements for representing an agent's clinical status and any disciplinary actions taken against the health professional by regulatory authorities.

Each of the schemas described in this section capture a variety of agent metadata often in a complex hierarchical structure. These are the schemas that seem most directly relevant to the context of professional regulation and workforce analysis. Only the schemas in this Agent as Resource category capture agent qualifications in sufficient detail to be of use in the evaluation of an individual's fitness to practice or in the assessment of health workforce supply and distribution.

5 Conclusion

The results of this research indicate that existing metadata schemas incorporating agents can be classified into different groups based on the agent's purpose in context and the granularity of agent data represented. Those that describe agents as resources best align with the representation of health professionals metadata for the purpose of health workforce research. The work reported here is a first step in ongoing research to define an agent metadata framework fit for global use in this area. Next steps will include the review of additional schemes and soliciting feedback from regulatory authorities and workforce researchers.

If health workforce research is to progress and become useful as a tool for correcting shortages and maldistributions, the promotion of an international standard for the collection of individual level data describing health professionals is crucial. Decades of work in the development of agent representations in various metadata schemas across a number of fields and contexts can provide guidance on the development of such a standard for the regulatory context. Metadata science can guide the development of health workforce informatics as an area of study that can inform policies to improve global health.

References

1. Diallo, K., Zurn, P., Gupta, N., Dal Poz, M.: Monitoring and evaluation of human resources for health: an international perspective. Hum. Resour. Health. **13**, 1–13 (2003). doi: 10.1186/1478-4491-1-3
2. Hawthorne, L.: The impact of skilled migration on foreign qualification recognition reform in Australia. Can. Public Policy **41**, S173–S187 (2015). doi:10.3138/cpp.2015-027
3. Hawthorne, L.: Recognizing Foreign Qualifications: Emerging Global Trends. Migration Policy Institute, Washington, D.C. (2013)
4. Dussault, G., Franceschini, M.C.: Not enough there, too many here: understanding geographical imbalances in the distribution of the health workforce. Hum. Resour. Health. **4**, 12 (2006). doi:10.1186/1478-4491-4-12
5. World Health Organization: Draft global strategy on human resources for health: workforce 2030 (2015)
6. Amorim Lopes, M., Santos Almeida, Á., Almada-Lobo, B.: Handling healthcare workforce planning with care: where do we stand? Hum. Resour. Health. **13**, 38 (2015). doi:10.1186/s12960-015-0028-0
7. Rea, S., Pathak, J., Savova, G., Oniki, T.A., Westberg, L., Beebe, C.E., Tao, C., Parker, C.G., Haug, P.J., Huff, S.M., Chute, C.G.: Building a robust, scalable and standards-driven infrastructure for secondary use of EHR data: the SHARPn project. J. Biomed. Inform. **45**, 763–771 (2012). doi:10.1016/j.jbi.2012.01.009
8. Driessen, J., Settle, D., Potenziani, D., Tulenko, K., Kabocho, T., Wadembere, I.: Understanding and valuing the broader health system benefits of Uganda's national Human Resources for Health Information System investment. Hum. Resour. Health. **13**, 49 (2015). doi:10.1186/s12960-015-0036-0
9. Waters, K.P., Mazivila, M.E., Dgedge, M., Necochea, E., Manharlal, D., Zuber, A., de Faria Leão, B., Bossemeyer, D., Vergara, A.E.: eSIP-Saúde: Mozambique's novel approach for a sustainable human resources for health information system. Hum. Resour. Health. **14**, 66 (2016). doi:10.1186/s12960-016-0159-y
10. Nuruzzaman, M.: Strengthening human resource information system at the Ministry of Health & Family Welfare of Bangladesh. Bangladesh Med. J. **44**, 1–2 (2015)
11. Tursunbayeva, A., Bunduchi, R., Franco, M., Pagliari, C.: Human resource information systems in health care: a systematic evidence review. J. Am. Med. Informatics Assoc., 1–22 (2016). doi:10.1093/jamia/ocw141
12. Credential Engine: Guide: Credential Transparency Description Language. http://credreg.net/ctdl/handbook
13. CASS Schema. http://schema.cassproject.org/
14. Library of Congress: MADS 2.0 - XML Format for Authorities Data. http://www.loc.gov/standards/mads/mads-doc.html
15. Staatsbibliothek zu Berlin: Encoded Archival Context for Corporate Bodies, Persons, and Families. http://eac.staatsbibliothek-berlin.de/
16. ICA Committee on Descriptive Standards: ISAAR (CPF): International Standard Archival Authority Record for Corporate Bodies, Persons and Families. International Council on Archives, Paris, France (2004)
17. Bizer, C., Eckert, K., Meusel, R., Mühleisen, H., Schuhmacher, M., Völker, J.: Deployment of RDFa, microdata, and microformats on the web – a quantitative analysis. In: Alani, H., et al. (eds.) ISWC 2013. LNCS, vol. 8219, pp. 17–32. Springer, Heidelberg (2013). doi: 10.1007/978-3-642-41338-4_2
18. Brickley, D., Miller, L.: FOAF Vocabulary Specification 0.99. http://xmlns.com/foaf/spec/

19. Bursa, O., Sezer, E., Can, O., Unalir, M.O.: Using FOAF for interoperable and privacy protected healthcare information systems. In: Closs, S., Studer, R., Garoufallou, E., Sicilia, M.-A. (eds.) MTSR 2014. CCIS, vol. 478, pp. 154–161. Springer, Cham (2014). doi: 10.1007/978-3-319-13674-5_15
20. Schema.org: Organization of Schemas. https://schema.org/docs/schemas.html
21. HR-XML Consortium: Recruiting Specification. http://www.hropenstandards.org/
22. European Centre for the Development of Vocational Training: Europass XML Schema Documentation, v3.3.0. http://interop.europass.cedefop.europa.eu/data-model/xml-resources/
23. PK20 W Education Standards Council: PESC Approved Standards. http://www.pesc.org/pesc-approved-standards.html
24. MedBiquitous: Professional Profile Schema and Specification. https://medbiq.org/working_groups/professional_profile/index.html

Promoting Semantic Annotation of Research Data by Their Creators: A Use Case with B2NOTE at the End of the RDM Workflow

Yulia Karimova$^{(\boxtimes)}$, João Aguiar Castro, João Rocha da Silva, Nelson Pereira, and Cristina Ribeiro

INESC TEC, Faculdade de Engenharia, Universidade do Porto,
Rua Dr. Roberto Frias, 4200-465 Porto, Portugal
ylaleo@gmail.com, joaoaguiarcastro@gmail.com, joaorosilva@gmail.com,
nelsonpereira1991@gmail.com, mcr@fe.up.pt

Abstract. Research data management is promoted at different levels with awareness actions carried out to encourage cooperation between researchers. However, data management requires tools to set the scene for researchers and institutions to disseminate the research data they produce. In this context good quality metadata play an important role by enabling data reuse. EUDAT is an European common data infrastructure, with integrated services for data preservation and dissemination. The TAIL project, at the University of Porto, proposes workflows based on Dendro, a collaborative environment that helps researchers prepare well described datasets and deposit them in a data repository. We propose a data deposit workflow use case for a small research project with emphasis in data annotation. Data is organized and described in Dendro; deposited in B2SHARE; and semantic annotation is performed with the new B2NOTE service from EUDAT.

Keywords: Research data management · Dendro · B2NOTE · Semantic annotation

1 Introduction

Research environments are characterized by a huge amount and wide variety of research data, but many issues are raised with respect to data access and data reuse [21]. Two motivators are prompting researchers to adopt a more active attitude into so-called open science practices: the compliance with funder requirements and the growing recognition of data as first-class research outputs. The fact that the main funding agencies in the US and EU now require researchers to attach Data Management Plans (DMP) to their grant applications is a clear statement of the importance of this topic. DMPs must specify the storage and long-time preservation conditions for the data during their lifecycle, as well as the representation of the data and the context of their creation. Without storage, one cannot recover the data in the long term, but the context is equally

© Springer International Publishing AG 2017
E. Garoufallou et al. (Eds.): MTSR 2017, CCIS 755, pp. 112–122, 2017.
https://doi.org/10.1007/978-3-319-70863-8_11

important to make data findable and to allow others to make sense of them, favouring reuse.

In this context, the wide adoption of research data management (RDM) best practices is an essential step towards data reuse. Yet, despite the increasing interest in making their data available [20] and the existing institutional infrastructures and workflows designed to support researchers in RDM activities [7], researchers still need to deal with several problems related to RDM, such as the inadequacy of existing tools to support metadata creation [17].

Even if research data gets to the publication stage, potential reusers are very likely to disregard them if they are not conveniently described [18], since metadata is a determinant in data reuse [23]. High quality metadata is a positive outcome from the involvement of researchers in data description, as they are expected to generate more specialized descriptions [22]. A promising investment in RDM is to guide researchers in self-publication of research data, both to engage them in data management and to integrate RDM into the research workflow, alleviating data curation costs. In short, data reuse depends on the involvement of researchers in RDM activities, namely on the enrichment of data with quality metadata.

At the University of Porto, under the TAIL project [16], we are exploring the integration of different tools to build RDM workflows that are suitable for research scenarios with the typical requirements of the long tail of science. The proposed workflows anticipate the description requirements prior to the deposit stage, supporting them via the Dendro platform[1], but as an alternative we are also proposing researchers to directly deposit and describe their data in a CKAN-powered data repository at our institution, INESC TEC[2].

We explore here the definition of a workflow that integrates our tools with the services from the EUDAT platform, illustrating it with the use case of an MSc. researcher from the University of Porto who generated a dataset as a result of academic work and explored the publication of the data before the final thesis delivery. In this workflow, data are first prepared and described in Dendro and then transferred to the B2SHARE repository, where they can be further annotated with B2NOTE. This enables data to be reused and cited, considering that the nature of data from this project is appealing to others [15]. The next section is an overview of the main issues regarding RDM workflows, including a brief presentation of the Dendro + B2SHARE workflow, followed by a more detailed description of the EUDAT B2NOTE service.

2   RDM Workflows

An RDM workflow is a "sequence of repeatable processes (steps) through which research data passes during their lifecycle, including the steps involved in its creation, curation, preservation and possible disposal" [1]. To improve the value of data in the long term, researchers should systematically perform management

---

[1] Link: https://github.com/feup-infolab/dendro.
[2] Link: https://rdm.inesctec.pt/dataset/cs-2017-005.

tasks throughout the data lifecycle, meaning that, among other tasks, they need to describe their data on a regular basis. However, more often than not, they find themselves without adequate RDM tools, leaving them to resort to ad-hoc RDM practices supported by any tools that they have at their disposal [22], often addressing personal and immediate needs [13].

If a researcher promptly addresses data description during the initial stages of the data lifecycle, most of the work will be done when data gets to the deposit stage. The advantages are that early descriptions are probably richer than those made long after data production and are also more likely to ensure compliance with an existing DMP.

When data get to the deposit stage, researchers need access to trusted data repositories. Moreover, to improve data findability, accessibility and reusability, RDM workflows have to ensure that metadata is interoperable and has comprehensive information, is open and complies with legal and ethical rules for encouraging reproducible science [11].

However, RDM workflows are often built around multiple RDM systems that are not fully integrated, and any communication gaps between these systems may erode the willingness of the researchers to deposit their data—this is especially true if their dedication in early stages leads to redundant RDM tasks later in the data lifecycle. To safeguard more data, it is therefore crucial to provide effective and well integrated tools to researchers, in order to simplify and streamline the whole RDM workflow, making the processes clearer to the researchers [1].

The EUDAT Collaborative Data Infrastructure[3] currently proposes a suite of services to address the full lifecycle of research data. The services used in our workflow are B2SHARE—a trusted repository to support sharing of long tail data, B2FIND—a multidisciplinary joint metadata catalogue to find and access data in EUDAT, and B2NOTE—a semantic annotation service. These services are evolving, while EUDAT aims to establish a common model and lead the development of an infrastructure of data management services to cover European research data centers and community data repositories [11].

Complete RDM Workflow with Dendro and B2SHARE

At the University of Porto, with the TAIL project, we are proposing workflows that integrate tools to support RDM during the research data lifecycle, with particular attention to the data description requirements from different research domains [16].

Figure 1 depicts a workflow consisting of the Dendro platform and the EUDAT B2SHARE service, which interact through an API. This connection is part of a Data Pilot established between the TAIL team and EUDAT to allow researchers to describe their data using generic and domain-specific vocabularies through Dendro, and to import the resulting data and metadata to B2SHARE [6].

In Dendro, description ideally occurs when the data is captured (Steps 1 and 2), considering that pertinent information about research data may be

---

[3] Link: https://www.eudat.eu/.

forgotten if not recorded right away. The purpose of data description in Dendro is to capture metadata for research datasets, based on ontologies [19], combining description elements from widely adopted metadata standards such as Dublin Core, for the sake of interoperability, with domain-specific elements for specificity. The latter can either be sourced from domain metadata standards, or otherwise defined in collaboration with the researchers after analysing the terms they already associate to their data [3,4]. For some of the domains tested with Dendro, controlled vocabularies were created to restrict the possible values for some fields to facilitate description and improve its quality [10]. Since Dendro is a collaborative platform, researchers can improve their metadata from feedback provided by others. This is implemented in Social Dendro [14], where researchers are notified when others *like, share or comment* their metadata. When researchers decide that their data are ready for deposit they can send them to a data repository that complies with their requirements. Dendro currently interfaces with CKAN, Zenodo, Figshare and EUDAT's B2SHARE, among others. Figure 1 shows a deposit in B2SHARE (Step 3). After the deposit, users can proceed to data annotation, this time with the B2NOTE service, using tags derived from controlled vocabularies, or free-text keywords and comments (Step 4).

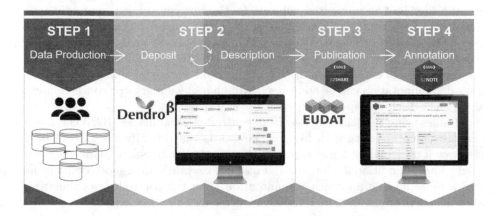

Fig. 1. Complete RDM workflow with Dendro and B2SHARE

This workflow illustrates that, while Dendro is intended for the organization and description of data, EUDAT B2SHARE is tasked with publishing and sharing data. B2NOTE complements the annotation of datasets at a post-deposit stage.

3 B2NOTE

B2SHARE, like most multidisciplinary data repositories, has no specific community in mind, assuming a generalist approach to data publication [2] reflected in its domain-agnostic deposit form.

B2NOTE is a standalone research data annotation service based on the W3C Web Annotation Data Model. It currently integrates with B2SHARE, and will integrate with other EUDAT services [5]. With a flexible approach to data annotation, B2NOTE appears as a post-deposit tool. In most systems, the metadata is not supposed to change after publication. Data annotation can be regarded as a source of community metadata, providing evidence of data usage and comments on their limitations, since it is available to users without mediation.

When used for specific metadata elements, controlled vocabularies can provide lists of terms that promote uniform descriptive cataloging, labeling, or indexing [8]. Controlled vocabularies are also expected to improve the quality of the descriptions added to research datasets by restricting the valid values of specific metadata elements. However, it has been observed that, while researchers are interested in using them, they are not widely implemented in data repositories [25].

Using B2NOTE, researchers can complement the information available in the metadata generated by the authors, using semantic tags, without changing the original data file and its description. These tags are filled by means of auto-completion boxes where terms from specific controlled vocabularies appear. These additional tags can help other users find, organize and aggregate files, datasets and documents. The goal is to improve retrieval, helping users find specific files by the annotated subject. In the current version, semantic tags are drawn from controlled vocabularies in the Bioportal repository, but more vocabularies will be considered by EUDAT, based on the analysis of controlled vocabularies already in use in research data repositories. Since there is risk of vocabulary fragmentation, the choice of the right vocabulary for multidisciplinary data annotation can be addressed through a social marketplace where users share their discipline-specific experiences [11,12].

Besides using the semantic tags from controlled vocabularies, B2NOTE users can also annotate data with free-text keywords that identify the subject of a resource if no semantic tag is appropriate, or include a free-text comment, open to any kind of additional information. Free-text keywords are a good complement and a more flexible approach to annotation than the controlled vocabularies, allowing users to classify and retrieve resources based on *folksonomies*. This can result in the expansion of the formal structured vocabularies with new terms [24]. However this approach has its own limitations, mostly related to issues with vague meaning, term variations, homonyms and polysemy, and may result in tags that only make sense to an individual user, making it difficult to build a hierarchy of concepts [9].

Free text comments capture non-structured, informal information, desirable for expressing opinion and recommendations. Free comments are open to all users and may be used to enable the collaboration between researchers.

4   Use Case

This use case illustrates a complete RDM workflow, from data description in the Dendro platform to data annotation using B2NOTE after publication.

Step 1. Data Production

Different types of data call for different management practices and data description requirements vary depending on the data type or discipline. In this case the
data were produced as part of an M.Sc. dissertation, focused in entity extraction
from Portuguese news articles. These entities can be names of persons, organizations, or places. The goal of the work was to select a tool for entity extraction that
can be adopted in projects with similar entity-related challenges, namely ANT[4].
The dataset contains models trained with a dataset created in the HAREM evaluation initiative[5]. The dataset that results from the trained models, *HAREM
NER Models*, is a valuable contribution since this kind of data is rare in the
Portuguese language.

Step 2. Deposit and Description

Deposit of the *HAREM NER Models* dataset in Dendro started with the creation of a project to organize the data and associated metadata. From there
the researcher managed the data exploring the four main sections (see Fig. 2):
user area (area **1**), the file manager (area **2**), the description zone (area **3**) and
the descriptor selection zone (area **4**). In the user area the researcher has created a folder named *HAREM NER MODELS*, where four files, corresponding to
the models, were deposited. Then, the researcher selected the vocabulary with
the concepts that better fit the data. In this case Dublin Core descriptors were
selected to describe the folder, namely *Title, Subject, Description, License, Format* and *Language*. Since each individual file has specific properties, a *Description* was added to each one. After the data were organized and described in
Dendro, the researcher sent a package, containing both data and metadata files,
to the B2SHARE data repository. This makes the data exposed to a larger community [18] and allows for data citation.

Fig. 2. Data deposit and description in Dendro

---

[4] Link: http://ant.fe.up.pt/.
[5] Link: http://www.linguateca.pt/aval_conjunta/HAREM/harem_ing.html.

Step 3. Publication

When a data package is transferred from Dendro to B2SHARE, the former automatically fills the metadata fields available in B2SHARE at the deposit stage. The remaining fields, present in Dendro but not ingestable by B2SHARE, are exported as an RDF file (see Fig. 3, area **1**), that can be consulted by the users to see more information about the data (area **2**) [18].

Fig. 3. Data package deposited in B2SHARE and additional metadata

This transfer takes advantage of the data description work the researcher has already performed in Dendro to fill in the metadata required in B2SHARE, while keeping the full metadata record from Dendro. However, this approach has its limitations since the information contained in the RDF file is not actually used for retrieval purposes in B2SHARE, and its format is not user-friendly. The ability to add annotations after the deposit stage, using B2NOTE, may alleviate some of this inconvenience.

Step 4. Annotation

After the data are published in B2SHARE, annotations in B2NOTE can add information to the metadata previously captured, and link resources within the EUDAT CDI or with external resources (see Fig. 4, area **1**). Annotations are saved in a machine-readable format, according to the W3C Web Annotation model, in order to be findable and viewable [5].

There are three types of annotations in B2NOTE: semantic tags, free-text keywords and free text comments (area **2**). In this case the researcher was aware that some information to be shared with potential users had not been captured during the preparation stage in the Dendro platform. Thus, the researcher used B2NOTE to add a reference to the open-source tool *OpenNLP* using a free-text keyword; OpenNLP is a tool that supports natural language processing,

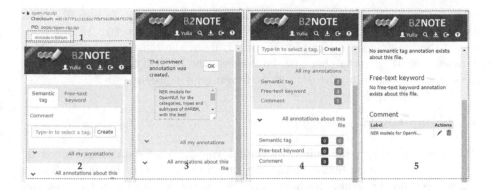

Fig. 4. Data annotation in B2NOTE

particularly entity extraction, used to analyze the Portuguese news articles. The free comment option was also used to comment about missing information in one of the files (area **3**). At this time there are no recommendations on how to write these comments; they can be regarded as personal notes used to provide more insight, or updates, to help others explore the data in a meaningful way.

The annotations made by the researcher are then displayed for all users, "*All annotations about this file*", and all registered users can make additional annotations to the data file. B2NOTE users can choose to visualize all comments or can choose to show only their own annotations, by clicking "*All my annotations*" (areas **4, 5**).

Registered users can also search the annotated file using "Search" (see Fig. 5, area **6**) and export results to JSON-LD or RDF files for their own purposes (areas **7, 8**). Searching is performed over semantic-tag and free-text keywords.

Fig. 5. Search, export results and annotation visualization in B2NOTE

Although users can add as much information as they see fit to any file (area **9**), they cannot edit annotations made by other users (area **10**). In our case, one of the users added a free-text comment about the reuse and utility of this dataset. The M.Sc. researcher may later access the B2NOTE platform and read the comments regarding the dataset and even reply to them.

5   Conclusions

Data reuse is strongly influenced by the information that data creators convey to others about the context of data they intend to share. Usually, research data deposit workflows resemble traditional publication ones, with the risk of essential metadata being lost, if captured at all.

The Dendro + B2SHARE + B2NOTE workflow presented here addresses this issue by covering important stages of the data lifecycle, reinforcing the notion that data description should appear on time in the research process to render good quality metadata. Furthermore, data annotation at the end of the workflow adds new pathways to the data, while also encouraging the exchange of ideas between researchers using more casual notes.

Tools and guidelines for better and clearer RDM encourage researchers to share their data on a broader scale. The overall workflow, and in particular the Dendro and the EUDAT services, are currently under development and are more likely to succeed if they evolve in close collaboration with researchers. For instance, at the time of writing, annotations made in B2NOTE are publicly available, yet in a future release researchers will have the option to keep them private, a requirement gathered from user feedback. It would also be useful for researchers if B2NOTE notifies them when new annotations occur. This kind of behaviour is explored in Social Dendro, a social extension for description in Dendro.

The use case in this paper is as close as possible to a real-world scenario, taking into consideration that the B2NOTE service is only available in a training instance of the B2SHARE platform. Therefore, there are aspects that will be interesting to assess as B2NOTE evolves. An evaluation of the use of annotations, for instance, and how they help users find data, can justify the effort of creating richer metadata. The need to update data and metadata, and their impact in the final stages of the data publication workflow, can also result from the observation of the annotation tool.

From the researcher perspective this case study was an opportunity to explore a set of RDM tools, according to users needs, rather than the execution of a designated set of tasks to evaluate tool performance. The researcher had the primary goal of publishing the project data. This led to a natural and low-effort exploration of the tools, using Dublin Core according to their needs. The obvious way to expand this work is to handle use cases that demand more specific metadata elements, clearly demonstrating the role that staging platforms, like Dendro, or annotation tools, as BNOTE, may have to alleviate the difficulties with metadata in generic data repositories.

Future work will be informed by further use cases resulting from data deposit needs derived from funder requirements, as a way to train researchers in RDM activities. This will make it possible to amass domain metadata and requirements stemming from the domain data types that are likely to improve RDM workflows.

Acknowledgements. This work is financed by the ERDF European Regional Development Fund through the Operational Programme for Competitiveness and Internationalisation - COMPETE 2020 Programme and by National Funds through the Portuguese funding agency, FCT - Fundação para a Ciência e a Tecnologia within project TAIL, POCI-01-0145-FEDER-016736. João Aguiar Castro is supported by research grant PD/BD/114143/2015, provided by the FCT - Fundação para a Ciência e a Tecnologia. We thank Yann Le Frank and the B2NOTE team for the availability of the beta version of B2NOTE and the helpful remarks.

References

1. Addis, M.: RDM workflows and integrations for higher education institutions using hosted services (2015). Arkivum white paper https://www.digital-science.com/resources/reports/
2. Assante, M., et al.: Are scientific data repositories coping with research data publishing? Data Sci. J. **15**(6), 1–24 (2016). https://doi.org/10.5334/dsj-2016-006
3. Castro, J.A., da Silva, J.R., Ribeiro, C.: Creating lightweight ontologies for dataset description. Practical applications in a cross-domain research data management workflow. In: IEEE/ACM Joint Conference on Digital Libraries (JCDL) (2014). https://doi.org/10.1109/JCDL.2014.6970185
4. Castro, J.A., et al.: Involving data creators in an ontology-based design process for metadata models. In: Malta, M.C., Baptista, A.A., Walk, P. (eds.) Developing Metadata Application Profiles, pp. 181–214. IGI Global (2017). https://doi.org/10.4018/978-1-5225-2221-8.ch008
5. EUDAT. Annotate your research data with B2NOTE (2017). EUDAT news https://eudat.eu/news/annotate-your-research-data-with-b2note
6. EUDAT. EUDAT as a long-term repository for the University of Porto (2017). EUDAT Data Pilot https://eudat.eu/communities/eudat-as-a-long-term-repository-for-the-university-of-porto
7. Van den Eynden, V., et al.: Managing and sharing data - best practice for researchers. UK Data Archive, pp. 1–40 (2011). ISBN: 1904059783
8. Hedden, H.: Taxonomies and controlled vocabularies best practices for metadata. J. Digit. Asset Manag. **6**(5), 279–284 (2010). https://doi.org/10.1057/dam.2010.29
9. Huang, S.-L., Lin, S.-C., Chan, Y.-C.: Investigating effectiveness and user acceptance of semantic social tagging for knowledge sharing. Inf. Process. Manage. **48**(4), 599–617 (2012). https://doi.org/10.1016/j.ipm.2011.07.004
10. Karimova, Y., Castro, J.A.: Vocabulários controlados na descrição de dados de investigação no Dendro. In: Cadernos BAD N.2, jul-dez, pp. 241–255 (2016)
11. Latif, A.: EUDAT: Research data infrastructure and European Open Science Cloud vision (2017). Team ZBW Mediatalk https://www.zbw-mediatalk.eu/en/2017/05/eudat-research-data-infrastructure-and-european-open-science-cloud-vision/
12. Le Franc, Y.: Organise, retrieve and aggregate data using annotations with B2NOTE (2017). EUDAT webinar https://eudat.eu/events/webinar/eudat-webinar-organise-retrieve-and-aggregate-data-using-annotations-with-b2note

13. Mayernik, M.S.: Metadata realities for cyberinfrastructure: data authors as metadata creators (2011). SSRN https://ssrn.com/abstract=2042653. https://doi.org/10.2139/ssrn.2042653

14. Pereira, N., da Silva, J.R., Ribeiro, C.: Social Dendro: social network techniques applied to research data description. In: Kamps, J., Tsakonas, G., Manolopoulos, Y., Iliadis, L., Karydis, I. (eds.) TPDL 2017. LNCS, vol. 10450, pp. 566–571. Springer, Cham (2017). https://doi.org/10.1007/978-3-319-67008-9_47

15. Pires, A.: Named entity recognition on Portuguese web text. Master thesis, Faculdade de Engenharia da Universidade do Porto (2017)

16. Ribeiro, C., et al.: Projeto TAIL - Gestão de dados de investigação da produção ao depósito e à partilha (resultados preliminares). In: Cadernos BAD N.2, jul-dez, pp. 256–264 (2016)

17. Shearer, K., Furtado, F.: COAR survey of research data management: results. Confederation of OpenAccess Repositories (2017). https://www.coar-repositories.org/files/COAR-RDM-Survey-Jan-2017.pdf

18. Silva, F., Amorim, R.C., Castro, J.A., da Silva, J.R., Ribeiro, C.: End-to-end research data management workflows: a case study with Dendro and EUDAT. In: Garoufallou, E., Subirats, C.I., Stellato, A., Greenberg, J. (eds.) MTSR 2016. CCIS, vol. 672, pp. 369–375. Springer, Cham (2016). https://doi.org/10.1007/978-3-319-49157-8_32

19. da Silva, J.R., et al.: The Dendro research data management platform: applying ontologies to long-term preservation in a collaborative environment. In: iPres 2014 Conference Proceedings (2014)

20. Tenopir, C., et al.: Changes in data sharing and data reuse practices and perceptions among scientists worldwide. Plos One 10(8) (2015). https://doi.org/10.1371/journal.pone.0134826

21. Vines, T.H., et al.: The availability of research data declines rapidly with article age. Curr. Biol. 24(1), 94–97 (2014). https://doi.org/10.1016/j.cub.2013.11.014

22. White, H.C.: Descriptive metadata for scientific data repositories: a comparison of information scientist and scientist organizing behaviors. J. Libr. Metadata 14(1), 24–51 (2014). https://doi.org/10.1080/19386389.2014.891896

23. Willis, C., Greenberg, J., White, H.: Analysis and synthesis of metadata goals for scientific data. J. Assoc. Inf. Sci. Technol. 63(8), 1505–1520 (2012). https://doi.org/10.1002/asi.22683

24. Zervas, P., Sampson, D.G.: The effect of users' tagging motivation on the enlargement of digital educational resources metadata. Comput. Hum. Behav. 32, 292–300 (2014). https://doi.org/10.1016/j.chb.2013.06.026

25. Zhang, Y., et al.: Controlled vocabularies for scientific data: users and desired functionalities. Proc. Assoc. Inf. Sci. Technol. 52(1), 1–8 (2015). https://doi.org/10.1002/pra2.2015.145052010054

A Review of Practices for Transforming Library Legacy Records into Linked Open Data

Ya-Ning Chen[✉]

Department of Information and Library Science, Tamkang University,
New Taipei City 25137, Taiwan, R.O.C.
arthur9861@gmail.com

Abstract. Current practices for transforming library legacy records into linked data for libraries were studied. The Linked Data Cookbook released by W3C was used as an analytical framework. A total of sixteen library linked data case studies focused on converting library catalogue data into linked open data were selected as subjects to analyze the details of transformation according to the following categories: identifying data, modeling data, naming with URIs, reusing existing terms, publishing human and machine readable descriptions, RDF conversion, license, download, host and announcement. It was found that although most tasks defined by the Linked Data Cookbook were adopted, some extensions and refinements were adopted to meet specific library-oriented requirements. Related issues including selection of data, selection of terms, 1-to-1 mapping principle and long-term preservation of library linked data are discussed.

Keywords: Library legacy records · Linked open data · Library linked data

1 Introduction

MARC has been used as a standard format to exchange library records over various information systems within the library community for a long time. Most MARC-based metadata records, either bibliographic or authority records, are locked in a closed system, and cannot be integrated into the web or found by search engines such as Google. Although a vast volume of records have been created and maintained by libraries, they are nearly all isolated from the web. Linked Open Data (LOD) has become the preferred approach for the conversion of MARC-based legacy library data into a part of the semantic web by libraries. Based on the principles of LOD, legacy records can be deconstructed into LOD data which can be enriched with various information by aggregating with other external resources and their contexts on the web. However, this approach still lacks a best practice and related issues to tell libraries how to convert library catalogue records into LOD.

2 Literature Review

In recent years, LOD has been used to associate related information with diverse viewpoints for the same resource, especially in the domain of cultural heritage. Traditionally,

© Springer International Publishing AG 2017
E. Garoufallou et al. (Eds.): MTSR 2017, CCIS 755, pp. 123–133, 2017.
https://doi.org/10.1007/978-3-319-70863-8_12

libraries have played the role of gatekeeper by providing information to support scholarly communication and research, but blocking these well-organized catalogue data through proprietary library information systems, and thus keeping them far away from users of the Internet. Libraries have shown great interest in freeing catalogue data to become part of the web, because these data, stored in a complicated format such as MARC, can enrich content and context for resources of the semantic web. According to the analysis of Baker et al. [1], datasets, value vocabularies and metadata element sets in libraries are available for Linked Data (LD) reuse. Terms from value vocabularies (e.g., terms of The Virtual International Authority File (VIAF) and Library of Congress Subject Headings) and metadata element sets (e.g., Dublin Core Element terms) can be used for description of LD, such as persons, organizations, geographic names, temporal periods, works, concepts, events, and so on.

According to the definition provided by Bernes-Lee [3], there are four principles for (LD) as follows: use URIs as names for identification of things, use HTTP URIs for looking up names, use standards such as RDF and SPARQL for provision of useful information, and link to more data with URIs. In order to facilitate wide free adoption and reuse of data, the concept of open data has been integrated with LD into a new concept, that is, LOD [27]. In fact, LD and LOD are used interchangeably. In this study LOD is used as a standard for both LD and LOD.

Although best practices have been released by W3C such as Hyland and Villazón-Terrazas [21] and Hyland et al. [20], there is a gap in the transfer "from theoretical discussion into practical implementation" of LOD for libraries as pointed out by Hanson [17]. In terms of metadata design and development, LOD is not only "a conceptual shift from document-centric to data-centric and metadata-based approaches" as stated by Di Noia et al. [11], but is also a data model that is distinct from that of library community as pointed out by Cole et al. [8] and Di Noia et al. [11]. According to the four principles of LOD, libraries have to transform current legacy records (e.g., MARC) stored in the catalogue into URI-based data. To do this, Hanson [17] regarded that libraries have to know how LOD are actually created and published in practice, and Bowen [6] also pointed out the significance of LOD, and the many unexpected issues faced by libraries, as exemplified in the current case studies. For example, in a case study that transformed the MARC-based authority files of the National Library and Archive of Iran into LOD, Eslami and Vaghefzadeh [12] pointed out that it is difficult for libraries to select exact terms and rules for data RDFization and linking for authoring LOD. In a case of the transformation of MARC records of 30,000 digitized books at the University of Illinois at Urbana-Champaign Library, Cole et al. [8] pointed out that there are no common consistencies in current examples of library LOD records based on cases of OCLC WorldCat and British Library's British National Bibliography (BL's BNB). They also further raised the issue of the lack of clear and consistent decisions for guiding libraries to integrate links and select the exact URIs. Furthermore, manual editing and intervention is needed for batch transformation from catalogue data into LOD as reported by Bowen [6], Lampert and Southwick [24], Park and Kipp [28] and Zeng et al. [35]. Therefore, there is an urgent need for customized LOD best practices and workflow for libraries as stated in several studies including Bowen [6], Cole et al. [8], Di Noia et al. [11], Hallo et al. [15], Hanson [17], Lampert and Southwick [24], and Southwick [30].

3 Methodology

Several types of documents, including Bauer and Kaltenböck [2], Heath and Bizer [19], Hyland et al. [20], Hyland and Villazón-Terrazas [21] and Hyland and Wood [22], can be regarded as useful references for authoring and publishing LOD. The document authored by Hyland and Villazón-Terrazas [21] is not only an official publication released by W3C, it has also been extended into several derivatives such as Hyland et al. [20] and Hyland and Wood [22], and the procedures are more abstract than those of Hyland et al. [20]. Thus, in this study, the Linked Data Cookbook authored by Hyland

Table 1. 16 cases of LLD practice for review

Case	Subject of LLD	Original format	Reference No.
BL's BNB	3 million records or so	MARC	Deliot [9]
Biblioteca Nacional de España (BNE)	7 million or so authority and bibliographic records	MARC	BNE [4], Vila-Suero and Rodríguez-Escolano [32], Vila-Suero et al. [33]
Bibliothéque nationale de France (BNF)	11 million pieces of bibliographic data (catalogue general), 0.15 million records (Archives and Manuscripts database), 2 million records (digital library collection), more than 2 million authority records	MARC, Dublin Core, EAD	BNF [5], Simon et al. [29], Wenz [34]
Deutsche National Biblothek (DNB)	National bibliographic and authority data	PICA/MARC	DBN [10]
Harvard Library Dataset	Over 12 million bibliographic records	MARC	Kumar et al. [23]
Music resources	64 MARC records of sound recordings and music score in OCLC WorldCat, and metadata of 20 digital music collections	MARC and non-MARC	Gracy et al. [13], Zeng et al. [35]
National Library and Archive of IRAN (NLAI)	982,892 authority records used in 3,175,125 bibliographic records of NLAI	MARC	Eslami and Vaghefzadeh [12]
National Polytechnic School in Ecuador (EPN)	Datasets and bibliographic metadata from the electrical engineering faculty of EPN	MARC	Hallo et al. [15]
North Carolina State University Libraries (NCSU Libraries)	Organization name authority metadata of E-Matrix	ERMS records	Hanson [17]
Puglia Digital Library	40 digital collections and 1700 resources	Unknown	Di Noia et al. [11]
Swedish Union Catalogue (LIBRIS)	6 million or so bibliographic records	MARC	Malmsten [25], Malmsten [26]
Talis approach	MARC records	MARC	Styles et al. [31]
Universidad de Alicante	200,000 catalogue records of Biblioteca Virtual Miguel de Cervantes	MARC	Candela et al. [7]
University Libraries, University of Nevada, Las Vegas (UNLV Libraries)	Digital collections of 45,000 items with Dublin Core based metadata	Dublin Core	Lampert and Southwick [24], Southwick [31]
University Library, University of Illinois at Urbana-Champaign (UIUC Library)	30,000 digitized books and their MARC records	MARC	Cole et al. [8]
eXtensible Catalog (XC) approach	MARC records	MARC	Bowen [6]

and Villazón-Terrazas [21] was selected as a framework to examine the characteristics and issues related to Library LD (LLD). The framework is composed of key components as follows: modeling (including identifying and modeling datasets), naming with URIs, reusing existing terms, publishing human and machine readable descriptions, RDF conversion, license, host and announcement. Based on the aforementioned framework, content analysis was used in this study as an approach to analyze the existing practices for transforming library data into LOD. In total, sixteen case studies were selected as subject, six national libraries, four university libraries, and six related LOD pilot projects and approaches (shown in Table 1). Each selected case study has to offer related information to reply to more than four components of the framework defined by Hyland and Villazón-Terrazas [21]. In addition to the published journal articles, LOD websites and their documents (e.g., ppt, specification, FAQ, about, data model, technical report, LOD web catalogs, example LOD datasets) offered by selected cases were also cross-checked.

4 Results

4.1 Identifying Data

Originally the principle defined by Hyland and Villazón-Terrazas [21] was to select real world objects of interest, but that has been adapted to include unique datasets for the public by Hyland et al. [20]. Eight cases (BNE, DNB, Harvard Library datasets, LIBRIS, Talis, Universidad de Alicante, UIUC Library and XC) addressed this task, and two (EPN and NCSU Libraries) selected the data for expected audience interest, and three (music resources, Puglia Digital Library, and UNLV Libraries) selected unique data for LLD. In addition to interest and uniqueness selection for LLD, data popularity (i.e., NLAI) and integration of data (i.e., BNF) are also regarded as selection criteria for identification of data. However, the selection principle has been extended in the case of British Library BNB into more detailed categories, including authority, consistency, vast amount and clear rights of data.

In terms of type of library legacy records, three patterns can be generalized as follows. The first is that most cases focus on bibliographic data and then extend to specific value vocabularies, including the following cases: BL's BNB, BNF, EPN, Harvard Library datasets, LIBRIS, music resources, Puglia Digital Library, UNLV Libraries Universidad de Alicante and XC. Second, in some cases authority data was selected as subject for LLD, including NCSU Libraries, NLAI and UIUC Library. Lastly, both bibliographic and authority data were selected for LLD in only three cases: BNE, DNB and Talis.

4.2 Modeling Data

Modeling data is required to express the relations between data and reuse existing terms from standards. There are three types of modeling data for LLD. The first is to select a reference model or an ontology as a basis for data modeling. As they have MARC-based legacy records, most cases have adopted Functional Requirements for Bibliographic Records (FRBR) for modeling data, including group 1 (i.e., work, expression, manifestation and item), group 2 (i.e., person, family and corporation body) and group 3 (i.e., subject). Some cases only focus on group 1 (i.e., EPN and LIBRIS), some on group 1 and 2 (i.e., Talis), and some on group 1–3 (BNE, BNF, music resources, NLAI, Universidad de Alicante and XC). On the other hand, one case (UNLV Libraries) used the European Data Model (EDM) to model data for LLD, one case adopted music ontology (i.e., music resources), and one case (Harvard Library datasets) employed PROV to model LLD with provenance. Second, in some cases more than two existing LOD terms from different standards were reused to model the data (i.e., BL's BNB, DNB, NCSU Libraries and Puglia Digital Library). Third, and most interestingly, MARC was converted into MODS format, and then existing terms were reused for LLD (i.e., UIUC Library).

4.3   Naming with URIs

All the cases developed their own URIs for LLD. In terms of URI expression, in most cases an URL was adopted for each piece of data, but in several cases special expressive methods, such as ARK (including BNF and UIUC Library), compact URI (i.e., BNE), and hash value were used (i.e., Talis). Furthermore, Bowen [6] suggested that libraries should use a metadata registry such as the NSDL Metadata Registry to register and reuse their LOD terms with URIs at no cost.

4.4   Reusing Existing Terms

Existing LOD terms (shown in Table 2) have been used to achieve two functions for LLD as follows: data modeling and linking to external resources. The former is used to describe the data, and the latter is employed to aggregate different information for the same resource. According to the selected practices for review by this study, there are three types of reuse of existing LOD terms for LLD, as follows: metadata elements, value vocabularies, and classes/entities and relations of conceptual reference models/ ontologies between resources. In order to describe data, in most cases, only an appropriate standard and its terms are selected. However, in a few cases, terms from more than two standards of metadata elements, value vocabularies and conceptual reference models/ontologies were adopted to aggregate with a broader range of information for LLD, such as the case of BL's BNB.

Table 2. Existing terms reused by LLD for data modeling and external linking

Case	Data modeling	External linking
BL's BNB	Bibliographic Ontology, DC, FOAF, Event Ontology, ISBD, OWL, SKOS	Dewey.info, Geonames, LCSH, Lexvo, MARC Country and Language codes, VIAF
BNE	DC, ISBD, RDA Group 2 Elements, Relationships for WEMI, MADS/ RDF, SKOS, OWL	DBpedia, GND, Lexvo, LIBRIS, SUDOC, VIAF, DCterms: lang
BNF	BNF specific vocs, Bnf-onto, DC, FOAF, OAI-ORE, MARC Relator, Music ontology, RDFS, RDA Group 1–2 elements, RDA Manifestation properties, Schema.org, SKOS, OWL	Agrovoc, DNB, DBpedia, Geonames, LCSH, MARC Country/Geographic areas/Language code, Rameau, VIAF
DNB	Bibliographic Ontology, DC, FOAF, ISBD, MARC Relator, RDA Group 1–3 properties, RDFS, Schema.org, Umbel	Dewey.info, OpenGIS
Harvard Library	Bibliographic Ontology, DC, FOAF, MARCOnt, RDA Group 1 Elements, PROV, VCard	DBpedia, VIAF
Music resources	Music ontology	
NLAI	FRBR properties, ISBD properties, OWL	DBpedia, LCSH, VIAF
EPN	Bibliographic Ontology, DC, FOAF, ORG ontology, RDFS, SKOS	Europeana, LCSH, Open Library
NCSU Libraries	DC, FOAF, Linked Open Vocabularies, OMR, RDFS, SKOS, OWL	DBpedai, Freebase, ISNI, LCNAF, VIAF
Puglia Digital Library	DC, DBpedia, FOAF, Geonames, LinkedGeoData, PICO Thesaurus, SKOS, Schema.org,	DBpedia, GTI LinkedGeoData, LOD, VIAF
LIBRIS	DC, FOAF, FRBR, RDFS, SKOS, OWL	DBpedia, LCSH
Talis	Bibliographic Ontology, DC, FRBR, MARCOnt	DBpedia, FOAF, Geonames, LCSH
Universidad de Alicante	OWL Time Ontology, RDA Group 1–2 Elements, RDA Group 2 Properties	DC, FOAF
UNLV Libraries	DC, EDM, FOAF	DBpedia, Europeana, FAST, LCAF, TGM, TGN
University of Illinois at Urbana-Champaign	MADS, MODS, SKOS, Schema.org, RDFA	LCSH, VIAF
University of Rochester	DC, RDA Group 1 Elements, RDA Group 2 Properties	Dewey.info

4.5   Other Steps

In addition to publishing machine readable descriptions for LLD in various formats such as RDF, JSON and Turtle, human readable descriptions are also important to enable users' to browse. Most cases are inclined to offer both human and machine readable descriptions, including BL's BNB, BNE, BNF, DNB, LIBRIS, NCSU Libraries, Puglia Digital Library, Universidad de Alicante and UNLV Libraries.

In terms of RDF conversion task, eleven cases (BL's BNB, BNE, BNF, EPN, Harvard Library datasets, LIBRIS, NCSU Library, Talis, UIUC Library, Universidad de Alicante, and XC) developed propriety software for conversion from library legacy records into RDFized form, in addition to open software like OpenRefine (i.e., UNLV Libraries). Furthermore, owing to the inconsistency of library catalogue data, manual intervention and editing are still required for RDF conversion. In releasing LLD, open licensing terms (i.e., Creative Commons 0) were selected in nine cases (BL's BNB, BNE, BNF, DNB, EPN, LIBRIS, NCSU Libraries, Puglia Digital Library, and Universidad de Alicante) to allow users to download RDF-based data for reuse. National libraries in particular, such as the British Library BNB, BNE, BNF, DNB, and LIBRIS have provided users a "data dump" service to download LLD by batch, rather than record by record. In 10 cases (BL's BNB, BNF, DNB, EPN, LIBRIS, NCSU Libraries, Puglia Digital Library, UIUC Library, UNLV Libraries, and Universidad de Alicante) a website was also provided as host and announcement for LLD.

5 Discussion

5.1 Selection of Data for LLD

According to the best practices provided by W3C, the principle of data selection for LOD is to "look for real world objects of interest" [21]. Naturally, selection policy is rooted in the library community for many professional tasks, such as collection development and cataloging. In the case of BNB, the British Library has attempted to develop library-oriented principles to identify data for LLD, including authority, consistency, vast amount and clear rights [9]. Although interests and uniqueness of data are important, quality data related to authority and consistency is also regarded as essential criteria to select data for LLD. Based on experiences learned from Bowen [6], Gracy et al. [13] and Zeng et al. [35], inconsistency in original library catalogue data will result in unsolved issues during conversion from MARC to RDF-based LLD. Fully automatic transformation from library legacy records into LLD is not possible without human intervention and editing, although mapping rules and specification have been defined and specified clearly. Usually the more consistent the data, the higher automatic conversion for LLD can achieve. Furthermore, clear rights are also the other important criteria for users to determine how to reuse these LLD for future extended applications. Therefore, achieving a common agreement about what criteria are essential for selection of data for LLD is an urgent issue for libraries.

5.2 Selection of Existing LOD Terms

Selection of appropriate existing terms from standards is fundamental for data modeling. How to select an appropriate standard and its terms consistently has also become a hot issue for LLD raised by Cole et al. [8], Deliot [9], Lampert and Southwick [24] and Park and Kipp [28], and Cole et al. [8] furthering highlighting that inconsistency will impact interoperability directly. According to the selection criteria for terms of best practices provided by Hyland et al. [20], terms should be documented, self-descriptive, described in more than one language, used by other datasets, accessible for a long period, published by a trusted group or organization, have persistent URLs, and provide a versioning policy. According to the information outlined in the selected cases studied here, long-term viability [28], authoritative source [9] and relevance [13] are another three criteria for LLD, in addition to popularity [12]. Traditionally, trusted metadata registries have been published and maintained to facilitate data interoperability, including the Open Metadata Registry, RDA Registry, and NSDL Metadata Registry. A trusted metadata registry of LLD terms composed from various standards (e.g., AAT, Bibliographic Ontology, Dewey.info, Dublin Core Terms, LCNAF, LCSH, TGN, ULAN, VIAF, MARC21's language/country/role and so on) provided by authoritative organizations is required for libraries. If LLD is an important approach to push library legacy records as part of the semantic web, trusted registries composed of terms from standards including metadata element sets, value vocabularies and conceptual reference models/ontologies (e.g., Bibliographic Ontology, FRBR and MARCOnt) need to be collected, created and maintained persistently in order to meet the aforementioned criteria defined by Hyland et al. [20] and pave a way for interoperability in the future.

5.3   1-to-1 Mapping Principle

Mapping is an essential task for the selection of the right standard and its terms for LLD. In the domain of the digital library, 1-to-1 mapping defined by Dublin Core is a widely accepted principle globally. In the case of Europeana, Haslhofer and Isaac [18] pointed out that the 1-to-1 mapping principle was not applied to the Europeana LOD Data Pilot as data can be applied to various resources resulting in complicated networks of aggregations. In other words, too many individual terms can be used for the same data. Furthermore, Deliot [9] emphasized that the BL's BNB has employed more than two individual terms from different standards for LLD. Therefore, apparently the 1-to-1 mapping principle is not entirely suitable to decide and select the right term for data modeling and external linking in LLD. It seems that "context" pointed by Gracy et al. [13], Hallo et al. [15], Han [16], Lampert and Southwick [24] and Zeng et al. [35] could be the key reason for this complicated issue in selecting the right terms for described resources. Therefore, a contextual mapping principle and its decision rules are required for judging and selecting the appropriate standards and their terms for LLD.

5.4   Long-Term Preservation of LLD

One of the essential requirements of LOD is to assign resources with URIs for facilitating aggregation of information from various sources. However, the changeability and vanishing of URLs has been an unsolved issue for a long time. If URLs can be not kept intact or persistent, the aggregated networked effects of LOD will diminish. According to a review of five case studies of LOD in digital libraries, Hallo et al. [14] suggesting that preservation of linked datasets should be considered as one of the tasks of a library. In order to play an infrastructure role in the semantic web, libraries need to evaluate feasible solutions to this issue.

6   Conclusion

Most of the tasks defined by Hyland and Villazón [21] are adopted by the 16 LLD cases examined for transforming library legacy records (e.g., MARC) into LOD. However, many cases have also developed policies that extend or refine the tasks defined by Linked Data Cookbook to meet their specific requirements of LLD. More studies are needed to investigate the decision principles and rules for selection of standards and their terms during data modeling for LLD. On the other hand, based on results of this study, the concept of application profile should be adopted to examine the application levels of tasks provided by Hyland and Villazón [21]. In the future, a library-oriented workflow for LLD will be developed from this study.

Acknowledgements. This paper was supported by the Ministry of Science and Technology of Taiwan under MOST Grants: MOST 105-2410-H-032-057.

References

1. Baker, T., Bermès, E., Coyle, K., Dunsire, G., Isaac, A., Murray, P., Panzer, M., Schneider, J., Singer, R., Summers, E., Waites, W., Young, J., Zeng, M.: Library linked data incubator group final report: W3C incubator group report (2011). https://www.w3.org/2005/Incubator/lld/XGR-lld-20111025/
2. Bauer, F., Kaltenböck, M.: Linked Open Data: The Essentials. Edition Mono, Vienna (2012). https://www.semantic-web.at/LOD-TheEssentials.pdf
3. Bernes-Lee, T.: Linked data (2006). https://www.w3.org/DesignIssues/LinkedData.html
4. BNE's Data model Homepage. http://www.bne.es/en/Inicio/Perfiles/Bibliotecarios/Datos Enlazados/Modelos/
5. BNF's semantic web and data model Homepage. http://data.bnf.fr/en/semanticweb#Ancre2
6. Bowen, J.: Moving library metadata toward linked data: opportunities provided by the extensible catalog. In: Proceedings of International Conference on Dublin Core and Metadata Applications 2010 (2010). http://dcpapers.dublincore.org/pubs/article/view/1010/979
7. Candela, G., Escobar, P., Marco-Such, M., Carrasco, R.C.: Transformation of a library catalogue into RDA linked open data. In: Kapidakis, S., Mazurek, C., Werla, M. (eds.) TPDL 2015. LNCS, vol. 9316, pp. 321–325. Springer, Cham (2015). https://doi.org/10.1007/978-3-319-24592-8_26
8. Cole, T.W., Han, M.-J., Weathers, W.F., Joyner, E.: Library marc records into linked open data: challenges and opportunities. J. Libr. Metadata **13**(2–3), 163–196 (2013)
9. Deliot, C.: Publishing the British National Bibliography as linked open data. Cat. Index **174**, 13–18 (2014). http://www.bl.uk/bibliographic/pdfs/publishing_bnb_as_lod.pdf
10. Deutsche National Biblothek: The linked data service of the german national library: modelling of bibliographic data (2016). http://www.dnb.de/SharedDocs/Downloads/EN/DNB/service/linkedDataModellierungTiteldaten.pdf?__blob=publicationFile
11. Di Noia, T., Ragone, A., Maurino, A., Mongiello, M., Marzoccca, M.P., Cultrera, G., Bruno, M.P.: Linking data in digital libraries: the case of purlia digital library. In: Proceedings of 1st Workshop on Humanities in the Semantic Web (WHiSe 2016) (2016). http://ceur-ws.org/Vol-1608/paper-05.pdf
12. Eslami, S., Vaghefzadeh, M.H.: Publishing Persian linked data of national library and archive of Iran. In: Proceedings of IFLA WLIC 2013 (2013). http://library.ifla.org/193/1/222-eslami-en.pdf

13. Gracy, K.F., Zeng, M.L., Skirvin, L.: Exploring methods to improve access to music resources by aligning library data with linked data: a report of methodologies and preliminary findings. J. Am. Soc. Inform. Sci. Technol. **64**(10), 2078–2099 (2013)

14. Hallo, M., Luján-Mora, S., Maté, A., Trujillo, J.: Current state of linked data in digital libraries. J. Inf. Sci. **42**(2), 117–127 (2016)

15. Hallo, M., Luján-Mora, S., Trujillo, J.: Transforming library catalogs into linked data. In: Proceedings of the 7th International Conference of Education, Research and Innovation (ICERI 2014), Seville, Spain, 17–19 November 2014, pp. 1845–1853 (2014). https://rua.ua.es/dspace/bitstream/10045/50586/1/transforming-library-catalogs-linked-data.pdf

16. Han, M.-J.: Linked data in library services: transforming the library catalog to linked data. In: Proceedings of Semantic Web in Libraries. Hamburg, 23–25 November 2015 (2015). http://www.bi-international.de/download/file/SWIB2015-MJHan-Report.pdf

17. Hanson, E.: A beginner's guide to creating library linked data: lessons from NCSU's organization name liked data project. Ser. Rev. **40**(40), 251–258 (2014)

18. Haslhofer, B., Isaac, A.: data.europeana.edu: the Europeana linked open data pilot. In: Proceedings of International Conference on Dublin Core and Metadata Applications 2011 (2011). http://dcpapers.dublincore.org/pubs/article/view/3625/1851

19. Heath, T., Bizer, C.: Linked Data: Evolving the Web into a Global Data Space, 1st edn. Morgan & Claypool, London (2011). http://linkeddatabook.com/book/

20. Hyland, B., Atemezing, G.A., Villazón-Terrazas, B.: Best practices for publishing linked data (2017). https://dvcs.w3.org/hg/gld/raw-file/cb6dde2928e7/bp/index.html

21. Hyland, B., Villazón-Terrazas, B.: Linked data cookbook: cookbook for open government linked data (2011). https://www.w3.org/2011/gld/wiki/Linked_Data_Cookbook

22. Hyland, B., Wood, D.: The joy of data – a cookbook for publishing linked government data on the web. In: Wood, D. (ed.) Linking Government Data, pp. 3–26. Springer, New York (2011). https://doi.org/10.1007/978-1-4614-1767-5_1

23. Kumar, S., Ujjal, M., Utpal, B.: Exposing MARC21 format for bibliographic data as linked data with provenance. J. Libr. Metadata **13**(2–3), 212–229 (2013)

24. Lampert, C.K., Southwick, S.B.: Leading to linking: introducing linked data to academic library digital collections. J. Libr. Metadata **13**(2–3), 230–253 (2013)

25. Malmsten, M.: Making a library catalogue part of the semantic web. In: Proceedings of International Conference on Dublin Core and Metadata Applications, pp. 146–152 (2008). http://dcpapers.dublincore.org/pubs/article/view/927/923

26. Malmsten, M.: Exposing library data as linked data. IFLA 2009 (2009). http://wtlab.um.ac.ir/images/e-library/linked_data/other/Exposing%20Library%20Data%20as%20Linked%20Data.pdf

27. Miller, P.: Linked data horizon scan (2010). http://cloudofdata.s3.amazonaws.com/FINAL-201001-LinkedDataHorizonScan.pdf

28. Park, H., Kipp, M.E.I.: Evaluation of mappings from MARC to linked data. In: Proceedings of 25th ASIS SIG/CR Classification Research Workshop (2015). http://journals.lib.washington.edu/index.php/acro/article/view/14908/12495

29. Simon, A., Wenz, R., Michel, V., Di Mascio, A.: Publishing bibliographic records on the web of data: opportunities for the BnF (French National Library). In: Cimiano, P., Corcho, O., Presutti, V., Hollink, L., Rudolph, S. (eds.) ESWC 2013. LNCS, vol. 7882, pp. 563–577. Springer, Heidelberg (2013). https://doi.org/10.1007/978-3-642-38288-8_38

30. Southwick, S.B.: A guide for transforming digital collections metadata into linked data using open source technologies. J. Libr. Metadata **15**(1), 1–35 (2015)

31. Styles, B., Ayers, D., Shabir, N.: Semantic MARC, MARC21 and the semantic web. In: Proceedings of Linked Data on the Web Workshop, 17th International World Wide Web Conference (WWW2008), Beijing, China, 22 April 2008 (2008). http://sunsite.informatik.rwth-aachen.de/Publications/CEUR-WS/Vol-369/paper02.pdf

32. Vila-Suero, D., Rodríguez-Escolano, E.: Linked data at the Spanish national library and the application of IFLA rdfs models. IFLA SCATNews **35**, 5–6 (2011)

33. Vila-Suero, D., Villazón-Terrazas, B., Gómez-Pérez, A.: Datos.bne.es: a library linked data dataset. Sem. Web J. **4**(3), 307–313 (2012)

34. Wenz, R.: Linked open data for new library services: the example of data.bnf.fr. JLIS.it **4**(1), 403–415 (2013). http://leo.cineca.it/index.php/jlis/article/viewFile/5509/7919

35. Zeng, M.L., Gracy, K.F., Skirvin, L.: Navigating the intersection of library bibliographic data and linked music information sources: a study of the identification of useful metadata elements for interlinking. J. Libr. Metadata **13**(2–3), 254–278 (2013)

Automatic Extraction of Correction Patterns from Expert-Revised Corpora

Giovanni Siragusa[1]([⊠]), Luigi Di Caro[1], and Marco Tosalli[2]

[1] Department of Computer Science, University of Turin,
Corso Svizzera 185, Turin, Italy
{siragusa,dicaro}@di.unito.it
[2] Nuance Communication Inc., Strada del Lionetto, 6, Turin, Italy
marco.tosalli@nuance.com

Abstract. In this paper, we first present the task of automatically extracting *correction patterns* from texts which have been manually revised by domain experts. In real industrial scenarios, raw texts obtained via surveys or web crawling often require manual intervention to flatten word capitalization, punctuation, linguistic variability and entity naming. In this context, we propose a distributional and language-independent approach that learns revision rules that also manages errors introduced by the experts themselves. We extensively evaluated our approach on more than 300,000 expert-revised sentences.

Keywords: Pattern extraction · Natural Language Understanding · Annotation learning · Correction patterns

1 Introduction

Natural Language Understanding (NLU) aims at analyzing textual data collected via parsing of large web corpora or through user surveys in order to produce semi-structured patterns, generalizing over the expressed semantics. Since collected texts usually present a very wide space of unexpected tokens, this task generally requires advanced techniques that pre-process the input to limit morphosyntactic variability while removing spelling errors and incoherence in the naming of entities. In particular cases (especially in industrial scenarios), parsed texts are additionally annotated by domain experts with revised expressions and tags. These high-quality pre-processed texts may only result from costly and time-consuming human intervention, where input (*raw*) texts are partially rewritten by annotators producing *clean* texts.

In this context, many tools have been created to simplify and lighten the annotation process. They generally show two panels to annotators: one containing the sentence to annotate and a *suggestion-panel* showing the same sentence with annotation suggestions obtained via machine learning algorithms or further information extracted from the web or social media. For example, Yimam et al. [12] proposed a machine learning algorithm for *WebAnno 1.0* [13] which

© Springer International Publishing AG 2017
E. Garoufallou et al. (Eds.): MTSR 2017, CCIS 755, pp. 134–146, 2017.
https://doi.org/10.1007/978-3-319-70863-8_13

is trained using both the training-set documents and new annotated documents as soon as they are completed by annotators. The tool supports only sequence classification tasks, such as *Part-Of-Speech* tagging, *Named Entity Recognition* and so forth. Hu et al. [6] described a tool called *DocRicher* for e-reader applications. The tool shows, in the above-called *suggestion-panel*, media and posts extracted from social media in order to enrich the information provided by the text. Moreover, the users can highlight portions of text and retrieve further information.

Although these tools can provide suggestions to annotators extracting information from a sentence or trying to solve well-known problems such as Part-of-Speech tagging, they lack of automatic ways of learning from human-provided corrections. Even if suggesting word corrections may be seen as the task called *spell-checking*, which includes those algorithms that learn from large corpora how to possibly correct wrong versions of input words, we here report a different and more complex case. In particular, the task of learning *revision rules* involves other factors such as the domain of application (e.g., domain vocabularies and ambiguities), the contexts of use (e.g., revisions may follow specific annotation methodologies), and annotators subjectivity (e.g., some rules are applied according to personal ideas or simple automatism). While spell-checkers deal with accidental errors, we instead focus on reasoned revisions.

In this contribution, we propose an innovative yet simple method to automatically learn revision rules (or *correction patterns*, from now on) at different levels of complexity from expert-revised examples, in a semi-supervised way. This is particularly useful for proposing suggestions to annotators as well as for automatic text revisions when dealing with large amount of data that must be later processed by NLU engines for deep semantic analysis. Still, learned revision rules could be adopted as a tool for evaluating the effort of annotation works.

With *correction patterns*, we mean automatically-generated rules of the form of *<expression, replacement>* pairs: the left element is an expression matching a determinate set of input raw-strings while *replacement* indicates how the matched string must be rewritten with a new (clean) string. *expression* and *replacement* have an extended variety of possible structured values, which are later detailed in the paper. Simple examples of correction patterns are *<sshow, show>*, *<Turn on, Turn it on>* and *<Activate wifi, Activate Wi-Fi>*.

The input data for the proposed extraction of correction patterns must thus provide a correspondence between raw texts and their manual replacements. Since such manual annotations are equally susceptible to errors, it is also important to avoid over-fitting and error propagation. In the light of this, a method should take into account the unpredictability of raw texts as well as errors inserted in the manual annotation phase.

Our approach, to the best of our knowledge, represents a novel method that fully complies with such requirements without relying on overly complex and language-specific[1] approaches. Generally speaking, our technique is based on a

---

[1] A part from some simple language-specific heuristics which are detailed later in the paper.

two-step process. The first one aims at finding a set of sub-string alignments between *raw* and *clean* texts. Sub-strings are unlimited and unconstrained with respect to characters, words, multi-words expressions and punctuation. The goal of the second step is to build a distributional profile of the sub-strings of the previous step over the aligned cleaned sub-strings. A clustering process on such distributional representations with a centroid-based feature selection finally generates the *replacement* part of the correction patterns.

2   Related Work

As previously mentioned in the Introduction, we adopt a statistical approach to learn relations between sub-string revisions in order to generate correction patterns able to simulate the manual intervention.

Our proposal has some similarity with the *spell-checking* task since they both suggest word corrections. To the best of our knowledge, current spell-checkers use a statistical approach, assigning a probability to candidate words and selecting the one with the highest value. Such probability is learned through a set of <*word, correct-word*> pairs. Differently, our approach proposes transformations by using a set of correction patterns that are unraveled in a semi-supervised fashion through automatic sub-string alignments between *raw*-sentences and manual revisions. Moreover, a clustering over the distributions of such multi-words alignments is used.

There exists a large literature concerning the correction of spelling errors. The Shannon's noisy channel model [10] is composed of an error model and a language model, and it has been successfully applied in several contexts. Kernighan et al. [8] proposed as error model a *confusion matrix* that computes candidates by looking at the probability of single edit-operations with the erroneous word. Brill and Moore [3] introduced an error model that calculates the posterior probability through candidate and error word partitioning. For the language model, Katz [7] proposed a method to compute *N-gram* probability recursively back to low order *N-gram*. It also used probability discount to smooth the probability of rare *N-gram* using a *modified Good-Turing smoothing*. Brants et al. [2] described a simplified model, called *Stupid Backoff*, that computes *N-gram* scores without applying discount and using relative frequencies. Furthermore, recent works focused on re-ranking candidates to increase the spell-checking accuracy. Zhang et al. [14] proposed a method based on *Support Vector Machines*.

Context-sensitive spelling correction aims to correct erroneous words using the surrounding context. Generally speaking, the task builds up a set of candidates for a word, called *confusion set*, taking all words that are "similar enough" to that word. Bassil and Alwani [1] proposed a spelling correction that uses *Google Web 1T 5-gram* dataset. Their model first detects an error word inside a sentence and retrieves correction candidates. Then, they substitute the erroneous word with a candidate word in the original sentence and compare this latter one with *Google 5-gram* sentences in order to score the candidate. Finally, the candidate with the highest score is selected as replacement of the erroneous word. Fossati and Di Eugenio [5] proposed a statistical method called *mixed trigrams model* which is based on the language model. Their language model is a combination of the word-trigram model and the POS-trigrams model. To find the candidate word they use the Markov Model approach applied to POS tagging to the mixed trigrams.

3   Data

In this section, we present the data that have been used to train and evaluate the proposed technique. The data[2] regard voice commands in the automotive context. Example types of such commands are *open app **, *change radio station to **, *read message from **, and so forth.

3.1   Revision Rules on Data

The *raw*-sentences contain a large set of linguistic variability (both lexical and syntactical) which needs steps of normalization, performed by human operators, in order to produce *clean*-sentences that can be efficaciously exploited by deep semantic analysis techniques.

These steps involve revision rules used by domain experts that transform the raw data. Our extraction of correction patterns represents a way to unravel them directly from the data, automatically. These operations may be of the following types:

word case words may be lower-cased or not, and this may differ for proper nouns rather than domain-specific keywords (e.g., raw=*"send poi"*, clean=*"send POI"*);

punctuation removal punctuation may be removed or not (e.g., raw=*"connect to Wi-Fi."*, clean=*"connect to WiFi"*);

word decomposition words may be decomposed or not. For example, an expert in a specific domain may have to separate the possessive case from a word with respect to later semantic analysis modules (e.g., raw=*"Katrina's phone"*, clean=*"Katrina 's phone"*);

deletion sentences may be modified eliminating words or letters (e.g., raw=*"No! Do not call John"*, clean=*"Do not call John"*);

insertion annotators can re-arrange sentences inserting words or letters (e.g., raw=*"zoom map"*, clean=*"zoom in on map"*);

ordering words and letters may be re-ordered (e.g., raw=*"Open folder music"*, clean=*"Open music folder"*);

spelling-errors spelling-errors are corrected by spell-checkers with the supervision of domain experts (e.g., raw=*"vall Paul"*, clean=*"call Paul"*); in this case, *spelling-errors* operation contains all cases that are not covered by *insertion*, *deletion* and *ordering*.

Such cleaning procedure produces very high-quality data, which is often crucial for advanced semantic analyses.

---

[2] The data are collected by Nuance Communications Inc. via web-based surveys.

3.2 Datasets

We experimented our approach on two English datasets, namely the original one ($D1$) and a surrogate dataset ($D2$). $D2$ dataset has been derived from $D1$ by using the revision history of some English sentences. In detail, we extracted the penultimate and the ultimate revision for each sentence and we treated them as $<raw, clean>$ pairs. This was done to further evaluate our method on sentence-pairs that were relatively close. Table 1 gives an overview of the two datasets. In the table, N_{raw} and N_{clean} represent the number of unique words, whereas $|V_{raw}|$ and $|V_{clean}|$ represent the number of unique non-stopword words.

Table 1. The table reports the information about the two datasets. N_{raw} and N_{clean} describe the number of unique tokens, while $|V_{raw}|$ and $|V_{clean}|$ describe the number of unique tokens which are not stopwords. ALR and ALC are the average length of raw and clean sentences respectively.

Dataset	# sents	ALR	ALC	# tok.s raw	N_{raw}	$|V_{raw}|$	# tok.s clean	N_{clean}	$|V_{clean}|$
D1	195,540	3.93	4.04	777,405	15,219	14,931	798,741	8,643	8,444
D2	131,915	4.1	4.28	540,620	12,890	12,612	565,254	7,056	6,861

4   Method Description

As previously mentioned in the Introduction, with correction patterns we mean $<expression, replacement>$ pairs. An *expression* is a string-matching pattern while the *replacement* is a string replacement triggered by the *expression*. The general architecture of the system is shown in Fig. 1. In detail, it includes four phases: (1) pre-processing (yellow box), (2) alignment (red box), (3) co-occurrence matrix construction (blue box), and (4) clustering (green box).

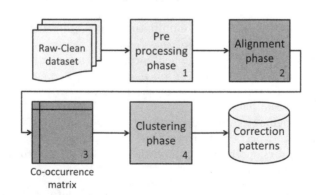

Fig. 1. The pipeline of the approach. (Color figure online)

In phase 1, we carried out three operations: (i) a text cleaning procedure which deletes consecutive duplicate words and punctuation, except for apostrophes, punctuation between numbers and hyphens (e.g., *"Turn on on the radio."* is re-written as *"Turn on the radio"*); (ii) the addition of a start-symbol $<s>$ at the beginning of raw and clean sentences (eg., raw=*"$<s>$Turn on the radio"*, clean=*"$<s>$turn on the radio"*); (iii) a transformation of numbers into a generic *NUM* string (e.g., raw=*"$<s>$station 43"*, clean=*"$<s>$station NUM"*). While duplicate words are always considered as writing errors[3], the start-symbol allows to find patterns which takes also into account the position of words within the sentences. Suppose we have the word *turn* and that each time *turn* starts a sentence it is rewritten as *auto turn*, while in other cases *turn* maintains its form. This allows to define two distinct patterns for the same word. For example, $<<s>turn, auto\ turn>$ if *turn* starts the sentence, and $<turn, turn>$ otherwise.

The alignment phase (2) is composed by two steps: the first one takes as input the result of phase 1 and it aligns each raw-element with one or more elements belonging to the clean sentence sharing the maximum number of characters. If a raw-element does not match with a clean-element, we align the raw-element with a special character (*) to mark the element as deleted. We used manually-defined heuristics to align each raw-element with its clean counterparts. Heuristics allow to easily extend the approach for multiple languages. In details, we defined three heuristics based on the score computed by *Smith-Waterman* edit distance [11]. First, we select a *raw*-element and we initialize the variable *maxScore* (which will maintain the maximum score) to $-\infty$ and *maxClean* (which will maintain the element with the maximum score) to *nil*. Then, for each *clean*-element we compute the *Smith-Waterman* distance between the *raw*-element and the latter one (we will label it with *swScore*) and we check the following heuristics:

1. if maxScore=$-\infty$ and swScore=0, we update its value to swScore and maxClean to the current *clean*-element. This heuristic strategy permits to match words with different accents.
2. if swScore=1 and length(*clean*-element)=2 and maxScore=0, we update maxScore value and maxClean. This heuristic allows to match words that contains apostrophe.
3. if swScore $>$ maxScore or *raw*-element is identical to *clean*-element, we update maxScore value and maxClean.

Finally, a filter operation is applied to remove wrong alignments, checking maxScore, maxClean length and *raw*-element length. The output of this phase is a set of $<expression, replacement>$ patterns, where more than one pattern may have the same *expression* or *replacement*. For example, given the raw-sentence *"Play audio book"* and the clean sentence *"play audiobook"*, we initially insert the start symbol $<s>$ to sentences, then we select a raw-element and iterate over the clean sentence to find a clean-element that is strictly related to the raw-element. First we select the raw-element $<s>Play$ attaching it to the clean-element $<s>play$, then we align *audio* and *book* with *audiobook* in the same way. The goal of

---

[3] This is an assumption that annotators jointly found reasonable in our context.

the second step is to link together, through the * symbol, *expression*-words with the same *replacement* or *replacement*-words with the same *expression*. This step allows to represent patterns that describe segmentations (e.g. <*Michelle's, Michelle*'s*>), insertions (e.g. <*please, car*please*>), deletions (e.g., <*scar*call, call*>) and spelling corrections (e.g. <*madia, media*>). For instance, since the two adjacent raw-elements *audio* and *book* are linked to the same clean-element in the previous example, they can be merged to build a single <*audio*book, audiobook*> pattern.

In phase 3 we build a *co-occurrence* model, i.e., a *sparse* numeric matrix capturing the distributional profile of each raw-element. In particular, each row of the matrix is a raw-element while each column is an aligned clean-element. Each cell of the matrix contains the correlation of a raw-to-clean alignment. This value is calculated with *Pointwise Mutual Information* (or *pmi*).

High *pmi* values mean strong correlations between the *raw*-element and the *clean*-element, whereas lower *pmi* values represent weaker alignments.

The distributional profiles of raw-elements are used to build correction patterns. In detail, for each raw-element, we pick the column with the highest *pmi* value. For example, let us suppose that the raw-element *wifi* co-occurs with the clean-element *WiFi* with a *pmi* value of 0.08 and with *WIFI* with a *pmi* value of 0.12. Suppose that *Wi-Fi* is correlated with *WiFi* with a *pmi* value of 0.10 and with *Wifi* with a *pmi* value of 0.15. Taking the alignment with the highest *pmi* value for *wifi* and *Wi-Fi* we can produce two different patterns: <*wifi, WIFI*> and <*Wi-Fi, Wifi*>. Although this method is fast and easy to apply, it may introduce inconsistent tokens into the vocabulary. To remove these inconsistencies, we applied the following phase.

The last phase (4) aims at grouping raw-elements with *similar distribution profiles* to elicit correction patterns. The centroids of the clusters[4] define *prototypes* of raw-elements which can be associated to a single *replacement* (i.e., that with the highest *pmi* value). Considering the previous example, the clustering algorithm groups together *wifi* and *Wi-Fi*, building the distributional profile of the centroid which has the following *pmi* values: 0.08 for *WiFi*, 0.06 for *WIFI* and 0.075 for *Wifi*. Then, taking the element with the highest *pmi* from the centroid we produce two correction patterns that have the same action: <*wifi, WiFi*> and <*Wi-Fi, WiFi*>.

After the clustering phase, we filter out all correction patterns having the same *expression* and *replacement* (e.g., <*WiFi, WiFi*> or <*turn, turn*>) because they have no effect in correcting the sentences.

For the test, we used *Scikit-learn* [9] and the *DBSCAN* clustering algorithm[5] [4].

---

[4] In some cases, the clusters contain only one element. These clusters are easily transformed into a single correction pattern where the *expression* is exactly the raw-element and the *replacement* is the clean-element with the highest pmi value.

[5] We set *radius* (or *eps*) and *min points* to 3 and 2 for each test set. The *eps* value was chosen analyzing the density distribution of each dataset. *Noise points* are not discarded, but are treated as single point clusters.

5   Evaluation

The used data present a great variety of lexical, syntactical and semantic variability. Moreover, domain experts had the possibility to completely change terms and structure of such sentences also adding (in some cases) errors[6]. Thus, our task of automatically extracting correction patterns must be seen as a real challenging one.

For the evaluation, we trained the software on a subset of the dataset in order to extract a set of correction patterns. Then, we applied the patterns over the *raw*-sentences of the remaining data, generating *pseudoclean*-sentences (labeled as *raw* and *AI* respectively from now on). Finally, we compared the latter ones with the actual *clean*-sentences produced by the domain experts (labeled as *HU*).

We evaluated the *<AI, HU>* pairs in terms of Precision-Recall and Edit Similarity. The reason of the double evaluation relies on the fact that on one hand Edit Similarity aligns two sentences at character-level and computes a score that represent how many characters have found their counterpart. However, it does not take into account when a word starts and ends. On other hand, Precision and Recall are focused at word level and use them to compute a score, although they are not able to capture sentence similarity in terms of Edit Distance. In our work, Precision measures how many *AI* words are present in *HU* while Recall measures how many words in *HU* are found in *AI* (normalizing by the number of words in *AI* and *HU* respectively). We counted 1 for exact match and 0.5 for case-insensitive match. For the Edit Similarity, we used the Smith-Waterman Edit Distance with a match and mismatch weight of 1 and -1 respectively. The Edit Similarity is normalized on the maximum length of the two sentences.

In order to compare the *raw*, *HU* and *AI* sentences, we filtered out the tags presented in *AI* splitting the sentences according to word spaces. Then, we passed the two split-sentences in input to Precision and Recall. For the Edit Similarity we performed an additional step, concatenating together all words in order to have no increment on the similarity due to spaces.

5.1   Baselines

We defined 3 baselines to evaluate the performances of our model:

human a simple baseline obtained aligning the raw-sentences with the HU-ones. It represents how human-annotators performed well in the task.

align baseline *align baseline* is a simple version of our method. First, this method tokenizes the sentences using *Spacy*[7]; then, it aligns each tokenized word in the *raw* part with its *HU* counterpart (in the same way as our method does) and counts how many times a *raw*-word is aligned with a *HU*-word. Finally, for each *raw*-word the method extracts the *HU*-word with the

---

[6] Even if domain experts have been sharing a set of correction rules, we identified some inconsistencies.

[7] https://spacy.io.

142 G. Siragusa et al.

highest frequency and uses it to form a <expression, replacement> pattern.
The extracted patterns are applied over the *raw*-sentences.

spellchecker As described in Sect. 2, our method presents some similarities
with *spell-checkers*; thus, we compared the two methods. We adopted the
one provided by Norvig at his page[8], substituting the sentences used to train
the spell-checker with our *HU*-ones.

5.2 Results

In order to evaluate our method, we shuffled the two datasets (*D*1 and *D*2)
and we splitted them in 80% for training (*trainset*) and 20% for test (*testset*).
During our experiments, we found that the method was heavily affected by poor-
quality raw-clean sentences. In particular, if the sentences (the *raw*-sentence
and the *HU*-one) have a low quality (e.g., raw=*"please car open folder musi"*,
clean=*"opren musi folder"*), the software cannot find proper alignments, adding
noise and outliers in the next phases. To limit the generation of noise and outliers,
we decided to filter out all sentences having a proximity score lower than a
threshold. Proximity score is the Edit Similarity with a less-grained sentence
cleaning method, which measures approximately how much the raw-sentence is
close to the HU-one. A proximity score of 1 means that the two sentences are
close and contain little noise (e.g., some typos), while a proximity score of 0
means that the two sentences are completely different. Therefore, we needed to
find proper threshold values: First, we computed the proximity score for each
sentence in the training set; Second, we plotted the scores in descending order.
Figures 2 shows the proximity score for all sentences in trainsets D1. From the
plots we chose the threshold values 0 (as baseline value), 0.9, 0.95 and 1.

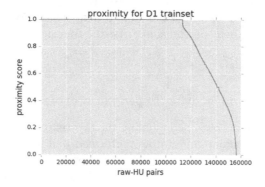

Fig. 2. Proximity score distribution for *D*1 trainset.

---

[8] http://norvig.com/spell-correct.html.

Table 2 shows the results for D1 trainset, while Table 3 shows the results for D2 one. The capital letters in the tables represent (in order of appearance): *T*hreshold, *E*dit Similarity, *P*recision, *R*ecall and *F*-measure[9].

We noticed that the increment of the threshold implies a substantial reduction of the deletion rules cluster (the cluster where the *replacement* is the symbol *). Supposing that deletion rules are heavily context dependent, we removed those ones and we applied the remaining patterns over the *raw*-sentences, generating the *AI*-sentences. Then, we evaluated the *AI*-sentences with respect to the *HU*-ones. The voice *"our method no deletion rules"* in Tables 2 and 3 shows the results for this experiment on D1 and D2 datasets. From the results, we can notice two interesting facts: (i) the results validate our assumptions, and (ii) for F-Measure, our method surpasses the spellchecker of 2 points in *D*1 and the align baseline of 1 point in *D*2. In this latter case, the *align-baseline* has an high score, compared with the others baselines, because it takes more advantage of the similarity between the <*raw, HU*> pairs.

Table 2. The table shows the results on D1 dataset. Numbers in bold represent the highest value.

Method	T	E	P	R	F1
Human	0	**0.90**	0.70	0.81	0.73
	0.9	0.90	0.70	0.81	0.73
	0.95	0.90	0.70	0.81	0.73
	1.0	0.90	0.70	0.81	0.73
Align baseline	0	0.30	0.24	0.46	0.28
	0.9	0.35	0.27	0.52	0.33
	0.95	0.38	0.30	0.56	0.36
	1.0	0.39	0.30	0.56	0.36
Spellchecker	0	0.47	0.73	0.81	0.75
	0.9	0.60	0.74	0.81	0.75
	0.95	0.60	0.74	0.81	0.75
	1.0	0.88	**0.74**	0.81	0.75
Our method	0	0.79	0.57	0.65	0.60
	0.9	0.85	0.63	0.72	0.65
	0.95	0.88	0.69	0.80	0.73
	1.0	0.89	0.71	0.82	0.74
Our method no deletion rules	0	0.87	0.64	0.67	0.68
	0.9	0.89	0.67	0.74	0.70
	0.95	0.90	0.71	0.82	0.75
	1.0	**0.90**	0.73	**0.84**	**0.77**

---

[9] The F-measure is the harmonic mean of Precision and Recall.

Table 3. The table shows the results on D2 dataset. Numbers in bold represent the highest value.

Method	T	E	P	R	F1
Human	0	0.88	0.70	0.81	0.73
	0.9	0.88	0.70	0.81	0.73
	0.95	0.88	0.70	0.81	0.73
	1.0	**0.88**	0.70	0.81	0.73
Align baseline	0	0.83	0.71	0.86	0.76
	0.9	0.85	0.71	0.86	0.76
	0.95	0.85	0.71	0.86	0.76
	1.0	0.85	0.71	**0.86**	0.76
Spellchecker	0	0.83	0.68	0.74	0.68
	0.9	0.83	0.68	0.74	0.68
	0.95	0.83	0.68	0.74	0.68
	1.0	0.83	0.68	0.75	0.69
Our method	0	0.78	0.59	0.67	0.61
	0.9	0.83	0.65	0.73	0.67
	0.95	0.83	0.66	0.77	0.69
	1.0	0.84	0.67	0.77	0.70
Our method no deletion rules	0	0.85	0.64	0.72	0.67
	0.9	0.87	0.69	0.79	0.72
	0.95	0.88	0.73	0.84	0.76
	1.0	**0.88**	**0.73**	0.85	**0.77**

For both datasets, it is evident that the increment of the threshold has an impact on the performance. We thus inspected both the sentences and the patterns, founding that half of the sentences in testsets have a proximity score of 1, which means the sentence pairs contain little typos. The patterns, instead, capture typos such as uppercase letters (e.g., raw=*CAll*, clean=*call*), wrong words decomposition (e.g., raw=*den ote*, clean=*denote*), deletions (e.g., raw=*overv*, clean=*overview*) and insertions (e.g., raw=*there*, clean=*there's*). This means that the software is able to move closer the distance between *raw* and *HU* sentences.

6 Conclusion

In this paper, we presented a novel method that extracts a set of correction patterns analyzing *raw*-sentences and their human-revised counterparts (i.e., the *clean*-sentences). As validated in Sect. 5, extracted patterns can be used to suggest text-revisions to annotators, lightening and speeding up their work.

These suggestions are an important key for annotation tasks, especially in industrial scenarios, since they allow to reduce linguistic variability and unravel high-quality patterns. Furthermore, correction patterns can be used to automatically revise sentences when dealing with large amounts of data, or for the evaluation of the work of annotators, which are often costly *black box* professionals.

The paper represents the first effort of a large-scale NLU project, with leaves many research questions open for future work. In particular, we will consider improvements such as others methods to ordering correction patterns, the weighting of correction patterns, context-aware replacements, and integration of topic modeling techniques.

References

1. Bassil, Y., Alwani, M.: Context-sensitive spelling correction using google web 1t 5-gram information. arXiv preprint arXiv:1204.5852 (2012)
2. Brants, T., Popat, A.C., Xu, P., Och, F.J., Dean, J.: Large language models in machine translation. In: Proceedings of the Joint Conference on Empirical Methods in Natural Language Processing and Computational Natural Language Learning. Citeseer (2007)
3. Brill, E., Moore, R.C.: An improved error model for noisy channel spelling correction. In: Proceedings of the 38th Annual Meeting on Association for Computational Linguistics, pp. 286–293. Association for Computational Linguistics (2000)
4. Ester, M., Kriegel, H.P., Sander, J., Xu, X.: A density-based algorithm for discovering clusters in large spatial databases with noise. In: Kdd, vol. 96, pp. 226–231 (1996)
5. Fossati, D., Di Eugenio, B.: A mixed trigrams approach for context sensitive spell checking. In: Gelbukh, A. (ed.) CICLing 2007. LNCS, vol. 4394, pp. 623–633. Springer, Heidelberg (2007). https://doi.org/10.1007/978-3-540-70939-8_55
6. Hu, Q., Liu, Q., Wang, X., Tung, A.K., Goyal, S., Yang, J.: Docricher: an automatic annotation system for text documents using social media. In: Proceedings of the 2015 ACM SIGMOD International Conference on Management of Data, pp. 901–906. ACM (2015)
7. Katz, S.M.: Estimation of probabilities from sparse data for the language model component of a speech recognizer. IEEE Trans. Acoust. Speech Sig. Process. **35**(3), 400–401 (1987)
8. Kernighan, M.D., Church, K.W., Gale, W.A.: A spelling correction program based on a noisy channel model. In: Proceedings of the 13th conference on Computational linguistics, vol. 2, pp. 205–210. Association for Computational Linguistics (1990)
9. Pedregosa, F., Varoquaux, G., Gramfort, A., Michel, V., Thirion, B., Grisel, O., Blondel, M., Prettenhofer, P., Weiss, R., Dubourg, V., Vanderplas, J., Passos, A., Cournapeau, D., Brucher, M., Perrot, M., Duchesnay, E.: Scikit-learn: machine learning in Python. J. Mach. Learn. Res. **12**, 2825–2830 (2011)
10. Shannon, C.E.: A mathematical theory of communication. ACM SIGMOBILE Mob. Comput. Commun. Rev. **5**(1), 3–55 (2001)
11. Smith, T.F., Waterman, M.S.: Identification of common molecular subsequences. J. Mol. Biol. **147**(1), 195–197 (1981)
12. Yimam, S.M., Biemann, C., de Castilho, R.E., Gurevych, I.: Automatic annotation suggestions and custom annotation layers in webanno. In: ACL (System Demonstrations), pp. 91–96 (2014)

13. Yimam, S.M., Gurevych, I., de Castilho, R.E., Biemann, C.: Webanno: a flexible, web-based and visually supported system for distributed annotations. In: ACL (Conference System Demonstrations), pp. 1–6 (2013)
14. Zhang, Y., He, P., Xiang, W., Li, M.: Discriminative reranking for spelling correction. In: Proceedings of the 20th Pacific Asia Conference on Language, Information and Computation, pp. 64–71. Citeseer (2006)

Enabling Analysis of User Engagements Across Multiple Online Communication Channels

Zaenal Akbar$^{(\boxtimes)}$, Anna Fensel, and Dieter Fensel

Semantic Technology Institute (STI) Innsbruck, University of Innsbruck,
Innsbruck, Austria
{zaenal.akbar,anna.fensel,dieter.fensel}@sti2.at

Abstract. The role of online communication channels, especially social media, has been developed from a platform for sharing information to a platform for influencing audiences. With the intention to reach the widest audience possible, organizations tend to distribute their marketing information to as many communication channels as possible. After that, they measure the performance of their marketing activities on every channel, where the typical measurement on how users perceived information is through engagement indicators. Measuring engagements across channels is challenging because the heterogeneity of engagement mechanism that can be performed by users on every channel. In this paper, we introduce a method to enable an analysis of those heterogeneous engagements which are distributed on multiple online communication channels. The solution consists of a conceptual model to uniformly representing user engagements on every channel. The model enables user engagements integration across channels, such that a more advanced user engagements analysis can be performed. We show how to apply our solution to analyze wide variety user engagements on popular social media channels from the tourism industry. This work brings us a step closer to realize an integrated multi-channel online communication solution.

Keywords: User engagement · Multi-channel · Data integration · Data analysis

1 Introduction

In marketing strategy of organization, multiple online communication channels especially social media has widened the marketing communications capability, maintaining relationships with customers, and increasing brand recognition [21]. It has a rich variety of information sources, where the quality of information is not solely determined by the quality of content, but also by links between content and the explicit quality ratings from members of the community (such as likes, comments) [1]. The effectiveness of online marketing communication is typically measured by the received user engagement [9]. User engagement can be seen as the quality reflection of the user experiences [14], where a total engagement with a marketing channel could lead to an e-commerce practice success [5]. Capability

© Springer International Publishing AG 2017
E. Garoufallou et al. (Eds.): MTSR 2017, CCIS 755, pp. 147–159, 2017.
https://doi.org/10.1007/978-3-319-70863-8_14

to measure, analyze and visualize these social data could help organizations to realize the value in all phase of their products or services life cycle, including to monitor changes in customer interests or to respond to crises quickly [10].

Social web platforms possess interoperability limitations [7], making user engagements integration across platforms problematic. Platforms are isolated from one to another, and there is no common standard for exchanging information or knowledge among them. Adoption of multiple-platform is increasing causing a high demand for cross-media content aggregation (merging, analysis, visualization) [6]. A channel might use different features and notions of engagement, limiting comparison of engagement dynamics across channels [19]. Besides the diversity of engagement metrics, user engagement also possesses different characteristics depending on the application [14]. Most recently, many social media tools have provided a capability to aggregate multiple channels as well as performing an analysis on them simultaneously. Klout [18] for example, provides a method to measure user influences across multiple channels.

Semantic web technologies [4] have been used to overcome the interoperability limitation by allowing the representation and exchange of information in a meaningful way, facilitating the integration of information from different sources. Friend-of-a-Friend (FOAF) and the Semantically-Interlinked Online Communities (SIOC) projects[1] are a few examples of existing works trying to eliminate the interoperability issues on the social web. In this work, we introduce a similar approach for interlinking social entities, but instead of focusing on the people and their activities, our approach is focused on the channel as the center of communication activities where content can be put and retrieved. Our approach enables us to interlinking user engagements across communication platforms for further analysis. To be precise, our main contributions are: (i) **a conceptual model**, focused on channels, to uniformly representing communication activities, (ii) **three forms of categorization** to integrate engagements across channels, (iii) **analysis results** of users engagements from several organizations in the tourism industry. The paper is organized as follows. Section 2 describes a few related works. Section 3 presents our conceptual model to represent communication activities uniformly. Section 4 describes our approach to integrate various user engagement through different forms of categorization. In Sect. 5, we show how to analyze user engagements from multiple channels in the tourism industry, and finally, we summarize our findings, conclusion and future work in Sect. 6.

2   Related Work

We align our work to two topics of the social semantic web including usage of semantic technologies in online communication and user engagement modeling.

Social Semantic Web Modeling. An approach for modeling social semantic web is by representing a "thing" and its actions as the core of the model. This

---

[1] http://www.foaf-project.org/, http://sioc-project.org/.

approach is known as "object-centered sociality" [7] is typically put people and their actions as the core. In this case, a model enables us to determine what content people have created together, which person is commenting on content created by someone else, which content they use in common, or which annotation they have used together, and so on. FOAF project was started in 2000 to create a web of machine-readable pages describing people, the links between them and the things they create and do. Its vocabulary enables to share and use information about people and their activities, for instance to interlinking people from multiple documents on the web [12]. SIOC ontology aims to enable the integration of the online community information in a way a new knowledge can be acquired [8], for example, to acquire user-generated content from various sites. Simple Knowledge Organization System (SKOS)[2] enables people to define controlled vocabularies in a way tags can be linked together. Provenance ontology[3] focused on the entities, activities, and people in producing data, which can be used to form an assessment of data quality, reliability or trustworthiness.

User Engagement Modeling. User engagement as a reflexion of user experiences [14] is critical to business as an indicator of marketing impact to the users. There have been many works dedicated to measure and analyze it, especially on how to maximize the engagement by fine tuning the disseminated content. In [17], different types of post categorization (e.g. announcement, question), post type (e.g. photo, link) were introduced including posting weekday and hour that can be used to analyze engagement. Social interactions also can be measured by categorizing them into several associated levels of engagement [16], for example, a "comment" has higher value than a "like" corresponding to a higher score. Specifically for social media analytics, to measure various social aspects such as user sentiment or likelihood to purchase a product/service, various metrics need to be considered including user backgrounds, interest, concerns, and the network of relationships [10]. Another engagement metrics also can be used to measure how much a site was used, how a site was used, and how often users return to a site, known as popularity, activity, and loyalty metrics respectively [14]. Common and comparable features (e.g. post count, post rate, post length) from different platforms can be identified and categorized them into social and content features and use them to analyze and mine engagement dynamics across channels [19].

Contribution. Our most significant contributions to these topics are: (i) the development of a conceptual model for the social web in the context of online communication especially marketing communication, (ii) the application of the model to analyze user engagements across multiple communication channels. In contrast with existing works were focused on person and their activities, our work was focused on communication channel, in a way heterogeneous engagements can be represented uniformly, enabling advanced user engagement analysis.

---

[2] https://www.w3.org/2004/02/skos/.

[3] http://www.w3.org/TR/prov-dm/.

3   Multi-channel Online Communication Model

In this section, we describe our conceptual model for multi-channel online communication. First, we introduce the main entities of the model followed by necessary entities to form a complete multi-channel model.

3.1   Communication Model

We started from the sender/receiver communication model of Shannon and Weaver [20], where three essential entities are composed: (1) the sender and receivers (human or software agent) that participate in communication activities, as **Agent**, (2) the message, exchanging during communication activities, as **Content**, (3) the channel or medium for exchanging message in communication activities, as **Channel**. With the advancement of web technologies, the current communication system can not be represented perfectly by using these three entities only; the model should be expanded.

The Internet has transformed marketing communication in a hypermedia computer-mediated environment (CME) into many-to-many form [13]. Social networks, in particular, extends the possibility of multi-modal and simultaneous communication with many members, with a possibility to communicate through different communication channels [15]. This multiple channel communication, as well as cross-platform interoperability including advertisement on social web platforms, has been identified as an important research issue especially in the tourism industry [22]. Many works have been invested in solving this issue, including how to distribute content to multiple channels through a rule-based system [2] and has been proved to be effective for hotel marketing [11], as well as to maximize publication flows among channels [3]. More than that, we also need to consider structural differences between CMEs including their interfaces, functionalities, as well as how members interact [23].

3.2   Multi-channel Support

By considering all information from the previous section, to reflect a complete multi-channel communication system, we introduced another three entities, namely "Post", "Platform", and "Act". The whole model is shown at Fig. 1.

Post. It can be seen as the representation of a Content on a particular Channel, owns two important properties: (i) A Post must have a Content and a Channel. We represent this case through "hasContent" and "hasChannel" properties which both have domain "Post" and value ranges "Content" and "Channel" respectively. (ii) A Post might be linked to another Post, such that one Post can be visited from another Post. We represent this case through "linkedTo" property which has domain and values ranges as "Post".

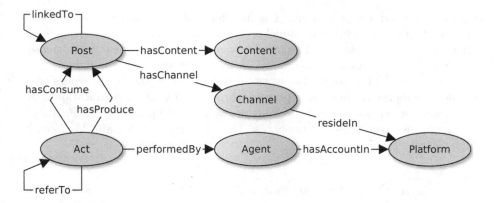

Fig. 1. Multi-channel online communication model

Platform. It is the entity that manages a collection of channels particularly for the access permission to certain channels, owns two important properties: (i) A Channel must reside in and only one Platform, but a Platform might contain one or more Channels. We represent this case through "resideIn" property which has domain "Channel" and value ranges "Platform". (ii) To perform specific actions to a Channel, Agent needs to have an account in the Platform where the Channel resides. We represent this case through "hasAccountIn" property which has domain "Agent" and value ranges "Platform". An Agent might have multiple accounts in a Platform, where each account bears different functions and permission.

Act. It can be seen as the (communication) action performed by Agent to specific Post, owns two important relationships: (i) An Act might consume a Post and produce one or more Post. We represent this case through "hasConsume" and "hasProduce" properties where both have domain "Act" and value ranges "Post". (ii) An Act might refer to another Act, such as an Act followed by another Act. For example on Facebook, commenting on a wall post can be described by an act "Commenting" that refers to an act "Posting". Reply to a comment can be described by an act "Commenting" that refers to another "Commenting", and so on. We represent this case through property "referTo" where its domain and values ranges are both "Act".

4   User Engagement Integration

In this section, we describe three forms of engagement categorization across platforms, derived from three entities in the communication model defined in the previous section, namely "Agent", "Act" and "Post". After explaining each form, we list and discuss our contributions.

Agent-Oriented Engagement. The first form of engagement categorization is oriented around users (in our model represented as Agent), where engagement can be seen as the reaction of users to the received information. In this case, the engagement represents the quality of user experience [14], or reflects user acceptance [10]. There are various ways for users to show their experiences on a channel. We represent this user experience through different communication acts. And since there are numerous acts available, we specify a property "hasPolarity" to express the level of user experiences. The property has domain "Act" with value ranges "Text".

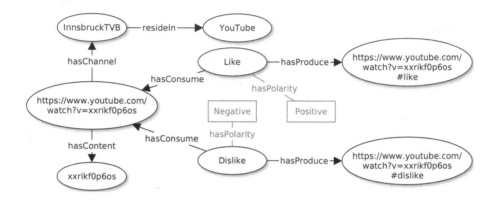

Fig. 2. An example to represent act polarity

Figure 2 shows an example of how to represent polarities on different acts. In this example, we have a video resource[4] located in channel InnsbruckTVB on YouTube. Two acts were applied, Like and Dislike with Positive and Negative polarities respectively, consumed the resource and produced different engagement indicators, namely the number of likes and dislikes. Two or more of those reactions can be represented with one type of polarity. User might enable/disable certain acts at post level as well as channel level, in a way users could not perform any engagement. For example, on a blog, the author might enable/disable act Comment for a specific post or the whole blog.

Act-Oriented Engagement. The second form of engagement categorization is oriented around Act. Two or more acts can be performed independently or consecutively. A Comment might be followed by another Comment, but Like could not be followed by another act anymore. We represent this case as "referred-ability', meaning that if an act has referred-ability, then one or more acts can be performed after it. If not, then there is no more act can be performed after it. In our model shown in Fig. 1, this situation is represented by property "referTo", which has domain and range values of "Act". This categorization can be used to distinguish which acts can drive other acts, and to what extent.

---

[4] https://www.youtube.com/watch?v=xxrikf0p6os.

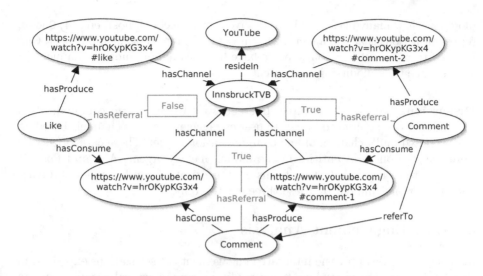

Fig. 3. An example to represent act referred-ability

Figure 3 shows two different acts (Like and Comment) applied to a video[5] which is available in channel InnsbruckTVB on YouTube. The Like increase the number of like to the video, but can not be followed by another act ("hasReferral" equal to False). On the other hand, the Comment produces a new text to the video, where another Comment replied to it, adding a new text to the video and at the same time producing a "referTo" relationship. In this case, we say that act Comment can be referred ("hasReferral" equal to True). This referred-ability property can be customized by users. For example, in a Blog, users might specify the maximum nested level for comment, indicates that this ability can be performed only until certain levels.

Post-oriented Engagement. The third form of engagement categorization is oriented around Post, where an act consumes an input post which contains content available on a certain channel. After the act has been performed successfully, a new post will be produced where its content (or its channel) might be not similar anymore to the input post. We use this condition to categorize communication actions as follow: (1) `View`, represent actions that will not affect the content as well as the channel of the input post. This category can be used to represent how many visitors have been visited a blog post or watched a video, etc. (2) `Share`, represent actions that will affect the channel but not the content of the input post. Can be used to represent how many blog posts have been shared on Facebook, or how many tweets have been re-tweeted, etc. (3) `React`, represent actions that will affect the content but not the channel of the input post. Can be used to represent how many comments have been received by a

---

[5] https://www.youtube.com/watch?v=hrOKypKG3x4.

blog post, how many likes have been received by a Facebook post, etc. (4) `Quote`, represent actions that will affect both content and channel of the input post. Can be used to represent how many posts have been shared on another channel and at the same time modifying its content.

Discussion. We explained three different ways to categorize communication actions that can be used to integrate user engagements across channels based on the proposed multi-channel online communication model. These categorizations were oriented on three entities in the model, namely Agent, Act, and Post. It is worthy to mention that other forms of categorization can be explored further and they are not limited by these three entities only.

5   User Engagement Analysis

In this section, we apply the integrated engagement categorizations explained in the previous section to analyze social media posting of several organizations in the tourism industry.

Dataset. To construct our dataset, we selected 3 of Destination Marketing Organizations/Tourismusverband (TVB) from the region of Tyrol, Austria[6] which have a relatively high number of posts on 5 platforms of social media, namely Facebook, Google+, Pinterest, Twitter, and YouTube. The data collection was performed during December 2016 until January 2017 through public API from each platform, limited to public posting only. In total, we collected 9189, 8229, 6055 posts from TVB Kitzbühel, Ötztal, and Innsbruck respectively.

Mapping. To align user engagements from every platform to our model, we constructed a mapping for every type of engagement. Table 1 shows the alignment of user engagements from five platforms to the proposed model. The mapping might differ from one application to another.

Integration. A row in the produced mapping denotes how the related engagement will be represented in three different types of integrated engagements. For example, if a video on YouTube has n-number of "like", then according to the mapping we will obtain n-engagements with positive polarity, n-engagements without referred-ability, and n-engagements in category 3 (react).

Result and Discussion. We limited our analysis to publicly available posts published on 2016. This time range can be defined for any time duration, for example, to analyze engagements during a campaign period.

Figure 4 shows plots of integrated user engagements for TVB Kitzbühel, Ötztal, and Innsbruck, where a point in the plots represents a single social media posting. Plots in the first row compare the average number of act polarities (Positive vs. Negative) for each TVB, while in the second row between

---

[6] https://www.tirol.gv.at/tourismus/tourismusverbaende/.

Table 1. Engagement and model alignment

No.	Platform	Engagement	Polarity		Referred-ability		Post Cat.
			Positive	Negative	True	False	
1.	Facebook	shares	✓		✓		2, 3, 4
		comments	✓		✓		3
		like, love, wow, haha, thankful	✓			✓	3
		sad, angry		✓		✓	3
2.	Google+	reply	✓		✓		3
		plusone	✓			✓	3
		reshare	✓		✓		2, 3, 4
3.	Pinterest	comment	✓			✓	3
		repin (save)	✓		✓		2, 4
4.	Twitter	favorite	✓			✓	3
		retweet	✓		✓		2, 3, 4
5.	YouTube	view	✓			✓	1
		like	✓			✓	3
		dislike		✓		✓	3
		comment	✓		✓		3

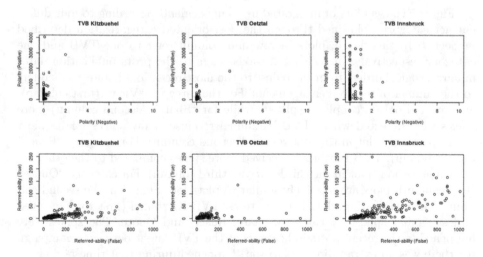

Fig. 4. Integrated user engagements (based on act polarity and referred-ability) of TVB Kitzbühel, Ötztal, Innsbruck

act referred-abilities (True vs. False). Several interesting results were detected: (i) TVB Innsbruck received a high number of positive polarity engagements as well as negative ones compared to the other TVB as shown in the top-right plot. (ii) TVB Innsbruck received a high number of engagements with referred-ability (most likely comments) compare to engagements without referred-ability as shown in the bottom-right plot.

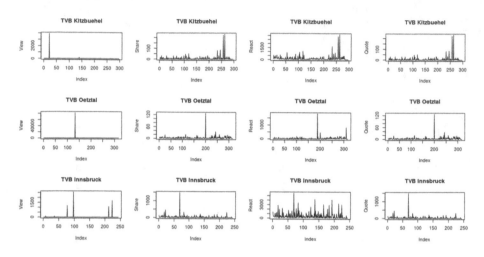

Fig. 5. Integrated user engagements (based on post-oriented Categorization) of TVB Kitzbühel, Ötztal, Innsbruck

Figure 5 shows plots of integrated user engagements according to four different act categories obtained through the post-oriented categorization described in Sect. 4. In this figure, plots in row and column refer to one TVB and one category respectively. In each plot, x-axis refers to the posts publication dates in chronological order (from the oldest to the most recent one), and y-axis refers to the number of received engagements. For the category "View" (first column), we detected only a couple of spikes[7], while for "Share" (second column) more spikes were detected where TVB Kitzbühel received many spikes for its most recent postings (plot in the first row and second column). For category "React" (third column), TVB Innsbruck received more spikes compared to the other for the whole period (plot in the third row and third column). For category "Quote" (last column), plots are relatively similar to plots for "Share" in the second column. When comparing plots between rows, TVB Kitzbühel (first row) received almost similar spikes for category Share, React, and Quote. The spikes were happened to the recent posts indicates that the TVB might perform a campaign (or there was an extraordinary occasion) happened during that time period.

---

[7] A spike is a vertical line from a point to the base (x-axis) which is deviate from the common values.

6   Conclusion

Analyzing user engagements across multiple online communication channels such as social media is a challenging task. Each channel maintains different types of engagements, and there is no proper way exists yet to interlinking them. In this paper, we presented a method to overcome this challenge by utilizing semantic web technologies. First, we defined a conceptual communication model (consists of six main entities: Agent, Content, Channel, Act, Post, and Platform) to represent user engagements uniformly. Then, numerous types of integrated engagements were constructed by using various forms of categorization, namely polarity, referred-ability, and post-oriented categorization.

We applied our method to analyze user engagements of three Destination Marketing Organizations from the region of Tyrol, Austria. For each organization, 20 types of engagements across five social media platforms were represented into three types of integrated engagements. Then, two visual exploratory analysis methods can be performed to identify different engagements patterns across organizations and platforms. The results indicate that the proposed method could bring benefits for monitoring online marketing activities on multiple channels, namely: (i) reducing the required time to monitor multiple channels simultaneously by integrating various types engagements across social media channels, (ii) engagement comparison can be performed not only between the types of integrated engagements within an organization but also across organizations.

We have demonstrated that semantic web technologies through a uniform representation across channels have enabled us to exchange information and perform an integrated analysis of user engagements on social media. In the future, we would like to find the correlation between identified integrated engagement patterns to online marketing strategies. For example, how a positive polarity trend engagement contributes to the marketing effectiveness.

Acknowledgements. This work was partially supported by the EU project EUTravel. We would like to thank all the members of the Online Communication (http://oc.sti2.at) working group for their valuable feedback.

References

1. Agichtein, E., Castillo, C., Donato, D., Gionis, A., Mishne, G.: Finding high-quality content in social media. In: Proceedings of the 2008 International Conference on Web Search and Data Mining, WSDM 2008, pp. 183–194. ACM (2008)
2. Akbar, Z., García, J.M., Toma, I., Fensel, D.: On using semantically-aware rules for efficient online communication. In: Bikakis, A., Fodor, P., Roman, D. (eds.) RuleML 2014. LNCS, vol. 8620, pp. 37–51. Springer, Cham (2014). https://doi.org/10.1007/978-3-319-09870-8_3
3. Akbar, Z., Toma, I., Fensel, D.: Optimizing the publication flow of touristic service providers on multiple social media channels. In: Inversini, A., Schegg, R. (eds.) Information and Communication Technologies in Tourism 2016, pp. 211–224. Springer, Cham (2016). https://doi.org/10.1007/978-3-319-28231-2_16

4. Berners-Lee, T., Hendler, J., Lassila, O., et al.: The semantic web. Sci. Am. **284**(5), 28–37 (2001)
5. Bilgihan, A., Okumus, F., Nusair, K., Bujisic, M.: Online experiences: flow theory, measuring online customer experience in e-commerce and managerial implications for the lodging industry. Inf. Technol. Tour. **14**(1), 49–71 (2014)
6. Bontcheva, K., Rout, D.: Making sense of social media streams through semantics: a survey. Sem. Web **5**(5), 373–403 (2014)
7. Breslin, J., Decker, S.: The future of social networks on the internet: the need for semantics. IEEE Internet Comput. **11**(6), 86–90 (2007)
8. Breslin, J.G., Harth, A., Bojars, U., Decker, S.: Towards semantically-interlinked online communities. In: Gómez-Pérez, A., Euzenat, J. (eds.) ESWC 2005. LNCS, vol. 3532, pp. 500–514. Springer, Heidelberg (2005). https://doi.org/10.1007/11431053_34
9. Calder, B.J., Malthouse, E.C., Schaedel, U.: An experimental study of the relationship between online engagement and advertising effectiveness. J. Interact. Mark. **23**(4), 321–331 (2009)
10. Fan, W., Gordon, M.D.: The power of social media analytics. Commun. ACM **57**(6), 74–81 (2014)
11. Fensel, A., Akbar, Z., Toma, I., Fensel, D.: Bringing online visibility to hotels with Schema.org and multi-channel communication. In: Inversini, A., Schegg, R. (eds.) Information and Communication Technologies in Tourism 2016, pp. 3–16. Springer, Cham (2016). https://doi.org/10.1007/978-3-319-28231-2_1
12. Finin, T., Ding, L., Zhou, L., Joshi, A.: Social networking on the semantic web. Learn. Organ. **12**(5), 418–435 (2005)
13. Hoffman, D.L., Novak, T.P.: Marketing in hypermedia computer-mediated environments: conceptual foundations. J. Mark. **60**(3), 50 (1996)
14. Lehmann, J., Lalmas, M., Yom-Tov, E., Dupret, G.: Models of user engagement. In: Masthoff, J., Mobasher, B., Desmarais, M.C., Nkambou, R. (eds.) UMAP 2012. LNCS, vol. 7379, pp. 164–175. Springer, Heidelberg (2012). https://doi.org/10.1007/978-3-642-31454-4_14
15. Musiał, K., Kazienko, P.: Social networks on the Internet. World Wide Web **16**(1), 31–72 (2013)
16. Peters, K., Chen, Y., Kaplan, A.M., Ognibeni, B., Pauwels, K.: Social media metrics a framework and guidelines for managing social media. J. Interact. Mark. **27**(4), 281–298 (2013)
17. Pletikosa Cvijikj, I., Dubach Spiegler, E., Michahelles, F.: Evaluation framework for social media brand presence. Soc. Netw. Anal. Min. **3**(4), 1325–1349 (2013)
18. Rao, A., Spasojevic, N., Li, Z., Dsouza, T.: Klout score: measuring influence across multiple social networks. In: 2015 IEEE International Conference on Big Data (Big Data), pp. 2282–2289. IEEE, October 2015
19. Rowe, M., Alani, H.: Mining and comparing engagement dynamics across multiple social media platforms. In: Proceedings of the 2014 ACM Conference on Web Science, WebSci 2014, pp. 229–238. ACM, New York (2014)
20. Shannon, C.E., Weaver, W.: The Mathematical Theory of Communication. University of Illinois Press, Illinois (1949)
21. de Vries, L., Gensler, S., Leeflang, P.S.: Popularity of brand posts on brand fan pages: an investigation of the effects of social media marketing. J. Interact. Mark. **26**(2), 83–91 (2012)

22. Werthner, H., Alzua-Sorzabal, A., Cantoni, L., Dickinger, A., Gretzel, U., Jannach, D., Neidhardt, J., Pröll, B., Ricci, F., Scaglione, M., Stangl, B., Stock, O., Zanker, M.: Future research issues in IT and tourism. Inf. Technol. Tour. **15**(1), 1–15 (2015)
23. Yadav, M.S., de Valck, K., Hennig-Thurau, T., Hoffman, D.L., Spann, M.: Social commerce: a contingency framework for assessing marketing potential. J. Interact. Mark. **27**(4), 311–323 (2013)

Lost Identity – Metadata Presence in Online Bookstores

Tjaša Jug[✉] and Maja Žumer

Department of Library and Information Science and Book Studies, Faculty of Arts,
University of Ljubljana, Ljubljana, Slovenia
{Tjasa.jug,Maja.zumer}@ff.uni-lj.si

Abstract. Book metadata plays an important role in discovering, identifying and selecting books in the online bookstores. While there is a link between good book description and sales, an insufficient description may make a book unfindable and therefore lost. There are many recommendations and guidelines regarding the book metadata to be included in the book description but not much is known about which information is actually available to end users. To get an overview of the current situation we conducted an expert study and examined American and Slovenian bookstores. We were mostly interested in the presence and the form of various metadata elements in online bookstores. The results show that all bookstores provide basic information, but many lack enhanced book information, which was evident especially in Slovenian sample. What is more, we found that metadata is mostly descriptive and does not allow users to navigate through the webpage and explore the collection. The results offer an insight in the actual situation on two book markets and open new research questions for publishers as well as for librarians.

Keywords: Book metadata · Online bookstores · Expert study

1 Introduction

With the emergence of the World Wide Web consumers have an opportunity to make a purchase from the comfort of their own homes. Online shopping allows us to search and get information about a wide variety of products from all over the world. Besides that, cost and time efficiency are one of the strongest motivations for people to shop online [1]. However, how do people find the products, that will suit them best and how do they know, what exactly are they buying? The answer is metadata.

Metadata, or data about data, represents structured information that describes, explains, locates, or otherwise makes it easier to retrieve, use or manage an information resource [2]. Various communities have adopted their own explanations and uses of this term. In the context of online shopping, metadata correspond to product description that includes item attributes and, hopefully, links to similar products. Depending on the nature of the products, elements and values in the description may vary. From this point of view, books are interesting, since each title and version of a book represents an individual product. While some readers are only interested in the experience with the content, others may want to obtain a particular version of the title, such as translation, leather bounded book or illustrated edition. Metadata should describe both of two natures

E. Garoufallou et al. (Eds.): MTSR 2017, CCIS 755, pp. 160–166, 2017.
https://doi.org/10.1007/978-3-319-70863-8_15

of the book and help readers to find a work and version that suits them best. Unfortunately, not much is known of which book information is actually available in online bookstores. In our study, we wanted to fill this gap and examine a presence and form of book metadata in online bookstores.

2   Book Metadata and Online Bookstores

Since the invention of the printing press, approximately 150 million of different book titles have been published worldwide [3]. In the online environment and in the flood of different titles, a book without an appropriate description is indiscoverable [4]. Libraries have a good practice in describing books by using well-established metadata standards, such as MAchine-Readable Cataloging (MARC). However, the current use of library catalogues is relatively low [5] as they lack the needed data and are difficult to use [6]. Therefore, people are searching for books on other book-related websites, including online bookstores. The advantage of these platforms is their capability to offer a rich set of metadata, which does not only display an appealing book description but also offer additional subjective information and information about related products [7].

There is also a connection between good book metadata description and sales [8], therefore publishers and booksellers should make an effort in creating quality and accurate book description. Similar to catalogues, online bookstores should support user tasks such as finding, identifying, selecting and obtaining the resources [9] and to explore related content [10]. Since consumers most frequently discover books by browsing [8], a good textual description should be enriched with connections and information about related products should be provided. There are many guidelines for booksellers on inclusion and quality of book metadata, such as Best Practices for Product Metadata [11] and The Metadata Handbook [7]. Moreover, some organizations award certificates to publishers who deliver good book information [6]. However, actual practice depends on the publisher and is different on various book markets. While in the USA many publishers are aware of the importance of the metadata and therefore use uniform standard ONline Information eXchange (ONIX) [12], on smaller book markets, such as Slovenian, they do not jet resort to the optimal metadata practice [13].

Nevertheless, we still do not know which metadata set booksellers provide to end users and how do this metadata helps to navigate in online bookstores and enable the discovery of new titles. While we have a quite good overview of book information in library catalogues [6, 14] there is a lack of studies on quality of metadata in online bookstores.

3   Research Questions and Methodology

Bookstores may expose different information to the readers. Since browsing is the most common way for people to discover books, we were mostly interested in which metadata allows users to navigate in online bookstores and which of this book information is displayed in the detailed book description page. We wanted to obtain the answers to following research questions:

- What are the most frequent search options in online bookstores?
- Which are the most frequent metadata elements that allow navigation in online bookstores?
- Are the values of navigational elements displayed in the detailed description of a titles?
- What is the ratio between the navigational and descriptive elements in online bookstores?
- What are the differences in presence of book metadata elements between Slovenian and American online bookstores?

For this purpose, we conducted an expert study of 33 Slovenian and 33 American online bookstores as this method allows researchers to quickly and easily analyze characteristics of information systems using a coding scheme. In our sample, we included publishers of fiction who own an online bookstore or a website that enables a book purchase. Furthermore, we selected only online bookstores that already have sufficient book description for identifying specific title and version of the book. Therefore, bookstores in our sample include at least following elements: *author, title, book cover, description, price, identifier* or *year of publication* and *form* or *medium*. Since Slovenia does not have many publishers, we selected every bookstore that meets these criteria, while American publishers where chosen from the *PublishersGlobal* webpage with *Fiction Publishers of United States* filter.

In the next step, we examined various resources, such as *ONIX for Books Codelists* [15], *Best Practices for Product Metadata* [12] and *The Metadata Handbook* [7] and identified 46 metadata elements that are important for finding, identifying and selecting a specific title. After we created a coding scheme, we investigated the presence of each book information element from our list and analyzed it in Microsoft Excel. In our study we examined the presence of book information elements from a user perspective. This means that we were interested in which book information is visible to an online bookstore visitor rather than if it is actually saved in a form of computer-processable metadata.

We evaluated each online bookstore by examining their search options, browse elements and detailed description pages of books and determined the presence of metadata elements from our list. We were also interested in the form of these metadata elements, since book information can be only descriptive or it may appear as a browsing category or internal link to related products. We named the metadata elements that were identified in the detailed description page of *descriptive elements*. Values of these elements serve for identification of the product which can lead to selection of a book. Meanwhile, we identified elements that appear as part of the facets, categories or values that contain internal links as *navigational elements*. These elements may appear anywhere in the online bookstore and allow users to explore, discover and find most suitable book. Individual element may also be marked as *descriptive* and *navigational* at the same time if it appears in the detailed description of a title and contains internal link to related products or additional book information.

Example in Fig. 1 shows that the many elements can be identified in the detailed description of a book. In this case we would identify descriptive elements: *title, binding, date, author, contributors (translator), cover, medium* (Hardcover, Paperback, Kindle), *rating, series, pages, language, publisher, dimensions, identifier* (ISBN), *topics* (categories), *short description, long description, praise, additional author information, customer reviews* and *books by same author.* Values that allow users to navigate and explore similar content are usually "clickable" and therefore also represent navigational elements. In this case these elements are: *author, contributors, medium, series, publisher, topics, books by the same author.*

Fig. 1. An example of descriptive and navigational metadata in online bookstore

In our study we particularly wanted to identify the most frequent navigational elements in online bookstores as they allow users to explore and discover new books. We compared the frequency of these elements with descriptive elements found in the book's detailed description page and examined the differences between Slovenian and American bookstores.

4   Results and Discussion

The results show that not all booksellers in our sample provide efficient tools for searching books. As you can see in Table 1, of 66 online bookstores, only 12 (3 Slovenian and 9 American) allow readers to use advanced search. What is more, 5 of examined websites do not even provide basic search and forces users to browse through the whole collection. Furthermore, only 44 bookstores allow readers to sort results according to their interests. As expected, the most frequent options for result organizing are *Date, Title, Author, Price* and *Popularity.*

From 46 examined metadata elements, Slovenian online bookstores provide on average 21 descriptive elements, while American bookstores display a bit more (24 elements). As we expected, the number of navigational metadata that appear as categories or internal links is even lower. There are approximately 9 metadata elements with this function in Slovenian and 13 in American bookstores. This indicates that the most of the book information is only descriptive.

Overall, in all 66 examined bookstores, *genre* (54), *target audience* (52), *author* (51), *date* (50), *books by the same author* (45), and *series* (45) are the most frequent elements that enable users to browse and navigate through the page. These elements were present in both samples approximately the same. It is also interesting that some of these elements, such as *genre*, *target audience* and *books by the same author* are frequent browse categories, however this information is often not available in a book's detailed description page (Fig. 2). In our opinion, this is not the best approach since this information is not only important to discover new books but also for their identification and potential selection.

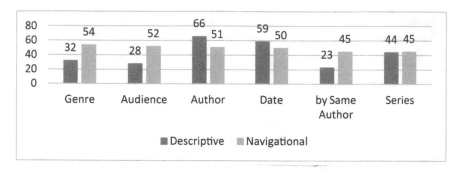

Fig. 2. Most frequent navigational elements

Meanwhile, there is the biggest difference between countries in frequency of navigational elements that represent additional book information and related work. As you can see in Fig. 3 navigational elements *additional author information*, *books on the same topic*, connection to *other formats*, *contributors*, *enriched information* and *other editions* of the same work are more common in the sample of American bookstores. These elements are also usually underrepresented as descriptive elements in Slovenian bookstores. Although differences for other elements are not so great, it is evident that Slovenian bookstores provide less book information in almost every case. There is only one navigational element that appears in Slovenian bookstores and is not so frequent in America. This is the *price* element which is present in 20 Slovenian and 12 American Bookstores. Most frequently it represents discount category on the homepage or is part of the facets.

Table 1. Search options in online bookstores.

Search options	US (33)	SLO (33)	Total (66)
Basic search	30	31	61
Advanced search	9	3	12
Sorting results	24	20	44

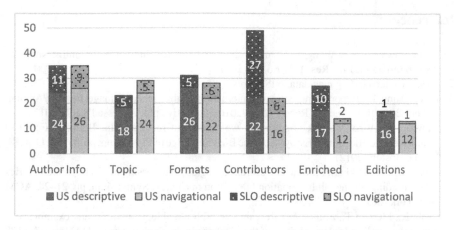

Fig. 3. Descriptive and navigational elements in US and SLO bookstores

Overall, the results show that booksellers could invest more time in creating rich book metadata. By doing so, even smaller publishers and booksellers could benefit and make their titles visible and therefore more competitive in the online environment as good book description can result in better sales [8]. Furthermore, converting descriptive information into computer-processable metadata enables people to discover suitable titles inside online bookstores as well as making them visible to the web search engines. Therefore, more attention should be devoted to adding additional book information, such as topic, target audience, rewards and related work, that would place the title among the online search results.

5   Conclusion

Online bookstores are the most important sources for searching books and discovering new titles. Booksellers should therefore put a lot of effort in creating and maintaining a good book description. The results of our study show that the most metadata in online bookstores is only descriptive. What is more, many online bookstores do not have efficient searching tools and do not provide enriched information, a rich set of categories and connections to related product that would allow users to explore their offer, which is evident especially in the Slovenian sample. We believe that our results could serve as a good starting point for other research on book information. Future research could include online bookstores from other countries and could also benefit from a qualitative approach. Since this study investigated the phenomenon from the user perspective, similar research on computer-processable metadata is suitable. In addition, a user study on the importance of the book metadata is needed, since more book information does not necessary mean a better description. Nevertheless, provided overview of the current situation in this field may be interesting for publishers as well as for librarians, who could get an insight in different practice of creating and displaying book information.

References

1. Katawetawaraks, C., Wang, C.: Online shopper behavior: influences of online shopping decision. Asian J. Bus. Res. 1(2), 66–74 (2011)
2. NISO: Understanding metadata. NISO Press (2004)
3. IPA Annual Report. https://www.internationalpublishers.org/images/reports/Annual_Report_2016/IPA_Annual_Report_2015-2016_interactive.pdf. Accessed 8 July 2017
4. Dawson, L.: What we talk about when we talk about metadata. In: Book: A Futurist's Manifesto: A Collection of Essays from the Bleeding Edge of Publishing, pp. 47–55. O'Reilly Media, Boston (2012)
5. Mikkonen, A., Vakkari, P.: Readers' search strategies for accessing books in public libraries. In: Proceedings of the 4th Information Interaction in Context Symposium, pp. 21–24. ACM, New York (2012)
6. Švab, K., Merčun T., Žumer, M.: Researching bibliographic data with users: examples of 5 qualitative studies. In: Proceedings of the Libraries in the Digital Age (LIDA), pp. 171–178. University of Zadar, Zadar (2014)
7. Register, R., McIlroy, T.: The Metadata Handbook. Datacurate, Columbus (2015)
8. Walter, D.: Nielsen Book UK Study: The Importance of Metadata for Discoverability and Sales. Nielsen Book Services Ltd. (2016)
9. Functional Requirements for Bibliographic Records: Final Report. K.G. Saur, Munich (1998)
10. Zeng, M., Žumer, M., Salaba, A.: Functional requirements for subject authority data (FRSAD). De Gruyter Saur, Berlin (2011)
11. Best Practices for Product Metadata: Guide for North American Data Senders and Receivers. Book Industry Study Group (2015)
12. EDItEUR. http://www.editeur.org/154/Users-and-Services-directory/. Accessed July 2017
13. Breznik Močnik, M., Trplan, T., Milohnić, A.: Model razvoja e-založništva v javnem interesu v Sloveniji ter primerjava s stanjem in podatki iz primerljivih evropskih držav. Ljubljana, Mirovni Inštitut (2013)
14. Pöntinen, J., Vakkari, P.: Selecting fiction in library catalogs: a gaze tracking study. In: Aalberg, T., Papatheodorou, C., Dobreva, M., Tsakonas, G., Farrugia, Charles J. (eds.) TPDL 2013. LNCS, vol. 8092, pp. 72–83. Springer, Heidelberg (2013). http://doi.org/10.1007/978-3-642-40501-3_8
15. ONIX for Books Codelists: http://www.editeur.org/files/ONIX%20for%20books%20-%20code%20lists/ONIX_BookProduct_Codelists_Issue_37.html. Accessed 7 July 2017

Collaborative Approach to Developing a Multilingual Ontology: A Case Study of Wikidata

John Samuel[✉]

CPE Lyon, Université de Lyon, Lyon, France
john.samuel@cpe.fr

Abstract. Last several years have seen the growing shift towards collaborative development of ontologies. Collaborative ontology development has become important particularly for large-scale projects involving multilingual contributors from different countries. Collaborators propose, discuss, create and modify ontologies and this whole process must be understood. In this article, Wikidata has been taken as an example to understand how community-driven approach is used to develop a multilingual ontology and in the subsequent building of a knowledge base.

1 Introduction

Ontology development is an important step for building a knowledge base and requires continuous feedback from domain experts and key players. Much recently, its development has shifted towards a community driven approach permitting collaborative authoring [3, 6, 7] especially, by those involved. But collaborative development is not easy to achieve and it becomes much more difficult when the goal is to build a multilingual ontology.

A major example of such a collaborative development and subsequent building of knowledge base is Wikidata[1]. Wikidata [9] is open, multilingual, free, collaborative, linked, multilingual and structured data store started in 2012. Like its sister project Wikipedia, it is also a community-driven project managed by thousands of contributors and bots around the world creating, editing and deleting numerous articles. This community-driven approach distinguishes it significantly from another similar project, DBpedia [1]. It is therefore very important to understand the overall process of building an ever-evolving Wikidata ontology targeting several domains.

Section 2 gives an overview of Wikidata and briefly presents how key elements of Wikidata are represented. It also presents a brief comparison to DBpedia focusing on the major differences between representing such information. The process of building a multilingual ontology is described in Sect. 3. We then focus on how domain-specific ontologies are built. We briefly discuss how structured data can be extracted from Wikipedia and fed to Wikidata. Finally Sect. 4 concludes the article.

---

[1] https://www.wikidata.org/.

© Springer International Publishing AG 2017
E. Garoufallou et al. (Eds.): MTSR 2017, CCIS 755, pp. 167–172, 2017.
https://doi.org/10.1007/978-3-319-70863-8_16

2   Wikidata

Wikidata has two types of pages: item pages and property pages. An item is identified by a number with a data format like $Q[1-9][0-9]*$, i.e., Q followed by a number. Similary a property has an identifier of the form $P[1-9][0-9]*$, i.e. P followed by a number. An item page describes an entity with a number of statements describing it. Example items include Douglas Adams (Q42), Wikidata (Q2013) etc. Examples of properties are 'instance of' (P31), 'subclass of' (P279). A statement is a triple; the item in question is the subject, followed by a property and a value. A property of an item may have multiple values. However, each such value along with the item and the property identifier form a single statement. Property values may be a constant (like a number) or identifier of another item. Every statement may be supported by one or more references. References include sources like the corresponding Wikipedia page, books, web pages etc. Additionally, a statement may have qualifiers, that are additional properties used along with a property, for example property 'height' (P2048) requires additional properties like units (P2237). Since items and properties are only identified by their identifiers, users can chose any language and item is described in the chosen language. Figure 1 shows a screenshot of the URL[2]. Every item page optionally has links to associated Wikipedia pages of different languages (see right hand side of Fig. 1).

Property pages are similar to item pages and are displayed in similar manner. A property is also described by a number of statements, the key statement being the allowed data type of the property values. Example property 'instance of' (P31)[3] is shown in Fig. 2. Every property and every item has a label, description and a number of aliases in every language supported by Wikipedia. These values

Fig. 1. Wikidata page for Wikidata (Q2013)

---

[2] https://www.wikidata.org/wiki/Q2013.
[3] https://www.wikidata.org/wiki/Property:P31.

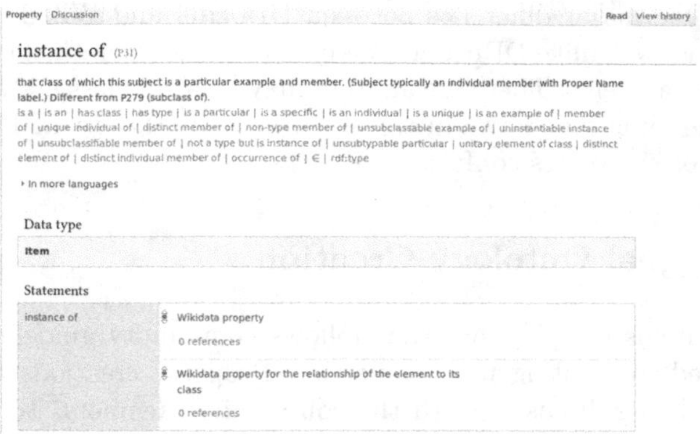

Fig. 2. Wikidata page for Property 'instance of'(P31)

are defined by the community members. An alias is another name for an item (or a property) in the respective language. Together, they are useful to build a multilingual user interface of Wikidata.

From the user interface, users can search for items and properties using labels, description and aliases and search results include the pages matching search queries. Similarly, while editing an item (or a property page) for adding a new statement or modifying an existing statement, the interface provides suggestions as user types in label (or aliases) and the user can choose the appropriate property (as shown in Fig. 3).

Properties may have constraints like distinct values constraints, allowed qualifiers constraint, type constraint etc. Some of the property constraints are not strictly followed, but data type and format constraint violations are not allowed. A detailed discussion on items[4] and properties[5] can be found on their talk pages. Like Wikipedia, there is historical information about all the edits made on a property or an item page. Wikidata also has several import and export options, thereby allowing users to get the complete Wikidata dump or use the query service[6] to selectively download a subset of data. Data formats like RDF, JSON, CSV, JSON-LD etc. are available. Note that these data-dumps are

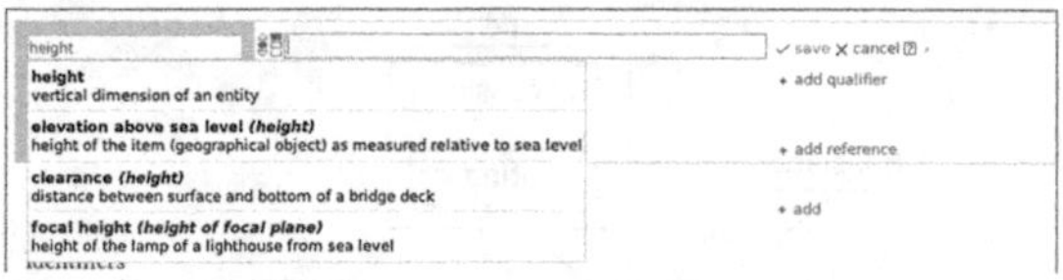

Fig. 3. Wikidata edit suggestions as user types 'height' on English user interface

---

[4] e.g., https://www.wikidata.org/wiki/Talk:Q2013.

[5] e.g., https://www.wikidata.org/wiki/Property_talk:P2302.

[6] https://query.wikidata.org/.

multilingual. One major difference between DBpedia and Wikidata is the way they handle classes. Unlike DBpedia, Wikipedia considers both classes and associated instances as items. Therefore an item may be a subclass (P279) of another item and at the same time be an instance (P31) of another item. This flexibility, though useful often creates confusion.

3   Multilingual Ontology Creation

Creating new items on Wikidata that follows community guidelines are much easier compared to creating new properties. Property creations and deletions are done after being discussed with the community members. To create a new property, a user must propose the property on a specific project proposal page[7]. The community member must choose an appropriate topic of the property (for e.g., person, event, sports, creative work etc.). Once the topic is chosen, the member must describe the new property, its data type (string, external identifier, integer, URL etc.), domain, examples, planned use etc. With the required values, the project proposal is put to discussion, whereby members have the option to support, oppose or ask for clarification etc. If there is enough support (though, there is no fixed number of votes), administrators finally create the new property and announce its creation to the community members. Entire process of property proposal to its final creation may take days, weeks or even months.

Despite its multilingual nature, property creation and discussion is usually carried out in English (however with options to get the discussion translated). Once a property has been identified by an identifier, community members label and describe it in different languages. Property statements and constraints are gradually added. As described above, Wikidata is also part of the linked, open data. Therefore, there are special properties that are identifiers to external data sources like Freebase, DBpedia, Twitter etc. New external identifers are added based on community suggestions with the same procedure described above.

Properties may have short life span, i.e., there are chances that a property can be removed. Community members can ask for property removal[8]. Figure 4 shows the major steps of property creation and removal in Wikidata.

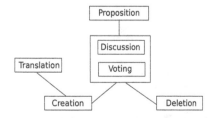

Fig. 4. Major steps of a Wikidata property creation or deletion

---

[7] https://www.wikidata.org/wiki/Wikidata:Property_proposal.
[8] https://www.wikidata.org/wiki/Wikidata:Properties_for_deletion.

Wikipedia infoboxes contain structured data and they have been used for a very long time for representing key information of different domains or topics (e.g., historical building, person, city, country etc.) Infoboxes contains property-value pairs. DBpedia that imported structured data from Wikipedia (infoboxes) made use of infobox properties [2] by creating (or performing appropriate mapping) new properties, as and when needed; a significant part of the process was automatic. But Wikidata doesn't permit this automated approach to property creation. Hence, one major limitation with the community-driven approach is the slow creation of new properties.

There are several domain-specific projects[9], where domain experts discuss to create properties for their respective domains. Nevertheless, these properties (in every language) need to be appropriately mapped to a Wikidata property (identifier). The main goal of Wikidata projects is to map the infobox properties to Wikidata properties and to identify whether new properties need to be created. The task is difficult when mappings between infoboxes different languages is unknown. Wikidata provides several online tools like HarvestTemplates[10] to extract structured infobox data from Wikipedia and feed them to Wikidata. But without correct mapping, it is difficult to fully automate the extraction of structured data from Wikipedia pages of all languages.

Collaborative ontology development [3,4,6,8] has been a research focus during the last few years. A community-driven approach from the ontology creation to feeding the knowledge base is explored [5,7] to understand community contribution to various aspects of a knowledge base. Nevertheless, contributions in the form of multilingual edits is still left unexplored.

4   Conclusion

Community-driven approach of Wikidata for ontology development is one of its key distinguishing characteristics compared to other similar projects like DBpedia. Despite some recent studies on collaborative approaches to ontological development, the multilingual aspects of ontology development have been overlooked. The development process of a new property in Wikidata consists of major steps like its proposition by a Wikidata contributor, community discussion and an eventual voting, creation of the property by Wikidata administrators and finally its translation to other languages. This article presented an overview of ontological development in Wikidata as part of an ongoing work to fully understand this development process.

References

1. Auer, S., Bizer, C., Kobilarov, G., Lehmann, J., Cyganiak, R., Ives, Z.: DBpedia: a nucleus for a web of open data. In: Aberer, K., et al. (eds.) ASWC/ISWC -2007. LNCS, vol. 4825, pp. 722–735. Springer, Heidelberg (2007). https://doi.org/10.1007/978-3-540-76298-0_52

---

[9] https://www.wikidata.org/wiki/Category:WikiProjects.

[10] https://tools.wmflabs.org/pltools/harvesttemplates/.

2. Auer, S., Lehmann, J.: What have innsbruck and leipzig in common? Extracting semantics from wiki content. In: Franconi, E., Kifer, M., May, W. (eds.) ESWC 2007. LNCS, vol. 4519, pp. 503–517. Springer, Heidelberg (2007). https://doi.org/10.1007/978-3-540-72667-8_36

3. Francescomarino, C.D., Ghidini, C., Rospocher, M.: Evaluating wiki collaborative features in ontology authoring (extended abstract). In: Mendling, J., Rinderle-Ma, S. (eds.) Proceedings of the 7th International Workshop on Enterprise Modeling and Information Systems Architectures, EMISA 2016, Vienna, Austria, October 3–4, 2016, vol. 1701. CEUR Workshop Proceedings, pp. 48–51. CEUR-WS.org (2016)

4. Mihindukulasooriya, N., Poveda-Villalón, M., García-Castro, R., Gómez-Pérez, A.: Collaborative ontology evolution and data quality - an empirical analysis. In: Dragoni, M., Poveda-Villalón, M., Jimenez-Ruiz, E. (eds.) OWLED/ORE -2016. LNCS, vol. 10161, pp. 95–114. Springer, Cham (2017). https://doi.org/10.1007/978-3-319-54627-8_8

5. Müller-Birn, C., Karran, B., Lehmann, J., Luczak-Rösch, M.: Peer-production system or collaborative ontology engineering effort: what is wikidata? In: Riehle, D. (ed.) Proceedings of the 11th International Symposium on Open Collaboration, San Francisco, CA, USA, August 19–21, 2015, pp. 20:1–20:10. ACM (2015)

6. Simperl, E., Luczak-Rösch, M.: Collaborative ontology engineering: a survey. Knowl. Eng. Rev. **29**(1), 101–131 (2014)

7. Strohmaier, M., Walk, S., Pöschko, J., Lamprecht, D., Tudorache, T., Nyulas, C., Musen, M.A., Noy, N.F.: How ontologies are made: studying the hidden social dynamics behind collaborative ontology engineering projects. J. Web Sem. **20**, 18–34 (2013)

8. Tonelli, S., Rospocher, M., Pianta, E., Serafini, L.: Boosting collaborative ontology building with key-concept extraction. In: Proceedings of the 5th IEEE International Conference on Semantic Computing (ICSC 2011), Palo Alto, CA, USA, September 18–21, 2011, pp. 316–319. IEEE Computer Society (2011)

9. Vrandecic, D., Krötzsch, M.: Wikidata: a free collaborative knowledgebase. Commun. ACM **57**(10), 78–85 (2014)

New Generation Metadata Vocabulary for Ontology Description and Publication

Biswanath Dutta[1](✉), Anne Toulet[2], Vincent Emonet[2],
and Clement Jonquet[2,3](✉)

[1] Documentation Research and Training Centre (DRTC),
Indian Statistical Institute, Bangalore, India
bisu@drtc.isibang.ac.in
[2] Laboratory of Informatics, Robotics and Microelectronics of Montpellier
(LIRMM) CNRS and University of Montpellier, Montpellier, France
{anne.toulet,emonet,jonquet}@lirmm.fr
[3] Center for Biomedical Informatics Research (BMIR),
Stanford University School of Medicine, Stanford, USA

Abstract. Scientific communities are using an increasing number of ontologies and vocabularies. Currently, the problem lies in the difficulty to find and select them for a specific knowledge engineering task. Thus, there is a real need to precisely describe these ontologies with adapted metadata, but none of the existing metadata vocabularies can completely meet this need if taken independently. In this paper, we present a new version of *Metadata vocabulary for Ontology Description and publication*, referred as MOD 1.2 which succeeds previous work published in 2015. It has been designed by reviewing in total 23 standard existing metadata vocabularies (e.g., Dublin Core, OMV, DCAT, VoID) and selecting relevant properties for describing ontologies. Then, we studied metadata usage analytics within ontologies and ontology repositories. MOD 1.2 proposes in total 88 properties to serve both as (i) a vocabulary to be used by ontology developers to annotate and describe their ontologies, or (ii) an explicit OWL vocabulary to be used by ontology libraries to offer semantic descriptions of ontologies as linked data. The experimental results show that MOD 1.2 supports a new set of queries for ontology libraries. Because MOD is still in early stage, we also pitch the plan for a collaborative design and adoption of future versions within an international working group.

Keywords: Metadata vocabulary · Ontology metadata · Semantic description · Ontology repository · Ontology reuse · Ontology selection · Ontology relation

1 Introduction

Since a few years, we can observe an increasing number of knowledge artifacts [7, 16] or knowledge organization systems [15] that are in use for various semantic applications. Researchers, academicians, practitioners and in general the semantic community across the fields (e.g., computer and information science, medicine, agriculture, economics) are engaged in producing these artifacts (in the rest of the paper these knowledge artifacts are referred with the global term of 'ontologies'). Today, a simple

© Springer International Publishing AG 2017
E. Garoufallou et al. (Eds.): MTSR 2017, CCIS 755, pp. 173–185, 2017.
https://doi.org/10.1007/978-3-319-70863-8_17

Google Search for "filetype:owl" returns around 3.4K results. Hence, this is important to describe ontologies with a high degree of accuracy and consistency to find and select them. And for this purpose, we need properly defined metadata. Metadata will facilitate the manual or automatic search, selection, and elicitation of ontologies. They will allow us to ask various questions on ontologies, for instance, who edited or contributed? When? What methodology or tool was used? Which natural language is used? etc. To describe the ontologies, ontology developers use a variety of metadata vocabularies[1] ranging from general purpose metadata (e.g., DC, DCT, PROV) to dataset specific metadata (e.g., VOID, DCAT, SCHEMA).[2] However, until recently the only ontology specific metadata vocabulary was OMV [4], first published in 2005, which is found to be hardly used by the community. The two main criticisms of OMV are: (i) the current metadata elements primarily allow to capture the provenance information of ontologies, while the other significant aspects, such as development aspect (e.g., curation, evaluation), operational, linguistic, etc. [10] are overlooked; and (ii) it has not reused any other existent relevant metadata vocabularies. Following OMV, in the literature we find a very few studies such as in [3, 8, 9] primarily focused on extending OMV. None of these works address the problems in totality. For instance, the various aspects of ontology descriptions (e.g., ontological relations, community contributions, content-based services) or, the alignment and reuse of other existing metadata vocabularies are not completely exploited. Our earlier work MOD 1.0 (the proposition for Metadata for Ontology Description and publication) in 2015 [2] was a step forward covering some of these limitations. But still there were issues with MOD 1.0 (as discussed in Sect. 2.1). In the current paper, we present our most recent and revised work on MOD (we refer it as MOD 1.2) acquired with the experience of building a brand new metadata model for the AgroPortal ontology repository [5, 13]. The revision carried out from multiple aspects (e.g., new labels, structural changes, and design principles) to overcome some of the limitations of MOD 1.0 and to enrich it further. In the current work, we also describe the application goals of the vocabulary and illustrate our experimental results with queries that can be run on properly defined metadata.

The main contributions of this work are: (1) the analysis of current ontology metadata practices by looking at the currently existing metadata vocabularies and how they are explicitly used by ontology developers and ontology libraries; (2) the introduction of MOD 1.2, a metadata vocabulary which is a new proposition to the community to harmonize and clarify ontology metadata descriptions, and (3) a use-case describing how to exploit MOD 1.2 ontology with a knowledge base consisting of metadata of eight ontologies originally downloaded from AgroPortal (http://agroportal. lirmm.fr) and new types of queries enabled.

The rest of the paper is organized as follows: Sect. 2 discusses the current ontology metadata practices; Sect. 3 discusses MOD 1.2 design methodology and illustrates the

---

[1] In this paper, we will use the word ontology to identify the subject that is described by metadata (e.g., Movie Ontology, Human Disease Ontology, MeSH thesaurus, etc.) and the word vocabulary to identify the objects used to described ontologies (e.g., OMV, DC, DCAT, etc.).

[2] Please refer to column 'prefix' of Table 2 all along the paper for acronyms definitions of metadata vocabularies.

MOD OWL model. Section 4 illustrates experimental results. Finally, Sect. 5 concludes and discusses our proposition for community involvement.

2 Analysis of Current Ontology Metadata Practices

2.1 Analysis of Existing Metadata Vocabularies to Describe Ontologies

Here, we describe the vocabularies that to some extent have been proposed to capture metadata about ontologies or that could be used with this purpose. Capturing the metadata about 'electronic objects' has been the original motivation of the DCMI [14]. The *Dublin Core* (DC) and *DCMI Metadata Terms* (DCT) are the results of these initiatives. Then we can cite the W3C Recommendations such as *Resource Description Framework Schema* (RDFS), *Web Ontology Language* (OWL) and *Simple Knowledge Organization System* (SKOS). Then the *Ontology Metadata Vocabulary* (OMV) produced in the context of several EU projects and published in 2005 [4]. OMV consists of 16 classes, 33 object properties, and 29 data properties. Unfortunately, the initiative stopped in 2007. One of the limitations of OMV was not to be aligned (or reuse) standard vocabularies at that time. This limitation has been partially addressed in our earlier work on the *Metadata for Ontology Description and publication* (now referred as MOD 1.0) [2]. It has been designed as an ontology consisting of 15 classes (mod:Ontology + 10 others + 4 from FOAF), 18 object properties (7 new ones compare to OMV) and 31 data properties. In MOD 1.0, some of the properties from SKOS, FOAF, and DC and DCT have been used and the vocabulary was not relying on OMV. However, MOD 1.0 still missed out numerous relevant properties as discussed later. In 2005, the quite simple but relevant *Vocabulary for annotating vocabulary descriptions* (VANN) was made available and quite used since then. In 2009, the *Descriptive Ontology of Ontology Relations* (DOOR) [1] has been published but never really used outside of the NeON project. It was a very formal vocabulary that described precisely and in a logical manner 32 relations between ontologies organized in a formal hierarchy. More recently, the *Vocabulary of a Friend* (VOAF) [10] was created to "describe vocabularies (RDFS vocabularies or OWL ontologies) used in the Linked Data (LD) Cloud." Although VOAF was developed to capture relations between ontologies, it makes no use or reference to OWL or DOOR (with which it shares a few properties). In 2014, the NKOS working group of the Dublin Core proposed the *NKOS Application Profile* which introduces 6 new properties and reused 22 properties from other vocabularies.

Ontologies share some characteristics with web datasets or data catalogs. In the semantic web vision, ontologies are themselves sets of RDF triplets. We thus argue that some properties that have been defined to describe web datasets are relevant to ontologies also. Among the recent work to describe "datasets," there are the *Vocabulary of Interlinked Datasets* (VOID) [6]. It allows describing two main objects void:Dataset and void:Linkset. *Data Catalog Vocabulary* (DCAT), a most recent W3C recommendation for metadata (and uses DCT), and its profile *Asset Description Metadata Schema* (ADMS), used to describe semantic assets (such as data models, code lists, taxonomies, etc.). Finally, *Schema.org* (SCHEMA) do include a dataset class.

To describe other kinds of resources, one will find the following vocabularies: *Friend of a Friend Vocabulary* (FOAF) or *Description of a Project* (DOAP) to describe documents and projects. The *Creative Commons Rights Expression Language* (CC) for licensed work. SPARQL 1.1 *Service Description* (SD) for describing SPARQL endpoints. And the *Provenance Ontology* (PROV) and *Provenance, Authoring and Versioning* (PAV) for describing provenance (PAV specializes terms from PROV and DCT). OboInOwl mappings [12] which convert OBO ontology header properties to OWL. This is not a standard but some of these properties are handled by the OBO Edit ontology editor, and therefore often used in annotating the ontologies by the ontology developers.

Lessons learned: this review clearly shows that there is a strong overlap in all the vocabularies studied. It shows that no currently existing vocabularies really covers enough aspects of ontologies to be used solely. We also see that despite a few exceptions metadata vocabularies do not rely on one another and redefine things that have already been described several times before (such as dates for which 25 properties are available among the previously listed metadata vocabularies). It is therefore important that a new effort such as MOD 1.2 shall focus on integrating and harmonizing previous ones rather than adding a new one to the list. It is crucial that MOD 1.2 relies on existing metadata vocabularies (preferably official recommendations as we will see later) and also proposes to fusion (and simplify) with the vocabularies that are specific to ontologies (i.e., OMV, MOD 1.0, DOOR, VOAF, VANN) and are not recommendations.

2.2 Analysis of Current Use of Metadata Vocabularies for Ontology Descriptions

To get a sense of the existing metadata vocabularies actually used by ontology developers, we downloaded and manually reviewed 222 OWL ontologies taken randomly from different sources (108 from the NCBO BioPortal (https://bioportal.bioontology.org), 53 from AgroPortal, 61 from searching on Google). We provide here the analysis of the study.

We found 23 ontologies (10%) without any description or annotation. For rest of the 199 ontologies, the number of properties used in describing the ontologies ranging from 1 to 20. For instance, out of the 53 ontologies retrieved from AgroPortal, there are two ontologies having only one metadata for each. There are eight ontologies, for which ten or more properties (and maximum 20) are observed. For rest of the 21 ontologies, the number of metadata per ontology ranges from 2 to 9. The similar trend is observed in ontology descriptions retrieved from BioPortal and the Web. We have also observed in total 32 metadata vocabularies that are being used to describe the ontologies. The 12 most frequently used vocabularies are exemplified in Table 1. Notice that of these most frequently used vocabularies, half of them are W3C or Dublin Core recommended vocabularies. The rest of the other 20 vocabularies form the long tail of the curve with a couple of uses or mostly only once. These include recommended standards (e.g., PROV, SCHEMA), community standards (e.g., VOID, ADMS, DOAP) or very specific vocabularies (e.g., PRISM, EFO, IRON, CITO).

Table 1. Most frequent used vocabularies over a corpus of 222 ontologies.

Prefix	Number	Properties used (number)
dc	294	creator (60), title (51), contributor (34), description (32), rights (20), date (19), subject (15), publisher (14), format (10), identifier (10), license (10), language (9), source (5), coverage (2), issued (1), modified (1), type (1)
rdfs	196	comment (110), seeAlso (23), label (58), isdefinedby (5)
owl	194	versionInfo (105), imports (70), versionIRI (16), priorVersion (3)
oboInOwl	181	hasOboFormatVersion (38), date (35), default-namespace (35), savedBy (31), auto-generated-by (27), namespaceIdRule (3), synonymtypedef (3), hassubset (2), typeref (2), data-version (1), id_space (1), subsetdef (1), treat-xrefs-as-genus-differentia (1), treat-xrefs-as-is_a (1)
dct	105	license (15), modified (15), creator (12), description (12), created (9), issued (8), title (8), subject (6), rights (4), contributor (3), identifier (3), publisher (3), alternative (1), available (1), hasPart (1), hasVersion (1), language (1), lastModified (1), type (1)
skos	27	definition (8), altLabel (6), prefLabel (6), editorialNote (4), historyNote (2), changeNote (1)
vann	21	preferredNamespacePrefix (11), preferredNamespaceUri (10)
cc	12	license (12)
protege	11	defaultLanguage (11)
dcat	9	landingpage (5), downloadURL (2), contactPoint (1), mediaType (1)
foaf	5	primaryTopic (2), homepage (1), maker (1), page (1)
pav	5	version (5)
void	5	subset (2), dataBrowse (1), dataDump (1), sparqlEndpoint (1)

The readers may also refer here [11] for a similar study consisted of a corpus of total 23 RDFS/OWL metadata vocabularies which came to comparable conclusions.

Lessons learned: (1) most of all these 32 vocabularies are general in purpose. The metadata vocabularies which were especially proposed with the purpose of annotating/describing ontologies (e.g., OMV, DOOR), are completely absent from the selected sample of our study; (2) two vocabularies among the most used (oboInOwl and protege) are present because they are automatically included in ontologies by ontology development softwares. We can see that rdfs:comment, owl:versionOf and owl:imports are the most frequently used metadata elements. The reason could be because of their ready availability in the ontology editors. For instance, a selected set of metadata elements from RDFS and OWL are made readily available in Protégé annotation tab which is quite handy; (3) multiple properties capture the same information. For example, in providing the name of the ontology, some have used dc: license, while some other have used cc:license; (4) there is a confusion between the use of DC and DCT as the latter includes and refine the 15 primary properties from the former;[3] (5) generic properties such as rdfs:comment or dc:date are used over more specific ones such as dc:description or dc:created/modified, respectively.

2.3 Analysis of Metadata Representation Within Ontology Repositories

We have studied some of the most common ontology libraries and repositories available in the semantic web community to understand: (i) how they are dealing with ontology metadata; and (ii) to which extent they rely on previously analyzed metadata vocabularies. We have explicitly reviewed: repository or portals including the NCBO BioPortal, Ontobee (www.ontobee.org), EBI Ontology Lookup Service (www.ebi.ac. uk/ols), MMI Ontology Registry and Repository (https://marinemetadata.org/orr), the ESIP Portal (http://semanticportal.esipfed.org), AberOWL (http://aber-owl.net/). Registries or catalogs including the OKFN Linked Open Vocabularies (http://lov.okfn. org), OBO Foundry (www.obofoundry.org), WebProtégé (http://webprotege.stanford. edu), VEST/AgroPortal Map of Standards (http://vest.agrisemantics.org), and BioSharing (https://biosharing.org).

Lesson learned: We have reviewed the metadata properties captured by all these libraries. The NCBO BioPortal which uses 66 metadata properties and partially reuse OMV served as reference as it was also our baseline when implementing a new metadata model with AgroPortal [5, 13], before MOD 1.2. We observe that each of the reviewed libraries uses, to some extent, some metadata elements but do not always use standard metadata vocabularies. For a recent review of ontology libraries and their metadata, the readers might also refer to [2] where we showed that ontology metadata vocabularies are rarely used by ontology libraries: 4 ontology libraries over the 13 studied have partially used the OMV.

3   Presentation of MOD 1.2

3.1   Design Methodology

From our previous reviews and analysis, we have come up with a list of 88 properties forming MOD 1.2 vocabulary (whereas MOD 1.0 offered 25) that would capture the information about an ontology. The criteria for inclusion were the following, consider by order of importance:

1. Relevance for describing an ontology – the property may have a sense if used to describe an ontology. For this purpose, we prepared a list of queries (aka competency questions) considering the varieties of use scenarios (or, tasks), for instance, an application developer searching for an ontology to use in an application he is developing, a user making a survey to find the existence of ontologies in his domain of interest, and an ontology developer searching for an ontology that he can refer as a gold standard to evaluate his ontology.

---

[3] http://wiki.dublincore.org/index.php/FAQ/DC_and_DCTERMS_Namespaces.

2. Semantic consistency – there must not be any conflict (e.g., disjoint classes) if someone would describe an ontology with all the listed properties. For instance, an ontology may be of type omv:Ontology, foaf:Document, owl:Ontology, prov:Entity.
3. Being included in a W3C or Dublin Core recommendation.
4. The frequency of use as found in the study presented in Sect. 2.2.
5. Priority to vocabularies specific for ontologies rather than to the ones specialized for the more general objects (cc:Work, dcat:DataSet, sd:Service, etc.).

From each of these vocabularies, we have selected the significant properties to describe objects where an ontology could be considered a certain type of e.g., dataset, an asset, a project or a document. For instance, an ontology may be seen as a prov:Entity object and then the property prov:wasGeneratedBy may then be used to describe its provenance. From RDFS and OWL, we have reviewed properties that can be used to describe rdfs:Resource, and owl:Ontology. From RDFS, we selected only one property rdfs:comment, whereas we considered the properties rdfs:seeAlso and rdfs:label are better represented by other properties. For instance, rdfs:label is better represented by dct:title. From OWL, we selected all the considered properties. From Dublin Core (assuming the domain of its properties is rdfs:Resource), we have selected 28 properties giving priority to DCT. From OMV, we have considered all the 37 properties for omv:Ontology but selected in MOD 1.2 only 20 as others can be represented by other properties matching more of our criteria. In a similar way, we have selected the number of properties from the other vocabularies as indicated in Table 2. Out of the total considered 244 properties (column #C) from 23 vocabularies, MOD 1.2 consisted of 88 properties (column #S) from 11 vocabularies, which includes 13 properties defined (Table 3) in mod namespace.

Table 2. Vocabularies studied and used within MOD 1.2. R column states if it is a W3C or DC recommendation (R) or note (N), or none of the two (blank). Colon (#S) is the number of property selected in MOD1.2 from this vocabulary. Colon (#C) is the number of property considered that are either selected or considered equivalent of another selected one.

Prefix	Namespace	Name	R	#S	#C
adms	http://www.w3.org/ns/adms#	Asset Description Metadata Schema	N	0	9
cc	http://creativecommons.org/ns#	Creative Commons Rights Expression Language		0	3
dc	http://purl.org/dc/elements/1.1/	Dublin Core	R	0	4
dcat	http://www.w3.org/ns/dcat#	Data Catalog Vocabulary	R	11	15
dct	http://purl.org/dc/terms/	DCMI Metadata Terms	R	18	34
doap	http://usefulinc.com/ns/doap#	Description of a Project		3	11
door	http://kannel.open.ac.uk/ontology#	Descriptive Ontology of Ontology Relations		0	6
foaf	http://xmlns.com/foaf/0.1/	Friend of a Friend Vocabulary	N	5	10
idot	http://identifiers.org/idot/	Indentifiers.org		0	4
mod	http://www.isibang.ac.in/ns/mod#	Metadata for Ontology Description & Publication 1.0		13	25

(*continued*)

Table 2. (*continued*)

Prefix	Namespace	Name	R	#S	#C
nkos	http://w3id.org/nkos#	Networked KOS Application Profile		0	4
oboInOwl	http://www.geneontology.org/formats/oboInOwl#	OboInOwl Mappings		0	4
omv	http://omv.ontoware.org/2005/05/ontology#	Ontology Metadata Vocabulary		20	37
owl	http://www.w3.org/2002/07/owl#	OWL 2 Web Ontology Language	R	7	7
pav	http://purl.org/pav/	Provenance, Authoring and Versioning		2	10
prov	http://www.w3.org/ns/prov#	Provenance Ontology	R	3	9
rdfs	http://www.w3.org/2000/01/rdf-schema#	RDF Schema	R	1	3
schema	http://schema.org/	Schema.org		0	31
sd	http://www.w3.org/ns/sparql-service-description#	SPARQL 1.1 Service Description	R	1	1
skos	http://www.w3.org/2004/02/skos/core#	Simple Knowledge Organization System	R	0	1
vann	http://purl.org/vocab/vann/	Vocabulary for annotating vocabulary descriptions		0	4
voaf	http://purl.org/vocommons/voaf#	Vocabulary of a Friend		4	5
void	http://rdfs.org/ns/void#	Vocabulary of Interlinked Datasets	N	0	7
TOTAL		**23 vocabularies, 12 used**	**12**	**88**	**244**

Table 3. MOD1.2 new created metadata properties (naae = not available anywhere else, ifbp = inspired from BioPortal, povnyi = present in other vocabularies not yet integrated in MOD).

Properties	Definition	Reason for creating
mod:competencyQuestion	A set of questions asked at design time to explain why the ontology is needed and explain its design	naae
mod:group	A group of ontologies that the ontology is usually considered into	naae, ifbp
mod:translation	A pointer to the translated ontology(ies) for an existing ontology	povnyi
mod:rootClasses	The root class(es) of an ontology. This could be automatically populated by taking the direct subclasses of owl:Thing. If the ontology is also defined as a unique skos:ConceptScheme, then this property becomes the equivalent of skos:hasTopConcept	naae
mod:browsingUI	The user interface (URL) where the ontology may be browsed or searched	naae, ifbp

(*continued*)

Table 3. (*continued*)

Properties	Definition	Reason for creating
mod:vocabularyUsed	The vocabularies that are used and/or referred to create the current ontology	povnyi
mod:sampleQueries	A set of queries (may be SPARQL, DL Queries) that are provided along with an ontology to illustrate use cases	naae
mod:ontologyInUse	An ontology that is used in a project.	naae, ifbp
mod:evaluation	An ontology that has been evaluated by an agent	ifbp, povnyi
mod:numberOfObjectProperties	The total number of object properties in an ontology. Refines omv:numberOfProperties	naae
mod:numberOfDataProperties	The total number of data properties in an ontology. Refines omv:numberOfProperties	naae
mod:numberOfLabels	Number of defined labels for any resources in an ontology (classes, properties, etc.)	naae
mod:byteSize	The byte size of an ontology file	naae

3.2 Mod 1.2

MOD 1.2 is defined in OWL with the namespace http://www.isibang.ac.in/ns/mod#. Figure 1 provides a representation of the model in terms of its main classes, object & data properties, including the constraints on its primary class mod:Ontology. The OWL file and versions are publicly available (https://github.com/sifrproject/MOD-Ontology).

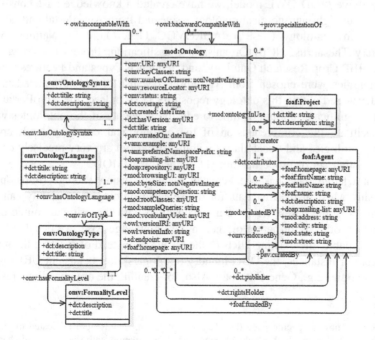

Fig. 1. A snapshot of MOD 1.2 (a complete diagrammatic representation is available here https://github.com/sifrproject/MOD-Ontology).

Classes: MOD 1.2 consists of 19 classes (where a class is a collection of things sharing common attributes) including three subclasses. The classes are derived by analyzing the selected properties and identifying the reusable ontological resources. Some of the exemplary classes (and their reusable resources) are mod:Ontology (e.g., Gene Ontology, Disease Ontology), mod:Group (e.g., OBO Foundry or OBO Library), foaf: Project (e.g., Planteome, AgroLD).

Object Property: MOD 1.2 consists of 28 object properties (which connects two resources belonging to two different, or same classes), for instances, mod:evaluatedBy, omv:endoresedBy, mod:ontologyInUse. Each object properties are defined with its domain and range e.g., the mod:ontologyInUse has a domain class mod:Ontology and a range class foaf:Project. An object property can have more than one domain and range.

Data Property: MOD 1.2 consists of 60 data properties (which connects a resource to a literal) to describe ontologies, for instances, omv:URI, mod:competencyQuestion, mod: sampleQueries. Besides, there are 9 other properties (e.g., foaf:name) included to facilitate the description of the related resources such as, foaf:Agent. Each data properties is specified with its domain and range. For instance, property mod:competencyQuestion has a domain class mod:Ontology and a range xsd:string. A data property can have more than one domain.

4   Illustration of Experimental Results

Using the above MOD OWL model, we have created a knowledge base consisting of metadata about eight agronomical ontologies selected from AgroPortal and defined as instance of omv:Ontology These are AGROVOC, Gene Ontology, National Agricultural Library Thesaurus, NCBI Organismal Classification, Protein ontology, AnaEE Thesaurus, IBP Crop Research Ontology, and Sequence Types and Features Ontology. These ontologies were chosen from AgroPortal because of the new metadata model recently developed within this ontology repository [13]. Indeed, the AgroPortal's team has spent a significant amount of time to edit the metadata of the ontologics with the goal to facilitate the comprehension of the agronomical ontology landscape [5].[4] Therefore, ontologies and vocabularies within AgroPortal are very precisely described still with another set of properties not yet aligned with MOD.

The knowledge base has been created manually using Protégé (https://protege. stanford.edu). Most of the metadata for the selected ontologies originally came from AgroPortal. In some cases, we have also consulted with the original source of those ontologies and other information online. In the knowledge base, we decided to reuse, wherever available, the existing URIs of the resources instead of creating them in mod namespace. For instances, the OBO foundry ontologies offer persistent URLs for each of their ontologies e.g., Gene Ontology. Also, for creating the organizational resources,

---

[4] AgroPortal has now a specific page (http://agroportal.lirmm.fr/landscape) dedicated to visualizing this landscape. It displays highly valuable synthetized information with diagrams and charts about the ontologies in agriculture. This was made possible by the new metadata model.

we have preferred to use DBPedia defined URIs. In the case of unavailability, we have used the organizational homepage URL as the resource URI. Similarly, in the case of people, we have preferred to use the ORCID IDs as URIs. In the case of unavailability, or any kind of ambiguity, we have created the resources in mod namespace. For language, we have used Lexvo vocabulary (www.lexvo.org). The same approach is followed for creating the other related resources, for examples, licensing (https:// creativecommons.org), vocabulary formality level (OMV), ontology types (http://w3id. org/nkos/nkostype), projects, and so forth. The current knowledge base consists of in total 1962 axioms, 20 classes, 33 objects and 69 data properties, and 217 individuals. The knowledge base is available and can be downloaded from https://github.com/ sifrproject/MOD-Ontolog with the main MOD 1.2 file.

The knowledge base supports the varieties of new queries, for instance, which is the most popular ontology editing tool? Who are the key contributors in a domain? How many ontologies are produced by OBO Foundry group? What are the projects using the Protein Ontology? *What are the ontologies endorsed by the RDA Wheat Data Interoperability Group (RDA WDI) and the National Science Foundation (NSF)?* These queries were expressed in SPARQL and successfully run over the knowledge base. The above *italicized* query is shown below. It returns the title and the creator of the ontologies endorsed by RDA WDI and NSF. A couple of such sample SPARQL queries are also available on GitHub.

```
SELECT DISTINCT ?Ontology ?Author
   WHERE {
       { ?x a mod:Ontology; omv:endorsedBy <https://www.rd-alliance.org/groups/wheat-
data-interoperability-wg.html> ; dct:title ?Ontology .}
   UNION
       { ?x a mod:Ontology; omv:endorsedBy
<http://dbpedia.org/resource/Category:National_Science_Foundation> ; dct:title
?Ontology .}
       OPTIONAL { ?x dct:creator ?Author .} }
```

Furthermore, our future goals are: (i) to automatize the process of creating mod: Ontology instances using the application programming interfaces of the main ontology libraries (e.g., BioPortal, AgroPortal, OBO Foundry). This will enable to export the content of these libraries without doing any change to their internal data models; (ii) to release knowledge base as Linked Open Data consisting of metadata for ontologies covering a significant amount of ontologies; and (iii) to offer a SPARQL endpoint to provide local and remote advanced queries on the knowledge base.

5   Conclusion and Proposition for Community Involvement

From our study and analysis (Sect. 2), we have seen that so far, the only ontology metadata vocabulary OMV (until the recent publication of MOD 1.0 in 2015) published in 2005 could make a very little impact on the community at least in terms of its use. According to us, among the main limitations of OMV that might explain why it is not really adopted today are: (i) it did not reuse any other existent relevant metadata vocabularies; (ii) it was never included in a common ontology editor like Protégé. It would have highly facilitated the adoption of the vocabulary if ontology editors would have had only to fill out a few forms directly in their preferred ontology edition software; (iii) the metadata properties were never really used and valorized by ontology libraries which would have been the best way to incite to fill them up; (iv) after 2009, there was no update and the development team has become less active.

MOD 1.2 is an initiative, a joint effort from ISI and LIRMM, which attempts to overcome some of the limitations of OMV and overall proposes a solution which shows the promises of satisfying the community needs for describing the ontologies from multiple aspects (e.g., provenance, developmental, linguistic, community). However, MOD 1.2 is still a temporary proposition. It is understandable that to achieve community adoption, this work needs to engage more people, with the ultimate goal of producing a community standard endorsed by a standardization body such as W3C. One of our objectives is to introduce MOD 1.2 to the Research Data Alliance recently re-configured Vocabulary and Semantic Services Interest Group (VSSIG - https:// www.rd-alliance.org/groups/vocabulary-services-interest-group.html). This group is a follow-up of the EUDAT Semantic Working Group Workshop from April 2017, where multiple interests on standardizing ontology metadata have been publicly expressed by the major ontology repository developers.

MOD is an open project described on GitHub and ResearchGate, so that the community can view, and participate in the discussions. We envision that the MOD 1.2, currently consisted of 88 properties, in the near future will turn to a collaborative extended version (MOD 2.0). One of our short-term objectives is also to propose an "application profile" for the description of ontologies that will be based on MOD and will serve ontology developers more easily than by creating mod:Ontology instances. Section 2.2 analysis has shown that it is the way adopted by ontology developers.

Acknowledgements. This work is partly achieved within the Semantic Indexing of French biomedical Resources (SIFR – www.lirmm.fr/sifr) project that received funding from the French National Research Agency (ANR-12-JS02-01001), the EU Horizon 2020 research and innovation programme under the Marie Sklodowska-Curie grant agreement No 701771, the NUMEV Labex (ANR-10-LABX-20), the Computational Biology Institute of Montpellier (ANR-11-BINF-0002) as well as by University of Montpellier and the CNRS. This work has also been partially funded by the Indian Statistical Institute under the Start-Up Grant project. We thank the National Center for Biomedical Ontology (NCBO) for latest information about the NCBO BioPortal.

References

1. Allocca, C., d'Aquin, M., Motta, E.: Towards a formalization of ontology relations in the context of ontology repositories. In: Fred, A., Dietz, Jan L.G., Liu, K., Filipe, J. (eds.) IC3K 2009. CCIS, vol. 128, pp. 164–176. Springer, Heidelberg (2011). https://doi.org/10.1007/ 978-3-642-19032-2_12
2. Dutta, B., Nandini, D., Kishore, G.: MOD: metadata for ontology description and publication. In: International Conference on Dublin Core and Metadata Applications, DC 2015, Sao Paulo, Brazil, pp. 1–9, September 2015

3. Fiorelli, M., Stellato, A., McCrae, John P., Cimiano, P., Pazienza, M.T.: LIME: the metadata module for OntoLex. In: Gandon, F., Sabou, M., Sack, H., d'Amato, C., Cudré-Mauroux, P., Zimmermann, A. (eds.) ESWC 2015. LNCS, vol. 9088, pp. 321–336. Springer, Cham (2015). https://doi.org/10.1007/978-3-319-18818-8_20
4. Hartmann, J., Sure, Y., Haase, P., Suarez-Figueroa, M.: OMV: ontology metadata vocabulary. In: Welty, C. (ed.) Workshop on Ontology Patterns for the Semantic Web, WOP 2005, p. 9. Springer, Galway, November 2005.
5. Jonquet, C., Toulet, A., Emonet, V.: Two years after: a review of vocabularies and ontologies in AgroPortal. In: International Workshop on Sources and Data Integration in Agriculture, Food and Environment Using Ontologies, IN-OVIVE 2017, p. 13. EFITA, Montpellier, July 2017
6. Keith Alexander, M.H.: Describing linked datasets - on the design and usage of void, the vocabulary of interlinked datasets. In: Linked Data on the Web Workshop, LDOW 2009, Madrid, Spain, April 2009
7. McGuinness, D.L.: Ontologies come of age. In: Spinning the Semantic Web: Bringing the World Wide Web to Its Full Potential, pp. 171–194. MIT Press (2003)
8. Min, H., Turner, S., de Coronado, S., Davis, B., Whetzel, P.L., Freimuth, R.R., Solbrig, H. R., Kiefer, R., Riben, M., Stafford, G.A., Wright, L., Ohira, R.: Towards a standard ontology metadata model. In: 7th International Conference on Biomedical Ontologies, ICBO 2016, Poster Session, CEUR, Corvallis, Oregon, USA, vol. 1747, p. 6, August 2016
9. Montiel-Ponsoda, E., de Cea, G.A., Suarez-Figueroa, M.C., Palma, R., Gomez-Pérez, A., Peters, W.: LexOMV: an OMV extension to capture multilinguality. In: Lexicon/Ontology Interface Workshop, OntoLex 2007, Busan, South-Korea, p. 10, November 2007
10. Obrst, L., Gruninger, M., Baclawski, K., Bennett, M., Brickley, D., Berg-Cross, G., Hitzler, P., Janowicz, K., Kapp, C., Kutz, O., Lange, C., Levenchuk, A., Quattri, F., Rector, A., Schneider, T., Spero, S., Thessen, A., Vegetti, M., Vizedom, A., Westerinen, A., West, M., Yim, P.: Semantic Web and big data meets applied ontology: the ontology summit 2014. Appl. Ontol. **9**(2), 155–170 (2014)
11. Tejo-Alonso, C., Berrueta, D., Polo, L., Fernandez, S.: Current practices and perspectives for metadata on web ontologies and rules. Metadata Semant. Ontol. **7**(2), 10 (2012)
12. Tirmizi, S.H., Aitken, S., Moreira, D.A., Mungall, C., Sequeda, J., Shah, N.H., Miranker, D. P.: Mapping between the OBO and OWL ontology languages. Biomed. Semant. **2**(S1/S3), 16 (2011)
13. Toulet, A., Emonet, V., Jonquet, C.: Modèle de métadonnées dans un portail d'ontologies. In: 6èmes Journées Francophones sur les Ontologies, JFO 2016, Bordeaux, France, October 2016. Best paper award
14. Weibel, S., Kunze, J., Lagoze, C., Wolf, M.: Dublin core metadata for resource discovery. Technical report RFC 2413, Internet Engineering Task Force, September 1998
15. Zeng, M.L.: Knowledge organization systems (KOS). Knowl. Organ. **35**(2–3), 160–182 (2008)
16. Dutta, B.: Examining the interrelatedness between ontologies and linked data. Libr. Hi Tech **35**(2), 312–321 (2017)

Track on Cultural Collections and Applications

Enriching Media Collections for Event-Based Exploration

Victor de Boer[1,4]([⊠]), Liliana Melgar[2,4], Oana Inel[1], Carlos Martinez Ortiz[3], Lora Aroyo[1], and Johan Oomen[4]

[1] Department of Computer Science, Vrije Universiteit Amsterdam,
Amsterdam, The Netherlands
{v.de.boer,oana.inel,lora.aroyo}@vu.nl
[2] Universiteit van Amsterdam, Amsterdam, The Netherlands
melgar@uva.nl
[3] eScience Center, Amsterdam, The Netherlands
c.martinez@esciencecenter.nl
[4] Netherlands Institute for Sound and Vision, Hilversum, The Netherlands
joomen@beeldengeluid.nl

Abstract. Scholars currently have access to large heterogeneous media collections on the Web, which they use as sources for their research. Exploration of such collections is an important part in their research, where scholars make sense of these heterogeneous datasets. Knowledge graphs which relate media objects, people and places with *historical events* can provide a valuable structure for more meaningful and serendipitous browsing. Based on extensive requirements analysis done with historians and media scholars, we present a methodology to publish, represent, enrich, and link heritage collections so that they can be explored by domain expert users. We present four methods to derive events from media object descriptions. We also present a case study where four datasets with mixed media types are made accessible to scholars and describe the building blocks for event-based *proto-narratives* in the knowledge graph.

1 Introduction

With the recent increase in availability of digital data relevant to humanities researchers, the term *digital humanities* is used to indicate the increased role that digital archives and computational tools play in scholarship. Different tools that cater to the different information needs of these scholars are often associated with specific phases in their research [7,24,25]. Such tools should support exploration of collections in early research phases, but also filtering of material during assembling or building the corpus, and during contextualization and analysis to identify links or commonalities between dataset items. During the process of information extraction and interpretation from such datasets, users identify connections between entities based on their specific domain knowledge. This creates a "narrative chain of events" that explains certain phenomena [27].

E. Garoufallou et al. (Eds.): MTSR 2017, CCIS 755, pp. 189–201, 2017.
https://doi.org/10.1007/978-3-319-70863-8_18

In most cases, the information needed to create such narratives are found in multiple collections that are heterogeneous in form and scope. To this end, many data curation efforts have turned to the principles of the Semantic Web and specifically the practice of Linked Data [5] as they provide key technologies to allow for data integration and re-usability. Linked Data is increasingly used to publish both archival (meta)data and datasets that are the result of curatorial and research activities. Linking such heterogeneous datasets allows for new types of analyses across collections, including event narrative creation.

However, a deeper integration of access to these heterogeneous linked datasets and the real praxis of humanities scholars still remains an open challenge for the field of digital humanities. Datasets often lack the structured metadata needed to identify the necessary links in order to investigate potential building blocks for event narratives. In previous work [2], we introduced the notion of 'proto-narratives', building blocks found in interconnected datasets that can serve as starting points for more elaborate narratives. Such proto-narratives are often based on events. In order to support scholars in making sense of these hetero-geneous data sources during their research by creating narratives, we observe that: (1) at the data level, these collections need to be integrated in a common semantic data model and enriched with event information, and (2) at the func-tionality level, scholars should be able to create their own links between entities and events by using navigation paths and annotations during their browsing and search activities. In this paper we focus on the first aspect, by investigating how we can use linked data principles to publish, enrich and connect heterogeneous datasets. Specifically, we describe:

- A simple and generic data model for connecting heterogeneous media datasets.
- A variety of methods to enrich media collections in such a way that they can be explored by cultural heritage scholars. These focus on identifying *events* and connecting them through shared persons, places and concepts.
- A case study in the context of the DIVE+[1] project where four heterogeneous datasets are enriched and interlinked using the proposed strategies.

2   Existing Data Enrichment Techniques and Modelling

Metadata schemas and vocabularies are key technologies for improving the access to cultural heritage collections and the cross-walks among their objects [4]. In this section we present an overview of existing data enrichment techniques that are further adapted and extended in our method (Sect. 4).

Machine Enrichment includes multi-modal information extraction tech-niques from free text, but also image or video content retrieval technologies. Specifically, Named Entity Recognition (NER) tools (for a review see [16]) typ-ically extract persons and organizations (actors), places, and to some extent temporal definitions from the texts. Such tools can be used to extract entities

---

[1] http://diveplus.beeldengeluid.nl.

from textual transcriptions of media objects (for example OCR'ed text for textual objects or subtitles for videos) or from descriptive metadata fields. Image analysis methods such as [28] or video analysis tools can be used to identify entities of different types in the visual content of media objects. Speech or speaker recognition can furthermore be used to identify entities in audio content.

While NER tools extract named entities such as actors and places with high accuracy, their performance in detecting events is still poor [16,20]. However, Natural Language Processing (NLP) techniques proved to be successful in event extraction tasks for specific domains such as the Biomedical domain [22]. More recently, advances have been made in the cultural heritage domain [26] as well. For the Dutch language, the FROG NLP suite [6] includes functionalities to identify Named Events in Dutch language texts. Such Named Events are denoted with proper names, in contrast to other pipelines that extract parts of sentences based on object-verb occurrences.

Human Computation includes crowdsourcing, but also smaller-scale annotation efforts by experts, games-with-a-purpose or nichesourcing [13]. The common factor here is that for specific enrichment tasks, human annotators outperform machines. This is the case for hard-to-extract entities, but it also depends on the quality of the source material. For example, if OCR'ed text is of low quality, off-the-shelf NER tools have a hard time accurately identifying entities [17], while humans are able to deal much better with the textual errors. Furthermore, since events are difficult to extract by machines, various crowdsourcing approaches have been defined [9,23].

Hybrid Methods combine both machine enrichment and human computation for effective and efficient optimization. Current research [21] showed that the performance of NER tools can be improved by allowing crowd workers to validate and correct their output. Furthermore, hybrid methods have been used for solving complex tasks of linking events with their participating entities [9].

Reusing event metadata. Though not an enrichment technique, a source for events can be existing structured metadata. Some metadata standards do have explicit modelling of events. For example, the LIDO metadata schema [8] allows for representing events as metadata for museum objects. The CIDOC-CRM metadata schema [14] or the Europeana Data Model [15] allow for event-centric modelling of cultural heritage content.

3 The Need for Event-Based Exploration of Collections

During the "Agora" project, historians and computer scientists laid the basis for the concept of *digital hermeneutics*, which couples exploration of cultural heritage collections via browsing tools with the interpretation needs of historians. Essential to *digital hermeneutics* is the concept of *event*, which is the building block of the interpretation process. Events add context to information objects in collections since they consist of the related entities extracted from these media objects (e.g., persons, locations, concepts). When two or more events are related to each other, they start to compose the so-called *proto-narrative*, in which relations can be observed between actors (e.g., F. de Casembroot, in a biographical proto-narrative), types (e.g., battles, in a conceptual proto-narrative), or places (e.g., Shimonoseki, in a topological proto-narrative) [2]. In this way, events are able to connect data and describe the relation between historical events and digital resources or objects [29].

The core of digital hermeneutics is formed by two components: *object-event relationships* and *event-event relationships*. By making explicit relationships between the objects and events, and between the events themselves we can facilitate users in their access and interpretation processes (i.e., in creating narratives) based on objects in online cultural heritage collections.

Several user studies with historians and other humanities scholars have shown the need for events in supporting meaningful browsing of cultural heritage collections, for instance, [1]. Recent studies in the context of the CLARIAH project[2] have also shown that media scholars and other scholars using mixed-media collections require to annotate their sources, which consists in great part of entity identification and linking [24]. Media scholars in these projects have also shown the need to identify media events and their different types (e.g., disruptive media events) [19]. While for concepts, places and persons structured data is often available, for events this is less the case. For this reason, we introduce our method for media data enrichment and event extraction in the next section.

4 A Method for Media Data Enrichment

In this section we present our generic method for connecting heterogeneous media collections, for enabling the explorative search as described above. Each subsection describes a specific step. In Sect. 5, we detail these steps for our specific case study in the DIVE+ demonstrator.

4.1 Collections and Vocabularies

We assume as input a number of collections consisting of Media Objects, curated by the providing institution. These can be text, audio, image, video, or multimedia. Furthermore, we assume that descriptive metadata is available in RDF form or that it can be converted to this format so that we have at least syntactic interoperability in this common data format. The metadata can be textual (descriptions, titles, among others) or other literal values (e.g., numbers) or it can contain values from controlled vocabularies. These can be either in-house vocabularies or can refer to external vocabularies. In these cases, we assume that these vocabularies are available and can be imported in the common framework.

---

[2] https://www.clariah.nl/en/.

4.2   Mapping to Generic Schema

The collection RDF metadata will be defined according to an (RDFS) metadata schema, listing the properties and classes used in that metadata. In order to link the schema-level information of the heterogeneous collections, we establish sub-property relations between the individual collections' properties and that of a generic schema and we do the same for the classes. Because of these relations, queries at the level of the generic schema can use information declared at the level of the individual collections, as outlined in [12].

This generic schema describes basic properties and classes that are to be used for the type of hermeneutical exploration we described above. It should at least contain the classes **Media Object**, **Person**, **Place**, **Concept** and importantly **Event** and properties relating these to each other. Furthermore, it should contain descriptive metadata properties for textual metadata about the media objects (title, description, dates, among others).

We base our generic model on the Simple Event Model (SEM) [18]. This model allows for the representation of events, actors, locations and temporal descriptions. One of its features is that it is a very basic event-centric model, but more complex relations between, for example, events and persons (such as the role that a person plays in an event) can also be expressed. We select this model over other event-models such as the aforementioned CIDOC-CRM or LODE because of its relative small size, flexibility and low ontological commitment, allowing for easy mapping of data with various heterogeneous data models. Furthermore, SEM includes explicit mappings to these models, making it easy to interpret the data integrated at the SEM level using CIDOC or LODE tooling. For a detailed discussion comparing SEM to other event models, we refer the reader to [18]. We furthermore use SKOS[3] to represent concepts from vocabularies and DCTerms[4] for the descriptive metadata of the objects. In order to visualize media objects in a tool, we define two relations to web-accessible resources:

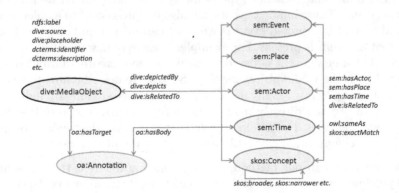

Fig. 1. Graphical representation of the generic data model.

---

[3] https://www.w3.org/2004/02/skos/.
[4] http://dublincore.org/documents/dcmi-terms/.

one for image thumbnails, one for large-sized image or video. We define additional generic relations (`isRelatedTo`) between these persons, places, concepts and objects and extend it with specific relations to relate media objects to entities depicted in the objects (`depicts` and `depictedBy`). Finally, to allow for metadata about user annotations, we use the Web Annotation datamodel[5]. Figure 1 shows the classes in the datamodel as well as properties that hold between them.

4.3 Constructing a Knowledge Graph

Schema-level mappings as described above are not sufficient to establish an explorable graph. For this, we need (a) instances of person, place, concept and event classes for media objects and (b) links between these instances.

Enrichment: Persons, Places, Concepts. Most collections come with structured metadata which includes persons, places and concepts related to collection items. In these cases, the values for these metadata fields are either literal values or RDF Resources from controlled vocabularies. In the first case, to allow for establishing links, these literal values can be converted to RDF resources which have as a label the original literal value. The resource type is mapped to one of the data model classes. This 'promotion' to resource results in a simple vocabulary. In the latter case, the vocabulary is simply loaded together with the object data. In cases where one or more entity types are missing from the original metadata (for example, no Persons, no Places), extra enrichment is needed. Here, we can build on existing strategies as listed in Sect. 2.

Enrichment: Events. As events play a key role for connecting media objects into larger storylines or proto-narratives, extraction of such events is key. For some objects, we can assume one or more events are represented in the content or in the metadata. One way these can occur is through properties denoting events, including object creation timestamps or even start- and end-times. For example in the MADS metadata schema[6], the property *creationDateStart* indicates such a creation event. These implicit events can also be 'promoted' to explicit events. A second type of interpreted event is when we can infer from the type of media object that an event is present. For example, in cases of news media objects, we can infer that a news event is described and therefore create an event resource associated with the media object itself. In Sect. 5, we describe how this is done for radio news bulletins. Finally, for cases where events are already indicated in the metadata, we can directly map them to SEM constructs, resulting in the required event entities. For media objects that lack such identifiable events, we apply human computation and NLP techniques as detailed in Sect. 5.

Hybrid pipeline. In our method, we also combine different strategies into a hybrid pipeline where machines and crowds collaborate in order to extract events and event related entities and find links between them [9]. First, we use various NER tools to extract the set of relevant concepts from object description. We

---

[5] https://www.w3.org/TR/annotation-model/.
[6] http://lov.okfn.org/dataset/lov/vocabs/mads.

reject the notion of majority vote and focus on harnessing the disagreement between different extractors to achieve a more diverse set of entities. In short, we preserve all the entities extracted by every NER tool, disregarding the number of tools that extracted them. Each media object description is then used in a crowdsourcing task where the crowd is asked to highlight events mentioned in the text. The NER and crowd output are then aggregated into a second crowdsourcing task that aims to create links between the detected events and their participating entities. We use the CrowdTruth platform[7] and methodology [3] in order to perform all the crowdsourcing steps and experiments.

Establishing Links. With structured metadata, including persons, places, concepts and events established, there still remains the task of interlinking these entities across the different collections and vocabularies. In some cases, existing alignments between controlled vocabularies exist, where in other cases -especially for the controlled vocabularies constructed in the process of enrichment- these need to be established. Different methods and tools for such alignment exist and include fully automatic tools. We mainly employ a transparent, interactive tool, CultuurLink[8], which allows collection managers and other experts to combine various string matching algorithms to build alignment strategies [10].

5 Case Study: Data Enrichments in the Dive+ Project

In this section we present a case study concerning the DIVE+ platform where we employ and validate the method described above. DIVE+[9] builds on research [2,9] supporting *digital hermeneutics* for historians and media scholars, through connected heterogeneous datasets and vocabularies. DIVE+ uses historical events and event narratives as context for searching, browsing and presenting

Fig. 2. Screenshot showing the current UI of the DIVE+ browser where an event (top) as well as related entities (bottom) are shown.

---

[7] http://crowdtruth.org/.

[8] http://cultuurlink.beeldengeluid.nl.

[9] http://diveproject.beeldengeluid.nl.

cultural heritage collection objects. The interface (Fig. 2) combines Web technology and theory of interpretation to allow for browsing this knowledge graph.

5.1   Four Datasets

We first list the datasets and their accompanying vocabularies. These openly licensed collections are curated by Dutch cultural heritage institutions.

OpenImages.eu broadcasts (OI). This collection is archived by the Netherlands Institute for Sound and Vision[10]. It consists of 3,220 videos published on the Openimages platform[11] from the period 1920–1980. Most of these videos are news items originally shown in movie theaters. For the structured metadata, the thesaurus Gemeenschappelijke Thesaurus Audiovisuele Archieven (GTAA)[12] is used containing 160,000 concepts, places and persons, but no events.

ANP Radio News Bulletins (NB). These are scans of typoscripts which were read aloud on broadcast radio in the period 1937–1984 and are now archived by the Dutch National Library[13]. In DIVE+ we ingested 197,199 digitized typoscripts with their OCR'ed content. The original metadata only contains dates and administrative metadata, but no persons, places, concepts or events. Where the other datasets were available as RDF, for NB we did a straightforward conversion to RDF from the XML output of the OAI-PMH API[14].

Amsterdam Museum collection (AM). This concerns an RDF version of the collection metadata of Amsterdam Museum [11]. It contains 73,447 cultural heritage objects[15]. The collection is described using the Amsterdam Museum Thesaurus, containing some 28,000 concepts, persons and places. It also includes 148 Events. The thesaurus was previously partially aligned with GTAA.

Tropenmuseum collection (TM). This consists of an RDF version of 78,270 cultural heritage objects from the collection of the Tropenmuseum[16] related to ethnological research. The collection is described using the SVCN thesaurus[17], which contains 3,896 places and 13,269 content subjects and was also previously aligned with GTAA. Again, in this thesaurus there are no events identified.

5.2   Mapping Schema

We established schema mapping files for each of the four datasets by inspecting the properties and classes used in those datasets and writing sub-property or

---

[10] http://www.beeldengeluid.nl.

[11] http://openimages.eu.

[12] http://gtaa.beeldengeluid.nl.

[13] http://radiobulletins.delpher.nl/.

[14] This conversion code is available at https://github.com/biktorrr/dive/.

[15] https://www.amsterdammuseum.nl.

[16] https://tropenmuseum.nl/en.

[17] http://svcn.nl.

sub-class links to the common DIVE+ schema as RDF triples. Very few of such links are required: for the three datasets OI, AM, TM, we respectively had to add 3, 12 and 18 sub-property or sub-class triples. For NB no extra triples were needed as these were converted in the scope of the project[18].

5.3   Enrichment and Linking

We here describe for each dataset the types of enrichment performed.

OI enrichment. For OI news videos, some structured metadata in the form of subject relations to GTAA terms existed. However, these do not include events and persons. For these entities, we deployed the hybrid pipeline as described in Sect. 4.3. NER and Event extraction tools for Dutch text are used including the xTas[19] and Opener[20] toolkits. In a second stage, crowdsourcing through the CrowdTruth platform is employed to have human-recognized entities and to refine the results from Natural Language Processing. For the extraction of the News Bulletins, we also use the results of the NER employed by the KB, which is based on the Stanford parser, optimized for Dutch texts. This results in a total of 11,474 individual annotations provided by the human annotators. These include 1,916 unique Events, 1,249 Actors, 1,412 Places and 162 Time annotations. We aligned the newly generated related entities to places, persons and concepts in the GTAA. For this, we used the CultuurLink alignment tool to develop a simple pipeline based on basic string matching. In total, we aligned 452 Places, 171 Actors and 117 Concepts with GTAA.

NB enrichment. To enrich the Radio News bulletins metadata, we used the original publishers' own enrichment services as described in [30], which include NER. At data-conversion time, for each record, we retrieve the content as well as the Named Entities (Person, Place, Organization, Unknown) which were then mapped to DIVE classes. This resulted in 54,571 Places, 197,200 Actors and 6,736 SKOS Concepts. Events are not returned by the NER module, however, here we can use our strategy of interpreting events. As every news bulletin object is actually a description of a newsworthy event, we can deduce that there is at least one event described by the media object. We therefore generate one Event object for each Media Object. The label of this Event object is derived from the OCR'ed description of the Bulletin using simple heuristics[21]. This generated event is then also related to the Actors, Places and Concepts that have been identified in the NER process. The Entities are aligned with GTAA to establish

---

[18] http://data.dive.beeldengeluid.nl/browse/list_triples?graph=http%3A//purl.org/collections/nl/am/am_additions.ttl shows the 12 triples added for Amsterdam Museum. These include mappings of object-image relations, object-entity relations as well as object classes.

[19] http://xtas.net.

[20] http://www.opener-project.eu/.

[21] http://tinyurl.com/diveplusexample2 shows an example event in the DIVE+ UI.

correspondences between the NB and OI datasets. Again, we used the Cultu-urLink tool to establish a simple string-matching based pipeline. This results in 3,223 Places and 3,130 Actor matches.

AM enrichment. For Amsterdam Museum, we already have identified Persons, Places and Events in the collection metadata. We therefore suffice by aligning the thesaurus terms to GTAA. We here reuse alignments between the AM thesaurus and GTAA that were established in [11]. In total this alignment contains 1,500 Place matches 5,301 Actor matches and 64 Concept matches.

TM enrichment. In the Tropenmuseum data and SVCN thesaurus, we find no Events. However, upon inspection, some of the item descriptions contain mentions of events. To identify these, we use the FROG Event extraction to extract named events from those descriptions. This results in 115 relations between Media Objects and Events. In total we find 16 of such Named Events (for example "Day of the Dead" or "Second South-New Guinea Expedition"). These events, as well as the places and concepts in SVCN are aligned with GTAA, again using the CultuurLink tool, resulting in 2,573 alignments.

5.4   Results

These enrichment strategies result in a large knowledge graph. Table 1 summarizes the results of the enrichment process for all datasets as well as the total. Table 2 shows the total number of links between different entity types and events in the whole dataset. These correspond to the building blocks for the exploratory

Table 1. Number of objects resulting from data conversion and enrichment

	Enrichment method	Media objects	Actors	Places	Events	Other
OI	Hybrid pipeline	3,204	1,249	1,412	1,916	185,846
NB	Interpreted + NER	197,200	194,890	54,571	197,200	6,736
AM	Original thesaurus	73,447	66,966	5,973	148	28,047
TM	Original thesaurus + NER	78,226	27,829	3,896	16	13,269
Total		352,077	290,934	65,852	199,264	233,898

Table 2. Links statistics in the total knowledge graph

Subject-Object	Property supertype	Count
Media Object-Event	`dive:depictedBy` or `dive:isRelatedTo`	199,233
Event-Actor	`sem:hasActor`	265,677
Event-Place	`sem:hasPlace`	220,726
Event-Concept	`dive:isRelatedTo`	230

browsing and to the establishment of proto-narratives. The data is stored in a public RDF Triple store[22] and is available at a public GIT repository[23].

6 Discussion and Future Work

In this paper, we showed the need for integrating heterogeneous media collections from a user perspective. To be able to deliver a usable exploratory functionality to our end-users, original collections need to be not only converted, but also enriched with structured metadata. Where existing methods often focus on persons, places, and concepts, we emphasize extraction of events and provided a number of methods to do this. By linking events with objects, persons and places, an interconnected knowledge graph is constructed, which has the required characteristics. Different errors or conflicting extractions can occur both based on automatic extraction, human intervention and in the hybrid method. A discussion on appropriate quality measures and the use of these measures to determine link quality is out of the scope for this paper. However, current work on this is to build on current work on harnessing disagreement [3].

The methodology described in this paper can be used for any heterogeneous cultural heritage linked data collection. We show how we validated this methodology in a specific use case, where we present enrichment statistics as well as explorable paths between entity types. Next steps include evaluation of these paths. For this, we are currently integrating annotation and improvement functionalities in the DIVE+ UI based on continuous user studies with scholars. This will allow for in-browsing crowdsourcing of annotations and corrections, and will provide a way to continuously update and upgrade our knowledge graph. The ability to develop storylines from this interconnected knowledge graph during exploratory search will be evaluated and mediated through the DIVE+ UI. Therefore, this also becomes another enrichment method as part of our methodology.

Acknowledgements. This work was partially supported by CLARIAH (http:// clariah.nl/) and by the Netherlands eScience Center (http://esciencecenter.nl/) DIVE+ project. We furthermore thank Victor Kramer, Jaap Blom and Werner Helmich.

References

1. van den Akker, C., van Nuland, A., van der Meij, L., van Erp, M., Legne, S., Aroyo, L., Schreiber, G.: From information delivery to interpretation support: evaluating cultural heritage access on the web. In: Proceedings of the 5th Annual ACM Web Science Conference, WebSci 2013, pp. 431–440. ACM, New York (2013)
2. Akker, C.v.d., Legêne, S., Erp, M.v., Aroyo, L., Segers, R., Meij, L.v.D., Ossenbruggen Van, J., Schreiber, G., Wielinga, B., Oomen, J., et al.: Digital hermeneutics: agora and the online understanding of cultural heritage. In: Proceedings of the 3rd International Web Science Conference, p. 10. ACM (2011)

---

[22] The triple store can be accessed at http://data.dive.beeldengeluid.nl/.
[23] https://github.com/biktorrr/diveplusdata/.

3. Aroyo, L., Welty, C.: The three sides of CrowdTruth. J. Hum. Comput. **1**, 31–34 (2014)
4. Baca, M.: Practical issues in applying metadata schemas and controlled vocabularies to cultural heritage information. Cat. Classif. Q. **36**(3–4), 47–55 (2003)
5. Bizer, C., Heath, T., Berners-Lee, T.: Linked data-the story so far. In: Semantic Services, Interoperability and Web Applications: Emerging Concepts, pp. 205–227 (2009)
6. van den Bosch, A., Busser, B., Canisius, S., Daelemans, W.: An efficient memory-based morphosyntactic tagger and parser for dutch. LOT Occas. **7**, 191–206 (2007)
7. Bron, M., van Gorp, J., de Rijke, M.: Media studies research in the data-driven age: How research questions evolve. J. Assoc. Inf. Sci. Technol. **67**(7), 1535–1554 (2015)
8. Coburn, E., Light, R., McKenna, G., Stein, R., Vitzthum, A.: LIDO-lightweight information describing objects version 1.0. ICOM International Committee of Museums (2010)
9. de Boer, V., Oomen, J., Inel, O., Aroyo, L., van Staveren, E., Helmich, W., de Beurs, D.: DIVE into the event-based browsing of linked historical media. Web Semant. Sci. Serv. Agents WWW **35**, 152–158 (2015)
10. de Boer, V., Priem, M., Hildebrand, M., Verplancke, N., de Vries, A., Oomen, J.: Exploring Audiovisual Archives Through Aligned Thesauri, pp. 211–222 (2016)
11. de Boer, V., Wielemaker, J., van Gent, J., Oosterbroek, M., Hildebrand, M., Isaac, A., van Ossenbruggen, J., Schreiber, G.: Amsterdam museum linked open data. Semant. Web **4**(3), 237–243 (2013)
12. de Boer, V., Wielemaker, J., Gent, J., Hildebrand, M., Isaac, A., Ossenbruggen, J., Schreiber, G.: Supporting linked data production for cultural heritage institutes: the amsterdam museum case study. In: Simperl, E., Cimiano, P., Polleres, A., Corcho, O., Presutti, V. (eds.) ESWC 2012. LNCS, vol. 7295, pp. 733–747. Springer, Heidelberg (2012). https://doi.org/10.1007/978-3-642-30284-8_56
13. Dijkshoorn, C., Leyssen, M.H., Nottamkandath, A., Oosterman, J., Traub, M.C., Aroyo, L., Bozzon, A., Fokkink, W., Houben, G.J., Hovelmann, H., et al.: Personalized nichesourcing: acquisition of qualitative annotations from niche communities. In: UMAP Workshops (2013)
14. Doerr, M.: The CIDOC conceptual reference module: an ontological approach to semantic interoperability of metadata. AI Mag. **24**(3), 75 (2003)
15. Doerr, M., Gradmann, S., Hennicke, S., Isaac, A., Meghini, C., van de Sompel, H.: The europeana data model (edm). In: World Library and Information Congress: 76th IFLA General Conference and Assembly, pp. 10–15 (2010)
16. Gangemi, A.: A comparison of knowledge extraction tools for the semantic web. In: Cimiano, P., Corcho, O., Presutti, V., Hollink, L., Rudolph, S. (eds.) ESWC 2013. LNCS, vol. 7882, pp. 351–366. Springer, Heidelberg (2013). https://doi.org/10.1007/978-3-642-38288-8_24
17. Grover, C., Givon, S., Tobin, R., Ball, J.: Named entity recognition for digitised historical texts. In: LREC (2008)
18. van Hage, W.R., Malais, V., Segers, R., Hollink, L., Schreiber, G.: Design and use of the simple event model (SEM). Web Semant. Sci. Serv. Agent World Wide Web **9**(2), 128–136 (2011)
19. Hagedoorn, B., Sauer, S.: Getting the Bigger Picture: Exploratory Search and Narrative Creation for Media Research into Disruptive Events. Utrecht (2017)
20. van Hooland, S., De Wilde, M., Verborgh, R., Steiner, T., van de Walle, R.: Exploring entity recognition and disambiguation for cultural heritage collections. Digit. Sch. Humanit. **30**(2), 262–279 (2013)

21. Inel, O., Aroyo, L.: Harnessing diversity in crowds and machines for better NER performance. In: Blomqvist, E., Maynard, D., Gangemi, A., Hoekstra, R., Hitzler, P., Hartig, O. (eds.) ESWC 2017. LNCS, vol. 10249, pp. 289–304. Springer, Cham (2017). https://doi.org/10.1007/978-3-319-58068-5_18

22. Kim, J.D., Ohta, T., Pyysalo, S., Kano, Y., Tsujii, J.: Overview of bionlp'09 shared task on event extraction. In: Proceedings of the Workshop on Current Trends in Biomedical Natural Language Processing: Shared Task, pp. 1–9. ACL (2009)

23. Lee, K., Artzi, Y., Choi, Y., Zettlemoyer, L.: Event detection and factuality assessment with non-expert supervision. In: EMNLP, pp. 1643–1648 (2015)

24. Melgar Estrada, L., Koolen, M., Huurdeman, H., Blom, J.: A process model of time-based media annotation in a scholarly context. In: ACM SIGIR Conference on Human Information Interaction & Retrieval (CHIIR), Oslo (2017)

25. Palmer, C.L., Teffeau, L.C., Pirmann, C.M.: Scholarly information practices in the online environment: themes from the literature and implications for library service development. Technical report, OCLC Research, Dublin, Ohio (2009)

26. Richards, J.D., Tudhope, D., Vlachidis, A.: Text mining in archaeology: extracting information from archaeological reports. In: Barcelo, J., Bogdanovic, I. (eds.) Mathematics and Archaeology, p. 240. CRC Press, Boca Raton (2015)

27. Sauer, S., de Rijke, M.: Seeking serendipity: a living lab approach to understanding creative retrieval in broadcast media production. In: Proceedings of the 39th International ACM SIGIR Conference on Research and Development in Information Retrieval, SIGIR 2016, pp. 989–992. ACM, New York (2016)

28. Schreiber, G., Amin, A., Aroyo, L., van Assem, M., de Boer, V., Hardman, L., Hildebrand, M., Omelayenko, B., van Osenbruggen, J., Tordai, A., et al.: Semantic annotation and search of cultural-heritage collections: the multimedian e-culture demonstrator. Web Semant. Sci. Serv. Agents World Wide Web 6(4), 243–249 (2008)

29. Shaw, R., Troncy, R., Hardman, L.: LODE: linking open descriptions of events. In: Gómez-Pérez, A., Yu, Y., Ding, Y. (eds.) ASWC 2009. LNCS, vol. 5926, pp. 153–167. Springer, Heidelberg (2009). https://doi.org/10.1007/978-3-642-10871-6_11

30. van Veen, T., Lonij, J., Faber, W.J.: Linking named entities in dutch historical newspapers. In: Garoufallou, E., Subirats Coll, I., Stellato, A., Greenberg, J. (eds.) MTSR 2016. CCIS, vol. 672, pp. 205–210. Springer, Cham (2016). https://doi.org/10.1007/978-3-319-49157-8_18

A Semantic Web Case Study: Representing the Ephesus Museum Collection Using Erlangen CRM Ontology

Tuğba Özacar[✉], Övünç Öztürk, Lobaba Salloutah, Fulya Yüksel,
Baraa Abdülbaki, and Elif Bilici

Department of Computer Engineering, Manisa Celal Bayar University,
45140 Manisa, Turkey
{tugba.ozacar,ovunc.ozturk}@cbu.edu.tr,
{lobaba.salloutah,fulya.yuksel,baraa.abdulbaki,
elif.bilici}@ogr.cbu.edu.tr

Abstract. Cultural heritage has recently become an important application area for Semantic Web technologies. Semantic Web technologies and ontologies provide a solution for intelligent integration of heterogeneous data about the cultural heritage. The objective of this paper is the construction of an ontology for the cultural heritage related to Selçuk region in Western Turkey. We use a subset of the Erlangen CRM as our ontology schema, then we populate the ontology with 814 objects in the Ephesus Museum. One of the objectives of this work is to integrate the ontology with other projects which use Erlangen CRM as ontology schema. Therefore, we present an integration case study that aggregates content from Ephesus Museum and British Museum.

1 Introduction

The data about the heritages in museums of Turkey is heterogeneous and fragmented. Worse still, a significant part of data is not digitized. This is a major obstacle to accessing and integrating the information. On the other hand, by its nature, cultural heritage is a domain with very dense interrelations within and between different heritages, which in the current situation are impossible to exploit [1]. The difficulty of finding and relating information in this kind of heterogenous content is an obstacle for end-users. Producing the contents is also another challenge to organizations and communities. Portals like Google Arts & Culture try to ease these problems by collecting content of various publishers into a single site [2].

Semantic Web technologies and ontologies provide a solution for intelligent integration of such heterogeneous information. An ontology provides formal, machine readable, and human interpretable representations of a domain knowledge. [3] discusses current shortcomings in the Semantic Web management of

This research was done while the 3rd, 4th, 5th and 6th authors were undergraduate students at Manisa Celal Bayar University.

cultural resources and future research directions. It specifies that the multidisciplinary nature of analytical data in cultural heritage field requires advanced techniques for optimal data integration and knowledge reuse. The merging and integration of this multidimensional information has the potential to uncover new knowledge about artworks. Semantic Web technologies play a crucial role in improving data integration as well as reasoning over dynamically evolving data via fuzzy inference rules. A major application type of Semantic Web in the cultural heritage domain has been semantic portals [4,5]. These portals often aggregate content from different organizations, thus providing cultural organizations with a shared cost-effective publication channel and the possibility of enriching collaboratively the contents of each other's collections [6].

In this work, we define the inventory records of the Ephesus Museum in a computer readable format using Semantic Web technologies and ontologies. The Ephesus Museum, located near the entrance to the Basilica of St. John in Selçuk/Turkey, displays excavations from the ancient city of Ephesus. The main highlights are two statues of the Ephesian Artemis, frescoes and mosaics. As a basis for the ontology schema, we chose the Erlangen CRM [7], which is an OWL implementation of the CIDOC Conceptual Reference Model [8]. The Erlangen CRM is used by various projects and initiatives, including The British Museum Ontology [9], SWAS (Sharing Ancient Wisdoms) Project [10], Synat Open Platform [11] and WissKI Project [12]. Then we populate the ontology with 814 objects exhibited by the Ephesus museum.

There are several similar works in literature. For example [13] applies linked open data methodologies to Greek vases. [1] compiles the knowledge around the cultural heritage related to Cantabria region in Spain. To the extent of our knowledge, this work is the first attempt to use Semantic Web technologies in a Turkish museum.

This work has three objectives: (a) specify the ontology schema which is a subset of the Erlangen CRM (b) Populate the ontology with class and property instances (c) Integrate the ontology with other projects which use Erlangen CRM as ontology schema. Section 2 represents the Erlangen CRM subset that is used in our work. Section 3 represents the individuals in our knowledge base. Section 4 describes how we define the interrelations between heritages in Ephesus Museum and the ones in the British Museum. Finally, Sect. 5 concludes the paper with summary and future directions.

2   The Ontology Schema

An important contribution of Semantic Web technologies in cultural domain is the CIDOC-CRM ontology. It is a formal ontology intended to facilitate the integration, mediation, and interchange of heterogeneous cultural heritage information. The Erlangen CRM/OWL is an OWL-DL 1.0 implementation of the CIDOC Conceptual Reference Model (CIDOC CRM). In this study, we used a subset of the standard Erlangen CRM ontology as our ontology schema. We identified the Erlangen CRM concepts that will be used in the ontology

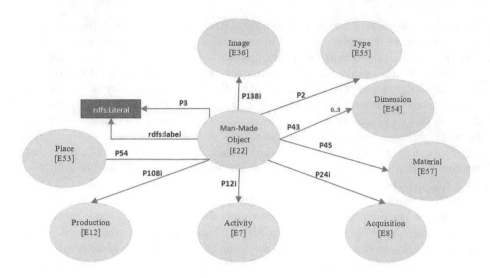

Fig. 1. E22_Man-Made_Object class.

schema according to two factors: (a) the available information of the objects in Ephesus Museum (b) the concepts used in the semantic representation of the British Museum collection. Using these two factors, each object in the museum is defined as an instance of the $E22\_Man-Made\_Object$ in Fig. 1. An instance of $E22\_Man-Made\_Object$ may have the following properties; type, image, material, label, description, dimension, production info, excavation info and acquisition info. The rest of this section presents the definition of each concept in Fig. 1. These definitions are taken from [7].

$E22\_Man-Made\_Object:$ This class comprises physical objects purposely created by human activity. For example: an inscribed piece of rock or a preserved butterfly are both regarded as instances of $E22\_Man-Made\_Object$.

$E38\_Image:$ This class holds the artifacts' images links as they are saved on a local host.

$E57\_Material:$ This class holds the materials consisting the artifacts. This class is a specialization of $E55\_Type$ and comprises the concepts of materials. Instances of $E57\_Material$ may denote properties of matter before its use, during its use, and as incorporated in an object.

$E55\_Type:$ This class holds the type of the artifact. This class comprises concepts denoted by terms from thesauri and controlled vocabularies used to characterize and classify instances of CRM classes.

$P138\_has\_representation$ (represents): This property links the artifacts with their images by establishing the relationship between an $E36\_Visual\_Item$ and the entity that it visually represents.

$P45\_consists\_of$ (is_incorporated_in): This property links the artifacts with their materials. This property identifies the instances of $E57\_Material$ of which an instance of *E18_Physical_Thing* is composed. All physical things consist of physical materials. *P45_consists_of* allows the different materials to be recorded.

P2_has_type (is_type_of): This property links the artifacts with their types. This property allows subtyping of CRM entities through the use of a terminological hierarchy, or thesaurus.

P54_has_current_permanent_location: This property stores the permanent museum location of the object. The range of the property is an instance of the *E53_Place* class. This property indicates the E53 Place currently reserved for an object, such as the permanent storage location or a permanent exhibit location.

P3_has_note: This property is a container for all informal descriptions about an object that have not been expressed in terms of CRM constructs. In particular it captures the characterisation of the item itself, its internal structures, appearance etc.

P43_has_dimension: This property records a *E54_Dimension* of an *E70_Thing* individual. An instance may have 0 to 3 dimensions.

P108i_was_produced_by(P108_has_produced): This property relates an instance of *E24_Physical_Man − Made_Thing* class to an instance of the *E12_Production* class. The instances of the *E12_Production* class stores the actor(s), place and time-span information related with the production process.

P12i_was_present_at (P12_occurred_in_the_presence_of): This property relates an instance of the *E77_Persistent_Item* to an instance of the *E5_Event* class. In our ontology, we used this property to relate an *E22_Man − Made_Object* to an excavation activity. In other words, this property is used to store the information about the excavation in which the object is found. The excavation information contains the actor(s), place (findspot) and time-span information related with the excavation activity.

P24i_changed_ownership_through(P24_transferred_title_of): This property is inverse of *P24_transferred_title_of*, which identifies the *E18_Physical_Thing* or things involved in an *E8_Acquisition*. In reality, an acquisition must refer to at least one transferred item. In our ontology we create an instance of *E8_Acquisition* class to store the acquisition date of an object in the museum. If there is an actor related with the acquisition (for example a person who donates the object to the museum), this is also stored in the *P14_carried_out_by* property of the acquisition instance.

Table 1 summarizes some metrics about the ontology schema.

Table 1. Ontology schema metrics.

# Classes		9
# Properties	# ObjectProperties	8
	# DatatypeProperties	2
Depth of Hierarchy		6

It is also important to note that, all concept and individual names in the ontology are also represented in Turkish. The name of the concept/individual in Turkish is stored using the "rdfs:label" attribute as in the following example (highlighted line):

```
<owl:NamedIndividual rdf:about=
        ''http://erlangen−crm.org/160714/Amulet_of_Female_Figure_2''>
  <rdf:type rdf:resource=
        ''http://erlangen−crm.org/160714/E22\_Man−Made_Object''/>
  <Erlangen CRM:P45_consists_of rdf:resource=
        ''http://erlangen−crm.org/160714/Terracotta''/>
  <Erlangen CRM:P2_has_type rdf:resource=
        ''http://erlangen−crm.org/160714/_amulet''/>
  <Erlangen CRM:P8i_witnessed rdf:resource=
        ''http://erlangen−crm.org/160714/6000−2600_BC''/>
  <Erlangen CRM:P1_is_identified_by>
     <owl:NamedIndividual rdf:about=
        ''http://erlangen−crm.org/160714/4625''>
        <rdfs:label xml:lang=''tr''>4625</rdfs:label>
        <rdf:type rdf:resource=
        ''http://erlangen−crm.org/160714/E42_Identifier''/>
     </owl:NamedIndividual>
  </Erlangen CRM:P1_is_identified_by>
  <rdfs:label xml:lang=''tr''>Amulet Kadın Figürü</rdfs:label>
</owl:NamedIndividual>
```

3   Populating the Ontology

Ephesus Museum exhibits 814 objects, including terrace houses findings, sculptures from the fountains, coins, tomb findings, etc. Ephesus Museum Ontology models these objects as instances of $E22\_Man-made\_Object$ class. All of these instances have the following properties filled in the ontology:

- $P138i\_has\_representation$ (image link)
- $P2\_has\_type$ (type of the object which is compatible with types used in British museum ontology; statue, plate, vase, earring, etc.)
- $P45\_consists\_of$ (material of the object such as bone, bronze, glass)
- $P108i\_was\_produced\_by$ links the object to the instances of $E12\_Production$ class. The instances of the $E12\_Production$ class stores the actor(s), place and time-span information related with the production process. The period of $Production$ (such as Hellenistic, Archaic) is an instance of the $E4\_Period$ class and defines the production period of the object.
- $rdfs:label$ (object name in Turkish)

In addition to the five properties described above, some objects may have the following extra properties: height, width, length ($P43\_has\_dimension$), date of arrival to the museum ($P24i\_changed\_ownership\_through$), permanent location in the museum ($P54\_has\_current\_permanent\_location$), findspot ($P12i\_was\_present\_at$) and description ($P3\_has\_note$) of the object.

The most important class in the ontology is $E22\_Man-Made\_Object$ with 814 individuals. If we ignore the extra properties of the objects with inventory information, then each object has five properties: period, type, material, label and image link. Therefore, we have over 4070 (814x5) property instances in the ontology. The other populated classes in the ontology ordered by their importance (by individual count) are $E4\_Period$ (310), $E55\_Type$ (112) and $E57\_Material$ (24). The total number of class individuals in the ontology is 1260. It is important to note that the number of property instances will be increased as we get the inventory records of the objects in the museum.

4   Integrating Ephesus Museum and the British Museum

In this section, we present a web application to introduce an integration case study that aggregates content from Ephesus Museum and British Museum. The web application provides two main functionalities: (a) querying the Ephesus Museum knowledge base (b) finding the most relevant objects in the British Museum with the selected object from the Ephesus Museum.

Figure 2 shows an example query, which returns all marble objects in the museum knowledge base. User can build a query using the period, type and material fields. These constraints are converted to a Gremlin query and the results are listed on the right of the screen. Each result shows the title and the image of a related object.

User can select and view the details of a result (Fig. 3). In this view, the image and the description of the object are shown on the left of the screen. All remaining properties of the object are listed on the middle part of the screen, including title, dimensions, period, material, findspot and permanent location in

Fig. 2. Querying the Ephesus museum knowledge base.

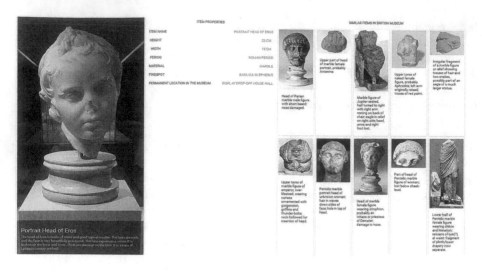

Fig. 3. "Show Details" screen.

the museum. The left and middle parts are the results of Gremlin queries that are sent to Ephesus Museum knowledge base. The right of the screen is used for listing similar objects from the British Museum. The list of these similar objects are obtained using British Museum SPARQL end-point. Then they are ordered from most to least relevant. The order is defined using "Algorithm Relevant_Object_Order", where p is the period, t is the type and m is the material of the object in the Ephesus Museum.

```
ALGORITHM RELEVANT_OBJECT_ORDER ( String p, String t, String m)
//returns the objects in the British Museum ordered by the their
//relevance of the current object c.
//The ordered results are returned in  Map<Key, Value>.
// p is the period of c, t is the type of c, m is the material of c.
//check(List ,obj) returns 1 if the obj is in the List, 0 otherwise
//merge(L_1, L_2, L_3) merges the three lists into one without repetition
//sort(Map<Key, Value>) sorts the elements in the Map by values
//in descending order

List_1= find the objects having period p in the British Museum
List_2= find the objects having type t in the British Museum
List_3=find the objects having material m in the British Museum
List=merge(List_1, List_2, List_3)
for each object obj in List
    weight_of_obj= check(List_1 ,obj)*weight_p + check(List_2 ,obj)*weight_t
                 + check(List_3 ,obj)*weight_m
    Map.Add<obj , weight_of_obj>
sort(Map<Key, Value>)
return Map
```

The knowledge base of the Ephesus Museum is stored in Cayley [14], which is an open-source graph database. Cayley is developed to be used in applications related with Linked Data and graph-shaped data. User interface is developed using Reactjs library [15]. Communication between Web application and Cayley Graph Database is implemented via Gremlin queries. Gremlin [16,17] is a domain specific language for traversing property graphs. This language has appli-

Fig. 4. Architecture of the web application.

cation in the areas of graph query, analysis, and manipulation. Figure 4 shows the architecture of the Web application.

5 Conclusion and Future Work

This work defines the inventory records of the Ephesus Museum in a computer readable format using Semantic Web technologies and ontologies. It also presents an integration case study that aggregates content from Ephesus Museum and British Museum.

One possible future work is to provide both a SPARQL and a Gremlin endpoint that will be used by other developers to integrate Ephesus Museum collection to their applications. Another possible future work is to increase the property count of the objects in the Ephesus museum by discussing domain experts.

To the extent of our knowledge, this work is the first attempt to use Semantic Web technologies in a Turkish museum. Therefore, we aim to extend this work to other museums in Turkey. The ultimate goal of the work is to create a tool, that enables any museum to easily create and publish its collection using Semantic Web technologies and to integrate its content with other museums having compliant knowledge bases.

Acknowledgement. We greatly appreciate Ephesus Museum Director Mr. Cengiz Topal for providing permission to photograph the items and to use of information about the collection. We are also thankful to archaeologist Dr. Gamze Günay Vonedlegraeve and archaeologist Hüseyin Özer for helping us during the studies in the museum.

References

1. Hernandez, F., Rodrigo, L., Contreras, J., Carbone, F., Botin, F.M.: Building a cultural heritage ontology for Cantabria. In: CIDOC Annual Conference, Athens (2008)
2. Tudhope, D., Binding, C., May, K.: Semantic interoperability issues from a case study in archaeology. In: Proceedings of the 1st International Workshop Semantic Interoperability in the European Digital Library (SIEDL 2008), associated with 5th European Semantic Web Conference, pp. 88–99 (2008)
3. Vavliakis, K.N., Karagiannis, G.T., Mitkas, P.A.: Semantic web in cultural heritage after 2020. In: What will the Semantic Web look like 10 years from now? Workshop held in conjunction with the 11th International Semantic Web Conference 2012 (ISWC 2012) (2012)
4. Schreiber, G., Amin, A., Aroyo, L., van Assem, M., de Boer, V., Hardman, L., Hildebrand, M., Omelayenko, B., van Osenbruggen, J., Tordai, A., Wielemaker, J., Wielinga, B.: Semantic annotation and search of cultural-heritage collections: The MultimediaN E-Culture demonstrator. Web Semant. Sci. Serv. Agents World Wide Web 6(4), 243–249 (2008). Semantic Web Challenge 2006/2007
5. Hyvönen, E., Mäkelä, E., Salminen, M., Valo, A., Viljanen, K., Saarela, S., Junnila, M., Kettula, S.: MuseumFinland - Finnish museums on the semantic web. Web Semant. Sci. Serv. Agents World Wide Web 3(2–3), 224–241 (2005)
6. Hyvönen, E.: Semantic portals for cultural heritage. In: Staab, S., Studer, R., (eds.) Handbook on Ontologies, pp. 757–778. Springer, Berlin (2009)
7. Schiemann, B., Oischinger, M., Görz, G.: Erlangen CRM/OWL (2013). http://erlangen-crm.org
8. Doerr, M.: The CIDOC conceptual reference module: an ontological approach to semantic interoperability of metadata. AI Mag. 24(3), 75–92 (2003)
9. ResearchSpace Project: British museum semantic web collection online (2017). http://collection.britishmuseum.org/
10. Tupman, C., Hedges, M., Jordanous, A., Roueché, C., Lawrence, K.F., Wakelnig, E., Dunn, S.: Sharing ancient wisdoms: developing structures for tracking cultural dynamics by linking moral and philosophical anthologies with their source and recipient texts. In: Digital Humanities (2012)
11. Ryzko, D.P., Mieczyslaw, M.: SYNAT - An Innovative Platform for Scientific Information Management. Part IV- Innovations for an Information Professional. Innovating Innovation: Essays on the Intersection of Information Science and Innovation, pp. 179–87 (2013)
12. Scholz, M., Goerz, G.: Wisski: A virtual research environment for cultural heritage. In: Raedt, L.D., Bessière, C., Dubois, D., Doherty, P., Frasconi, P., Heintz, F., Lucas, P.J.F., (eds.) ECAI. Frontiers in Artificial Intelligence and Applications, vol. 242, pp. 1017–1018. IOS Press (2012)
13. Gruber, E., Smith, T.J.: Linked open greek pottery. In: CAA2014 (Computer Applications and Quantitative Methods in Archaeology) (2014)
14. Community: CayleyIO (2014). https://cayley.io/
15. Jordan Walke and community: Reactjs. "Releases- facebook/react". GitHub (2011)
16. Apache TinkerPop of the Apache Software Foundation: Gremlin (2009). https://github.com/tinkerpop/gremlin/wiki
17. Rodriguez, M.: The gremlin graph traversal machine and language. In: Proceedings of the ACM Database Programming Languages Conference (2015)

The Semantic Enrichment Strategy for Types, Chronologies and Historical Periods in Searchculture.gr

Haris Georgiadis[✉], Agathi Papanoti, Maria Paschou, Alexandra Roubani, Despina Hardouveli, and Evi Sachini

National Documentation Centre, National Hellenic Research Foundation, Athens, Greece
{hgeorgiadis,apapano,mpasxo,arouba,dxardo,esachin}@ekt.gr

Abstract. Most aggregators face challenges regarding searchability, discoverability and visual presentation of their content due to metadata heterogeneity. We developed an innovative metadata enrichment and homogenization scheme that is both effective and user-friendly and we embedded it in the ingestion workflow of searchculture.gr, the cultural heritage aggregator of National Documentation Centre (EKT). Two key components of the enrichment scheme are semantics.gr, a platform for publishing vocabularies that contains a tool for massive semantic enrichment, and a parametric tool embedded in the aggregator for chronological normalization. We enriched and homogenized the aggregated content with respect to types and chronological information which subsequently allowed us to develop advanced multilingual search and browsing features, including hierarchical navigation on types and historical periods, searching and faceting on type, time span and historical period, a tag cloud of types and an interactive timeline.

Keywords: Aggregator · Semantic enrichment · Linked data · Automatic categorization · Vocabularies · Thesauri · Cultural heritage · Historical periods · Time-driven search · Temporal coverage · Timeline

1 Introduction

National Documentation Centre (EKT) has created a cultural content aggregation infrastructure [1] that collects content from digital repositories and libraries and publishes it in a central public portal, www.searchculture.gr. Soon our aim became to increase searchability and discoverability by providing new means of search, filtering, browsing and visual presentation of the content, based on two key types of metadata, item type (dc:type) and chronological information (dc:date, dcterms:created or dcterms:temporal, depending on the collection). However, the original documentation is extremely heterogeneous across the collections making impossible to support these features without intensive semantic enrichment and homogenization.

The heterogeneity of dc:type derives from term variations (different languages, synonyms, mixing plural and singular etc.) and from different documentation methodologies (ranging from extremely general terms, such as "exhibit", to very specialized terms, such as "oenochoe", a specific type of vase). When it comes to temporal fields, some providers use *period labels* (as problematic as the aforementioned type labels),

© Springer International Publishing AG 2017
E. Garoufallou et al. (Eds.): MTSR 2017, CCIS 755, pp. 211–223, 2017.
https://doi.org/10.1007/978-3-319-70863-8_20

but most of them use *chronological values*, such as dates, centuries, years and their *interval* counterparts which are also highly heterogeneous due to the use of different time encodings, languages, time granularity or literal descriptors (e.g. "Early").

As a solution we developed a semantic enrichment and homogenization scheme. It is based on www.semantics.gr, a platform for publishing vocabularies and thesauri that includes *a mapping tool for content enrichment* and contextualization. The tool sets mapping rules from multiple metadata field values to vocabulary terms. It uses a self-improving automatic suggestion mechanism and additionally supports the curator when intervening in the enrichment process. We also extended our aggregator infrastructure with a *parametric tool for the normalization of chronological values* which is based on regular expression processing. As a result the content of searchculture.gr was enriched and homogenized in respect to types, chronologies and historical periods, allowing us to publish it as Linked Open Data and to enhance the portal with new multilingual search and navigation features.

2 Related Work

Many aggregators use semantic enrichment techniques to deal with heterogeneity. Europeana [3], aggregation platforms such as MoRe [2], MINT [11] and LoCloud [12] and research projects such as PATHS [8] use automatic enrichment with terms of established vocabularies. Complete automated enrichment on structured fields (such as dc:type) adopts an "enrich-if-you-can" strategy, horizontally, resulting in low enrichment coverage and high percentage of mistakes [6]. Automated annotation methods on more descriptive fields (such as dc:title) also yield relatively poor results [8]. As a result, homogenization is not achieved and this is why aggregators usually avoid offering advanced ways of exploration (browsing, faceting), that would improve the discoverability and the visual presentation of the aggregated content. TMP tool [13] of the AthenaPlus project is a platform for creating vocabularies that offers a mapping functionality which allows users to define equivalent relations between concepts from different vocabularies. However, unlike semantics.gr, it supports only SKOS vocabularies (which is not very suitable for time periods) while the mapping tool cannot perform more complex mappings (such as mappings from multiple fields, mappings from keywords contained in descriptive fields, use of logical expressions for filtering) and does not have a self-improving auto-suggestion mechanism.

Particularly for temporal enrichment, some aggregators enrich items described with period labels using timespan vocabularies (e.g. [3]), suffering, though, the abovementioned problems. Some attempt to homogenize chronological values to some extend as far as they conform to specific date formats [2, 11]. In either case, unlike our enrichment scheme, they don't handle items with temporal information uniformly, i.e. they don't assign period labels to items described with chronologies (a complex and error-prone task as highlighted in [9, 10]) and vice versa (chronologies to items described with period labels). Our enrichment scheme supports chronological search and browsing both by year ranges and historical periods across all items with chronological metadata, either explicit (temporal fields) or implicit (e.g. keywords in titles), regardless whether they were originally described with chronologies or with period labels.

3   The Semantic Enrichment Scheme Used in Searchculture.gr

Searchculture.gr is based on an aggregator infrastructure that contains a tool for harvesting metadata and digital files (OAI-PMH harvester), a system for validating content against specific requirements (validator), a platform that implements the ingestion workflow (aggregator) and the public portal [1]. The search engine of the public portal is based on the Apache Solr[1] indexing system. The internal data model used for metadata storage is compatible with the EDM schema [4]. The aggregator was recently enhanced with a semantic enrichment scheme. We enriched the aggregated content with terms from a vocabulary of cultural item types, with homogenized chronological values (years or year intervals) and with terms from a vocabulary of greek historical periods. Both vocabularies were created with specific assumptions to facilitate the enrichment process. Metadata records are enhanced with three separate *EKT fields*. Note that the original documentation is not modified and is normally indexed and searchable.

3.1   The Mapping-Based Enrichment Tool of Semantics.gr

Semantics.gr was initially created by EKT as a platform where institutions can create and publish RDF-based vocabularies and thesauri of any kind (concepts, timespans, agents, places) or any schema (parametric schema definition support). The platform was enhanced with a mapping tool that allows aggregators to enrich their collections with vocabulary and thesaurus terms [5, 7].

The tool has a GUI environment with advanced automated functionalities that help the *curator* easily define *Enrichment Mapping Rules (EMR)* per collection from distinct metadata values to vocabulary terms. The tool accesses collection metadata via OAI-PMH harvesting. After setting the EMR, they can be served on request via a REST API in json format. Subsequently, the EMR can be used by an aggregator to enrich the collection in a bulk and straightforward one-pass fashion.

The EMR are defined per distinct value of a predefined metadata field (for example dc:type or dcterms:temporal), which is called *primary field*. In special cases the curator can choose a second metadata field (for example dc:subject) to create more precise EMR in case the documentation of the primary field is poor. We call this metadata field *secondary field* and its values filters. For example, a metadata record may have a dc:type value "folklore object" but a dc:subject value "Jewel" that reveals a much more accurate type. The enrichment tool supports automatic suggestion of EMR which by default is based on string similarity matching between metadata field values and indexed labels of vocabulary entries (e.g. skos:prefLabel and skos:altLabel). The automatic mapping suggestion is very effective and efficient leveraging the indexing system of semantics.gr search engine, namely Apache Solr. The tool can be easily configured to be loosely

---

[1] http://lucene.apache.org/solr/.

coupled to the aggregator search portal (using deep linking) allowing the curator to easily search the collection for items having the specific values on primary and secondary fields. The curator can create complex logical expressions on the filters of a vocabulary entry assignment in order to create finer and more precise EMR and avoid false positives. For instance, they can use the logical NOT operator for setting exceptions.

When the automatic suggestion function fails to produce correct rules, the curator can set mappings manually. The enrichment tool "remembers" manual assignments in order to improve the effectiveness of auto-suggestion in future.

In certain cases, the curator can choose a highly selective *descriptive* field (the number of its distinct values approaches the number of all items) as a secondary field, such as dc:title or dc:description, if the values contain words or phrases that can reveal the appropriate vocabulary entry. For example a dc:title "An amphora from Attica" implies that the item is a vase. The tool searches inside such values for specific words or phrases derived from the vocabulary terms and then exposes only the matches as filters (instead of the entire field values).

3.2   The Enrichment Strategy for Item Types

We enriched and homogenized the aggregated content of searchculture.gr using a hierarchical bilingual SKOS vocabulary of item types that we created and published in semantics.gr[2]. The vocabulary consists of 414 terms, many of them linked to Getty AAT[3] (via skos:exactMatch). Eventually, metadata records were enriched with a separate field *EKT type* that holds references to the vocabulary. The type enrichment of a collection involves the following actions: (i) examination of the documentation quality of the collection to decide whether a secondary field is needed or not (ii) registration of the repository in semantics.gr (iii) creation of EMR for the collection (iv) ingestion (or re-indexing) of the collection in the aggregator in order for the actual enrichment to take place. Depending on the collection, the enrichment is based on original values of "dc:type" and, for special cases, of "dc:subject" or "dc:title". Table 1 summarizes 3 different documentation qualities, namely Type-A, Type-B and Type-C, and the respective mapping methodology.

Table 1. Documentations classes & type enrichment methodologies.

Class	Documentation quality class description	Methodology
Type-A	Good documentation of dc:type.	**EMR**: primary field
Type-B	Insufficient documentation on dc:type for part or all the collection, useful dc:subject	**EMR**: primary and **secondary** fields
Type-C	Insufficient documentation on dc:type for part or all the collection, useful dc:title or dc:description	**EMR**: primary field and **descriptive secondary** field

---

[2] http://www.semantics.gr/authorities/vocabularies/ekt-item-types/vocabulary-entries/tree.

[3] The Getty Art & Architecture Thesaurus, http://www.getty.edu/research/tools/vocabularies/aat/.

We will demonstrate the mapping process with the following example. Suppose that an aggregator-institution wishes to enrich its collections with references to a SKOS vocabulary (*V*) previously published in semantics.gr. Vocabulary *V* contains the following 5 entries:

→ **http://scs.gr/sculpture** **skos:prefLabel** "Sculpture"@en | "Γλυπτό"@el
  → **http://scs.gr/figurine**   **skos:prefLabel** "Figurine"@en | "Ειδώλιο"@el
→ **http://scs.gr/Jewellery** **skos:prefLabel** "Jewellery"@en | "Κόσμημα"@el
→ **http://scs.gr/vessel** **skos:prefLabel** "Vessel"@en | "Σκεύος"@el
  → **http://scs.gr/vase**   **skos:prefLabel** "Vase"@en | "Αγγείο"@el

For a *Type-A* collection, the curator initializes a new EMR form in the enrichment tool where he/she sets the metadata field dc:type as the primary field and choose *V* as the target vocabulary. Then, the enrichment tool harvests metadata records from the repository and creates a list of distinct dc:type values with their cardinalities (1st column of Table 2). Next, the curator triggers the auto-suggestion functionality which successfully maps 3 distinct dc:type values to the correct vocabulary entries. The curator assigns the correct vocabulary term for the remaining value manually. Finally, the curator confirms the EMR and the mapping phase is completed. In Table 2, label "auto" indicates that the EMR was automatically created.

Table 2. EMR for a Type-A collection

dc:type value	Entry from vocabulary *V1*	
sculpture art *(120 items)*	http://scs.gr/sculpture	Auto
greek vases *(230 items)*	http://scs.gr/vase	Auto
jewelleries *(135 items)*	http://scs.gr/Jewellery	Auto
amphora *(100 items)*	http://scs.gr/vase	Manual

Type-B collection has insufficient documentation of the primary field (either for all or for some of the items) but has another metadata field (secondary) that can contribute in the enrichment process. An example is shown in Table 3. Focus on the first mapping rule for dc:type value "ceramic objects": a metadata record with this dc:type value will be enriched with the reference http://scs.gr/vase only if it has one of the following dc:subject filters: "vase" or "amphora" or with the reference http://scs.gr/figurine if it has a dc:subject value "figurine". The auto-suggestion mechanism can easily set this EMR as long as there are vocabulary matches for these filters. Items with dc:type value "exhibits" will be enriched with http://scs.gr/vase if they have a dc:subject "amphora" but they do NOT have a dc:subject "earing" (suppose that an image shows an earring shaped as an amphora).

In a *Type-C* collection, the documentation of dc:type is very poor for some items, but its dc:title values may contain useful words or phrases. The enrichment tool will search all titles against a set of words derived from all the labels of *V* (e.g. skos:prefLabel and skos:altLabel) as well as the keywords from previous EMR assignments and will

Table 3. EMR for a Type-B collection

dc:type	Filters (dc:subject)	Entry from vocabulary *V1*	
ceramic objects *(101 items)*	amphora, vase, statuette ...	http://scs.gr/vase if filter in ["vase", "amphora"]	auto auto
		http://scs.gr/figurine if filter in ["statuette"]	auto auto
exhibits *(55 items)*	earing, amphora, ...	http://scs.gr/Jewellery if filter in ["earing"]	auto auto
		http://scs.gr/vase if filter in ["amphora"] & **NOT** in ["earing"]	auto manual

set only the matching words as available filters for each dc:type value. The rest of the mapping process is identical with the one described for *Type-B* collections.

3.3 The Enrichment Strategy for Chronologies and Historical Periods

We enriched the aggregated content with homogenized (normalized) chronologies and with historical periods using a hierarchical bilingual vocabulary of Greek historical periods. Metadata records are enriched with two separated fields, *EKT chronology* and *EKT historical period*.

Depending on whether the original temporal documentation is based on period labels or chronologies, we adopted two fundamentally different enrichment strategies, *historical period-driven enrichment* and *chronology-driven enrichment*, respectively. The former involves setting EMR in the enrichment tool of semantics.gr, similarly to the enrichment procedure for types; items originally described with period labels, are mapped to vocabulary terms but now they are also enriched with the respective year ranges. In the chronology-driven enrichment, chronological values are being homogenized into years or year ranges and then, based on the results, the items are enhanced with the corresponding terms from the historical periods vocabulary. The enrichment is based on the original values of a temporal field ("dc:date", "dc:created" or "dcterms:temporal", depending on the collection) and in special cases taking into account keywords in descriptive field values, such as of "dc:description" and "dc:title".

Table 4 summarizes 4 typical collection types, namely *Temp-A*, *Temp-B*, *Temp-C* and *Temp-D*, their qualitative characteristics with respect to temporal documentation and the enrichment methodologies used. The methodologies used for *Temp-A* and *Temp-B* fall into the historical period-driven enrichment strategy, while the methodology used for *Temp-C* falls into the chronology-driven one. *Temp-D* collections are handled using both strategies: items described with period labels are handled as *Temp-A* or *Temp-B* and items described with chronologies are handled as *Temp-C*. We use regular expressions to distinguish chronologies from period labels.

Table 4. Documentations classes & temporal coverage enrichment methodologies.

Class	Documentation quality class description	Methodology
Temp-A	Temporal field (dcterms:temporal) with period labels (e.g. "archaic era")	(1) **EMR**, primary field (EKT historical period) (2) extract year span from voc term (EKT chronology)
Temp-B	Insufficient documentation on temporal field for part or all the collection, useful titles (e.g. "<u>archaic</u> vase", "sculpture from the <u>hellenistic</u> period")	(1) **EMR**, primary field, descriptive secondary field (EKT historical period) (2) extract year span (EKT chronology)
Temp-C	Temporal field (dc:date, dcterms:created or dcterms:temporal) with chronologies (e.g. "1981", "late 12th c. AD", "1100–1200 AD")	(1) **Normalization of chronology values** (EKT chronology) (2) Enrich with EKT historical period
Temp-D	Temporal field (dcterms:temporal) with some values containing historical periods and others containing chronologies	Items with chronological values are handled as Temp-C and the remaining as Temp-A or Temp-B

The vocabulary of Greek Historical Periods. We created a Greek historical periods vocabulary that ranges from 8,000 BC (Mesolithic Period) to present and we published it in semantics.gr[4]. It is hierarchical and bilingual (Greek and English) consisting of 94 distinctive terms. The schema of the vocabulary conforms to the edm:Timespan contextual class introduced by Europeana [4]. For each term, apart from the different labels (skos:prefLabel, skos:altLabel) the year range is also defined in properties edm:begin and edm:end.

We created the thesaurus taking into consideration reputable sources about Greek history as well as established vocabularies such as Getty AAT. Some periods have a strict local scope (e.g. minoan, cycladic and helladic periods) and as a result their year ranges tend to overlap. We call those periods *relative*. The rest of the periods cover the entirety of Hellenic territory and are less debatable with respect to their timespans. We call those *absolute*. In our vocabulary, absolute periods have neither overlaps nor gaps when they have the same parent and relative periods have at least one absolute ancestor.

Historical period-driven enrichment. The aggregator enriches items originally described with period labels with the mapped historical periods from the vocabulary (step 1) and computes their chronologies according to the assigned periods (step 2). The temporal enrichment of a collection involves the following actions: (i) registration of the repository in semantics.gr, (ii) creation of the EMR for the time field of the collection in the enrichment tool, as described in Sect. 3.2 (only for the period label values; if there are chronological values as well, these are automatically ignored by the mapping tool using regular expression filtering) (iii) ingestion (or re-indexing) of the collection in the aggregator in order for the actual enrichment to take place. Tables 5 and 6 illustrate examples of *Temp-A* and *Temp-B* collections. The result of each enrichment step is presented for each item.

---

[4] http://www.semantics.gr/authorities/vocabularies/historical-periods/vocabulary-entries/tree.

Table 5. Enrichment steps for a Temp-A collection

dcterms:temporal	Step 1: EMR - primary field (EKT historical period)	Step 2: extract year span (EKT chronology)
Post-Byzantine period	→ Ottoman period	→1453/1821
Middle - Late hellenistic years	→ Middle Hellenistic period - Late hellenistic period	→-220/-31

Table 6. Enrichment steps for a Temp-B collection

dc:title, dc:description (secondary field)	Step 1: EMR -primary & descriptive secondary field (EKT period)	Step 2: extract year span (EKT chronology)
Archaic vase	→ Archaic period	→ -700/-480
Hellenistic sculpture	→ Hellenistic period	→ -323/-31

Chronology-driven enrichment. The effectiveness of chronology-driven enrichment is heavily based on the normalization of chronological values. We developed a parametric tool which is based on regular expression processing that can handle 4 classes of chronological patterns, namely, "century range", "century", "year range" and "year/ date". An authorized user can create many regular expression patterns for each class in order to capture as many chronological formats as possible. A chronological pattern can include custom and predefined placeholders that are associated with lists of keywords in many languages thus eliminating the number of different patterns needed for each class. Predefined placeholders affect the actual normalization algorithm. For example the "early" placeholder, which applies to patterns of "century range" and "century" classes, may have custom keywords "early", "beginning of" and the Greek counterparts. We created 30 different chronological patterns[5] and we arranged them in a specific order, from the stricter to the most ambiguous. When a chronological value is to be normalized, it passes through all the chronological patterns (or a subset of those that is set for the particular collection) sequentially, until the first match is found. Based on that pattern, the normalized year or year range is calculated. Table 7 shows some normalization examples per pattern class.

Table 7. Normalization of chronologies using regular expression matching

Chronological pattern class	Examples
century range	2nd half of 5th c. BC until 4th c. BC → **-450/-301**
century	early 18th century → **1700/1730** first half of 5th c. BC → **-500/-451**
year range	1342/48 → **1342/1348** 1342–1654 → **1342/1654**
date/year	526 BC → **-526**

---

[5] Available at https://www.searchculture.gr/aggregator/resource/docs/Chronological_Patterns. pdf.

The aggregator normalizes the original chronologies (step 1) and based on the year or year ranges, chooses the corresponding *absolute* historical periods from the vocabulary (step 2). We did not use the *relative* historical periods, since we did not always have spatial information [9]. For example, Middle Bronze Age is an absolute period, covering the timespan 2000–1580 BC. It includes Middle Minoan, Middle Cycladic and Middle Helladic periods which are marked as relative since they refer to different civilisations that flourished in different territories. Therefore, an item dated in 1700 BC will be assigned with the Middle Bronze Age term. The chronological-driven enrichment is completely automated since there is no need for creating EMR. Table 8 illustrates an example of a *Temp-C* collection.

Table 8. Enrichment steps for a Temp-C collection

dc:date, dctemrs:created or dcterms:temporal	Step 1: Normalize chronologies (EKT chronology)	Step 2:Enrich with corresponding period (EKT historical period)
Late 5th century	→ 471/500	→ Early Byzantine Period
7th c. B.C-mid 6th c. BC	→ -700/-551	→ Early Archaic - Middle Archaic Period
03/11/1980	→ 1980	→ Regime change

3.4   EKT Fields: Encoding and Indexing

The visual representation of EKT type field (as shown in the item page of searchculture.gr) consists of one or more types (e.g. "Figurine, Souvenir"). However, in order for the search engine to support advanced hierarchical searching and faceting on types, we index super (more general) types as well using a separate auxiliary Solr field.

For the EKT chronology field, we used the Date Range Field of Apache Solr which supports time interval indexing, time range queries and interval facets[6]. Regarding the EKT historical period field, its visual representation consists of either one (e.g. "Hellenistic Period") or two – in case of period intervals – historical periods (e.g. "Middle Archaic Period – Late Hellenistic Period"). In order for the search engine to support advanced hierarchical searching and faceting on periods, we index implying periods (e.g. those between the upper and lower bounds of a period interval) as well as both super (ancestor) and sub (descendant) periods in separate auxiliary Solr fields.

4   Enriching the Content of Searchculture.gr – The Results

More than 150 K items of searchculture.gr - 98% of the content - were classified into a compact and balanced set of 130 types. Table 9 illustrates the number of collections and enriched items per documentation class (Sect. 3.2).

---

[6] https://cwiki.apache.org/confluence/display/solr/Working+with+Dates.

Table 9. Collections and number of items per type documentation class

Documentation class		# of collections	# of items
Type-A:	sufficient existing dc:type values	27	42583
Type-B:	insufficient dc:type values – useful dc:subject	24	60181
Type-C:	insufficient dc:type – resorting to dc:title values	4	55912
Total		55	158676

After the type enrichment, searchculture.gr was enhanced with new multilingual search and browsing functionalities that improve discoverability including searching by type using a list of values, hierarchical navigation and faceting on types and an inter-active tag cloud (Fig. 1). The enrichment improved remarkably the searchability of the content as illustrated in the experiment shown in Fig. 2(a) where we compared the number of search results returned by searchculture.gr for 6 search keys in Greek before and after the enrichment. Then we repeated the experiment, this time using the same search keys in English, as shown in Fig. 2(b). Since the majority of the items were documented only in Greek, the improvement was even more impressive.

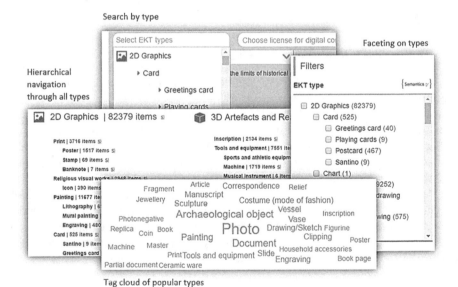

Fig. 1. Bilingual search, filtering (facets) and navigation (browsing) on types

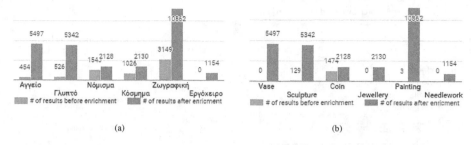

(a)
(b)

Fig. 2. Type enrichment: improve in searchability of 6 types in Greek (a) and in English (b)

A total of 107,003 items of searchculture.gr - the 66% of the aggregated content - were enriched with normalized chronologies and assigned with historical periods. Note that 63,234 items did not have any explicit temporal information, however, we managed to enrich 8,387 of them by identifying keywords in their titles or other descriptive fields. Table 10 illustrates the number of collections per documentation class as introduced in Sect. 3.3 and the total of enriched items per class.

Table 10. Collection and number of items per temporal documentation class

Documentation class		# of collections	# of items
Temp-A	Temporal field (dcterms:temporal) with period labels	4	6870
Temp-B	Insufficient temporal field, useful titles or descriptions	3	6646
Temp-C	Temporal field with chronologies	44	81813
Temp-D	Mixed values: historical periods and chronologies	2	11674
Total		53	107003

After the temporal enrichment, searchculture.gr was enhanced with advanced time-driven multilingual search and browsing functionalities including searching by historical period and by year range, hierarchical navigation by historical periods, faceting on year-range and historical period and an interactive histogram-timeline (Fig. 3).

Thanks to our EKT chronology and historical period indexing scheme (Sect. 3.4), users can choose between two modes for year or period interval search. In the "loose" one temporal search returns items with a year or period interval that overlaps that of the search criterion. For example, for a search criterion: "1500–1600 AD", an item dated "1550–1750 AD" will appear in the results. Similarly, for a search criterion "Classical Period", an item dated "From Classical to Hellenistic period" will also appear in the results. In the "strict" mode, temporal search is more precise bringing only items with a year or period interval strictly within or coinciding the one defined by the search criterion. For example, for a search year range: "1500–1600 AD", an item dated "1550–1750 AD" will not be included in the results, while an item with "1550–1570 AD" date will. Similarly, for a search criterion "Classical Period", an item dated "From Classical to Hellenistic period" will not be included in the results, while an item dated "Early

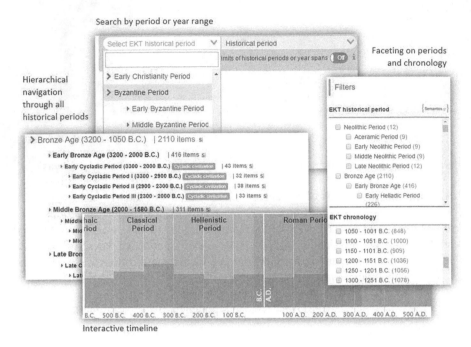

Fig. 3. Bilingual search, filtering (facets) and navigation (browsing) on periods and chronology

Classical Period" will. The "strict" mode is very useful when the user want to find items dated exclusively within as specific year or period interval.

Our future plans focus on extending the enrichment scheme in order to deal with spatial information and subjects. This will allow the enhancement of searchculture.gr with new features such as map-based navigation as well as searching, browsing and faceting on subject headings. Moreover, the multi-dimensional semantic enrichment will facilitate the creation of thematic exhibitions and "similar object" functionality.

Acknowledgments. The work presented in this article has been partly supported by the project "Platform for provision of services for deposit, management and dissemination of Open Public Data and Digital Content" of the Operational Programme "Digital Convergence" (NSFR), co-funded by Greece and the European Union. We would also like to thank Dimitra Pelekanou, the graphic designer of searchculture.gr.

References

1. Georgiadis, H., Banos, V., Stathopoulou, I.O., Stathopoulos, P., Houssos, N., Sachini, E.: Ensuring the quality and interoperability of open cultural digital content. In: IISA, pp. 178–183 (2014)
2. Gavrilis, D., Ioannides, M., Theofanous, E.: Cultural heritage content re-use: An aggregators's point of view. In: ISPRS, vol. II-5/W3, pp. 83–87 (2015)

3. Stiller, J., Petras, V., Gäde, M., Isaac, A.: Automatic enrichments with controlled vocabularies in europeana: challenges and consequenceS. In: Ioannides, M., Magnenat-Thalmann, N., Fink, E., Žarnić, R., Yen, A.-Y., Quak, E. (eds.) EuroMed 2014. LNCS, vol. 8740, pp. 238–247. Springer, Cham (2014). http://doi.org/10.1007/978-3-319-13695-0_23
4. Europeana Data Model Primer. http://pro.europeana.eu/page/edm-documentation
5. Georgiadis, H., Papanoti, A.: Semantics.gr: Information system for vocabularies & semantic enrichment. Technical report, EKT (2016). http://helios-eie.ekt.gr/EIE/handle/10442/15446
6. Manguinhas, H., Freire, N., Isaac, A., Stiller, J., Charles, V., Soroa, A., Simon, R., Alexiev, V.: Exploring comparative evaluation of semantic enrichment tools for cultural heritage metadata. In: Fuhr, N., Kovács, L., Risse, T., Nejdl, W. (eds.) TPDL 2016. LNCS, vol. 9819, pp. 266–278. Springer, Cham (2016). http://doi.org/10.1007/978-3-319-43997-6_21
7. Georgiadis, H., Papanoti, A., et al: Semantics.gr: A self-improving service to repositories and aggregators for massively enriching their content. In: Proceedings of DHC Workshop of MTSR (2016)
8. Agirre, E., Barrena, A., de Lacalle, O.L., Soroa, A., Fernando, S., Stevenson, M.: Matching cultural heritage items to wikipedia. In: Proceedings of the LREC 2012, Istanbul, Turkey (2012)
9. Rabinowitz, A.: It's about time: historical periodization and Linked Ancient World Data. ISAW Papers 7.22 (2014)
10. Doerr, M., Kritsotaki, A., Stead, S.: Which period is it? A methodology to create thesauri of historical periods. In: Proceedings of CAA2004 (2004)
11. MINT: MINT Metadata Interoperability Services (2013). http://mint.image.ece.ntua.gr/
12. LoCloud enrichment. http://www.locloud.eu/Resources/LoCloud-enrichment-services
13. Coudyzer, E., et al: The terminology management platform: a tool for creating linked open data. In: TOTh Workshop (2014)

Linked Data in Libraries' Technical Services Workflows

Philip E. Schreur[✉] and Nancy Lorimer

Stanford University, Stanford, CA 94305, USA
pschreur@stanford.edu

Abstract. Linked Data for Production (LD4P) is a collaborative project between six institutions (Columbia, Cornell, Harvard, the Library of Congress, Princeton, and Stanford) to begin the transition of the production workflows of their libraries Technical Services Departments to ones rooted in Linked Open Data (LOD). Each institution is focused on a different domain or facet of the problem to move us together as a group more quickly. As a whole, the six institutions will focus on four main areas of development. First will be the establishment of the ability to create linked open data communally. Second, in collaboration with external standards organizations such as the Program for Cooperative Cataloging and linked data projects such as BIBFLOW, will be the establishment of common procedures and protocols for the creation of library metadata as linked data. Third will be the expansion of the BIBFRAME ontology to better encompass subject domains such as art and music. And last will be the transition of a selection of current library workflows to ones based in linked open data. The projects will make use of a collection of preliminary tools and adopt them for production work in their individual environments and, through feedback, assist in the development of the tools.

Keywords: BIBFRAME · Linked data · Ontology · Cataloging

1 Background

Libraries worldwide rely upon Machine-Readable Cataloging (MARC)-based systems for the communication, storage, and expression of the majority of their bibliographic data. MARC 21 [1], created by the harmonization of U.S. and Canadian MARC, is a variant of an early communication format originally developed in the 1960s to enable machine manipulation of the bibliographic data previously recorded on catalog cards. Connections between various data elements within a single catalog record, such as between a subject heading and a specific work or between a performer and piece performed, are usually not expressed, since it is assumed that a human being will be examining the record as a whole and making the associations between the elements for themselves. But as libraries transition to a linked-data based architecture that derives its power from extensive machine linking of individual data elements, this former reliance on human interpretation at the record level to make correct associations between individual data elements becomes a critical issue. And although MARC metadata can be converted to linked data, many human-inferred relationships are left unexpressed in the new environment. The converted data are functional as linked data, but incomplete.

© Springer International Publishing AG 2017
E. Garoufallou et al. (Eds.): MTSR 2017, CCIS 755, pp. 224–229, 2017.
https://doi.org/10.1007/978-3-319-70863-8_21

In 2012, the Library of Congress (LOC) began a project to end libraries isolation from the semantic web through the creation of a new communication format, called BIBFRAME [2], as a replacement for the MARC formats. BIBFRAME continues to have a complex development as its creators try to balance the need to capture the data encoded in MARC, the constraints of RDF [3], and input from the community it hopes to serve. Libraries survive in their current environment by adhering to structural and data quality standards to facilitate the easy exchange of metadata for commonly held resources. These standards also allow metadata from various institutions to be quickly combined into large discovery interfaces. As libraries transition from their current environment to a more complex one based on entities, these standards must be rethought and re-envisioned. The collaborative project, Linked Data for Production (LD4P) [4], is designed to turn this new vision into a series of practical standards and workflows to make the transition possible.

This paper will first explore the overall goals of LD4P and the immediate needs that it is trying to fulfill. The following sections will focus on the specific subprojects created to support those goals and the progress that has been made to date. Finally, the conclusion will articulate the key challenges LD4P faces and future issues to be resolved.

2   Linked Data for Production: Goals

In order to begin the transition from a MARC-based environment, Stanford University proposed a grant to the Mellon Foundation in 2015 called Linked Data for Production. LD4P is a collaboration between six institutions (Columbia, Cornell, Harvard, LOC, Princeton, and Stanford) to begin the transition of the production workflows of their libraries Technical Services Departments to ones based in LOD. This first phase of the transition focuses on the development of the ability to produce metadata as LOD communally, the enhancement of the BIBFRAME ontology to encompass the multiple resource formats that academic libraries must process, and the engagement of the broader academic library community to ensure a sustainable and extensible environment. As its name implies, LD4P focuses on the immediate needs of practical metadata production such as ontology coverage and workflow transition. The efforts of the LD4P partners are based, in part, on a collection of tools that currently exist, such as the converter and editor developed by the Library of Congress (used by LOC and Stanford) or Vitro [5] (developed by Cornell and used by Cornell and Columbia). The cyclical feedback of use and enhancement requests to the developers of these tools allows for their enhancement based on use in an actual production environment. The focus of LD4P is on the integration and adoption of this current tool suite for immediate production needs.

3   Subproject Descriptions

Individual subprojects at each institution focus either upon the processing of special, local collections or the conversion of local workflows for more traditional materials. Library workflows are often particular to that institution. They develop organically from a complex mixture of institutional policies, vendor services, choice of ILS (and its capabilities), and accepted standards (Resource Description and Access (RDA)) [6], the Program for Cooperative Cataloging's Bibliographic Standard Record (BSR) [7], etc. The individual projects have two goals; the first being more straightforward. Although identical workflows cannot be developed for all institutions, standards for the **output** of those workflows can be. This meets the basic need of a library to be able to ingest and use metadata created at other institutions. By focusing on different subject domains (e.g., cartographic, music, rare books), the group is trying to standardize the metadata output for the most common types of resources they will need to process.

The second is more complex. Two institutions (LOC and Stanford) chose to look at the conversion of their local workflows to linked data as their institutional project. The benefits of these projects are numerous. First, they demonstrate that the conversion of a workflow from acquisition through discovery is possible. They identify the separate elements of the workflow that must be considered/converted, and produce solutions to the various elements of their workflows that can become models for how other institutions could approach similar issues. And as they work through these workflows, LOC and Stanford can do it in consultation with the other LD4P members so that common standards and protocols can be developed even if explicit workflows cannot be copied from institution to institution.

The focus of the individual projects center on two main themes. The first is the development of the BIBFRAME ontology and its extension into various subject domains. The second is the transition of selected workflows and the development of the technology stack needed to support them. The following section highlights the work of LD4P in those areas.

3.1 BIBFRAME 2.0

The latest iteration of BIBFRAME (BIBFRAME 2.0) is key to the work of most of the partners. Although originally created by the LOC, it is intended to be a community developed and maintained ontology. BIBFRAME is also intended to be a core ontology; specific subject domains such as music or art are intended to be developed by experts in those fields. As work on the subprojects continue, the members give informed feedback to the LOC for the refinement of BIBFRAME. To date, the LOC has completed the BIBFRAME Vocabulary 2.0 specification, published the ontology and namespace document, and shared draft specifications for the conversion of bibliographic data from MARC to BIBFRAME. In addition, the LD4P partners have extended the BIBFRAME ontology into a number of specific subject domains outlined below.

BIBFRAME and Art. Over the years, the museum and library communities have developed separate descriptive cataloging practices even though many museums hold library objects and many library collections contain museum objects. Libraries have frequently used their ILS system and the MARC 21/AACR2 [8] cataloging tradition to describe these art objects along with their traditional library materials. The Columbia BIBFRAME evaluation group is focusing on testing the suitability of the BIBFRAME ontology for the description of art objects. Currently the metadata for their art objects are captured in spreadsheets following conventions developed by the art community. This data is being mapped into BIBFRAME and an extension to BIBFRAME will be proposed for missing properties to cover essential data elements in the spreadsheet.

To date, the Columbia LD4P team has mapped existing Art Properties data (a local data model for art objects) to BIBFRAME 2.0 and identified resultant gaps, reconciled the Art Properties data with external data sources (such as the Art & Architecture Thesaurus) using Open Refine [9], and analyzed existing art ontologies (Visual Resources Association RDF [10], CIDOC-CRM [11]).

BIBFRAME and Rare Materials. Working with the Rare Books and Manuscripts Section-Bibliographic Standards Committee, Princeton, and Columbia, Cornell is defining an extension ontology to BIBFRAME for the description of rare materials. The data particularly relevant to rare materials often pertain to the instance and item level; however, item level data (e.g. provenance, binding) are not well defined by current library linked data models. So far, they have explored how to model and describe related events (tours, performances), complex attributions (people working under multiple names), annotations, provenance, and other item-specific details such as signed and numbered copies.

In March 2015, Princeton acquired the personal library of the Algerian-born French philosopher Jacques Derrida (1930–2004). Of the roughly 16,000 published books and other items in the library, a significant number have been heavily annotated. To date, approximately three thousand items with dedications have been identified. In addition to helping with the rare materials extension to BIBFRAME, Princeton's contribution to this effort focuses on the fusion of BIBFRAME with the Web Annotation Data Model [12]. To date, Princeton has digitized a sample set of 500 objects from the Derrida collection, compared and reconciled 235 transcriptions, and manually created forty five sample annotations.

BIBFRAME and Cartographic Resources. This sub-project of LD4P explores best practices for creating linked data descriptions for library cartographic resources including printed maps, atlases, digital geospatial datasets, and other cartographic information resources. The project is evaluating BIBFRAME's effectiveness as a data model for describing cartographic materials for research needs (including concepts such as projection, scale, and relief) and is comparing BIBFRAME's effectiveness versus other available linked data descriptive schemas. In addition, the group is evaluating the thesauri and controlled vocabularies associated with the description of cartographic resources to identify those vocabularies best suited to describe cartographic resources in a linked data environment.

BIBFRAME and Performed Music. The Performed Music Ontology project aims to develop a BIBFRAME ontology extension for performed music in all formats, with a particular emphasis on clarifying and expanding on the modelling of works, events, and their contributors. In this particular domain extension, the key domain stakeholders are the Music Library Association (MLA) [13] and the Association of Recorded Sound Collections (ARSC). [14] So far, the PMO group has gathered and enhanced use cases for performed music metadata, has surveyed existing linked data efforts related to performed music, has written a preliminary position paper on titles, and has added classes and properties relevant to performed music to BIBFRAME. In addition, the group has modeled performed-music-specific concepts including the extension of the BIBFRAME event model, medium of performance, thematic catalog and opus numbers, musical key and mode, and has done some preliminary modelling of aggregate and other complex works.

3.2   Workflow Transition

Production workflows contain the most complex problems in the transition to linked data, involving issues such as metadata of record, tool development, entity reconciliation, and provenance, among others. In this first phase of LD4P, the partners are experimenting with multiple existing tools, engaging in tool development, and designing the architecture needed to complete these sample workflows from beginning to end in a lightweight fashion.

BIBFRAME and RDA. The LOC is exploring the BIBFRAME and RDA data models and best practices for creating linked data descriptions for LOC resources in monographic, serial, notated music, and cartographic formats. These are data types that are most actively using the RDA cataloging provisions and this project is investigating the compatibility of the RDA and BIBFRAME models. The LOC has trained approximately seventy of its staff to create cataloging data directly in RDF using the BIBFRAME ontology and their editor.

Tracer Bullets. Stanford has chosen to transition four MARC-based workflows to ones rooted in linked data, two for traditional materials (vendor-supplied cataloging through the Acquisitions Department and original cataloging) and two for digital materials (deposit of a single item into the Digital Repository, and the deposit of a collection of resources into the Digital Repository). These four tracer bullets follow the life cycle of a resource, from its acquisition to discovery. Each process along the way is converted to a linked data strategy. These processes simply need to be good enough to support an experimental workflow. Requirements for a full production workflow will be gathered iteratively. The Tracer Bullet projects have mapped Stanford's vendor-supplied copy cataloging and original cataloging workflows, and completed the conversion of their copy-cataloging workflow to RDF (Tracer Bullet 1). In addition, they have evaluated and tested a new tool called CEDAR [15] for metadata template creation. The original pipeline for Tracer Bullet 1 is currently being rewritten to support the bulk processing of pre-existing MARC data. They are making use of Kafka [16] and Spark [17] to automate the workflow for large-scale data processing.

4   Conclusions

Key challenges for LD4P center on the enormous amount of library legacy data in the MARC formats and the intricate ecosystem of vendor-supplied services built upon MARC as the communication format. In addition, new tooling must be developed both to convert the MARC data to linked data and create the capability to create new data directly in RDF.

LD4P has experimented with various MARC to BIBFRAME converters, including one designed by the LOC and one designed by Casalini Libri and @cult called ALIADA [18]. In addition, the group is experimenting with a BIBFRAME editor designed by the LOC and the previously mentioned editor being developed at Stanford called CEDAR. Cornell is spearheading the development of both a new converter and BIBFRAME editor that is more in line with the needs of LD4P.

LD4P is currently working with the Mellon Foundation for funding for the second phase of the project. This phase will focus on the expansion of Tracer Bullets 1 and 2 to become more robust pipelines and the expansion of LD4P to include more libraries within the United States through a joint project with the Program for Cooperative Cataloging. Since we are hoping to move from a library-centric to a web-centric focus, another key element will be to develop close ties with similar European efforts underway and to develop the capability of sharing library data as linked data at a global scale.

References

1. MARC Homepage: https://www.loc.gov/marc/. Accessed 01 June 2017
2. BIBFRAME Homepage: https://www.loc.gov/bibframe/. Accessed 01 June 2017
3. RDF Homepage: https://www.w3.org/RDF/. Accessed 01 June 2017
4. LD4P Homepage: https://wiki.duraspace.org/display/LD4P
5. Vitro Homepage: http://vitro.mannlib.cornell.edu. Accessed 02 June 2017
6. RDA Toolkit Homepage, http://www.rdatoolkit.org. Accessed 02 June 2017
7. Program for Cooperative Cataloging Homepage. https://www.loc.gov/aba/pcc. Accessed 02 June 2017
8. AACR2 Homepage. http://www.aacr2.org. Accessed 02 June 2017
9. Openrefine Homepage. http://www.openrefine.org. Accessed 02 June 2017
10. Visual Resources Association VRA Core Homepage. http://www.vraweb.org/author/vra-core/. Accessed 02 June 2017
11. CIDOC-CRM Homepage. http://www.cidoc-crm.org. Accessed 01 June 2017
12. Web Annotation Data Model Homepage. https://www.w3.org/TR/annotation-model/. Accessed 16 Aug 2017
13. Music Library Association Homepage. https://www.musiclibraryassoc.org. Accessed 02 June 2017
14. ARSC Homepage. http://www.arsc-audio.org/index.php. Accessed 02 June 2017
15. CEDAR Homepage. https://med.stanford.edu/cedar.html. Accessed 02 June 2017
16. Kafka Homepage. https://kafka.apache.org/. Accessed 16 Aug 2017
17. Spark Homepage. https://spark.apache.org/. Accessed 16 Aug 2017
18. ALIADA Homepage. http://www.atcult.it/en/products/aliada/. Accessed 16 Aug 2017

The Combined Use of EAD and METS for Archival Material

An Integrated Toolkit

Ricardo Eito-Brun[✉]

Universidad Carlos III de Madrid, c/Madrid 126, Getafe, Madrid, Spain
reito@bib.uc3m.es

Abstract. Information professionals have at their disposal a complex ecosystem of standards and tools designed with specific focus by different user groups. In the case of the Cultural Heritage projects, there are different metadata schemas aimed to support the efficient creation, storage and distribution of content and digital assets. But the use of these metadata schemas, and the software tools that make their use and deployment possible, are sometimes restricted to well-limited areas. As an example, the EAD schema is widely used by archivists for describing fonds and records, TEI is mainly applied for encoding textual corpus, and METS is bounded to the digitization of ancient books. A major permeability and reuse of metadata schemas and tools in different contexts is needed, as information professionals and user communities can leverage their capability to exchange and disseminate assets, gain independence from proprietary software solutions and platforms and make possible an unlimited, global access to our communities' Cultural Heritage. This paper describes the development of a technical solution that integrates the use of EAD with METS for the digitization and description of archival records. With the proposed solution archivists obtain the benefits of both standards using a common, integrated process and tools.

Keywords: Records management · EAD · Mets · Metadata integration

1 Introduction

In the last years, the metadata schemas for describing, managing and preserving digital assets have consolidated. Information professionals have at their disposal a complex set of standards and tools for describing both physical and digital assets: Encoding Archival Description (EAD), Metadata Object Description Standard (MODS), MARCXML, VRA-Core, etc. Additional schemas were designed for keeping the digital objects' technical characteristics (TextMD, MIX, AudioMD, ALTO, etc.) and to support their long term preservation (PREMIS) [1, 2].

Although all these schemas converge for an efficient management of Cultural Heritage assets, they were designed by different user groups having different focus in their minds. Due to this historical reason, and to the availability of different tools that provide partial solutions to the problems and challenge that entities managing our

© Springer International Publishing AG 2017
E. Garoufallou et al. (Eds.): MTSR 2017, CCIS 755, pp. 230–236, 2017.
https://doi.org/10.1007/978-3-319-70863-8_22

Cultural Heritage face, the use of these metadata schemas is often restricted to well-limited, specific areas. For example, the EAD schema is widely used by archivists for describing records; the TEI (Text Encoding initiative) is used in different context (e.g. for encoding textual corpus), and METS (Metadata Encoding and Transmission Schema) is a wrapper schema used by projects centered on the digitization of different materials. Studies [3, 4] demonstrate the possibility of combining these schemas.

Although these schemas have been created to be easily interconnected and integrated (for example, METS has the <dmdSec> to incorporate descriptive metadata encoded in any other schema such as EAD, MODS or MARCXML, there exist a compartmentalization of the different metadata schemas (different communities and groups of users tend to apply and focus on the use of specific schemas). Entities and professionals are missing the benefits that can be obtained with an integrative approach. A major permeability and reuse of metadata schemas and tools in different contexts would report additional benefits, and information professionals and user communities could leverage their capability to exchange and disseminate assets, gain greater independence from proprietary software solutions and make possible an unlimited, global access to our communities' Cultural Heritage assets.

One possible reason for restricting the use of metadata schemas to a particular context or user community is the lack of tools that integrate them. Tools must reduce the perception of complexity that is tied to metadata schemas offering user friendly, easy-to-use interfaces that make the use of the metadata transparent for the information professionals. In the particular case of archives – where EAD is widely adopted for describing fonds and records -, support to other schemas like METS and those designed for managing technical metadata should be considered as part of the components of an integrated technical solution.

This paper describes the development of a technical solution that integrates the use of EAD and METS for managing the digital representations of the archival materials and their descriptions. The rest of the paper is structured as follows: (a) problem description, (b) technical basis and approach; (c) conclusions.

2   Problem Description

Archives need to manage the long-term preservation of records and ensure that user communities can access these assets. These are ensured through a combination of different standards (ISO13636, OAIS, PREMIS, PROV, etc.) and digital preservation policies. Metadata has also a relevant role in digital preservation initiatives.

The description of archival materials is based on international standards like ISAD(G) and EAD. In European countries archivists and software-based solutions tend to use ISAD(G) based solutions, and the use of EAD is more extended in the US. EAD, whose current version - EAD 3 [5] - was released in August 2015 is aligned with other archival description standards like ISAD(G), RAD (*Rules for Archival Description*), and APPM (*Archives, Personal Papers and Manuscripts*). It supports multilevel archival description and the traceability between EAD elements and ISAD(G) documentation. The schema allows references to external binary files, and this feature is used to link the descriptive metadata in the EAD document with digital representations of the materials being described or, at least, to some representative samples.

Digitization projects executed by archives in the last years have moved the focus from the description of the records to the management of complex digital objects. The movement toward a strategy where digital materials are more relevant imposes new requirements to archivists, who must consider which are the features that their tools and supporting IT infrastructure must offer. The capabilities offered by EAD to link digital representations of records to their descriptions are not sufficient to deal with the management of complex digital objects. Aspects like the structural organization of the digital representations of files, the need of keeping different representations for archiving, web access, thumbnails, etc., textual transcriptions, etc., led us to consider the need of using other metadata schemas more adequate for these purposes.

METS offers an XML schema for the exchange of complex, digital objects. One digital object can be made up of several files in different formats. For example, the digital representation of one file can include several image files in TIFF format, text files generated by an optical character recognition (OCR) process or by the human transcription of the document content. The possibility of combining – in a single package – a set of related files opens new possibilities to archives, as additional information like voice materials can be attached to the digital representations -. METS features allow keeping additional information regarding how those files must be displayed and shown to the user in a coordinated way, keeping the metadata for the structure of complex, digital documents. They are XML documents that can include all these data:

- The list of files that are part of the digital object.
- The logical organization of these files, including the sequence in which the files must be shown, their organization into groups and sections, as well as the parallelism between them (for example, the parallelism between a digitized image and the text file with their transcripts).
- The descriptive metadata of the object and its constituent parts.
- Administrative metadata for the digital object as a whole, or for any of its parts. This include rights management, provenance, and origin of the digital representations, data about the digitized document, etc.
- Hyperlinks between the different parts of the digital object.

The METS schema offers a way to encode different information about a digital object and its representation and combine different metadata. In the particular case of the descriptive metadata, the schema includes the <dmdSec> element. This element can either include a reference to an external file containing the metadata - <mdRef>, or embed them in a <mdWrap> element. METS gives the choice of using different descriptive metadata schemas, so it is possible to use EAD, MARCXML, MODS or any other alternative.

3   Technical Basis of the Proposed Solution

The proposed solution uses METS capabilities to embed descriptive metadata to combine – in a single metadata file - EAD descriptive metadata within the list of digital files that compose the representation of the records.

The drivers of the design were the following:

- Archives usually have detailed descriptions of their records in ISAD(G) based databases. These descriptions can be easily converted into EAD format, due to the traceability defined between these metadata schemas.
- They also maintain digitized representations of part of their fonds and files, which are the result of digitization programs completed in the last years.
- Descriptive metadata and digital representations of records are kept separately, which translates in restricted capabilities to access the information.
- The lack of established relationships between the digital representations and the descriptions makes difficult the diffusion of the content through the web.

The use of popular open source tools (e.g. Archivist Toolkit, Archon or Archivespace) do not offer a complete solution to deal with the complexity associated to the management of digital objects. These tools are oriented toward the publication of archival descriptions and accompanying images, but publication is just one of the steps in the life cycle of archival data.

Considering these aspects, the requirements to be implemented by the proposed solution include:

- Having a tool supporting the description of the archival materials using the EAD standard, fully compatible with ISAD(G).
- Keep all the data in standard formats.
- Easy publication of the records' descriptions and their digital representations in the web:
  - using different output formats (HTML, PDF).
  - With a look and feel aligned with the corporate image of the archive or the institutions it depends on.
  - Showing explicitly the hierarchical arrangement of the archival materials.
  - Offering full-text search capabilities.
- Capability of reusing, exporting and exchanging the metadata.

The design and implementation of the technical solution is divided into three parts or components:

- Content edition tool, with support to the creation of EAD and METS files.
- Content repository, based on a native XML database.
- Content publication tool, based on XSLT stylesheets.

The content edition tool was based on a custom development built on top of a free XML editor, Altova Authentic (a similar deployment just focused on the management of EAD data is described in [6]). Using these tool it is feasible to create templates that hide the complexity of XML mark-up to the end-users. Two separate templates where created: one for editing the EAD files – that are incorporated in the <dmdSec> element of the METS file -, and another one for keeping the information about the list of digitised files, their structure and order and hyperlinks. In the list of files, a distinction is made between the images used for publishing in the web, the thumbnails and the images in high resolution.

The resulting XML files are stored in a native XML repository based on Berkeley DB XML. The integration of the XML content editor with the database makes possible a smooth integration of the activities made by the archivists and the repository.

The final component of the solution is the publication module. This module includes separate XSLT stylesheets that process each METS file separately to generate different views of the data.

In the case of files, the stylesheets are run to generate several HTML pages:

- One with the descriptive metadata contained in the <dmdSec> element, based on EAD.
- A second one with the list of thumbnails for the different images of the digital representation.
- A set of pages for each page in the document.

The XSLT templates are modular, to separate the code that is used to generate the elements of the layout that depend on the corporate image of the institution (page header, lateral menus and page footer) and the code that is used to process the elements of the METS and EAD schemas. This modularity permits the reuse of the XSLT files in different projects, as customizing the look and feel of the resulting site only requires the update of the XSLT files that generate the header, footer and lateral menus.

Fig. 1. Web page showing a page of the file and thumbnails for the rest of the pages in the file.

Figure 1 show the custom look and feel of the pages generated for the proof of concept completed in the project (based on the archival descriptions provided by a Spanish archive holding historical records of the mining industry).

The content publication module follows a typical "staging" approach: XML content are moved from the database to a separate area where the XSLTs stylesheets are run to generate the set of HTML pages in a batch process. Then, these HTML pages are copied to the target web site. The web site integrates Google search – limited to the site of the target domain – to support full text searching.

4 Conclusions

Due to the relevance of digital materials in today's information management practices, archivists and information professionals need to consider additional requirements for storing, describing and delivering content. In the case of archives, traditional descriptive metadata - ISAD(G) and EAD – can be combined with other standards and technologies to support the diffusion, administration and long-term preservation of Cultural Heritage assets. The lack of tools that offer a smooth integration between metadata standards initially designed for different needs is one of the main constraints that professionals must face. The paper reports the development of an XML-based solution that integrates EAD descriptive metadata and METS to handle the digital representation of records and archival materials. The tool offers an integrated solution to manage these kind of assets, which are usually managed as separate entities, with no explicit links between them. The proposed solution streamline the dissemination of these assets and ensures a central-ized management based on the use of standards. The need of these tools has been recog-nized by archivists with implementations like those developed in the Archives Portal Europe [7] and the E-ARK (European Archival Records and Knowledge Preservation) project [8] for managing and displaying digital objects.

References

1. Dappert, A., Enders, M.: Using METS, PREMIS and MODS for archiving eJournals. D-Lib Mag. 14(9/10), 1082–9873 (2008)
2. Caplan, P., Guenther, R.S.: Practical preservation: the PREMIS experience. Libr. Trends 54(1), 111–124 (2005)
3. Gaitanou, P., Gergatsoulis, M., Spanoudakis, D., Bountouri, L., Papatheodorou, C.: Mapping the hierarchy of EAD to VRA Core 4.0 through CIDOC CRM. In: Garoufallou, E., Subirats Coll, I., Stellato, A., Greenberg, J. (eds.) MTSR 2016. CCIS, vol. 672, pp. 193–204. Springer, Cham (2016). https://doi.org/10.1007/978-3-319-49157-8_17
4. Eito-Brun, R.: Description of engineering artifacts and archival data: EAD meets VRA. Proc.-Soc. Behav. Sci. 147, 341–344 (2014)
5. Allison-Bunnell, J.: Review of encoded archival description tag library–version EAD3. J. W. Arch. 7(1) (2016)
6. Eito-Brun, R.: A metadata infrastructure for a repository of civil engineering records: EAC-CPF as a cornerstone for content publishing. J. Arch. Organ. 12(1–2), 62–76 (2014)

7. Peroni, S., Tomasi, F., Vitali, F.: The aggregation of heterogeneous metadata in web-based cultural heritage collections: a case study. Int. J. Web Eng. Technol. **8**(4), 412–432 (2013)
8. Maemura, E., Moles, N., Becker, C.: Organizational assessment frameworks for digital preservation: a literature review and mapping. J. Assoc. Inf. Sci. Technol. (2017)

Track on European and National Projects

Developing Quiz Games Linked to Networks of Semantic Connections Among Cultural Venues

Abdullah Daif[1]([envelope]), Ahmed Dahroug[2], Martín López-Nores[1],
Alberto Gil-Solla[1], Manuel Ramos-Cabrer[1], José Juan Pazos-Arias[1],
and Yolanda Blanco-Fernández[1]

[1] AtlantTIC Research Center, Department of Telematics Engineering,
University of Vigo, Vigo, Spain
adaif@uvigo.es,adrady@gmail.com,
{mlnores,agil,mramos,jose,yolanda}@det.uvigo.es
[2] Arab Academy for Science, Technology and Maritime Transport, Alexandria, Egypt
adahroug_87@aast.edu

Abstract. Existing general-purpose and domain-specific resources of the Semantic Web provide the foundations to discover connections between any two concepts of interest. The EU project CROSSCULT seeks to exploit that possibility in order to spur a change in the way citizens appraise history and culture, by means of web and mobile apps that will let them explore cross-border interconnections among cultural venues and their collections of heritage items. In this paper, we present a tool for experts to collaboratively develop the networks of semantic associations that will drive the gameplay or the storytelling of the apps. This tool includes reasoning aids to discover associations, to identify the most relevant ones in relation to selected topics, and to develop quiz tests involving the chosen entities (heritage items, characters, events or locations).

Keywords: Cultural heritage · Semantic associations · Association discovery and ranking · Reflective topics

1 Introduction

History is a huge mesh of interrelated facts and concepts, entwined with all other areas of human knowledge. However, this vision is neither commonplace at schools, nor in most of the cultural media that offer interpretation and dissemination to the wide public. On the contrary, History is typically presented in a siloed, simplistic and localistic manner that (i) promotes memorising rather than understanding, (ii) does not account for cross-border cultural aspects and (iii) prevents history, culture and even science from being viewed as a shared, global experience. For decades, many authors have called to implement student-centered and citizen-centered approaches in order to stimulate knowledge integration, reflection and retention in teaching and dissemination [1,2]. Nowadays,

© Springer International Publishing AG 2017
E. Garoufallou et al. (Eds.): MTSR 2017, CCIS 755, pp. 239–246, 2017.
https://doi.org/10.1007/978-3-319-70863-8_23

the advent of *Digital Humanities* is convincing more and more stakeholders that Information and Communication Technologies are mature enough to start realising the change [3].

The EU project CROSSCULT (www.crosscult.eu) seeks to create an open platform for web and mobile applications to deliver new experiences in line with the aforementioned vision, bringing together recent advances in the areas of semantic reasoning, recommendation/personalisation and digital storytelling. The cornerstone of the platform is a knowledge base that interrelates existing Linked Data resources with newly-developed ones (see [4]), based on the CIDOC *Conceptual Reference Model* (CRM)[1] that is progressively becoming the reference framework for cultural heritage information services [5]. On these grounds, the project partners have implemented a range of *association discovery* algorithms (based on successive rounds of SPARQL queries as in [6] and graph-traversal agents [7]) that provide semantic paths interrelating any entities of interest. In this paper, we present a web application that, taking those paths as input, allows humanities experts to collaboratively develop the networks of semantic associations that will drive the gameplay or the storytelling of the apps, exposing curated cross-border interconnections among cultural venues and their collections of heritage items.

The paper is organised as follows. Section 2 provides an overview of the experts' application. Section 3 presents the new mechanisms in place to identify the most relevant semantic paths in relation to the selected reflective topics, and to develop quiz tests involving some of the entities appearing in the paths. Section 4 presents early results about the perceived value of this tool among humanities experts from different venues that collaborate with CROSSCULT. Finally, Sect. 5 summarises our conclusions and describes our ongoing work.

2 A Tool to Design CROSSCULT Experiences

The motivation for writing an application to develop the networks of connections for the CROSSCULT experiences arose from the fact that, given a set of cultural venues, the association discovery algorithms may come up with tens or hundreds of semantic paths linking their heritage items. However, in order to deliver clear messages that instigate reflection and are easy to retain, it is up to experts to specify the *reflective topics* pursued and to select only the most relevant connections to develop each. Besides, it is not guaranteed that all the automatically-discovered connections be relevant (even if trivial connections are discarded straightaway, as explained in [7]) or correct (notable Linked Data resources have been criticised for the quality of the knowledge they capture in relation to humanities [8]), so qualified human supervision is needed. Experts can also enter new connections —not previously captured in any ontology— owing to their knowledge about the heritage collections in question.

Once the venues involved in a new experience have been selected, choosing from among the ones registered in the CROSSCULT platform, the experts can

---

[1] http://www.cidoc-crm.org/.

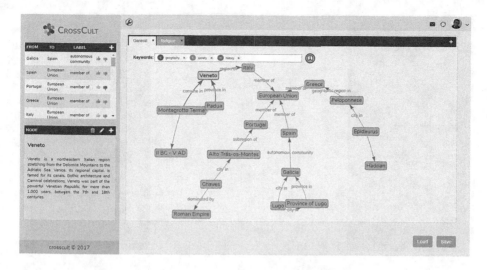

Fig. 1. Edition of topics and connections.

specify different types of target users according to any traits captured in the user profiles, which include demographic data (age, gender, marital status, ...), levels of knowledge about different subjects, personality and cognitive patterns (see [9] for details). Following that, the main screen of the experts' tool displays the elements that can be seen in Fig. 1:

- On top of the window, there appear as many tabs as reflective topics have been defined, each one characterised by a title and a number of keywords taken from EuroVoc vocabularies[2], and optionally the user types to which the topic is aimed.
- In the center of the screen, a graph visualisation contains the nodes and connections defined for the selected reflective topic. The experts can create new nodes and edges, edit and remove existing ones, drag the nodes around, zoom in/out, etc.
- On the left hand side, a table lists the triples that make up the semantic paths provided by the association discovery algorithms, ordered by their relation to the keywords of the selected reflective topic and the keywords that define the areas of competence of the expert (also taken from EuroVoc vocabularies). The ordering is computed by an *Associations Recommender* component, whose operation is summarised in Sect. 3. The experts can browse the list, drag-and-drop triples or paths into the graph visualisation, and right-click to tag triples or paths as *"worth considering"* or *"irrelevant"*.
- At the lower right corner there are buttons to load/save experience definitions from/to the CROSSCULT central repository.

---

[2] http://eurovoc.europa.eu/.

Fig. 2. Edition of informational snippets and multiple-choice questions.

As shown in Fig. 2, the nodes of the graph can be linked to snippets of information, containing text and/or multimedia contents to elaborate the narrative of the reflective topic, plus an optional number to specify their overall sequencing. Besides, the nodes can be turned into multiple-choice questions displaying text and images, timelines (when the original entity and the alternatives relate to time instants or periods) or geographical maps (when the choices correspond to locations). The alternatives to the original entity may be entered manually or suggested by a *Multiple Choices Recommender* component. As explained in Sect. 3, this component can deliver different recommendations upon successive clicks of the *"Get recommendation"* button. The expert can tag each recommended alternative as *"sure to use"*, *"makes sense"* or *"irrelevant"*, so that new clicks on the *"Get recommendation"* button only change the latter two (the *"makes sense"* alternatives may reappear later, whereas the *"irrelevant"* ones are discarded).

3   The Embedded Recommenders

Both the Associations Recommender and the Multiple-Choice Recommender rely on the word embeddings of *word2vec* [10], pre-trained on part of Google News dataset (about 100 billion words)[3]. In the current version of the CROSS-CULT platform (actually the first, released in May 2017), the computations go as follows:

- The Associations Recommender takes as input a collection of semantic paths and puts them on a list by decreasing relevance. To this aim, it simply rates

---

[3] The pre-trained embeddings were directly downloaded from https://code.google.com/archive/p/word2vec/.

each semantic path by the product of two averages of *word cosine distances*, as indicated by Eq. (1):

$$rating(\mathcal{P}, \mathcal{T}, \mathcal{X}) = \frac{1}{\#\mathcal{E}(\mathcal{P}) \cdot \#\mathcal{K}(\mathcal{T})} \cdot \left(\sum_{e \in \mathcal{E}(\mathcal{P})} \sum_{k \in \mathcal{K}(\mathcal{T})} WCD(e, k) \right)$$
$$\cdot \frac{1}{\#\mathcal{E}(\mathcal{P}) \cdot \#\mathcal{K}(\mathcal{X})} \cdot \left(\sum_{e \in \mathcal{E}(\mathcal{P})} \sum_{k \in \mathcal{K}(\mathcal{X})} WCD(e, k) \right) \quad (1)$$

where WCD denotes a word cosine distance; $\#$ denotes the cardinality of a set; $\mathcal{P}$ denotes a semantic path and $\mathcal{E}(\mathcal{P})$ the set of entities in it; $\mathcal{T}$ denotes the reflective topic and $\mathcal{K}(\mathcal{T})$ is the set of its defining keywords, and $\mathcal{X}$ denotes the expert with $\mathcal{K}(\mathcal{X})$ representing the set of keywords in his/her profile.

– The Multiple Choices Recommender takes one entity as input and provides three related alternatives, picking from any relevant *wikicategory* that contains the original entity.[4] First of all, the relevance of the wikicategories in relation to the current reflective topic and the expert's areas of competence is computed as indicated by Eq. (2), where $\mathcal{W}$ denotes a wikicategory and $\mathcal{C}(\mathcal{W})$ is the set of entities included in it:

$$rel(\mathcal{W}, \mathcal{T}, \mathcal{X}) = \frac{1}{\#\mathcal{E}(\mathcal{W}) \cdot \#\mathcal{K}(\mathcal{T})} \cdot \left(\sum_{e \in \mathcal{E}(\mathcal{W})} \sum_{k \in \mathcal{K}(\mathcal{T})} WCD(e, k) \right)$$
$$\cdot \frac{1}{\#\mathcal{E}(\mathcal{W}) \cdot \#\mathcal{K}(\mathcal{X})} \cdot \left(\sum_{e \in \mathcal{E}(\mathcal{W})} \sum_{k \in \mathcal{K}(\mathcal{X})} WCD(e, k) \right) \quad (2)$$

Once the four most relevant wikicategories have been found, the Multiple Choices Recommender puts all the entities contained in them into a unique set, from which it later picks alternatives to the original entity whenever requested by the expert. The selection is driven by the levels of knowledge indicated in the definitions of types of target users (Sect. 2), in the sense that lower levels of knowledge lead to the selection of alternatives which are further from the original entity (again, using word cosine distance) than in case of high levels.

4 Preliminary Evaluation Results

The tool and the recommenders presented in the preceding sections have hitherto been assessed by a team of experts who developed the contents for the Cross-Cult pilot experience called *"Many small venues"*. This pilot aims to highlight the connections among the Roman healing spa of Lugo (Spain), the thermal spa

---

[4] Wikicategories are groupings of Wikipedia pages on similar subjects. A global index of such groupings in English can be found at https://en.wikipedia.org/wiki/Wikipedia:Quick_cat_index.

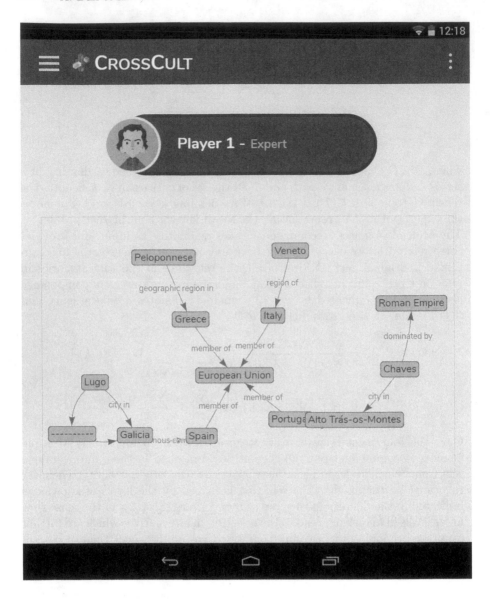

Fig. 3. The mobile app of the *"Many small venues"* pilot.

of Chaves (Portugal), the archæological site of Montegrotto Terme (Italy) and the ancient theater of Epidaurus (Greece), focusing on the reflective topics of *"Health"*, *"Leisure & daily life"*, *"Religion & pilgrimage"*, *"Trips & communication routes"* and *"Waters"* (see [11] for motivation and details). The experience is delivered by a mobile app that allows individual visitors or groups to explore the graphs of concepts and connections of the successive topics, browse the linked multimedia contents and fill in some nodes that appear blank by replying to the corresponding multiple-choice questions (a snapshot is given in Fig. 3). The reflective topics displayed and the choices included in the questions are selected according to two users types ("*knowledgeable*" and "*not-so-knowledgeable*"); the type of a given user is decided from his/her answers to a questionnaire about Classical Antiquity that appears right after logging in the mobile app.

The experts have rated aspects of perceived value on a Likert scale from 1 (lowest) to 5 (highest). Despite their lack of familiarity with graph visualisations and Semantic Web artifacts, we got the following average evaluations: 3.33 for "*the tool is intuitive and easy to use*", 4.17 for "*the tool is useful to develop connections among multiple venues*", 4.17 for "*the recommended associations are useful to develop the reflective topics*" and 4.00 for "*The tool facilitates the creation of multiple-choice questions that foster reflection*".

5   Conclusions and Future Work

We have created the first prototype of a tool for humanities experts to develop networks of semantic associations to drive the gameplay or the storytelling of apps intended to foster reflection about cultural heritage and history. The concept has been positively evaluated by a first group of experts, pending some improvements in terms of usability, the implementation of new features (e.g. widgets to link content from third-party collections and repositories of multimedia contents) and refinements in the association discovery and recommendation processes based on semantic reasoning. New teams will be involved in the development of other CROSSCULT pilot experiences and new initiatives in the context of a Living Lab starting in June 2017.

Regarding the improvements to the semantic reasoning aids, we plan to check whether different formulae that Eqs. (1) and (2) would provide better results (e.g. involving geometric or harmonic averages, thresholds and some notion of popularity for the terms in the Wikicategories). Likewise, we want to assess the impact of using different word embeddings (e.g. like the recent ones of ConceptNet Numberbatch [12]) or word2vec itself but trained on collections of documents focused on cultural heritage and history, like the ones gathered by Europeana Collections[5].

Acknowledgment. This project has received funding from the European Union's Horizon 2020 research and innovation programme under grant agreement No 693150.

References

1. Hafizur, R., Beng-Kiang, T.: Interpreting digital heritage: A conceptual model with end-users' perspective. Int. J. Architectural Comput. **9**(1), 99–114 (2011)
2. Maloy, R., Laroche, I.: Student-centered teaching methods in the history classroom: Ideas, issues, and insights for new teachers. Soc. Stud. Res. Pract. **5**(2), 46–61 (2010)

---

[5] http://www.europeana.eu/.

3. Bodenhamer, D.: The spatial humanities: space, time and place in the new digital age. In: History in the Digital Age. Routledge (2012)
4. Vlachidis, A., Bikakis, A., Terras, M., Naudet, Y., Deladiennee, L., Kyriaki-Manessi, D., Vasilakaki, E., Padfield, J., Kontiza, K.: Upper-level cultural heritage ontology. CROSSCULT Deliverable 2.3 (2017). http://www.crosscult.eu/en/resources/deliverables/
5. Myers, D., Dalgity, A., Avramides, I.: The arches heritage inventory and management system: a platform for the heritage field. J. Cult. Heritage Manage. Sustain. Dev. **6**(2), 213–224 (2016)
6. Heim, P., Hellmann, S., Lehmann, J., Lohmann, S., Stegemann, T.: RelFinder: Revealing relationships in RDF knowledge bases. In: Chua, T.-S., Kompatsiaris, Y., Mérialdo, B., Haas, W., Thallinger, G., Bailer, W. (eds.) SAMT 2009. LNCS, vol. 5887, pp. 182–187. Springer, Heidelberg (2009). https://doi.org/10.1007/978-3-642-10543-2_21
7. Bravo-Quezada, O., López-Nores, M., García-Nogueiras, I., Perdiz-Gradín, D., Blanco-Fernández, Y., Pazos-Arias, J., Gil-Solla, A., Ramos-Cabrer, M.: A semantics-based exploratory game to enrich school classes with relevant historical facts. In: Proceedings of 11th International Workshop on Semantic and Social Media Adaptation and Personalization (SMAP), Thessaloniki, Greece, pp. 128–132, October 2016
8. Berry, D. (ed.): Understanding Digital Humanities. Palgrave Macmillan, London (2012)
9. Vassilakis, C., Deladiennee, L., López-Nores, M., Giménez-Molina, R.: Programmer's guide for data management and service invocation - first version. CROSSCULT Deliverable 4.3 (2017). http://www.crosscult.eu/en/resources/deliverables/
10. Mikolov, T., Chen, K., Corrado, G., Dean, J.: Efficient estimation of word representations in vector space. CoRR abs/1301.3781 (2013)
11. Jones, C., Vlachidis, A., Bikakis, A., Lykourentzou, I.: Pilot specifications. CROSSCULT Deliverable 2.1 (2016). http://www.crosscult.eu/en/resources/deliverables/
12. Speer, R., Chin, J., Havasi, C.: Conceptnet 5.5: An open multilingual graph of general knowledge. In: Proceedings of 31st AAAI Conference on Artificial Intelligence, San Francisco (CA), USA, pp. 4444–4451, February 2017

Metadata for Nanotechnology: Interoperability Aspects

Vasily Bunakov[✉] and Brian Matthews

Science and Technology Facilities Council, Harwell, OX11 0QX, UK
{vasily.bunakov,brian.matthews}@stfc.ac.uk

Abstract. The work outlines the landscape of emerging metadata models for nanotechnology. A gap analysis and possible cross-walks for a few metadata recommendations are presented. The role of interoperability in the design of metadata for nanotechnology is discussed.

Keywords: Nanotechnology · Metadata models · Metadata interoperability

1 Introduction

Nanotechnology is no more a futuristic vision but established a permanent presence in the economy [1]. The fast pace of nanotechnology innovation blurs boundaries between research and industry; another noticeable trend is an intensive use of computer simulations for modeling nanomaterials which requires computation on the industrial scale.

Nanotechnology research and innovation deal with substantial amounts of data of all sorts. It may be data about nano-materials (either physical or computer-simulated) or it may be contextual data that is important for the research or industrial management, for complying with health and safety regulations, as well as for keeping records about the provenance of materials and products. Managing these various data requires good metadata which presents challenges both from a metadata design perspective and from an operational perspective of metadata quality and its semantic interoperability.

This work presents the effort of the Nanostructures Foundries and Fine Analysis (NFFA-EUROPE) project [2] on metadata design and, specifically, on the relation of this effort to other metadata initiatives. The main purpose of this work is to reflect on the position of the NFFA metadata model in a bigger landscape of metadata for nanotechnology and identify possible connections of the NFFA model to the elements of this landscape that can be further discussed with the respective projects and initiatives.

We first outline the design of the NFFA metadata model [3] and give reasons why it was required, then introduce other metadata models for nanotechnology with possible cross-walks between each of them and the NFFA model, then discuss the strengths of each metadata model and refer to the auxiliary collaborative effort that can contribute to the design of quality metadata for nanotechnology.

© Springer International Publishing AG 2017
E. Garoufallou et al. (Eds.): MTSR 2017, CCIS 755, pp. 247–252, 2017.
https://doi.org/10.1007/978-3-319-70863-8_24

2   NFFA Metadata Model

The Nanostructures Foundries and Fine Analysis (NFFA-EUROPE) project [2] brings together European research laboratories with the aim to provide seamless access to experimental equipment and computation for nanoscience researchers across the borders. The project organizational and IT infrastructure offers a single entry point for research proposals, and a common platform for the access to data resulting from the research. Both physical and computational experiments are intentionally in scope, as they often complement each other.

A novel metadata model has been developed in NFFA as a part of a Joint Research Activity that unites, on one hand, organizations that develop an IT infrastructure and on the other hand, the project partners who are involved in the actual running of physical or computational experiments and therefore can supply their requirements for metadata design and then validate the resulted model.

The main reason why a new metadata model was required is that it should be able to support a research lifecycle and data curation needs of what is called "facilities science" or "lab science" [11] when researchers apply for the timeslots in different facilities using a common portal for their research proposals. Another reason was to better cater for computational experiments so that metadata could accommodate the notions of both physical and computational experiments for nano-science.

The collaborative and multi-aspect process of metadata design in NFFA involved the development of a common vocabulary in the first place which served as a cornerstone for the loosely-coupled but semantically unambiguous enterprise architecture with the inclusion of both technological and organizational aspects of the project. The vocabulary was designed and validated with multiple stakeholders in order to ensure that common concepts can cover both physical and computational experiments.

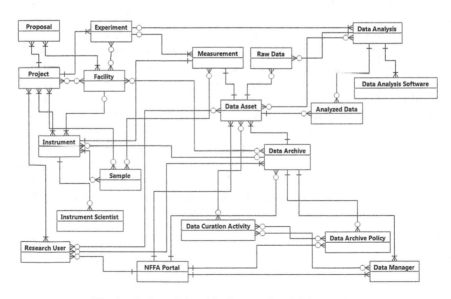

Fig. 1.   Entity-relationship diagram for NFFA metadata.

The common vocabulary was then used for the definition of information entities with clear semantic boundaries, and for the definition of relationships between them. The resulted entity-relationship diagram is presented in Fig. 1.

Such entities as Proposal, Project, Facility, Research User or Instrument Scientist represent organizational aspects of nanoscience experiments. Such entities as Experiment, Measurement, Instrument and Sample relate to the actual conduct of the experiment. Other entities represent data management, data curation and data analysis aspects of the experiment. These three interconnected aspects: organizational, experimental and data-related are conceptual pillars of the NFFA metadata model with its main purpose to capture all significant aspects of the experiment so that data stored in the common archive could be given a rich context required and serve a variety of business cases in cross-facilities experiments.

Overall the NFFA data model is aimed at a contextually rich description of nanoscience experiments lifecycle, with data management and data analysis considered to be essential parts of this lifecycle. The model is designed to reflect on both physical and computational experiments and on data resulted from them. The more detailed description of the model and its design considerations is given in [3]. Based on this model that can be considered a meta-model, various serializations (metadata formats) can be developed for their implementations in particular IT platforms.

3 Other Metadata Models and Semantic Assets for Nanotechnology

A significant effort has been made by CODATA [6] and VAMAS [7] who established a joint working group for the development of a uniform description system for nanomaterials. The group was international, also multi-discipline with the inclusion of representatives from physics, chemistry, pharmacology, ecology, engineering and other branches of research and technology. Through a number of workshops, the working group developed an elaborated recommendation [4] which, similarly to the NFFA metadata model [3], does not specify a data format but rather presents a structure of concepts that can be applicable for developing data formats and ontologies, for reporting research results, and for other practical uses.

The main focus of the CODATA-VAMAS model is on a nano-object with the metadata categories (sections) for the description of the object shape, size, physical structure, chemical composition, crystallographic structure and surface description. The model also pays attention to characterization of a collection of nano-objects with the captured concepts of a collection composition, size distribution, association type and topology. The model attempts to address the problem of the nano-objects production and testing, too, describing typical steps involved in those processes.

Cross-walks between NFFA and CODATA-VAMAS models are possible using three NFFA model entities: Sample, Experiment and Measurement. Sample can be related to nano-objects and collections of them in the CODATA-VAMAS model, Experiment can be related to nano-object production steps and Measurement to testing steps. To enable metadata cross-walks, either the respective entities of the NFFA model can be developed and presented as containers that include metadata definitions copied from CODATA-VAMAS model, or alternatively, these entities can serve as wrappers with pointers to the uniquely identifiable instances defined by the use of CODATA-VAMAS model, so that the respective part of the NFFA model devoted to nano-sample is just an annotation of an external CODATA-VAMAS description.

Another prominent effort has been made by NOMAD (NOvel MAterials Discovery) Laboratory, a European Centre of Excellence (CoE) [8] and is focused on modelling the computation for nanoscience. NOMAD maintains a large repository of input and output files for computer-simulated materials, and has developed metadata for it [5]. Unlike NFFA where metadata model has been derived through rounds of communication with nanoscience practitioners and IT architects, the NOMAD approach to metadata design is quite different and can be called opportunistic, as metadata elements are defined looking into the actual results of computational experiments. The NOMAD call this *a posteriori* approach with the main advantage of it that all significant properties of data can be captured as key-value pairs.

In order to implement this opportunistic or *a posteriori* approach, NOMAD construct the names of metadata elements on-the-fly depending on the concepts discovered in the results (data output) of a particular computational experiment. In addition to these metadata elements that can be called "topical keys", e.g. "energy_total_potential" name is a key for the corresponding data value, NOMAD consider a hierarchy of descriptors for the runs (executions) of a computer program that are related to particular software configurations, to the results of computation, as well as to theoretical methods used. This gives very context-rich descriptions of the computations actually performed.

Cross-walks between NFFA model and NOMAD one are possible via the NFFA Experiment entity that can relate to NOMAD "topical keys" that describe a particular experiment, as well as NFFA Measurement entity that can be related to the NOMAD definitions of program runs. The Sample entity of the NFFA model can relate to input data in NOMAD, and Data Asset to the output of NOMAD computation.

The identified cross-walks across the models are compiled in the Table 1.

Table 1. Cross-walks across NFFA, CODATA-VAMAS and NOMAD metadata models.

NFFA concept	CODATA-VAMAS concept	NOMAD concept
Experiment	Nano-object production steps	Series of s/w runs
Measurement	Nano-object testing steps	S/w run
Sample	Nano-object or collection of objects	Input data
Data Asset		Output data

It is noticeable that CODATA-VAMAS model is focused on the description of Samples (nano-objects) and the processes directly related to Samples such as production or testing steps but it does not care about data management.

On the opposite, the NOMAD model cares a lot about data; especially about Data Assets resulted from the computational experiment as this data is a source for the extraction of key-value metadata pairs in NOMAD.

Neither CODATA-VAMAS nor NOMAD care much about the organizational environment where experiment is conducted, whilst the NFFA model pays a detailed attention to such environment with a few entities like Facility, Proposal or Project catering for this. The data lifecycle in the archive has decent means of its description in the NFFA model but not as such in CODATA-VAMAS or NOMAD model.

Overall, the three models have some overlaps which make it possible to specify the above mentioned crosswalks but otherwise the models are complementary to each other. The levels of coverage of a few key aspects of nanotechnology by the three models is presented in Table 2 with the following gradations: Conceptual coverage (where there is at least one concept that can be potentially expanded), Detailed coverage (where there is enough interconnected concepts to cover the aspect) and Unadressed (when there is nothing or very little in the model to address the aspect).

Table 2. Conceptual coverage of nanotechnology experiments by NFFA, CODATA-VAMAS and NOMAD metadata models.

Nanotechnology aspect	NFFA model	CODATA-VAMAS model	NOMAD model
Nano-object	Conceptual	Detailed	Detailed[a]
Computation	Detailed[b]	Unaddressed	Detailed
Experiment lifecycle	Detailed	Conceptual	Conceptual
Data lifecycle	Detailed	Unaddressed	Conceptual

[a]For in silico (computer simulated) nano-objects only but key-value metadata pairs are potentially applicable to physical objects, too.
[b]As all NFFA model concepts are formulated in view of their dual application to physical and computational experiments.

Apart from the NFFA, CODATA-VAMAS and NOMAD metadata models, other semantic assets such as vocabularies and ontologies can be used to complement or augment the meaning of metadata concepts or their particular attributes. To better address the metadata interoperability challenge, the collaboratively developed semantic assets should be given a preference before the industry-led specifications. The Research Data Alliance [9] can be the right forum for such collaborations, with the particularly relevant effort of RDA/CODATA Materials Data, Infrastructure & Interoperability Interest Group [10] and RDA Materials Registry Working Group [11].

4   Conclusion

What we have considered in this work is the problem of interoperability of the NFFA metadata model with other prominent metadata models for nanotechnology that are not immediately represented in the NFFA project but can contribute to quality metadata design.

We look forward to fruitful discussions with the CODATA-VAMAS and NOMAD communities, as well as with the relevant RDA groups and other metadata practitioners in nanotechnology and material science who can contribute to the design of interoperable metadata.

Acknowledgements.   This work is supported by Horizon 2020 NFFA-Europe project www.nffa.eu under grant agreement no. 654360.

References

1. Vance, M.E., Kuiken, T., Vejerano, E.P., McGinnis, S.P., Hochella Jr., M.F., Rejeski, D., Hull, M.S.: Nanotechnology in the real world: redeveloping the nanomaterial consumer products inventory. Beilstein J. Nanotechnol. **6**, 1769–1780 (2015). https://doi.org/10.3762/bjnano.6.181
2. Nanostructures Foundries and Fine Analysis (NFFA-EUROPE) project. http://www.nffa.eu
3. Bunakov, V., Griffin, T., Matthews, B., Cozzini, S.: Metadata for experiments in nanoscience foundries. In: Kalinichenko, L., Kuznetsov, Sergei O., Manolopoulos, Y. (eds.) DAMDID/RCDL 2016. CCIS, vol. 706, pp. 248–262. Springer, Cham (2017). https://doi.org/10.1007/978-3-319-57135-5_18
4. Uniform Description System for Materials on the Nanoscale, Version 2.0. CODATA-VAMAS Working Group on the Description of Nanomaterials, 25 May 2016. https://doi.org/10.5281/zenodo.56720
5. NOMAD Meta Info. https://metainfo.nomad-coe.eu/nomadmetainfo_public/info.html
6. CODATA: Committee on Data for Science and Technology. http://www.codata.org
7. VAMAS: Versailles Project on Advanced Materials and Standards. http://www.vamas.org/
8. NOMAD (NOvel MAterials Discovery) Laboratory, a European Centre of Excellence (CoE). https://nomad-coe.eu/
9. Research Data Alliance. https://www.rd-alliance.org
10. RDA/CODATA Materials Data, Infrastructure and Interoperability Interest Group. https://www.rd-alliance.org/groups/rdacodata-materials-data-infrastructure-interoperability-ig.html
11. RDA Materials Registry Working Group. https://www.rd-alliance.org/group/international-materials-resource-registries-wg/post/rda-materials-registry-working-group

Data, Metadata, Narrative. Barriers to the Reuse of Cultural Sources

Jennifer Edmond(iD) and Georgina Nugent Folan(✉)(iD)

Trinity College Dublin, Dublin, Ireland
{edmondj,nugentfg}@tcd.ie

Abstract. The networking of objects facilitated by the Internet of Things isn't new. Every object that is catalogued for display within a GLAM institution is assigned entry-level data, along with further data layers on that object that each interactive agent (researcher) will draw upon to create their research narratives, irrespective of their disciplinary background or bias. Within the community of researchers working with cultural data in particular, the desire to compare and aggregate diverse sources held together by a thin red thread of potential narrative cohesion, is only increasing. This poses challenges to information retrieval and contextualization in the digital age, it forces us to reassess the value and cost of metadata, and the consequences that accompany the use and reuse of digital data in a humanities or cultural research context. This paper discusses a number of the key barriers to the digital representation of complex cultural data and presents the preliminary findings and recommendations of the EU Commission's Horizon 2020 funded KPLEX project (kplex-project.eu) in the field of knowledge complexity and cultural data.

Keywords: Narrative · Data · Metadata · Cultural computing · Digital humanities

1 Introduction

The networking of objects facilitated by the Internet of Things isn't new: in fact, the artifacts, nature and man-made, that inhabit the anthroposphere have always been connected by webs of information. Take, for example, a simple seashell. Any given seashell can be said to have certain core properties about which there is likely to be broad consensus: it is hard, it is hollow, is has a certain color. But these core properties have the potential to take on—or be attributed with—very different meanings depending on who or what interacts with them, and what interpretation they lay over these core properties. A child, for example, will appropriate it for use in a manner that is very different from that of a hermit crab. A fashion designer may take the item and, by inscribing designs on the shell, fundamentally alter the makeup of the item in and of itself, a factor that would influence how a museum cataloguer, working decades later, might catalogue the item for display within a GLAM institution.

© Springer International Publishing AG 2017
E. Garoufallou et al. (Eds.): MTSR 2017, CCIS 755, pp. 253–260, 2017.
https://doi.org/10.1007/978-3-319-70863-8_25

Put another way, each of the agents encountering the shell creates a **narrative**, capturing the meaning of the shell for them and for the moment in which they appropriate it. Narrative can here be understood as the story we tell about our data. As Jesse Rosenthal puts it

> narrative flaunts its human mediation. The term suggests communication—between a narrator and an implied narratee—and intention. More importantly, narrative declares itself as a retelling of something that had already existed in another form [2].

Roughly at the intersection of these narratives—these stories, or layers of human mediation—are, however, some shared essentials that all narratives draw upon. There is a **data layer** that narratives will share to some extent, though perhaps not equally, for example, a blind child won't know the color. In addition, in the course of the object's path through these narratives, it may be enhanced, altered or otherwise **transformed** in ways that are driven by specific agents or external forces, but which may not be apparent to later finders: the decorative layer added by the designer may or may not appear to a later user as the result of human intervention.

This metaphor of the seashell with its layers of data, narrative, and transformation may seem an overly charged one, but the same forces that circulate around such evocative objects shape our relationships to digital objects. Their interplay is not only useful for reimagining some of the challenges of information retrieval and contextualization in the digital age, but also for progressing an understanding of the value and cost of metadata and the use and reuse of digital data in a humanities or cultural research context.

2   Data: Slippery as a Fish?

An agent encountering an object or its representation perceives and draws upon the data layer they apprehend to create their own narratives. But any agent will likely perceive this data layer differently and, as a result, they retroactively think and speak about the data differently; identifying different "core principles" as input to their multiple narratives. A key facet of this problem is that the term data is ubiquitous, but is consistently interpreted differently, used in different contexts, or to refer to different things. Daniel Rosenberg [1] outlines the early history of "data" as a concept prior to the 20th century, and explores how it acquired its "pre-analytical, pre-factual status," while also clarifying that "facts are ontological, evidence is epistemological, data is rhetorical." Rosenthal [2] similarly presents data as an entity that "resists analysis." Christine Borgman [3] elaborates, stating that "Data are neither truth nor reality. They may be facts, sources of evidence, or principles of an argument that are used to assert truth or reality." Speaking in the context of data's relationship to fictional literary narratives, Rosenthal identifies data as a "fiction": "The fiction of data, the illusion of data" [2]. In addition, Rita Raley [4] posits data as "performative" because "our data bodies [...] are repeatedly enacted as a consequence of search procedures. Data is in this respect performative." Anything can *be data* once it is entered into a system *as data*.

A problematic facet of the discourse on data is that the language used is often overly theoretical and alienating, and therefore not necessarily accessible to the practitioners looking to make data findable, accessible, reusable, and interoperable. Given the cross-disciplinary nature of "data" this is problematic and potentially alienating to those approaching these debates from an information or computer science background which may not encourage cross-disciplinary dialogue. More assured definitions, as Borgman [3] observes, are to be found in business: "The most concrete definitions of data are found in operational contexts." However, operational definitions of data are necessarily pragmatic and, for the most part, discipline specific, which means that the problems encountered on a discipline-specific small scale environment will be magnified on an inter-disciplinary level. How a representative of the seafood industry speaks about seashells will be different to how an archivist working within a Natural History Museum speaks about them. So these operational definitions of data are not definitions *per se*, but discipline or industry-specific archival principles. Concordantly, they are often unclear in relation to what is and is not data; and arguably they also delimit the re-interpretability of the data by presenting it in the context of a specific database or dataset. Further still, because it is often the entity's placement within a database or other knowledge organization framework that causes it to be viewed as having the status of data, there is a high degree of contextual input, with the metadata taking on a prominent role in the assignation of data *as data*.

If left unaddressed, the confusion and disorganization brought about by this over-determined network of data definitions will have significant impact on future research programs and research infrastructures.[1] In order to better facilitate large-scale inter- or trans-disciplinary research infrastructures then, there needs to be consensus in terms of what we speak about when we speak about data, irrespective of how difficult it is to "define" it when it comes to the diverse cultural resources that fuel humanities research.

3   Metadata and the Shifting Sands of Meaning

To return to our shell analogy, aside from the object itself, we have the entry-level data, the data layer or layers on that object that each interactive agent will draw upon to create their narratives, irrespective of their disciplinary background or bias. Oftentimes, a necessary part of the process of moving from data to narrative involves moving from the **object** to a **document**.

Suzanne Briet, in her groundbreaking work Qu'est-ce que la documentation? identifies the presence of this process when she makes her distinction between entity and document:

> Une étoile est-elle un document? Un galet roulé par un torrent est-il un document? Un animal vivant est-il un document? Non. Mais sont des documents les photographies et les catalogues d'étoiles, les pierres d'un musée de minéralogie, les animaux catalogués et exposés dans un Zoo [5].
> (Is a star a document? Is a pebble rolled by a torrent a document? Is a living animal a document? No. But the photographs and the catalogues of stars, the stones in a museum of mineralogy, and the animals that are catalogued and shown in a zoo, are documents.) [6].

---

[1] See [13] for a discussion on the impact of the absence of standardisation on the interoperability of historical trade data.

The thing itself may be found, by chance, and be essentialized down to its manifestation(s) as data, but only on an individualized, perhaps haphazard basis. Facilitating wider reuse and integration into digital systems requires systematization, but how do we capture the richness of these items in a computerized environment?

This is where the question of metadata comes in. The goal of metadata is to align and describe the data layers of objects so that researchers can find the material they need or the material that is relevant to their research. Metadata supports, or should support, the formation of these narratives. According to William Uricchio [7] "data would be meaningless without an organizing scheme." Metadata is the "organizing scheme" that facilitates accessibility and discoverability of data, and its transformation into narratives. To a certain extent, metadata also influences the data it organizes and can thus be said to behave in a performative manner, having the potential to situate proto-data as data proper.

A rich information environment requires us to seek ways to reduce noise and enhance signal: this is what metadata does, but also data visualization, distant reading, semantic uplift, or any number of other strategies to focus on patterns within a text. But whose signal? Whose noise? Registries of digital objects created to mimic analogue finding aids are an essential part of the information retrieval landscape researchers face today. But they are also holdovers from a time when the affordances of the dominant technology were very different, and where a "natural curation" resulted from demographic and technological factors of the day. In the current context of largely unfettered access to digital data, this metadata can, as David Ribes and Steven Jackson [8] observe about data, "become a sort of actor, shaping and reshaping the social worlds around them" shaping and reshaping those fundamentals that underpin the range of possible narratives that can be created. Metadata standards have a mediating effect on the data that are accessible within the archive. They influence how we approach and conceptualize data. A failure to flag or fully account for data complexity leads to blinds spots within the archive. There is naturally a dual-threat here in the form of over- or under-describing: Over-describing risks losing the central signal from the material, while under-describing naturally results in reduced findability. It is necessary then to interrogate metadata's capacity to both delimit and flag data complexity and concordantly, to identify pragmatic approaches that avoid delimiting data while endeavoring at all times to maintain the capacity for the data within a given archive to display and communicate optimum semantic complexity. This is the sweet-spot that balances curation and complexity.

Not every person who approaches our seashell will be interested in the seashell in and of itself, just as not every agent that approaches an object within an archive has the same motives. For some then, the interest lies not in the data per se, but in how it's used. These are the things metadata can leave out or, in the case of the Shoah Foundation Visual History Archive (VHA), the metadata can be tailored to accommodate the interests of its primary audience. In "The Ethics of the Algorithm" Todd Presner [9] provides detailed analyses of "the meta-data scaffolding and data management system [...] that allows users to find and watch testimonies" of Holocaust survivors. These include human-assigned "hierarchical vocabularies to facilitate searching at a more precise level" [9]. Presner's concern is with the ethical implications of disassociating content and form: "Such a dissociation is not unique to the VHA but bespeaks a common practice in digital library systems and computation more generally, stretching back to Claude Shannon's theory of information as content neutral" [9]. Again however, this alternative metadata is tailored to a specific audience, and even within this purposefully curated system designed to counteract "the impulse to quantify, modularize, distantiate, technify, and bureaucratize the subjective individuality of human experience," [9] it is still possible to hide materials that do not align with your usage-intention such as for example any "content that the indexer doesn't want to draw attention to (such as racist sentiments against Hispanics, for example, in one testimony)" [9]. This again highlights the implications of "natural" curation via human limitations.

4   The Barnacled Shell: When Narrative Becomes Data

The urge to create narrative from data is deeply set in human nature [10]. Less recognized is what appears to be an equally innate ability to view what we find as somehow pristine, untouched by narratives: as data. In reality, the truth is often anything but: the shell we find takes its interesting shape and color from the barnacles that have colonized it, yet the data we find is still somehow "raw," as though untouched by the hands or subjectivities of others. Brine and Poovey [11] capture this paradox in their description of the so-called "data scrubbing" or "data cleaning" process as one "of elaboration and obfuscation"; it elaborates certain facets of the material, and obfuscates others. Borgman makes explicit that each and every decision made in the handling and rendering of data has consequences:

> Decisions about how to handle missing data, impute missing values, remove outliers, transform variables, and perform other common data cleaning and analysis steps may be minimally documented. These decisions have a profound impact on findings, interpretation, reuse, and replication [3].

In the sciences cleaning/scrubbing of data is considered standard practice; so much so that it is often taken as a given and, as noted above, minimally documented.[2] While the knowledge that data is always already "cleaned" or "scrubbed" is implicit in disciplines such as economics, in the humanities, cleaning of data does not receive as much (or any) attention or acknowledgement. Contradictions and confusions are rampant across humanities disciplines not only with respect to what data is, how data becomes data (whether it needs to be cleaned or scrubbed, whether the fact that this scrubbing takes place is or is not implicit to the discipline) and whether original context, abstraction, or recontextualizing are integral functions for the treatment of data. How do we retain cognisance of that which has been scrubbed away?

As Jennifer Edmond notes in "Will Historians Ever Have Big Data?" semantically and contextually complex cultural data is precisely the material humanities researchers thrive on; and again this presents us with a huge problem in terms of information systems management and curation:

---

[2] See [8] for further discussion of the cleaning that takes place in long-term data gathering projects.

> How is this level of uncertainty, irregularity and richness to be captured and integrated, without hiding it "like with like" alongside archival runs with much less convoluted narratives of discovery? Who is to say what […] is "signal" and what "noise"? Who can judge what critical pieces of information are still missing? [12].

If the interrogability of data makes everything potentially accessible, if the interests of humanities researchers makes every unit of data hold speculative value for the researcher, then we can no longer rely on "natural" curation via human limitations. After all, Raley [4] notes that "Data cannot 'spoil' because it['s value] is now speculatively, rather than statistically, calculated." It can, however, become hidden, or be rendered latent within an archive as a result of the very information architecture employed to facilitate its inclusion and findability within that archive.

Scholars have acknowledged the issues surrounding data cleaning and processing, particularly in the sciences, but there appears to be a lack of material addressing, acknowledging, and accounting for data processing in the humanities where machinations and re-shapings or re-contextualization of data are under-acknowledged, rarely explained or justified, and often not reversible. What also needs to be addressed then is whether the cleaning data undergoes is (or should be) reversible in a manner skin to the material recorded using NASA's Earth Observing System Data Information System (EOS DIS),[3] where, as Borgman [3] notes "Data with common origin are distinguished by how they are treated." This sees data defined by what researchers do to the data to make it data. In accordance with the EOS DIS, a researcher can opt for data at levels between 0 and 4, or even further back than the 0 phase, opting instead for native data (level pre-0 data?).

The EOS DIS is perhaps one of the most functional definitions of data available because it not only acknowledges the levels of processing material undergoes to become data, but tiers this scrubbing or cleaning process, therein acknowledging that some material undergoes more extensive modification than others, and maintaining traceability to the source context or environ wherein the "native data" was extracted from. That said, this approach is not without its problems. Firstly, it is incomplete because of the presence of a level that precedes "level 0"; data that precedes "level 0" is referred to in passing by Borgman as "native data," a phrase that is both problematic (having as it does unpleasant connotations akin to those that accompany the use of the term "primitive" or "primitivism" in art) and acute. "Native data" retains emphasis on the importance of context apropos data, whether that context be "native" or in the form of the context(s) it acquires when it transitions from a native to a non-native environment: "Some scientists want level 0 data or possibly even more native data without the communication artefacts removed so they can do their own data cleaning" [3]. However, while the distinctions between levels are relatively explicit, they only pertain to the onset of the research, the point where data is *gathered*. Thereafter the data is considered raw, until it is subjected to further processing:

> Although NASA makes explicit distinctions between raw and processed data for operational purposes, *raw* is a relative term, as others have noted […] What is 'raw' depends on where the

---

[3] "NASA EOS DIS Data Processing Levels," https://science.nasa.gov/earth-science/earth-science-data/data-processing-levels-for-eosdis-data-products.

inquiry begins. To scientists combining level 4 data products from multiple NASA missions, those may be the raw data with which they start. At the other extreme is tracing the origins of data backward from the state when an instrument first detected a signal [3].

It remains to be seen as to how the EOS DIS table would look had it been compiled for the purpose of humanities research. Interestingly, not one of the categories employed has an analogous one in the humanities (aside from the rather loose concept of primary, secondary and tertiary sources), though that is not to say that a clear, lucid gradation of data that distinguishes how the material has been treated, or at least flags the fact that the data has been subjected to transformations, would not be beneficial for humanities researchers.

5   Conclusion and Recommendations

The challenges we present are not new: but the fact that they are acknowledged does not mean that they have no negative effect on our ability to access and reuse data, or that we are moving steadily toward their resolution. Certainly within the community of researchers working with cultural data, the desire to compare and aggregate diverse sources held together by a thin red thread of potential narrative cohesion, is only increasing. The KPLEX project (kplex-project.eu) is investigating these barriers to meaning-making. Our team has adopted a comparative, multidisciplinary, and multi-sectoral approach to this problem, focussing on key challenges to the knowledge creation capacity of cultural data such as the terms we use to speak about data in a cultural context, the manner in which data that are not digitised or shared become "hidden" from aggregation systems, the fact that data lacks the objectivity often ascribed to the term and the subtle ways in which data that are complex almost always become simplified before they can be aggregated.

Our initial results would suggest that the following measures contribute greatly to meaningful findability in cultural collections. First: we need to build upon existing momentum toward standardization, not necessarily of metadata approaches, but for the automatic uplift and storage to linked open data of information that might facilitate the serendipitous discovery of connections between otherwise dissimilar documents. Second: we must build upon existing provenance work for RDM such as the W3C standard for provenance (https://www.w3.org/TR/prov-overview/), or the activities of the RDA working group on Research Data Provenance. We must be more rigorous about documenting and sharing information about the transformations applied to data, so that we can access not just the data as it is now, but retrace its journey to its current state via a sort of "data passport." Third, we must work toward a state where cultural heritage institutional finding aids are able to converge with the secondary literature that discusses the collections represented there. The historic separation between scientific publishers and cultural heritage institutions is a huge barrier to an obvious opportunity to enhance the big data of the catalogues with the rich data of scholarly production. Finally, we must recognize that not everything of value for the study of human culture can or will be digitized. The digital record must somehow incorporate that which is hidden to the digital eye. This may seem a paradox, or at least a challenge, but it will be a key underpinning for scholarship in the future that does not end up writing only the history of those on the winning side of the digital divide. Just as the sound of the sea is intrinsic to the curve of the seashell, we must also invent new shapes for the future of documentation that speaks both of itself and of its context, its origin, its journey to your hand.

Acknowledgements. This work has been funded by the European Commission as a part of the Knowledge Complexity (KPLEX) project, contract number 732340. It bears an intellectual debt to Dr. Michelle Doran of the KPLEX project team.

References

1. Rosenberg, D.: Data before the fact. In: Gitelman, L. (ed.) "Raw Data" is an Oxymoron, pp. 15–40. MIT Press, London (2013)
2. Rosenthal, J.: Introduction: "Narrative against Data." In: Genre 50.1, pp 1–18. Duke University Press, 1 April 2017. https://doi.org/10.1215/00166928-3761312
3. Borgman, C.L.: Big Data, Little Data, No Data: Scholarship in the Networked World. MIT Press, Cambridge (2015)
4. Raley, R.: Dataveillance and Countervailance. In: Gitelman, L. (ed.) "Raw Data" is an Oxymoron, pp. 121–145. MIT Press, Cambridge (2013)
5. Briet, S.: Quoted in Day RE. Indexing It All: The Subject in the Age of Documentation, Information, and Data, p. 156. MIT Press, Cambridge (2014)
6. Briet, S., et al.: What Is Documentation? English Translation of the Classic French Text, p. 10. Scarecrow Press, Lanham (2006)
7. Uricchio, W.: Data, culture and the ambivalence of algorithms. In: Schäfer, M.T., van Es, K. (eds.) The Datafied Society: Studying Culture through Data, pp. 125–138. Amsterdam University Press, Amsterdam (2017)
8. Ribes, D., Jackson, S.J.: Data bite man: the work of sustaining a long-term study. In: Gitelman, L. (ed.) "Raw Data" is an Oxymoron, pp. 147–166. MIT Press, Cambridge (2013)
9. Presner, T.: The ethics of the algorithm: close and distant listening to the shoah foundation visual history archive. In: Fogu, C., Kansteiner, W., Presner, P. (eds.) Probing the Ethics of Holocaust Culture. Harvard University Press, Cambridge (2015)
10. Kahneman, D.: Thinking Fast and Slow. Farrar, Straus & Giroux Inc., New York (2013)
11. Brine, K.R., Poovey, M.: From measuring data to quantifying expectations: a late nineteenth-century effort to marry economic theory and data. In: Gitelman, L. (ed.) "Raw Data" is an Oxymoron, pp. 61–76. MIT Press, Cambridge (2013)
12. Edmond, J.: Will historians ever have big data? In: Bozic, B., Mendel-Gleason, G., Debruyne, C., O'Sullivan, D. (eds.) CHDDH 2016. IAICT, vol. 482, pp. 91–105. Springer, Cham (2016). https://doi.org/10.1007/978-3-319-46224-0_9
13. Kirwan, L.: Databases for quantitative history. In: Proceedings of the Third Conference on Digital Humanities in Luxembourg with a Special Focus on Reading Historical Sources in the Digital Age, Luxembourg, December 5–6, CEUR Workshop Proceedings, 1613 (2013)

Validating the Ontology-Driven Reference Model for the Vocational ICT Curriculum Development

Mohammad Hadi Hedayati[1(✉)] and Mart Laanpere[2]

[1] Computer Science Faculty, Kabul University, Kabul, Afghanistan
hdhedayati@gmail.com
[2] School of Digital Technologies, Tallinn University, Tallinn, Estonia
martl@tlu.ee

Abstract. In the globally standardized domain of ICT, the vocational education curricula have to balance the requirements of fast-evolving international standards with unique local cultural traditions and socio-economic needs. This paper summarizes the results of a case study that tackled this challenge by developing and validating a reference model for ontology-driven curriculum development in the context of vocational ICT education in developing countries a case study about Afghanistan. We have demonstrated that even in the most challenging socio-economic and cultural context, semantic technologies have potential to represent, organize, formalize and standardize the knowledge in ICT domain so that it can be built, shared and reused in the curriculum process by different stakeholders like teachers, employers, alumni and deans. The final stage of our iterative design-based research focuses on development and validation of Ontology-Driven Curriculum (ODC) reference model based on results of our previous research.

Keywords: ICT · Vocational education · Curriculum · Ontology · Semantic web · Metadata · Knowledge management · Knowledge sharing · Job market · Reference model

1 Introduction

The fifty years of ICT development had a remarkable impact on ordinary peoples' lives and jobs even in the poorest countries such as Afghanistan. In spite of the recent downturn in the ICT markets, this area continues to be expected to provide a large number of new jobs over the coming years even in the most impoverished economies. Today, ICTs are relevant and important in nearly every business sector. Hence, the demand on the labor market for ICT education and employees with up-to-date ICT end-user skills is always growing. In developing countries, where youth unemployment in general is significantly higher than in European countries, the graduates of ICT study programs are in high demand among employers. However, our earlier research [11, 12] demonstrated that such a high demand towards ICT specialists has allowed vocational institutes of developing countries to supply ad-hoc, irrelevant study programs in the domain of ICT. Without national-level curriculum guidelines and pedagogical/curriculum competences, the low-qualified vocational ICT teachers tend to copy and teach the reduced

E. Garoufallou et al. (Eds.): MTSR 2017, CCIS 755, pp. 261–272, 2017.
https://doi.org/10.1007/978-3-319-70863-8_26

versions of the university courses, although the employers expect quite different competencies from vocational school graduates [11].

Job market in ICT sector is one probably the most influenced by the impact of international standardization resulting from globalization. Internet, computers and typical software is the same all in majority of workplaces around the world, both in developed and developing countries. Therefore, vocational education systems in all countries must increasingly take responsibility for providing to the next generation of students an updated set of ICT skills in line with fast developing international qualification and competence standards, as the domain knowledge and job profiles evolve constantly in the field of ICT. This implies the need for continuous curriculum innovation in vocational schools to maintain alignment with global standards. On the other hand, curriculum theorists [12] stress the importance of deliberative and inclusive curriculum design process that takes into consideration the specific local cultural and socio-economic factors, which are quite different in developing countries and their labor markets [9].

In order to address to the abovementioned challenge, we suggest a method of ontology-driven modeling of the vocational ICT curricula in developing countries, using easy-to-use semantic web tools such as Semantic MediaWiki and concept maps [33]. This paper summarizes the results of the design science research that aimed to develop and validate a reference model and related set of semantic tools that can be used in vocational schools to balance the global and local requirements for ICT curriculum development in developing countries.

Reference model is a generic meta-model of a domain that expresses an enterprise and its information system. Reference models enable the users to select relevant parts of the entities in the domain and adapt the parts in order to reduce the efforts during creation of application-specific models and related information systems [5]. There are many advantages of using reference model. First, reference models enable the developers to consider standards for objects and their relationships. The second advantage of reference model makes easy the communication of stakeholders to save the time and the cost. We use reference model for designing processes, artifacts ant tools to support curriculum development, implementation and evaluation processes that engage teachers, employers, alumni and administrators. Another advantage of reference model is helping curriculum developers to break down a big problem into smaller problems which can be refined and solved.

The study focused on the following research problem: how can semantic technologies help to balance the requirements of international qualification and competence standards in the domain of ICT with local cultural and socio-economic factors in the process of developing vocational ICT curricula in a developing country such as Afghanistan?

Our approach made use the potential of domain ontology and related semantic web technologies to structure and organize the data in the way it is understandable for ICT teachers in vocational schools in developing countries. Ordinary vocational school teachers are not knowledge engineers and are unable to directly contribute to ontology engineering and maintenance, but their engagement can be increased with the help of simple ontology-driven tools such as Semantic MediaWiki and concept maps.

This research was guided by the following research questions:

1. What are the preliminaries for modeling vocational ICT education in developing countries?
2. What are the layers, components and attributes of ontology-driven modeling for vocational ICT curriculum development?
3. Is the proposed reference model valid for vocational ICT curriculum development in the given context?

In order to answer these research questions, we carried out a review of related research, developed a reference model for vocational ICT curriculum development, instantiated this model with a demo application based on Semantic MediaWiki and conducted in a case study for evaluation of the model.

2   Context and Background

There are no professional qualification standards for ICT professionals or other national-level competence frameworks for ICT specialists in developing countries. On the other hand, European policies in vocational ICT education are guided by a set of well-defined job profiles in 14 generic work areas at sub-degree levels. These job profiles have been developed and constantly revised by representatives of educators, employers and standardization bodies in the field of ICT. However, we cannot take it for granted that developing countries should just copy the guidelines, qualification standards and study programs from Europe, as the job market needs might be quite different there. The European e-Competence Framework (e-CF) [25] provides a set of forty competences required and applied at the workplace, using a common language for competences, skills and capability levels that can be understood across Europe. The e-CF is a component of the European Union's strategy on e Skills for the 21st Century; it supports key policy objectives of the Grand Coalition for Digital Jobs launched in March 2013. While e-CF targets mainly higher education in ICT domain, another framework called EUCIP (European Certification of Informatics Professionals) was created specifically for vocational education [26]. EUCIP is a competence model, which offers the definitions and measurement indicators of ICT skills and is currently used as the basis for the provision of certification and services in ten countries across Europe. In some European countries there are national-level ICT skills framework such as eCCO in Italy and eSkillsUK in UK. Such frameworks are used for improving the match between what is taught in vocational schools and what skills are needed on the job market. Ontology-driven approach to modeling ICT competences and job profiles allows also to compare ICT curricula in different countries, enhance cross-border mobility and accreditation of ICT professionals, find and recommend relevant learning resources, make accreditation of prior learning and experience more reliable [27, 28]. This is why our research has been focused on ontology-driven modeling of vocational ICT curricula in developing countries while trying to balance the global vs. local needs in ICT education with the help of semantic technologies. This research is a continuation of our previous studies and in line with the model curricula [9] proposes to use ontological principles for the modeling the culturally-sensitive vocational ICT curriculum development process.

3   Related Research

Ontological model can be adapted for modeling as the computing with competencies e.g. [35] used for generic framework. Ontology-driven modeling has been applied in various research fields and application areas [10], including knowledge engineering, database design and integration, information retrieval and education. Some recent research done on ontology-based structured development focusing on data acquisition system e.g. [36] presented functional evaluation in clinical domain. Their result is highly agreeable to automatic analysis. Formalized and standardized model ICT curricula have been created by organizations like ACM and IEEE. Ontology is the pillar of semantic web and its applications used in various field and disciplines including education [2]. Semantic web enables us to reform the current web by adding layers to provide advanced automatic processing of web content, to enable the simultaneous access, analysis and enrichment of the data by both human and machine. Semantic web technologies make the computers to "understand" the web content and to help the human users with finding and interpreting relevant information and combining information in new ways to support knowledge based tasks such as authoring, planning, navigation, knowledge management and research [1]. The vision of Educational Semantic Web was proposed by researchers [4] already more than a decade ago, suggesting a service-based interoperability framework that could open up, share and reuse educational systems' content and knowledge components. They also proposed ontology-driven authoring tools that support automation of the complex learning resource authoring tasks [4].

Semantic MediaWiki (SMW) is one of such lightweight semantic tools that are created for collaborative knowledge management; its effectiveness has been demonstrated by several researchers. For instance, [3] used SMW for tracking internalization of new knowledge in a realistic course setting enhanced by assimilation and accommodation prompts and resulting with enhancing the learning.

There are different approaches to ontology driven modeling and one of them is building ontology reference models which can be used as blueprints [13, 14] and prototypical models [5] of information systems in different fields [6, 15, 22] demonstrated that use of reference model leads to high quality domain models on high and medium enterprise architecture levels [7]. Reference models have been created and validated by researchers in different areas like e-commerce [16], e-learning [20], information and library science [22], cloud computing [23], 3D modeling for cultural artifacts [17], workflow automation in multimedia production [19], competence modeling at vocational education programs [21] and sustainable development [18]. One research project that was close to our focus was carried out in University of Duisburg-Essen for integrating ontology-driven competence modeling into the European water sector by transferring the European Qualification Framework (EQF) and the German Reference Model for the Competence into Vocational Education and Training (VET) standards [21]. This project reference model for guiding identification of the VET needs by employees and learners, of required competences and qualifications at specific working places [21]. While there are several modeling languages exist for Enterprise Architecture and software, most of the reference models seem to use a language that is custom-made to the specific knowledge domain [21, 25].

Another significant study suggested the GCS (generic competency schema) model of generic competency to specify the requirements and offers shared built in computational semantics. They represented the needs of relationships among competencies to specify stages of competency elements [35].

Evaluation of reference models has been conducted by researchers using different approaches, e.g. [19, 29] describe three alternatives based on the model's features, ontology and cognitive psychology and suggested a Bunge ontology for the evaluation of reference models [31] used simpler approach for evaluation of reference models aligned by the heuristic criteria such as semantic correctness, applicability and adaptability of the model.

In general, we found out that most of previous related research on evaluating reference models has been dedicated to evaluation of conceptual model evaluation or to testing of a modeling language. The evaluation perspectives were guided by either linguistic categories (syntax, semantics and pragmatics), or dealt with users' perception diffusion at most or evaluating certain model's relationship to real world situation. Ontology can be seen as a valuable contribution to more elaborative and convincing evaluation [8].

On the long run, the value of a reference model depends on how the community sees it and accepts it as a useable one. But for a start, a simple heuristic evaluation by a group of potential target group members could help researchers to evaluate model by identifying the main strengths and weaknesses of a model in order to improve it.

4 Proposed Reference Model

Technology and a shared language enable the institutions to design pedagogical programs through collaboration with stakeholders [24]. The domain ontology can be used as a foundation for building a foundation for this shared language to bring together the stakeholders and technical standards to build shareable and machine-readable representations of knowledge objects, skills, and competences for the development of ICT vocational education program.

Underlying domain ontology together with the reference model could guide both development of software applications, information systems and institutional processes in the context of curriculum development. Hence, we propose a reference model that is based on our previous research on ontology-driven curriculum development; we call it Ontology-Driven Curriculum (ODC) reference model.

The proposed ODC reference model provides collaboration and support to stakeholders to develop, implement and validate the curriculum. The ODC reference model enables the vocational institutes to reform the processes of curriculum development. The model has two dimensions: the horizontal dimension contains the three phases of curriculum process, and the vertical dimension describes the layered structure of ontology-driven curriculum development.

The basic type and essential meta-model of ODC reference model showed in Fig. 1. The objects differentiate between three layers: the process layer, the semantics layer, and the services layer. Within each layer, the model reflects components mapped to three phases of curriculum process: curriculum development, curriculum implementation, and curriculum evaluation. Every layer is a means to provide services to the next upper level where the highest level provides process services to the stakeholders.

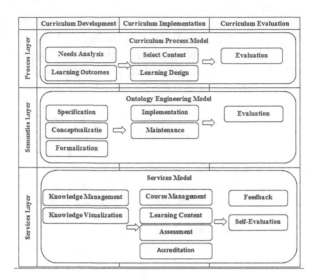

Fig. 1. Proposed ODC reference model

Within the process layer, we defined the component based on Hilda Taba's curriculum model [32]. In the curriculum implementation phase, the process layer suggests engaging different stakeholders in needs analysis and defining the goals and objectives of the curriculum. In the next phase curriculum implementation, the learning goals and outcomes are defined, after that the learning contents are selected and organized by participants of the curriculum process. It enables the administrators to guide and monitor the curriculum implementation process, to build and apply quality assurance mechanisms, to find out taught, learned and assessed curricula. Eventually, in the evaluation phase the curriculum needs to be evaluated by engagement of different stakeholders like administrators, employers, deans, alumni and so on.

Structure and components of the semantic layer of ODC model was guided by Methontology, one of the most popular reference models for ontology engineering. The first two components of Methontology are ontology specification and ontology conceptualization. For the specification, we used international standards in ICT education and other, related ontologies in educational and ICT domains. In the conceptualization phase, we engaged representatives of various stakeholder groups in concept mapping activities that resulted with initial conceptual models of ontology-driven ICT curriculum. In our earlier research, we used OWL and Protégé for ontology formalization. The semantic layer of ODC reference model will help to make curricula in different vocational institutes comparable and allows discovery of overlaps or uncovered topics in curricula in comparison with international qualification standards or job market needs. The semantic layer, ODC reference model helps the educational institutions to produce high quality curricula that can better address the labor market needs and match the international standards. In order to assure the ongoing relevance and quality of curricula and underlying domain ontologies in a fast-developing domain such as ICT, the ontology has to be regularly maintained and evolved. Ontology evaluation component will address this need.

Within the service layer, the knowledge management and visualization components are suggested in the curriculum development phase. In our earlier research, we used Semantic MediaWiki to build a collaborative knowledge management service called VocITwiki. The concept mapping plugin for Semantic MediaWiki was used for building the visualization service. Feedback service (for collecting data from students) and staff's self-evaluation service are already quite common in the vocational institutes of Afghanistan as case study, but ODC reference model and underlying ontology helps to create more effective and comparable evaluation services.

Figure 1 illustrates the phases, layers and components within each layer of the proposed ODC reference model.

5   Research Design

This paper reflects on the final stage of iterative design-based research that led us to development of the ODC reference model for ontology-driven vocational ICT curriculum development in developing countries. The three phases of this iterative study are reflected in [9, 11, 12] and visualized in Fig. 2 below.

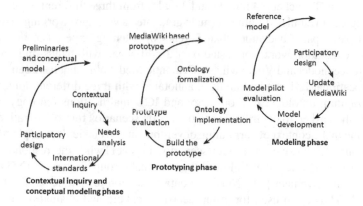

Fig. 2. Process model of research-based design phases

In the contextual inquiry and conceptual modeling phase we analyzed the local cultural context, the job market needs, related research and international standards in order to define the preliminaries and conceptual model.

In the prototyping phase we designed and tested the ontology-driven curriculum development scenarios engaging various stakeholders. It resulted with an initial prototype of collaborative knowledge management tool VocITwiki, which was built with

Semantic MediaWiki and made use of three formalized domain ontologies: curriculum ontology, computing ontology and ICT qualifications ontology.

The current paper reflects upon the modeling phase, where we created the generic reference model based on our experience of VocITwiki and validated it through case study that engaged a group of potential users. The following figure shows the VocITwiki interface.

Figure 3 shows the VocITwiki web interface of prototype which is human and machine readable and was pilot-tested by various stakeholder groups in authentic settings of vocational ICT curriculum development.

Fig. 3. The web interface of VocITwiki prototype

The finalized reference model was evaluated during case study involving a sample of 8 persons: 7 ICT teachers (4 female and 3 male) from three different technical voca-tional institutes of Kabul and 1 alumni (male graduated a year ago) working in the public sector. All participants had more than 5 years of teaching experience in vocational school. The evaluation workshop lasted over 2 h, it began with hands-on introduction of the reference model and VocITwiki – a Semantic MediaWiki that has been populated with the vocational ICT curriculum data, annotated with three different domain ontol-ogies (curriculum ontology, ICT ontology and ICT qualifications ontology, see [9]). Users were then asked to contribute to two real-life scenarios for collaborative knowl-edge building in the context of curriculum development and curriculum implementation. After an hour of intensive work with scenarios in VocITwiki, the respondents went through a group interview that followed the Nominal Group Technique (NGT) as key stakeholders' involvement [34]. NGT is a data collection technique similar to Delphi technique. NGT is often used for group decision making and evaluation, it proceeds through five phases [30]: (1) Introduction by facilitator, (2) Silent generation of ideas, (3) Sharing the ideas on the whiteboard, (4) Group discussion, and (5) Voting and ranking. In our case, the participants were asked to evaluate the reference model together with its prototype implementation VocITwiki against the three criteria suggested by [31]: (1) syntactic and semantic completeness and correctness, (2) adaptability and (3) applicability. In the eventual ranking list, the item that was of the highest priority for a respondent scored 3 points, the second one 2 and the next one 1 point, while the rest of items scored 0 points. Scores were summarized across all respondents and final ranking list was discussed once more to reach consensus with the group.

6   Results and Discussion

The validation of ODC reference model aimed to find out its semantic correctness, applicability and adaptability discussed in a focus group interview with eight participants. The results are shown and discussed below.

The results of group evaluation based on NGT are summarised in Table 1. The top score for both *Correctness* and *Applicability* criteria was expression of hesitation by participants, who thought that more experience in long-term use with a fully localised version of the model in a real-life context is needed before the judgement about can be confirmed. Yet, the next positions in ranking lists showed positive attitudes of respondents both towards *Correctness* (Comment: *"Good enough"*) and *Applicability* (Comment: *"Helps in sharing experience"*) of the reference model. The group discussion confirmed that learning from each other using ontology-driven modelling of curriculum development and implementation is seen as the main value of the model. However, the participants repeatedly voiced their concerns about poor ICT infrastructure and skills of staff in vocational schools that would reduce applicability of the reference model and VocITwiki in any other department than ICT or computer science in vocational schools of developing countries. While evaluating *Adaptability* of the reference model, the focus of participants was shifting more towards the adaptability of the VocITwiki and its underlying domain ontology, which received highly positive comments from the majority of participants (*Easy to visualise, Easy to change structure, Easy to change layout, Interoperability*). In the final discussion, the group reached consensus on correctness, applicability and adaptability of the reference model that could definitely help them to improve the quality of vocational ICT education in developing countries even if it is not possible yet to transfer to other domains of vocational education.

Table 1. The ranking list resulted from NGT.

Criterion	Comments from participants	Persons	Score
Correctness	Not sure before full localization and use	7	15
Correctness	Good enough	3	9
Correctness	Some terms are unfamiliar	6	6
Correctness	Some terms are irrelevant	2	2
Applicability	Undecided, should try in authentic context	7	19
Applicability	Helps sharing experience	3	15
Applicability	Localization would improve applicability	3	8
Applicability	Applicable only in IT domain	5	5
Applicability	Easy to use	1	3
Adaptability	Easy to add visualizations	4	8
Adaptability	Easy to change structure	2	5
Adaptability	Interoperability	5	3
Adaptability	Easy to integrate with other systems	4	2

As the result of evaluation showed, the main strength of the ODC reference model is its potential to redesign the curriculum process and related information systems in vocational schools of developing countries so that it balances the international standards with local cultural and socio-economic context, while engaging various stakeholders in collaborative knowledge-based curriculum process.

The main weaknesses of the model were related to its abstract level and partly unfamiliar vocabulary. Localization of ontology and building bilingual thesauri might help to address this issue in the future.

7   Conclusion

The reference model for ontology-driven modeling of vocational ICT curricula was composed through iterative design-based research and evaluated using a scenario-based pilot-test followed by a focus group interview.

Our case study involved a purposive sample of eight participants (seven ICT teachers from three different technical vocational institutes of Kabul and one alumni working in the public sector) in a focus group interview based on Nominal Group Technique. The aim of the interview was validation of the ODC reference model and related collaborative knowledge management tool VocITwiki in the context of vocational ICT curriculum development.

The results of our study showed that the main strength of the ODC reference model is its potential to improve the curriculum development by engaging various stakeholders in collaborative knowledge-based curriculum process. Although the case study had some methodological limitations regarding generalizability due to small and biased sample, the validation results were quite convincing. The study resulted with a set of preliminaries for ontology-driven curriculum modeling as well as the changes in the implementation scenarios of the reference model, which was positively received by the interview participants. The future research should involve a long-term and full-scale implementation of the reference model along with its representation in the form of Semantic MediaWiki in the context of radical redesign of an ICT curriculum in one of the vocational institutes in developing countries tackling with similar challenges.

References

1. Singh, G., Jain, V., Singh, M.: Ontology development using Hozo and semantic analysis for information retrieval in Semantic Web. In: Proceedings of the 2013 IEEE Second International Conference on Image Information Processing (ICIIP-2013) (2013)
2. John, S.: Development of an Educational Ontology for Java Programming (JLEO) with a hybrid methodology derived from conventional software engineering process models. Int. J. Inf. Educ. Technol. **4**(4), 308 (2014)
3. Kump, B., Moskaliuk, J., Dennerlein, S., Ley, T.: Tracing knowledge co-evolution in a realistic course setting: a wiki-based field experiment. Comput. Educ. **69**, 60–70 (2013)
4. Aroyo, L., Dicheva, D.: The new challenges for e-learning: the educational semantic web. Educ. Technol. Soc. **7**(4), 59–69 (2004)

5. Ramesh, B., Jarke, M.: Toward reference models for requirements traceability. IEEE Trans. Softw. Eng. **27**(1), 58–93 (2001)
6. Barhak, J.: The reference model uses object oriented population generation. In: Mittal, S., Moon, I.C., Syriani, E. (eds.) Proceedings of the Conference on Summer Computer Simulation (SummerSim 2015), pp. 1–6. Society for Computer Simulation International, San Diego, CA, USA (2015)
7. Becker, J., Delfmann, P.: Reference Modeling: Efficient Information Systems Design through Reuse of Information Models. Physica-Verlag GmbH, Heidelberg (2007)
8. Janulevičius, J., et al.: Enterprise architecture modeling based on cloud computing security ontology as a reference model. In: Open Conference of Electrical, Electronic and Information Sciences (eStream). IEEE (2017)
9. Hedayati, M.H., Laanpere, M.: Ontology-driven modeling for the culturally-sensitive curriculum development: a case study in the context of vocational ICT education in Afghanistan. In: 2016 3rd International Conference on Computing for Sustainable Global Development (INDIACom). IEEE (2016)
10. Zhang, L., et al.: Exploring ontology-driven modeling approach for multi-agent cooperation in emergency logistics. JCP **9**(2), 285–294 (2014)
11. Hedayati, M.H., Laanpere, M.: Identifying requirements for vocational ICT curriculum in development countries. J. Techn. Educ. Train. (JTET) **7**(1), 35–49 (2015)
12. Hedayati, M.H., Laanpere, M.: Analyzing the skill gaps of the graduates of vocational ICT programs in Afghanistan. In: IFIP TC3 Working Conference "A New Culture of Learning: Computing and next Generations" (2015)
13. Frank, U., Strecker, S.: Open reference models-community-driven collaboration to promote development and dissemination of reference models. Enterp. Model. Inf. Syst. Architect. **2**(2), 32–41 (2015)
14. Novotný, O.: A reference model for information systems. FAIMA Bus. Manag. J. **3**(2) (2015)
15. Vesterager, J.: 32 fast tracking ICT infrastructure. In: Collaborative Business Ecosystems and Virtual Enterprises, Sesimbra, Portugal, vol. 85. Springer (2013)
16. Aulkemeier, F., et al.: A service-oriented e-commerce reference architecture. J. Theor. Appl. Electron. Commer. Res. **11**(1), 26–45 (2016)
17. Sikos, Leslie F.: Rich semantics for interactive 3D models of cultural artifacts. In: Garoufallou, E., Subirats Coll, I., Stellato, A., Greenberg, J. (eds.) MTSR 2016. CCIS, vol. 672, pp. 169–180. Springer, Cham (2016). https://doi.org/10.1007/978-3-319-49157-8_14
18. Saghafi, F., et al.: Offering the reference model of backcasting approach for achieving sustainable development. J. Futures Stud. **18**(1), 63–84 (2013)
19. Stracke, C.M.: The benefits and future of standards: metadata and beyond. In: Sánchez-Alonso, S., Athanasiadis, I.N. (eds.) MTSR 2010. CCIS, vol. 108, pp. 354–361. Springer, Heidelberg (2010). https://doi.org/10.1007/978-3-642-16552-8_32
20. Stracke, C.M.: Competences and skills in the digital age: competence development, modelling, and standards for human resources development. In: García-Barriocanal, E., Cebeci, Z., Okur, M.C., Öztürk, A. (eds.) MTSR 2011. CCIS, vol. 240, pp. 34–46. Springer, Heidelberg (2011). https://doi.org/10.1007/978-3-642-24731-6_4
21. Gaitanou, P., Gergatsoulis, M.: A semantic mapping of VRA Core 4.0 to the CIDOC conceptual reference model. In: García-Barriocanal, E., Cebeci, Z., Okur, M.C., Öztürk, A. (eds.) MTSR 2011. CCIS, vol. 240, pp. 387–399. Springer, Heidelberg (2011). https://doi.org/10.1007/978-3-642-24731-6_39

22. Papadakis, I., Kyprianos, K., Karalis, A.: Highlighting timely information in libraries through social and semantic web technologies. In: Garoufallou, E., Subirats Coll, I., Stellato, A., Greenberg, J. (eds.) MTSR 2016. CCIS, vol. 672, pp. 297–308. Springer, Cham (2016). https://doi.org/10.1007/978-3-319-49157-8_26

23. Wang, X., Tiropanis, T., Tinati, R.: WDFed: exploiting cloud databases using metadata and RESTful APIs. In: Garoufallou, E., Subirats Coll, I., Stellato, A., Greenberg, J. (eds.) MTSR 2016. CCIS, vol. 672, pp. 345–356. Springer, Cham (2016). https://doi.org/10.1007/978-3-319-49157-8_30

24. Laanpere, M.: Pedagogy-driven design of virtual learning environments. Tallinn University, Doctorate thesis (2013)

25. European e-Competence Framework: Building the e-CF - a combination of sound methodology and expert contribution (e-CF 2.0 CWA Part III September 2010). EU: European e-Competence Framework (e-CF) (2010)

26. Vrtacnik, M., et al.: Response of slovene informatics teachers to the EUCIP on-line course. Comput. Technol. Appl. **3**(3), 268–278 (2012)

27. Povalej, R., Weiss, P.: Conceptual frameworks for the modeling of ICT competence profiles (2007)

28. Pernici, B., Locatelli, P., Marinoni, C.: The eCCO system: an ecompetence management tool based on semantic networks. In: Meersman, R., Tari, Z., Herrero, P. (eds.) OTM 2006. LNCS, vol. 4278, pp. 1088–1099. Springer, Heidelberg (2006). https://doi.org/10.1007/11915072_11

29. Fettke, P., Loos, P.: Classification of reference models: a methodology and its application. Inf. Syst. e-Bus. Manag. **1**(1), 35–53 (2003)

30. Stewart, D.W., Shamdasani, P.N.: Focus Groups: Theory and Practise. Sage Publications, Thousand Oaks (2004)

31. Mišic, V.B., Leon, J.: Evaluating the quality of reference models. In: Laender, A.H.F., Liddle, S.W., Storey, V.C. (eds.) ER 2000. LNCS, vol. 1920, pp. 484–498. Springer, Heidelberg (2000). https://doi.org/10.1007/3-540-45393-8_35

32. Taba, H.: Teachers' Handbook for Elementary Social Studies. Addison-Wesley, Reading (1967)

33. Hedayati, M.H., Laanpere, M., Ammar, M.A.: Collaborative ontology maintenance with concept maps and Semantic MediaWiki. Int. J. Inf. Technol. **9**, 1–9 (2017)

34. Pauline, F., Smith, A.B.: Prioritizing the patient voice in the development of urologic oncology research. Urol. Oncol. Semin. Orig. Invest. **35**, 548–551 (2017). Elsevier

35. García-Barriocanal, E., Sicilia, M.A., Sánchez-Alonso, S.: Computing with competencies: Modelling organizational capacities. Expert Syst. Appl. **39**(16), 12310–12318 (2012)

36. Gonçalves, R.S., et al.: An ontology-driven tool for structured data acquisition using Web forms. J. Biomed. Semant. **8**(1), 26 (2017)

Track on Open Repositories, Research Information Systems and Data Infrastructures

Building Scalable Digital Library Ingestion Pipelines Using Microservices

Matteo Cancellieri[✉] ⓘ, Nancy Pontika ⓘ, Samuel Pearce ⓘ,
Lucas Anastasiou ⓘ, and Petr Knoth ⓘ

CORE, The Open University, Milton Kenyes MK7 6AA, UK
theteam@core.ac.uk
http://core.ac.uk/

Abstract. CORE, a harvesting service offering access to millions of open access research papers from around the world, has shifted its harvesting process from following a monolithic approach to the adoption of a microservices infrastructure. In this paper, we explain how we re-arranged and re-scheduled our old ingestion pipeline, present CORE's move to managing microservices and outline the tools we use in a new and optimised ingestion system. In addition, we discuss the inefficiencies of our old harvesting process, the advantages, and challenges of our new ingestion system and our future plans. We conclude that via the adoption of microservices architecture we managed to achieve a scalable and distributed system that would assist with CORE's future performance and evolution.

Keywords: Harvesting · Repositories · Microservices · Infrastructure · Software architecture

1 Introduction

Aggregators are being used in many aspects of everyday life, from newspapers to traveling websites and from movies' reviews to social networking services. In the constantly growing scholarly communications environment, plenty of aggregators were developed due to the large amount of scientific knowledge published each year and the scholars' need to discover and extract the knowledge included in them. Moreover, the recent shift of sciences to interdisciplinarity created the need for a seamless tool that would make the retrieval of scientific literature from various subject fields possible.

Aggregators can collect, enrich and clean metadata to harmonise their access, allow a uniform search across a variety of platforms increasing the content's visibility, and bring to the end user an advanced discovering experience, by showcasing new trends in sciences and growth [1]. Due to their role, aggregators must be capable of processing large amounts of data and be developed in a scalable and sustainable infrastructure over time.

The transition process to microservices is described via a real life scenario, the CORE project, a global harvesting service aggregating millions of open access

© Springer International Publishing AG 2017
E. Garoufallou et al. (Eds.): MTSR 2017, CCIS 755, pp. 275–285, 2017.
https://doi.org/10.1007/978-3-319-70863-8_27

research papers. In the past, CORE's harvesting infrastructure was designed in a rather monolithic approach. Even though the scaling up and the continuation of its use was possible, the architecture suffered from complexity and maintenance issues, especially when facing a larger and extended amount of data, and had strong interdependent components that challenged its sustainability. Being in a need to restructure the current system and make it easier to scale, we introduced a microservices architecture, which is defined as small, autonomous components in a larger infrastructure that harmoniously work together [2]. This technology is lately widely used due to the advancement of the available software and resources. A benefit of the microservices is that programmers are able to efficiently focus on the implementation of the components performed in a single brief task.

In this paper we describe the evolution of a monolithic harvesting infrastructure to the creation of a microservices oriented architecture. Although migrating from a monolithic architecture to a microservices one is already covered in the literature, we believe that our contribution is worth to be described; our specific use case is applied to a combination of metadata harvesting, full text collection, crawling and enrichments of research outputs. The main contributions of this paper are outlined as follows:

- Define the requirements for designing a scalable aggregation infrastructure.
- Guided by the requirements, we propose a design based on microservices that can be applied to any aggregation and digital library infrastructure.
- Describe our experience migrating from a monolithic architecture to a microservices orientend one, in a real life scenario of the CORE project.

1.1   Related Work

The design of an aggregation system is usually conducted from square one, due to the variety of the application scenario per each project (or use case), which is defined both by the availability of resources and the flexibility of the distribution [3]. So far a number of architectural solutions have been released; some of them focusing on specific use cases, while others aim to address and solve the lack of reusable infrastructures. The D-NET component infrastructure, which is developed and implemented by the OpenAIRE project [4], addresses similar complexities to the ones we are encountering in our harvesting process and their proposed solution is very similar to CORE's infrastructure. The harvesting is accomplished using the Open Archives Initiative Metadata Harvesting Protocol (OAI-PMH) [5] and the harvested metadata are converted into XML files, creating a graph model information structure. Nonetheless, OpenAIRE's aim is to connect publications, data set repositories and Current Research Information Systems (CRIS) [6], therefore its main interest is to collect and enrich metadata only. On the other hand, CORE's focus lies both in crawling metadata pages and discovering the full text.

Another aggregation infrastructure has been implemented by the SHARE project [7]. Although the project focuses more on aggregating information about research activity metadata, its pipeline and the technologies used have main similarities with the processes we are describing in this paper. For example, the SHARE infrastructure uses RabbitMQ [8] as a messaging system and a Celery scheduler [9], which arranges how the workers will be collecting, normalising and making the content searchable via the ElasticSearch [10] index. Nonetheless, SHARE's architecture does not extend to providing tools for crawling and enriching full text documents as well. The BASE project [11], is another metadata aggregator facilitating search via repositories. The harvesting infrastructure implemented by BASE is similar to the aforementioned aggregation infrastructures; data is harvested via the OAI-PMH endpoint and the metadata are exposed and made searchable through the SOLR [12] index.

Commercial solutions, such as Google Scholar and Microsoft Academic Graph, use search engine crawl facilities to recognise full text and index it. Nonetheless, both of them limit user access at the granularity level with no access to raw data [13]. CiteSeerX [14], a metadata and full text harvesting service, defines three components of a scalable system that is capable of crawling citations from full text; harvester, document archive and search interface. With this system, the issue of scalability is approached horizontally, mirroring the servers and the locations that scale up the system.

All the aforementioned projects describe scalable architectures, but, there is no specific reference explaining a transition from a monolithic architecture to a microservices approach. In addition, CORE's case is unique, because it combines (a) metadata harvesting, (b) full text crawling and (c) enrichments in the same infrastructure while the other projects architectures are mostly oriented on aggregating metadata and enriching metadata. Furthermore, no previous work refers to scalability from the aggregation point of view of harvesting and enriching the content; the aforementioned literature describes the scalability approach following the front end availability only.

1.2 Real-Life Scenario: CORE

CORE harvests open access (OA) journals and repositories, institutional and disciplinary, from all over the world and provides seamless access to millions of OA research papers. (OA is defined as content offered digital, online, free of charge and free of most copyright restrictions [15]). While the OA movement is gradually growing, the amount of available scientific information follows this growth. CORE attempts to address this flourishing availability of OA content by aggregating large volumes of OA research papers and offers them via its search engine and other services, e.g. API and Dataset. As of March 2017, CORE harvested content from 6,000 OA journals and 2,437 repositories and offered access to 70 million metadata records and over 6 million full text PDFs. In addition, it provides its content via three access levels [13] and demonstrates the granulated structure of the raw data, the scientific papers and the collections as a whole. By taking into consideration the various research stakeholders who can benefit from CORE, the service offers (1) raw data access, (2) transactional and (3) analytical information access, addressing the needs of (1) text miners, digital libraries, developers, (2) researchers, students, general public and (3) funders and repository managers, respectively.

To collect its metadata, CORE uses the OAI-PMH, a widely supported protocol for collecting and exposing metadata records. In most cases, these metadata are mostly formatted using the Dublin Core schema [16]. In addition, CORE expands its use by supporting other standards as well, such as the Metadata Encoding and Transmission Standard [17], the RIOXX Metadata Application Profile [18], and the OpenAIRE Guidelines for Literature Repositories [4].

CORE is not merely a metadata aggregation service, but it expands also to aggregating and caching the full text. In an effort to solve the lack of an existing standard for harvesting a paper's full text, CORE has established a methodology and follows various procedures: (a) recognising the full-text links in the metadata record, (b) performing a crawling technique from an online resource to derive to the link of a specific paper, (c) composing the full-text link by using recognised patterns, which are obtained by analysing the structure of our data providers and (d) following other custom built approaches, whereby the machine readable structures of specific content providers are being examined.

Until recently, CORE was operating in a rather monolithic approach. Even though it was in position to process simultaneously several repositories, the harvesting pipeline was centralised around each repository. All these years CORE has progressed and custom solutions were applied to: (a) improve the harvesting process and growth of our collection, (b) address technology advancement issues, such as repository software updates and the establishment of new metadata profiles like RIOXX, and (c) assist with the integration of new and emerging services. The accumulation of all these lines of code and the unavoidable high code coupling, would often prove to be difficult to manage, require an extra effort of constant fixes and affect the capabilities and strengths of our performance. As a result, we experienced challenges in efficiently managing all the existing services and fear that the quality of our services would decline. Availability was also an issue; the services designed for public use were strongly coupled to the harvesting infrastructure, thus an overload of the system while harvesting would impact directly the overall availability of the service.

1.3 Ingestion Pipeline

CORE's ingestion pipeline currently consists of five tasks, but is in principle extensible to more tasks. The process can be described as a pipeline, a concept first introduced in computer science by the UNIX operating system and then extended to software architectures models as for example in Doberkat [19], and on a context similar to our use case by Abrams et al. [20]. Each task performs a certain action, while the result of each one of them creates the corpus of a full record, including of metadata and full text, available in the CORE collection (Fig. 1).

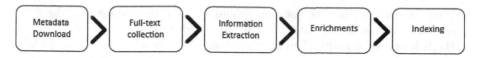

Fig. 1. CORE's ingestion pipeline.

1. Metadata Download
   (a) Extraction: The metadata of a journal or repository, institutional or disciplinary, (thereafter called only "repository") are downloaded and extracted in the CORE database for local storage.
   (b) Cleaning: The data is being processed for cleaning, such as performing an author name normalisation. The data is also standardised and normalised across the various supported standards.
2. Full-text download: CORE downloads and stores a cached version of the downloaded full-text in its database.
3. Information extraction
   (a) Text extraction: To enable full text searching, the downloaded PDFs are analysed and the full text is extracted into a text file.
   (b) Language detection: Performed to offer a filtering option for advanced searches.
   (c) Citation extraction: CORE cross-matches whether the referenced paper is available and provided by our service. If the paper is available, then the two papers are linked. If it is not, CORE receives the referenced papers Digital Object Identifier (DOI) via the CrossRef service [21].
4. Enrichment
   (a) Duplicates detection: CORE detects duplicate records and marks these files in its database.
   (b) Related Content Identification: With the use of information retrieval procedures, CORE matches the semantically related papers. (CORE's recommender, a plug-in for repositories and open journal systems, is highly dependent on this task.)
5. Indexing: This is the last step in the ingestion pipeline, which empowers the search functionality, while it supports the use of the CORE API and the CORE Dataset.

2   Scalable Infrastructure Requirements

Abstracting from our real life use case, we have defined a set of requirements that are generic and can be used in any aggregation or digital library scenario. Taking into consideration the features of the CiteSeerX [14] architecture, we built our requirements on a generic distributed system and we extended them focusing on systems that follow specific workflows and need to interact with a number of external services. In the initial phase we developed a set of requirements that the infrastructure had to support:

- **Easy to maintain**: The solution should be easy to manage and the code should be accessible for maintenance, fixes, and improvements.
- **High levels of automatisation**: We should be able to achieve a completely automated harvesting process allowing also a manual interaction.
- **Fail fast**: Items in the pipeline should be validated immediately after a task is performed, instead of having only one and final validation at the end of the pipeline. This has the benefit of recognising issues early in the process and programmers are notified earlier of possible failures and issues.
- **Easy to troubleshoot**: Possible bugs in the code should be easily discerned.
- **Distributed and scalable**: The addition of new nodes in the system should allow scalability, be transparent and replicable.
- **No single point of failure**: A single crash should not affect the whole ingestion pipeline, but tasks should work independently.
- **High availability**: The infrastructure containing services designed for public use should not be attached to the harvesting pipeline and be invariably available.
- **Recoverable**: When a harvesting task stops, either manually or due to a failure, the system should be able to recover and resume the task without intervening manually.

2.1 The CORE HARvesting System (CHARS)

The design of the architecture is based on the following main components (Fig. 2):

1. Worker (W_i): an independent and standalone application capable to execute a specific task and communicate via a queue;
2. Task Coordinator (scheduler): it becomes active when a task starts or finishes and coordinates the task workflow in the system;
3. Queue Handling System (Q_n): a messaging system that assists with the communication between the components;
4. Cron Scheduler: lines up tasks periodically;
5. Harvesting endpoint (supervisor): an API endpoint that facilitates the submission of task in the system and therefore works as an entry point for new harvesting requests.

All Workers (1) share the same lifecycle after receiving a task (Table 1). The lifecycle has been designed to be simple, generic and easy to troubleshoot.

The Event Scheduler (2), decides how the tasks should be moving and chooses the next task to run in the ingestion pipeline. If there are enough resources available in the system, i.e. idle Workers, the Scheduler adds new harvesting tasks based on the following policy: first, is adds repositories in the queue with metadata records older than a certain time window and, second, includes new repositories if no other priorities are being met. With this policy, our goal is to efficiently use all the available resources without overloading our system. Since

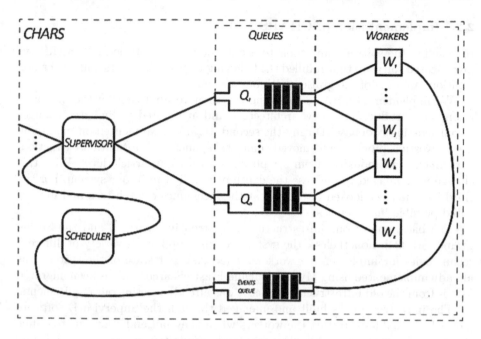

Fig. 2. CHARS architecture

Table 1. Worker lifecycle

Item	Description
0	Notify start
1	Collect data to perform task
2	Perform task
3	Finalise execution and collect metrics
4	Assess results (success or failure)
5	Notify end

our aim is to keep the content in our collection as fresh as possible, we periodically re-harvest repositories and add new ones without them interfering with the existing procedures.

The communication infrastructure is accomplished via a publish/subscribe pattern [22]. The Workers with the ability to perform a metadata download task express interest in the concept of metadata download and, when a producer submits a message, a Worker will be notified and act on it. A message is an item that is transmitted between components, such as a task definition or a start/finish event. When a CORE staff member wishes to harvest a repository, s/he needs to send a message to the harvesting endpoint by clicking a button in the administrator console. The task will then be created and submitted to the queue system.

2.2 Implementation of CHARS

In deciding the software and tools to use in the implementation of CHARS, we investigated software that fulfilled the following two requirements; out-of-the box solution and ease of integration with our system.

We implemented CHARS following an iterative approach; in the first iteration, we introduced the new architecture and attempted to limit the changes to our existing codebase. During the second iteration, we focused on modifying the harvesting pipeline and moved some tasks, such as information extraction, enrichment and indexing, from a repository level to an article level. With this change we managed to increase the depth of parallelism in our system. For the third iteration, we looked into detail at the mechanics of each task and investigated possible inefficiencies.

The backbone of our infrastructure is written in Java [23] and the Spring Framework [24]; nonetheless, the system equally supports a variety of different technologies for implementing workers. The persistent state of the system was already implemented using MySQL [25] and ElasticSearch and has been migrated as it is from the old infrastructure, since it was already meeting our requirements.

The infrastructure is built and managed through the SupervisorD software [26], which is able to restart the workers when they fail and allows us to define event based actions. SupervisorD uses a static configuration per server, meaning that we are able to define the amount of workers running on a single server based on its hardware specifications. As an alternative to SupervisorD, we explored the possibility of adopting container-based microservices using Docker and Kubernetes [27]. A container-based approach would allow a reusable microservices implementation with a dynamic and fine-grained management of the workers based on the available resources. One disadvantage, though, is that their configuration and usage would have increased the level of complexity of our infrastructure. In the end, we decided to postpone this approach and adopt a container-based microservices approach in a future iteration of the CHARS infrastructure.

2.3 Queuing System

For the queue message system, we explored two solutions, RabbitMQ [8] and Kafka [28]. Even though the latter has superior performance in terms of message rate [29], nonetheless it offers less out-of-the-box functionalities. Although Kafka performed better in the message rate, our use case did not need a system that could process an extremely high number, for example millions, of messages per second. Therefore, we decided to adopt RabbitMQ, which was easier than Kafka to configure and could be integrated with our existing infrastructure and code base. An additional functionality of RabbitMQ was the out-of-the-box support for message priorities. Prioritising in harvesting is necessary, since we often receive requests from our data providers to re-harvest repository collections in order to capture record updates, metadata and full text. Similarly, while fixing and resolving technical harvesting issues, we need to re-harvest a repository more than once, and we need to skip the existing queue.

3   Discussion

CORE has been using the new microservices architecture for the past year. During that time, our collection doubled; we now have 70 million metadata records and 6 million full text PDFs (Table 2). Although we cannot correlate the content increase with the introduction of the new microservices infrastructure, nonetheless we realised that we achieved a reduction in the consumption of staff time with regards to maintenance tasks, which favored the uptake of new duties.

One of the lessons we have learnt is that, by dividing the monolithic code into small components with specific operations, we were able to maintain and troubleshoot our system easier and more efficiently comparing to the past. In addition, when an issue arises, programmers can focus on small problematic units of code instead of going through the whole monolithic code base. Another improvement in the system's efficiency relates to recoverability. CORE harvests some large repositories and a task can run for a long time, even days for large data sets. In our new infrastructure cases of failure or re-deployment of an improved version of the code are treated differently; the task is not lost and it automatically resumes without any manual intervention.

By moving the monolithic harvesting approach to a microservices application, we were able to focus on the quality and performance of each single task establishing valid measures, such as success or failure. For example, in our earlier infrastructure it was problematic to focus on issues, such as delays and quality assurance control, whereas, currently, we are in position to decide whether we should direct more effort and resources in specific tasks.

The introduction of microservices allowed us to work in a more scalable and distributed environment. Scaling up in the old infrastructure required the addition of new resources or a new server. With the new architecture we are able to shuffle our services efficiently within the existing hardware infrastructure and transform it according to our needs.

While introducing microservices in CORE, we also separated our harvesting infrastructure from our publicly available services. Right now our public services are connected to the harvesting back-end only through our ElasticSearch index. The advantages of this distinction, between our front-end and back-end services, resulted in an increase in the amount of uptime of our services.

Despite the aforementioned advantages, new challenges have emerged. The first relates to the difficulty of estimating the optimal number of workers in our system to efficiently run. While the worker allocation is still largely done using

Table 2. CORE's metadata and full text volume

Year	Metadata	Full text
2015 Apr	23,006,000	2,091,334
2016 (Jan - Dec)	66,137,655	4,626,215
2017 (Jan - Mar)	68,387,703	5,852,274

a trial and error approach, we are investigating more sophisticated approaches based on formal models of distributed computation, such as Petri Nets [30]. For example, we are looking into formally modeling our system to find valid heuristics for dynamically allocating or launching workers to optimise the usage of our resources.

The designed architecture has been built with an evolutionary approach slowly removing the dependencies from the monolithic system. This introduced a complexity in the production of a formal evaluation framework of our architecture, one that would not require plenty of time and effort. However, with building the aforementioned formal model we will be also able to validate the quality of our approach in an experimental way.

This architecture highlighted an issue of cost-effective resource allocation in our system. Our previous architecture was designed for a monolothic approach, where servers were allocated in full for the harvesting process. With the introduction microservices we were able to fine-grain resource allocation and implement different ways of collecting hardware resources, such as using cloud services for storage and computational power.

With regards to CORE's internal infrastructure, we need to improve the overall performance of our system and, thus, we are now collecting metrics; CPU, memory and network usage, freshness of content and quality of full-text crawling. These metrics will help us define new performance key indicators and improve our services. Moreover, we are exploring ways of optimising the use of the resources in an highly efficient way. Even though, our new infrastructure enabled us to scale up faster than expected, nonetheless we are now facing other issues, such as error detection in the harvesting process, full text crawling efficiency and deduplication improvements. All these are currently highlighted in our system and need to be addressed in future work.

4   Conclusion

In this paper we outlined the requirements of a scalable aggregation system and by following them we designed a microservices architecture that could be applied to any aggregation service or digital library. We presented how CORE's harvesting process migrated from a monolithic to a microservices approach, explained the harvesting workflow, and the technology used in the real life implementation of the architecture. Finally, we discussed the advantages and disadvantages of our new infrastructure and presented future work.

References

1. Knoth, P., Anastasiou, L., Pearce, S.: My repository is being aggregated: a blessing or a curse? In: Open Repositories (2014)
2. Newman, S.: Building Microservices: Designing Fine-Grained Systems. O'Reilly Media Inc., Sebastopol (2015)

3. Manghi, P., Artini, M., Atzori, C., Pegano, P., Bardi, A., Mannocci, A., La Bruzzo, S., Candela, L., Castelli, D., Pagano, P.: The D-NET software toolkit: a framework for the realization, maintenance, and operation of aggregative infrastructures. Prog. Electron. Libr. Inf. Syst. **48**, 4 (2014). https://doi.org/10.1108/PROG=08-2013-0045
4. OpenAIRE Guidelines. https://guidelines.openaire.eu/en/latest/
5. Open Archives Initiative Protocol for Metadata Harvesting. https://www.openarchives.org/pmh/
6. Joint, N.: Current research information systems, open access repositories and libraries: ANTANEUS. Libr. Rev. **57**, 8 (2008). https://doi.org/10.1108/00242530810899559
7. SHARE 2.0 Documentation. http://share-research.readthedocs.io/en/latest/
8. Rabbit MQ. https://www.rabbitmq.com/
9. Celery period tasks. http://docs.celeryproject.org/en/latest/userguide/periodic-tasks.html
10. Elastic. https://www.elastic.co/
11. Lösch, M.: A multidisciplinary search engine for scientific open access documents. In: Depping, R., Christiane, S. (eds.) Elektronische Schriftenreihe der Universitäts- und Stadtbibliothek Köln. vol. 2, pp. 11–15 (2011)
12. Indexing and basic data operations. https://cwiki.apache.org/confluence/display/solr/Introduction+to+Solr+Indexing
13. Knoth, P., Zdrahal, Z.: CORE: three access levels to underpin open access. D-Lib Mag. **18**, 11–12 (2012)
14. Li, H., Councill, I., Bolelli, L., Zhou, D., Song, Y., Lee W-G, Sivasubramaniam, A., Giles, L.: CiteSeerX: A scalable autonomous scientific digital library. In: INFOSCALE 2006: Proceedings of the First International Conference on Scalable Information Systems, 29 May–1 June (2016)
15. Suber, P.: Open Access. Essential Knowledge Series. MIT Press, Cambridge (2012)
16. Dublin CORE Metadata Initiative. http://dublincore.org/
17. Metadata Encoding and Transmission Standard. http://www.loc.gov/standards/mets/
18. The RIOXX Metadata Profile and Guidelines. http://rioxx.net/
19. Doberkat, E.: Pipelines: modelling software architecture through relations. Acta Informatica **40**, 1 (2003). https://doi.org/10.1007/s00236-003-0121-z
20. Abrams, S., Cruse, P., Kunze, J., Minor, D.: Curation micro-services: a pipeline metaphor for repositories. J. Digit. Inf. **12**, 2 (2011)
21. Crossref: Metadata Enables Connections. https://www.crossref.org/
22. Birman, K., Joseph, T.: Exploiting visual synchrony in distributed systems. SIGOPS Oper. Syst. Princ. **21**, 123–138 (1987). https://doi.org/10.1145/41457.37515
23. Java Software. https://www.oracle.com/java/index.html
24. Spring Framework. https://spring.io/
25. MySQL. https://www.mysql.com/
26. Supervisor: a process control system. http://supervisord.org/
27. Kubernetes. https://kubernetes.io/
28. Apache Kafka. https://kafka.apache.org/
29. Kreps, J., Narkhede, N., Rao, J.: Kafka: a distributed messaging system for log processing. In: NetDB: 6th Workshop on Networking meetsDatabases (2011)
30. Petri, C.: Communication With Automata: Volume 1 Supplement 1. DTIC Research Report AD0630125 (1966)

Semantic Attributes for Citation Relationships: Creation and Visualization

Sergey Parinov[1,2(✉)] (iD)

[1] Central Economics and Mathematics Institute of RAS, Moscow, Russia
sparinov@gmail.com
[2] Russian Presidential Academy of National Economy and Public Administration,
Moscow, Russia

Abstract. This paper presents a method to process a content of research papers in binary PDF format at a server side that gives research information systems new features of citation content analysis. This method efficiently generates JSON versions of PDF documents that allows an easier recognition of papers' references, in-text references, citation context, etc. As a result, one can parse an extended set of citation data, including a location of citations in a research paper's structure, frequency of mentioning for the same references, style of reference mentioning and so on. Based on these data we upgrade traditional citation relationships by adding some semantic attributes. Formatting these semantic data according W3C Web Annotation Data Model and integrating the data with some annotation tools, we visualize citation relationships, its semantic attributes and related statistics as annotations for readers of PDF documents from a research information system.

Keywords: Research information system · PDF.js · PDF to JSON conversion · Citation relationships · Semantic attributes · Citation content analysis · Visualization

1 Introduction

A basic concept of this paper is that "a citation implies a relationship between a part or the whole of the cited document and a part or the whole of the citing document" [1]. Working with citations in a research information system (RIS), we can define a citation relationship as a pair of paper's ID, one of which is an ID of the citing paper and another – ID of the cited paper. These IDs can specify a part or the whole paper.

We also share Eugene Garfield's basic assumption that "citing and cited references have a strong link through semantics" [2]. In this paper, we present a new approach to creating data for testing this assumption by extracting different semantic attributes for citation relationships from research papers' content.

© Springer International Publishing AG 2017
E. Garoufallou et al. (Eds.): MTSR 2017, CCIS 755, pp. 286–299, 2017.
https://doi.org/10.1007/978-3-319-70863-8_28

Currently, many RIS, like Google Scholar, Web of Science (Clarivate Analytics), Scopus, RePEc/CitEc, etc. generate the citation relationships. Usually they use already well-developed procedure [3] with the two main steps:

(1) extraction – a research papers' content processing with the focus to its "References" section to extract bibliographic data about each reference;
(2) linking – a search of extracted reference data (data about cited paper) in a RIS database and, if the search was successful, taking the cited paper ID for linking it with the citing paper's ID.

In this way, new citation relationships emerge in RIS.

This traditional method gives data for building different citation indexes (e.g. see the basic citation impact indicators in [4, pp. 13–15]). However, research papers typically contain much more citation data, which potentially can also be useful, e.g. for studying semantic links between citing and cited papers, for a citation content analysis, for improving accuracy of already existed citation indicators and results of research assessment and evaluation procedures, etc. The Citation Counting and Context Characterization Ontology (C4O) provides a classification[1] of some additional citation data.

A diagram at the Fig. 1 illustrates different types of dependencies between parts of a research paper, which can be semantically associated with the citation relationships. Alschner and Umov [5] provide even more complex picture of paper's parts and their interdependences.

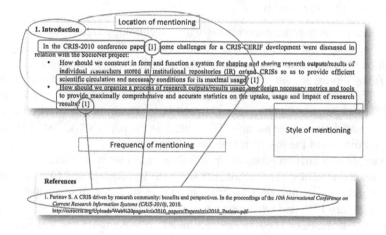

Fig. 1. Sources of semantics for a citation relationship

The Fig. 1 contains two fragments of the same paper[2]: (1) at the bottom - a reference, which has the number "1" in a list of references; (2) at the top – a text fragment, where a reference with the number "1" has been mentioned three times.

---

[1] C4O, the Citation Counting and Context Characterization Ontology. http://purl.org/spar/c4o.
[2] http://dspacecris.eurocris.org/bitstream/11366/526/1/CRIS2016_paper_40_Parinov.pdf.

There are two ways to denote that a reference is mentioned in a paper text[3]: (1) "in-text citation"; or (2) "in-text reference". Below in this paper we use the second term.

As it is shown on the Fig. 1, if we can recognize in a paper's text the in-text references, we can count a frequency of mentioning the same references in a paper and even in all papers at RIS.

One-two sentences to the left and to the right from each in-text reference give us a context of using references in a paper. Analyzing the context data [3], we can assess a style of its mentioning, e.g. how the cited paper was used in the citing paper, and many others.

Taking into account in what paper's section the in-text references are, we know its location in a paper's structure [6]. Such location data currently is a point for interesting scientometric studies [7].

All these context data potentially can influence the improving of a quality of citation indicators, e.g. by more accurate weighting of citations [8, 9].

Authors of the Citation Content Analysis (CCA) Framework in their paper [8] specified, as a part of their code book for the CCA, the following attributes of the cited papers, which in general are very similar to presented at the Fig. 1:

- Location of mentioning: (1) Abstract; (2) Introduction; (3) Literature Review; (4) Methodology; (5) Results/discussion; (6) Conclusion; (7) Others.
- Frequency of mentioning: (1) Once; (2) 2 to 4 times; (3) 5 times or more.
- Style of mentioning: (1) Not specifically mentioning; (2) Specifically mentioning but interpreting; (3) Direct quotation.

This paper presents some experiments with a technology created by the CitEcCyr project[4] (funded by RANEPA[5]) for RIS Socionet[6] and RePEc[7]. The technology allows an extraction of semantic attributes from a paper's text for each reference.

The Table 1 presents our abstract model of a citation relationship with semantic attributes. The citation relationship (as a pair of IDs of the citing paper "A" and the cited paper "B") has some in-text reference as an attribute. The in-text reference has an ID, which is a composition of the paper's "B" number in the paper's "A" list of references and text coordinates of the in-text reference in the paper "A".

An example of a citation relationship at Table 1 has one in-text reference attribute with four semantic values: (1) location, (2) style, (3) left context and (4) right context. This paper aims to demonstrate how one can extract such semantic attributes and its values from binary PDF and what new ways of visualization for citation relationships with semantic attributes can be implemented in RIS like Socionet and RePEc.

In the next section, we discuss a PDF conversion method, which uses the PDF.js module[8] as a processor. We discuss two solutions. Both of them: (a) are applicable for a regular processing of large sets of research papers in PDF that is a typical task for RIS

---

[3] http://www.monash.edu.au/lls/llonline/writing/science/3.3.xml.

[4] https://github.com/citeccyr.

[5] http://www.ranepa.ru/eng/.

[6] https://socionet.ru/.

[7] http://repec.org/.

[8] https://github.com/mozilla/pdf.js.

like RePEc and Socionet; and (b) allow producing JSON versions of PDF documents containing data sufficient for parsing semantic attributes for the citation relationships.

Table 1. A citation relationship with semantic attributes

Citing paper	Semantics of a citation relationship		Cited paper
Paper "A"(ID)	in-text reference(ID)	**location**: a set of values, like "introduction", "review", "methodology", "results/discussion"," conclusion", "other"	Paper "B"(ID)
		style: a set of values, like "unspecific", "interpreted", "quotation"	
		left context: a set of words on the left from the in-text reference	
		right context: a set of words on the right from the in-text reference	

The third section provides details on citation data parsing from JSON version of PDF documents. The CitEcCyr project also provided to public a set of XML files with extracted citation data. We used some of these files to create semantic attributes for citation relationships of real research papers available at Socionet RIS.

In the section four, we demonstrate a method of visualization of the citation relationships with semantic attributes as annotations. It became possible, because Socionet RIS includes an annotation tool developed by Hypothes.is, which also used the PDF.js module to display annotations of PDF documents. Since for the most PDF papers in Socionet we can present citation data as annotations, we can also give authors of these papers an ability to manage the annotations, e.g. to correct errors or to enrich these data.

At the conclusion, we discuss a further development of RIS features based on the extended citation data.

2   PDF Conversion

PDF is binary data file. To extract and parse data from such files one has to convert PDF to some text format.

At the Fig. 2, there is a small fragment of a PDF document, the same as on Fig. 1. The fragment of a document includes a page number, a header, a section title and some text of a document including one in-text reference.

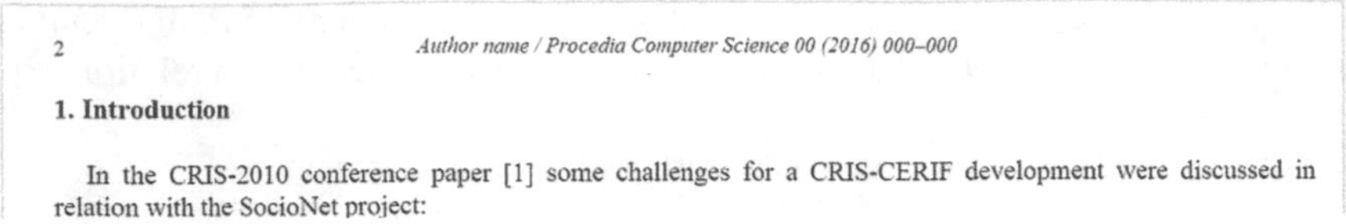

2   *Author name / Procedia Computer Science 00 (2016) 000–000*

1. Introduction

In the CRIS-2010 conference paper [1] some challenges for a CRIS-CERIF development were discussed in relation with the SocioNet project:

Fig. 2. A fragment of a PDF with a header, a section title and an in-text reference

To analyze a content of a PDF document one typically convert the PDF document to its plain text version. There are many free utilities[9] to do such conversion to the plain text or to HTML versions. After conversion to the plain text, a content presented at the Fig. 2 will look like at the Example 1 below.

Example 1. A plain text version of a PDF document fragment

```
    2 Author name / Procedia Computer Science 00 (2016) 000-000 1. Intro-
duction In the CRIS-2010 conference paper [1] some challenges for a
CRIS-CERIF development were discussed in relation with the SocioNet
project:
```

The plain text version allows more or less accurate parsing of a list of references that is typically enough for traditional citation analysis. At the same time, it is a very difficult task to recognize headers/footers and title of sections within the plain text version of a PDF document. Although they are very well visible in the document at the Fig. 2, because of their specific spatial arrangement on a paper's page.

Currently, there are at least two open source programs making the PDF conversion with a preservation of spatial arrangement attributes for all parts of a content like headers/footers, title of sections, etc. The both programs use a combination of the PDF.js Java-script module with the Node.js platform[10]. The PDF.js works as a processor to create an attributed text from PDF documents and Node.js allows running this Java-script module at the server side. As a result, at the output, we have a PDF document content as a JSON file includes some useful additional attributes.

One of these software programs is PDF2JSON[11]. It is used, e.g. for reconstructing semantic structure of documents [10]. If we process by this software the PDF document, partly presented at the Fig. 2, at the output we have a JSON file, a fragment of which is at the Example 2. This JSON fragment contains following data: a page number, a part of a header, a section title and a part of a text fragment from Fig. 2 including an in-text reference.

Example 2. JSON version of PDF document created by PDF2JSON, a fragment[12]

---

[9] E.g. the PDFMiner at http://www.unixuser.org/~euske/python/pdfminer/.

[10] https://nodejs.org/.

[11] https://github.com/modesty/pdf2json.

[12] The whole is at https://socionet.ru/citmap/convertedPDF/test_cris2016.json.

```
 "Texts":[
  {"x":3.8,"y":2.58,"w":0.5,"sw":0.32553125,"clr":0,"A":"left","R":
[{"T":"2","S":-1,"TS":[0,36,0,0]}]},
   {"x":12.23,"y":2.58,"w":5.516,"sw":0.32553125,"clr":0,"A":
"left","R":[{"T":"Author%20name%20","S":-1,"TS":[0,36,0,0]}]},
   ...
   {"x":3.8,"y":4.05,"w":0.766,"sw":0.32553125,"clr":0,"A":"left","R":
[{"T":"1.","S":-1,"TS":[0,45,1,0]}]},
   {"x":4.442,"y":4.05,"w":5.523,"sw":0.32553125,"clr":0,"A":"left","R":
[{"T":"Introduction","S":-1,"TS":[0,45,1,0]}]},
   {"x":4.544,"y":5.565,"w":1.099,"sw":0.32553125,"clr":0,"A":"left","R"
: [{"T":"In%20","S":-1,"TS":[0,44,0,0]}]},
   {"x":5.345,"y":5.565,"w":1.489,"sw":0.32553125,"clr":0,"A":"left","R"
: [{"T":"the%20","S":-1,"TS":[0,44,0,0]}]},
   {"x":6.39,"y":5.565,"w":2.266,"sw":0.32553125,"clr":0,"A":"left","R":
[{"T":"CRIS","S":-1,"TS":[0,44,0,0]}]},
   {"x":7.779,"y":5.565,"w":0.333,"sw":0.32553125,"clr":0,"A":"left","R"
: [{"T":"-","S":-1,"TS":[0,44,0,0]}]},
   {"x":7.987,"y":5.565,"w":10.984,"sw":0.32553125,"clr":0,"A":"left","R
": [{"T":"2010%20conference%20paper%20%5B1%5D%20","S":-
1,"TS":[0,44,0,0]}]},
   {"x":15.218,"y":5.565,"w":9.085,"sw":0.32553125,"clr":0,"A":"left","R
":[{"T":"some%20challenges%20for%20a%20","S":-1,"TS":[0,44,0,0]}]},
```

PDF2JSON site at GitHub provides explanations and meanings of all attributes in the Example 2:

As one can see at the Example 2, the JSON format, comparing with the plain text, provides a highly fragmented paper content. Values of the "T": attributes presents the text content of a paper. And PDF2JSON software replaces in the content all symbols like a space, a bracket and some others by their "percent-encoding"[13] values.

Data of each document's page starts in JSON as the "Texts": attribute. To recognize a page number and/or a header/footer one should attributes "x": and "y":, which are vertical and horizontal coordinates of each text fragment.

A recognition of the section title can use values of the "TS": attribute, which includes data about the font size and the formatting style (bold, italic). E.g. in the JSON code at the Example 2 the section title "1. Introduction" is splitted between two "T" attributes: "T":"1." and "T":"Introduction". The TS attribute of both "T" shows the font size 45 and the bold style of its formatting. Since the above and below text lines according the text "1. Introduction" have smaller font size and have no the bold highlighting, we can assume it is the section title. Spatial arrangement attributes "x": and "y": also can be used in this analysis.

A JSON version of a PDF document also allows extraction of in-text references and its context in a more accurate way, than using the plain text version. The citation context extraction typically means taking 1–2 sentences before and after the in-text reference [5]. If we make this extraction using the plain text version, a text at the left and at the right from the in-text reference may include some extra data, like a header, a section title, etc. Exactly this problem appears, if we, using the plain text of the Example 1, extract the citation context at the left from the in-text reference denoted as [1]. As

---

[13] https://en.wikipedia.org/wiki/Percent-encoding.

described above, using a JSON version, we can recognize headers and section titles and exclude this data from the citation context.

There is also another PDF to JSON conversion program built by the CitEcCyr team. It is also an open source software and available at GitHub as PDF-STREAM module[14]. According information from this project, they are using PDF-STREAM to create a public source with an open data for citation content analysis for research papers available at Socionet RIS.

In our experiments, PDF-STREAM worked faster on 2–3 s in average, then PDF2JSON. It makes a conversion of one PDF file in average for 1.7 s. PDF-STREAM also produces smaller size of JSON files, since it provides less attributes and excludes some useless metadata. We found that a conversion by PDF-STREAM provides enough data for parsing the citation attributes needed for our purposes.

The Example 3 presents a JSON version produced by PDF-STREAM for the same PDF document fragment as in the Example 2.

Example 3. JSON version of PDF document created by PDF-STREAM, a fragment[15]

```
{"page":2,"textContent":{"items":[
{"str":"2","dir":"ltr","width":3.96,"height":62.7264, "trans-
form":[7.92,0,0,7.92,64.8,788.72],"fontName":"g_d0_f3"},
{"str":" ","dir":"ltr","width":1.98,"height":62.7264, "trans-
form":[7.92,0,0,7.92,68.8,788.72],"fontName":"g_d0_f1"},
{"str":"Author name ","dir":"ltr","width":43.57584000000001,
"height":62.7264,"transform":[7.92,0,0,7.92,199.6743,788.72],
"fontName":"g_d0_f1"},
    ...
{"str":"1.","dir":"ltr","width":7.539408,"height":96.8256, "trans-
form":[9.84,0,0,9.84,64.8,765.2],"fontName":"g_d0_f4"},
{"str":" ","dir":"ltr","width":2.73552,"height":96.8256, "trans-
form":[9.84,0,0,9.84,72.3,765.2],"fontName":"g_d0_f5"},
{"str":"Introduction","dir":"ltr","width":54.45456,
"height":96.8256,"transform":[9.84,0,0,9.84,75.07832,765.2],
"fontName":"g_d0_f4"},
{"str":" ","dir":"ltr","width":2.46,"height":96.8256, "trans-
form":[9.84,0,0,9.84,129.5314,765.2],"fontName":"g_d0_f4"},
{"str":"In","dir":"ltr","width":10.845648,"height":96.8256, "trans-
form":[9.84,0,0,9.84,76.6999,740.96],"fontName":"g_d0_f3"},
{"str":"the ","dir":"ltr","width":14.722608,"height":96.8256, "trans-
form":[9.84,0,0,9.84,89.5246,740.96],"fontName":"g_d0_f3"},
{"str":"CRIS","dir":"ltr","width":22.250208000000004,"height":96.8256
, "transform":[9.84,0,0,9.84,106.236,740.96],"fontName":"g_d0_f3"},
{"str":"-","dir":"ltr","width":3.27672,"height":96.8256, "trans-
form":[9.84,0,0,9.84,128.4675,740.96],"fontName":"g_d0_f3"},
{"str":"2010 conference paper [1] ","dir":"ltr",
"width":113.736624,
"height":96.8256,"transform":[9.84,0,0,9.84,131.7975,740.96],"fontName":
"g_d0_f3"},
{"str":"some challenges for a ","dir":"ltr",
"width":95.45784000000002, "height":96.8256, "trans-
form":[9.84,0,0,9.84,247.4958,740.96],
```

[14] https://github.com/citeccyr/pdf-stream.
[15] The whole is at https://socionet.ru/citmap/convertedPDF/cris2016.json.

Comparing the code of the Examples 2 and 3 one can see that there is a difference in the attributes names. PDF-STREAM makes the text of the converted PDF document in the "**str**" attributes. To analyze document elements, like headers/footers, section titles, etc. we can use attributes as "page", "transform", "fontName", etc.

In June 2017, the CitEcCyr project provided for public use about 10 K of JSON files produced by PDF-STREAM software. A source of PDF documents is the archive NEICON[16] that contained about 150 collections of research papers with about 65 K papers in total. The results of this conversion are available at https://socionet.ru/~cyrcitec/json/spz/neicon/. It includes initial PDF documents and its JSON versions stored in folders of the NEICON collections. The PDF/JSON file names in the folders used handles (IDs) of the same papers at Socionet.

3   JSON Parsing: Citation Data and Semantic Attributes

We used an approach and a software developed by the CitEcCyr project to parse JSON files, to extract needed citation data and to store it as XML files. Victor Lyapunov made needed software.

As a source for our experiments, we used the same JSON file produced by PDF-STREAM for the PDF document, a fragment of which is on the Fig. 2.

The Example 4 provides extracted data about a single reference with the number "1" in a References section of a paper. Exactly this reference is shown at the bottom at the Fig. 1.

Example 4. Extracted data about a reference, a fragment[17]

```
<refer-
ence num="1" start="26962" end="27226" url="http://eurocris.org/Uploads/
Web\20pages/cris2010_papers/Papers/cris2010_Parinov.pdf" author="Parinov
S." title="A CRIS driven by research community benefits and perspec-
tives" year="2010">
          <from_pdf>Parinov S. A CRIS driven by research community: ben-
          efits and perspectives. In the proceedings of the 10th Interna-
          tional Conference on Current Research Information Systems (CRIS
          2010),                                                     2010.
          http://eurocris.org/Uploads/Web\20pages/cris2010_papers/Papers/c
          ris2010_Parinov.pdf</from_pdf>
    </reference>
```

The XML data of the Example 4 includes following subtags and attributes:

(a) subtag <from_pdf> - extracted raw data of a reference;
(b) attribute num - a serial number of the reference in the list;

---

[16] Available at https://socionet.ru/collection.xml?h=spz:neicon.
[17] The whole is data at http://no-xml.socionet.ru/citmap/outputs/cris2016-refs.xml.

(c) attributes `start` and `end` - text coordinates of the reference, which are numbers of the first and the last symbols of the reference counted from the beginning of the initial PDF document's text;

(d) attribute `url` - contains a proper URL, if there is one in data of the tag `<from_pdf>`;

e) attributes `author`, `title` and `year` are extracted from the row reference data in the tag `<from_pdf>` and using for different purposes, e.g. for searching in-text references by author names, for linking the reference with metadata of the same paper (creating a citation relationship for this reference), etc.

The Example 5 illustrates extracted data about in-text reference and its context. The parsing research paper has only one type of in-text references marked as a reference number in square brackets, like [1].

Example 5. Extracted data about an in-text reference, a fragment[18]

```
<intextref>
        <Reference>1</Reference>
        <Exact>[1]</Exact>
        <Start>2126</Start>
        <End>2128</End>
        <Prefix>In the CRIS-2010 conference paper</Prefix>
        <Suffix> some  challenges  for  a  CRIS-CERIF  development  were
        discussed  in  relation  with  the  SocioNet  project:  •How  should  we
        con</Suffix>
</intextref>
```

Extracted data includes:

(a) a number of the in-text reference, see the tag `<Reference>`;

(b) symbols of how this in-text reference is occurred in a paper, the tag `<Exact>`;

(c) text coordinates of the in-text reference, tags `<Start>` and `<End>`;

(d) a context located at the left, the tag `<Prefix>`, and at the right, the tag `<Suffix>`, according the in-text reference. By default to parse a context, an algorithm takes 200 symbols before and after the string in the tag `<Exact>`.

In the Example 5 a length of the left context text string in the tag `<Prefix>` is less than 200 symbols. It is so, because the parsing algorithm excludes from it a header and a section title. Example 6 shows parsing data about a section title.

Example 6. Extracted data about a section title

---

[18] The whole is at http://no-xml.socionet.ru/citmap/outputs/cris2016-intext.xml.

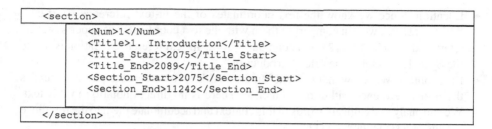

```
<section>
        <Num>1</Num>
        <Title>1. Introduction</Title>
        <Title_Start>2075</Title_Start>
        <Title_End>2089</Title_End>
        <Section_Start>2075</Section_Start>
        <Section_End>11242</Section_End>
</section>
```

Extracted data about the section includes: (a) serial number of a section; (b) its title; (c) text coordinates for the title; and (d) text coordinates for the whole section.

Using the extracted citation data of Examples 4–6 we can build semantic attributes of a citation relationship. The result is in the Table 2.

Table 2. An example of citation relationship with semantic attributes

Citing paper	Semantics of a citation relationship		Cited paper
Title: "SocioRePEc CRIS with an interactive mode of the research outputs usage", ID: `repec:rus:mqijxk:43`	**in-text reference:** ID: [num: 1, start-end: 2126-2128]	**location:** [number of section: 1, title: "1. Introduction", start-end: 2075-11242]	Title: "A CRIS driven by research community: benefits and perspectives", ID: `repec:rus:mqijxk:23`
		style: interpreted	
		left context: "In the CRIS-2010 conference paper"	
		right context: "some challenges for a CRIS-CERIF development were discussed in relation with the SocioNet project"	

We have a citation relationship between the citing paper "SocioRePEc CRIS with an interactive mode of the research outputs usage", having Socionet ID: `repec:rus:mqijxk:43`, and the cited paper "A CRIS driven by research community: benefits and perspectives" with ID: `repec:rus:mqijxk:23`.

The citing paper with ID: `repec:rus:mqijxk:43` has an in-text reference denoted by symbols [1] with text coordinates start = 2126, end = 2128, which refer to the cited paper with ID: `repec:rus:mqijxk:23`, because it has the number 1 in the reference list.

Using data of Examples 4–6 for this in-text reference, we can build following semantic attributes:

- Location. Since we know the text coordinates of the in-text reference (start-end: 2126-2128), we can comparing them with the text coordinates of paper's section (start-end: 2075-11242), and conclude that the in-text reference location is inside the Sect. 1, which has the title "Introduction".
- Left context. We know that the text "In the CRIS-2010 conference paper" precedes the in-text reference within one sentence. There is no direct quotation in this text. We can analyze significant words in this context and accumulate them to the reference as tags or a semantic halo [11].
- Right context: We know that the text "some challenges for a CRIS-CERIF development were discussed in relation with the SocioNet project" goes right after the in-text reference as a rest of the same sentence. There is no direct quotation in this text. We can process significant words the same as for the left context.
- Style. Since the left and the right context has no the direct quotation, we can conclude that the citation style is the "interpreted".

If a reference has many mentions as an in-text reference in one or in different papers available at RIS for the citation data extraction, we can collect for each paper its semantic attribute statistics and present it, e.g. as frequency distributions.

4   Citation Data Visualization

Some very popular tools to annotate PDF documents use the PDF.js module. For example, the Hypothes.is open source annotation software[19] used it. RIS Socionet integrated the Hypothes.is annotation tool into its environment[20] to give users ability to annotate all available research papers in PDF.

Since we are using the PDF.js module to convert and to display PDF documents, it gives us an opportunity to visualize the citation data extracted from the converted PDF as annotations of these PDF. Sergey Pertov made software needed for this visualization.

We are formatting the citation data according the Web Annotation Data Model[21]. To create an annotation according this data model, which should be associated with some in-text reference, one should make a JSON record as it is illustrated at the Example 7. A JSON record of an annotation from the Example 7 is based on the data of the in-text reference from the Example 5 and the Table 2.

Example 7. Illustration of annotation data for some in-text reference, a fragment

---

[19] https://github.com/hypothesis/pdf.js-hypothes.is.
[20] https://sparinov.wordpress.com/2016/05/27/comments-within-full-texts-in-pdf/.
[21] https://www.w3.org/TR/annotation-model/.

```
{"target": [
   {"source": "…CRIS2016_paper_40_Parinov.pdf",
    "selector": [
            {"type": "TextPositionSelector", "end": 2126, "start": 2128},
            {"exact": "[1]"}
            ]
   "tags": [we can insert here Semantic Halo tags],
   "text": "we can insert here statistics about this in-text reference"
}]}
```

The attribute `source` provides an URL of the annotated PDF document (in the Example 7 the URL is truncated). The attribute `selector` includes a data array specified what should be annotated in the PDF document content. The annotation will be at the text specified by the attribute `exact`, it is [1], and the first symbol of which has the number `"start"`: 2128, and the last - `"end"`: 2126. The attributes `tags` and `text` specify how the text in `exact` will be annotated, i.e. what a user will see when he/she click on this annotation.

The Fig. 3 presents a fragment of a PDF document with annotated in-text references. One can see in the document content three the same highlighted in-text reference with symbols [1]. The data of the Example 7 creates one of these annotations, exactly one at the top of the Fig. 3.

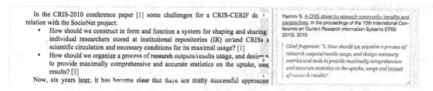

Fig. 3. A fragment of a PDF document with annotated in-text references

At the right side of the Fig. 3, one can see an information box, which appears on a screen after clicking on the annotation. Attributes `tags` and `text` from the Example 7 define what user sees in this box. Currently, it is just an information about the cited paper. In the future, it could be different statistics about this reference, including semantic attributes from the Table 2.

Extracted data about a reference presented at the Example 4 allow creating annotations for the references. The Fig. 4 illustrates this. An the right side of the Fig. 4 there is a text box with information about the reference, which annotation was clicked. Currently this text box shows information about its in-text reference, including their left/ right context. In the future, the box can provide different aggregated statistics about citing this reference in RIS papers.

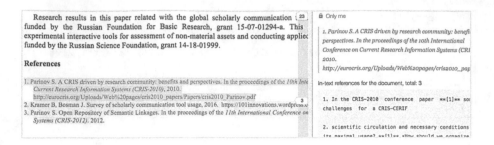

Fig. 4. A fragment of a PDF document with annotated references

5   Conclusion

A method of parsing an extended set of citation data and experiments with updating citation relationships of a real research paper by semantic attributes demonstrate an existing opportunity for research information systems to move from traditional citation analysis to the citation content analysis. Such, the content-based citation analysis offers multiple benefits for users of research information systems and authors of research papers. It includes the citation semantic attributes summarization, information retrieval based on the citation context, citation recommendation and prediction services, enhanced knowledge graph and conceptual networks, etc. [9].

Acknowledgments. A part of this research (related with the annotation tool development) is funded by Russian Foundation for Basic Research, grant 12-07-00518-a. Another part – the approach development for extracting citation content data with focus on the supercomputer simulation of interactions among the agents and research community environment is funded by RSF grant (project No. 14-18-01968).

References

1. Smith, L.C.: Citation analysis. Libr. Trends **30**(1), 83–106 (1981)
2. Garfield, E.: The relationship between citing and cited publications: a question of relatedness (1994). Originally published in the Current Contents
3. Barrueco, J.M., Krichel, T.: Building an autonomous citation index for grey literature: the economics working papers case. In: Proceedings GL6: Sixth International Conference on Grey Literature (2004). http://core.ac.uk/download/pdf/11878095.pdf
4. Waltman, L.: A review of the literature on citation impact indicators. J. Inf. **10**(2), 365–391 (2016)
5. Alschner, W., Umov, A.: Towards An Integrated Database of International Economic Law (IDIEL) Disputes (2016)
6. Bertin, M., Atanassova, I.: A study of lexical distribution in citation contexts through the IMRaD standard. PloS Negl. Trop. Dis. **1**(200,920), 83–402 (2014)
7. Bertin, M., Atanassova, I., Gingras, Y., Larivière, V.: The invariant distribution of references in scientific articles. J. Assoc. Inf. Sci. Technol. **67**(1), 164–177 (2016)

8. Zhang, G., Ding, Y., Milojević, S.: Citation content analysis (CCA): a framework for syntactic and semantic analysis of citation content. J. Am. Soc. Inform. Sci. Technol. **64**(7), 1490–1503 (2013)
9. Ding, Y., Zhang, G., Chambers, T., Song, M., Wang, X., Zhai, C.: Content-based citation analysis: the next generation of citation analysis. J. Assoc. Inf. Sci. Technol. **65**(9), 1820–1833 (2014)
10. Oevermann, J.: Reconstructing semantic structures in technical documentation with vector space classification. In: SEMANTiCS (Posters, Demos, SuCCESS) (2016)
11. Dix, A., Levialdi, S., Malizia, A.: Semantic halo for collaboration tagging systems. In: The Social Navigation and Community-Based Adaptation Technologies Workshop, 20 June 2006

Toward a Metadata Framework for Sharing Sensitive and Closed Data: An Analysis of Data Sharing Agreement Attributes

Sam Grabus[✉] and Jane Greenberg

Metadata Research Center <MRC>, College of Computing
and Informatics (CCI), Drexel University, Philadelphia, PA, USA
{sam.grabus, janeg}@drexel.edu

Abstract. Legal and policy-oriented restrictions often hamper if not inhibit well-intended efforts to share sensitive or restricted data. The research reported on in this paper is a part of a larger initiative to develop a prototype system for automatically generating data sharing agreements that address privacy, legal concerns, and other restrictions. A content analysis was conducted, examining a sample of 26 data sharing agreements. The results include 6 high level categories, 15 mid-level attributes, and over 90 lower-level specific attributes, a portion of which can help to expeditiously support the automatic development of data sharing agreements. The paper presents background information, research questions and methods, results, and a discussion. The conclusion summarizes our results and identifies next steps.

Keywords: Metadata · Closed data · Data sharing agreements · Restricted data · Privacy and data sharing

1 Introduction

Big data and the subsequent proliferation of data science and data analytics have bolstered data as a major avenue of research. These new disciplines offer the potential and promise to use data for gaining new insights and addressing societal and environmental problems locally and worldwide. As data has become a first-class information object, there is an increased drive to share data, and the open data movement has progressed as a significant development [1]. There is also a growing desire to share data that is sensitive or restricted, although this development has not progressed at the same pace, due to legal concerns and other restrictions [2–4].

The predicament with sharing closed or sensitive data is particularly detrimental when industry or government pursue an academic data sharing partnership and the plans fall apart, after considerable time and effort have been directed to the endeavor. This case is all too frequent, which results in a waste of resources, due to the legal fees and time commitments for those seeking the data sharing agreement. Another common scenario is that the data sharing negotiation simply takes too long, so that by the time the agreement is finally confirmed, the data being considered is no longer desirable. Again, the financial, time, and human resources expended are seen as a drain on those involved.

© Springer International Publishing AG 2017
E. Garoufallou et al. (Eds.): MTSR 2017, CCIS 755, pp. 300–311, 2017.
https://doi.org/10.1007/978-3-319-70863-8_29

Closed data sharing challenges were a major focus under a set of sessions entitled "War Stories" at the "Enabling Seamless Data Sharing in Industry and Academia" workshop, held at Drexel University (Fall 2016). The workshop also covered cases in which data sharing agreements were, in fact, successful, and presenters provided insight into lessons learned. An important outcome at this workshop was unanimous agreement regarding the need for a system that could automatically generate data sharing agreements. This outcome defines a key goal of "A Licensing Model and Ecosystem for Data Sharing" [5] initiative, being pursued as an NSF Spoke research project that is part of the North East Big Data Innovation Hub (NEBDIH) [6].

Many digital library and repository technologies provide options for secure, password-protected access, as well as controlling selected aspects of privacy, although these systems do not integrate fully with secure licensing models. The NSF Spoke research project (A Licensing Model and Ecosystem for Data Sharing) seeks to address this need by integrating data sharing and license development processes that extend beyond open creative commons standards. The Spoke research is being pursued through a collaboration involving Massachusetts Institute of Technology, Computer Science and Artificial Intelligence Laboratory (MIT/CSAIL), Drexel University's Metadata Research Center, and Brown University's Computer Science department. We are working toward an environment that will leverage existing de-identification and anonymization developments, and integrate with the DataHub platform [7]. The research presented in this paper is part of this larger effort to advance approaches for sharing closed data and ensuring security throughout the data-lifecycle.

The goal of the research presented in this paper is to identify metadata categories and attributes that will automatically and expeditiously support the development of data sharing agreements in closed and restricted environments. Specifically, the paper reports on a content analysis examining a sample of 26 data sharing agreements, and the identification of metadata categories and attributes. The paper that follows includes background information on open data, closed data, and data sharing; presents our research questions and methods; reports the first phase results; and includes a contextual discussion. The conclusion notes key findings and next steps.

2 Data Access and Sharing: A Simplified Continuum

Data access is directed by both contractual and technical factors. At the contractual level, there is a range of permissions, policies, legal considerations, personal and organizational preferences, and other factors that impact the data access rights. Rights, in this context, may cover permissions to view, use, reuse, repurpose, or distribute data. Metadata attributes, such as "rights management," can be assigned to data manually or automatically. When applied, rights management indicates data access status and use conditions. Data can be published or released under recognized licenses [8, 9], which may be documented in the rights-oriented attribute, or appended to the data in another way. These conventions are primarily contractual, and inform technical aspects of system design. More significantly, such conventions have helped to advance data access and sharing across a broad range of communities. Progress aside, it is important to realize that the amount of data published and released represents only a fraction of the vast quantities of data generated daily, including valuable data that owners may like to share, but can't, due to a myriad of restrictions. To understand the complexities of data access, both contractual and technical, it is helpful to first review the status of data access — specifically, what is meant by open and closed data.

2.1   Open Data

Open data is "data that anyone can access, use or share" [10]. More precisely, the Open Data Handbook explains that "open data is data that can be freely used, reused and redistributed by anyone — subject only, at most, to the requirement to attribute and sharealike" [11]. This resource elaborates on this definition by explaining important qualities, such as the practice that open data must be available and accessible, reusable, and redistributable, without restriction [11]. The absence of restriction surrounding open data extends to any endeavor, including commercialization. As noted, there are a range of licenses that data producers or data hosts append to data, indicating open access. The Creative Common Zero [12] is perhaps the most commonly known set of licenses.

While open data is increasingly lauded as beneficial and necessary to advance solutions for societal problems, the bioinformatics data community is arguably becoming more closed, due to the increasingly private nature of the data itself [13]. The sensitive nature of bioinformatics data falls into the category of closed data, given the need to protect individuals from potential exploitation and the harm that could result from research subject re-identification.

2.2   Closed Data

Closed data is data that often contains private or sensitive information. Closed data extends across a wide range of entities, topics, and environment. Examples of closed data include personal, institutional, or industry data identifying financial resources (e.g., sums, transactions, account numbers), personal information relating to health and well-being, or status (e.g., married, single, divorced). Data may be designated as closed, or regulated by controlled access, due to legal restrictions or organizational policies protecting current or predicted value. More specifically, data access is often restricted because of a known or perceived competitive advantage, and the associated risks with making it public, including misuse, if the data falls into the hands of the wrong person, office, or organization.

The last several years, there have been a series of data breaches exposing closed data, causing mayhem and outcomes that been ruinous to individuals. A case in point, the Ashley Madison hack [14], in which a torrent was used to publish user profiles, transactions, credit card data, and a wide range of other sensitive data, including associated metadata. Ashley Madison's core mission is to arrange extramarital relations between married individuals, and the breach exposed the private lives of thousands of people, damaging the reputation and status of people who used their work email addresses to use the website.

There are also cases that raise concern about potential exploitation, in which private data is shared between organizations without the consent of the data subject.

For example, UK's National Health Service allegedly violated data protection laws by sharing patient health data with Google's DeepMind [15]. Examples of medical data sharing frequently raise public concern, particularly with an increase of more than 20% in cases of medical identity theft between 2013 and 2014 [16].

These examples of sharing closed data demonstrate potentially harmful impacts, but this does not mean that closed data should not be shared, considering the immense societal advantages and innovation potential from new insights.

2.3   Data Access Status: Fuzzy Boundaries

To be clear, closed data is accessible to individuals or organizations who have the appropriate permissions. In other words, access and use are conducted in a tightly controlled, secure environment. Additionally, technical system features are implemented to support and maintain the controlled environment, albeit sometimes hackable, as demonstrated in the above and other cases. A common scenario is that data may initially be closed, marked by an embargo period, and then later be released as open. This option is one seen in the Dryad data repository [17], for published data that underlies published research. Additionally, data that is designated open may have components that need to remain closed, such as personally identifying information (PII). This is often the case when personal health data is made available for medical research. For example, the progression of a disease is important for research, but individuals who have certain disorders may want to protect their identity [18]. Approaches to sharing sensitive data include anonymization and de-identifying personal information [19], allowing some, but not all, of the data to be shared. This example, and others alluded to here, demonstrate the fuzzy boundary between open and closed data, and impact the increasing trend toward data sharing.

3   Data Sharing Practice and Needs

For the last decade and a half, extensive energy has been directed toward cultivating and sustaining open research and the sharing of creative output. Many of the ideas stem from the open source community, and the notion of wisdom of the crowds [20]. Simply put, the more people contributing to R&D, the better the end results. Additionally, open sharing environments keep people from reinventing the wheel. Specific to science, there have been considerable efforts to build cyberinfrastructure for sharing scientific and scholarly outputs [21], with data becoming a key focus.

Another significant motivator of data sharing has been the data deluge—that is, the sheer amount data generated through scientific research and other endeavors, and the unprecedented capacity to support data-driven science [22]. These ideas stem from Jim Gray's notion of the Fourth Paradigm enabling highly efficient access to data and analysis tools [23].

Data sharing in the closed environment has benefitted open data developments, where tools and technologies developed can be used and made secure. Even so, the rate of progress is hampered by legal and logistical challenges. Although useful infrastructure can help facilitate secure data sharing, a range of regulations and policies (e.g.,

HIPAA, institutional policies) complicate closed data sharing, impeding or otherwise delaying the process.

Research needs to be directed toward developing solutions to address these data sharing challenges in the closed environment. Metadata has been identified as part of the solution to addressing these challenges [24]. To move forward with metadata solutions, more analysis is needed to determine researcher data sharing needs. The research that follows takes initial steps toward addressing this need.

4 Research Questions

The overriding goal of this research is to advance metadata practices that can facilitate data sharing efforts in environments where the data is not necessarily open. The specific goals were to identify metadata categories and attributes that will, more expeditiously, support the development of data sharing agreements in these environments. The research was guided by two questions:

1. What high-level metadata categories are found in data sharing agreements?
2. What elements and attributes are found across data sharing licenses with sensitive information; what are the most common?

The next section reports methods and the steps taken to investigate our questions.

5 Methods and Procedures

To address the questions posited above, we conducted a content analysis following the general eight steps outlined by Zhang and Wildemuth [25]. Our research protocol involved the following steps:

1. *Data collection*: A sample of 26 data sharing agreements from industry, academia, and government was obtained. These agreements were collected via a solicitation, following the NE Big Data Hub's Data Sharing Workshop, and other communications through the NSF Big Data Innovation Hub Program, and in connection within the Research Data Alliance. The data sharing agreements were acquired through a two-step process. First, a number of licenses were found through online searching, which typically yielded templates containing useful language, along with sections to be completed by the parties involved in the data sharing. Second, a call was distributed to the diverse community that participated in the workshop, with members from industry, government, and academia. Achieving a representative sample across all sectors was a challenge; and our sample emphasized academic partnerships. Additionally, agreement dates were difficult to confirm. Despite these issues, the convenient sample of 26 agreements included representation from multiple sectors, including industry, and was deemed sufficient for our research.
2. *Content analysis:* The language of these licenses was first examined for overall clarity and to confirm data sharing support; then, a focused examination was pursued. The language was parsed for higher-level general categories, as well as mid

and lower-level attributes, which are the detailed license specifications for data handling. The full collection of categories and attributes make up the sample for the study reported on in this paper.

3. *Language clustering:* The high-level general categories and lower level attributes were organized on a spreadsheet in a hierarchical arrangement.

4. *Metadata labeling:* The language of the categories and attributes was refined. These results will be used to help build the infrastructure that will assist with the minting of data sharing agreements.

6   Data Analysis

The data analysis was carried out to answer our two questions, looking at high-level categories for sharing data, as well as common elements and attributes among the data sharing agreements. In answer to question 1, we found that the agreement attributes fit into 6 high-level broad categories, listed in Fig. 1 below. This categorization is the first iteration of refinement, and as such, we recognize that there may be some dependencies or overlap:

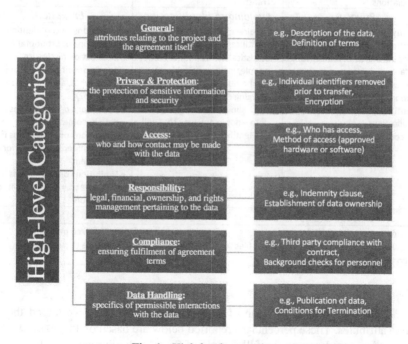

Fig. 1. High-level categories

In addressing question 2, we discovered 15 common mid-level elements (e.g., Legal, Termination), and over 90 lower-level attributes that address the specific data sharing needs (e.g., Who has access to proprietary information, Merging data with other sets).

Following the high-level categories, Table 1(below) presents detailed results for "Privacy & Protection," and Table 2 presents details of "Data Handling." The common elements were gleaned from the 26 data sharing licenses across the full sample.

Table 1. Privacy & Protection attributes

Privacy & Protection		
Sensitive Information		
Regulations	*Preparing data*	*Access*
• Regulation used to define sensitive data (e.g., HIPAA, FERPA, etc.) • Compliance with federal/state/international data protection laws and regulations	• Identification of confidential/special categories of information (e.g., pii, proprietary) • Individual identifiers removed/anonymized prior to transfer	• Who has access to pii/confidential data • Who has access to proprietary information
Privacy	*Avoiding re-identification*	*Exceptions*
• Anonymization of data • Confidentiality and safeguarding of PII/sensitive data • Removal/nondisclosure of company/personnel identification in materials and publications • No contact with data subjects	• No direct/indirect re-identification • Statistical cell size (how many people, in aggregated form, can be released in groups) • Merging data with other sets (e.g., allowed with aggregated data—not in any way that will re-identify)	• Exceptions to confidentiality • Conditions of proprietary information disclosure • Conditions of pii disclosure (who, what, and for what purpose?) • Limitations on obligations if data becomes public • Limitations on obligations if data is already known prior to agreement • Limitations on obligations if data given by 3rd party without restriction
Security		
• Sharing non-confidential data • Password protection/authentication of files • Encryption	• Security training for involved personnel • Establishing infrastructure to safeguard confidential data	

In addition to the identification of categories and attributes, we tallied the most common attributes. These percentages reported below are based on the 90+ lower-level attributes discovered among the full sample of 26 data sharing agreements:

- Most common attributes pertaining specifically to protecting sensitive information were adherence to federal/state/international data protection laws and regulations, as well as explicitly prohibiting direct or indirect re-identification of data subjects, found in over half the sample of agreements (16 of 26, 61.5%).

Table 2. Data Handling attributes

Data Handling		
Use		**Physical**
• Each data field/elements to be accessed • Use of data: only for project-specific/research, or analytical use • Documenting all projects using the data	• Modification of data • Compliance with data updates (changes, removal, corrections) • Sharing data	• Copy/reproduction of data • Storage of data • Transfer of data (e.g., allowed methods)
Results		**Personal Gain**
• Presentation of data • Publication of data (e.g., prior approval needed or right to publically disclose publication)	• Results/reports and associated documents (e.g., must be provided copies) • Right to remove/delete confidential data from proposed publications	• Sale of/profit from data (e.g., noncommercial use only) • Licensing of data • No reverse engineering
Termination		
• Conditions for termination • Destruction or return of data after agreement • 3rd party destruction or return of dataset • Confirmation of data destruction	• Data retained or used for period of time after termination • Which rights and obligations remain in effect after termination	

- Agreements involving industry had the highest instances of the data ownership attributes.
- The most common attribute found among general data handling practices, across the sample, was the return or destruction of data after the agreement ends (88.4%).
- Over half (61.5%) of all agreements specify which rights and obligations will remain in effect after termination.
- Over half (65.3%) of all agreements specify that the data should only be used for the specific research and analytic uses agreed upon through the license.
- Almost half (46.1%) of data sharing agreements include an indemnity clause, specifying that the other party will be held responsible for damages involved with the data usage.
- The most common privacy laws applicable to the data sharing agreements are HIPAA (Health Insurance Portability and Accountability Act) and FERPA (The Family Educational Rights and Privacy Act).
- Only 15.3% of the agreements specify whether the data can be merged with other sets (in aggregated form or otherwise).
- Only 4 (15.3%) of the agreements required source acknowledgement for use of the data.

7 Discussion

The results presented above are important to the research being conducted as part of the "A Licensing Model and Ecosystem for Data Sharing" project. Our results can connect with efforts underway with the Dataverse system, where a color-coded tag system has been developed to designate degree of data access [26]. One end of the spectrum is a light blue, to designate open access, and at the other end is a deep crimson red, indicating "maximally restricted," with access requiring a "Two-factor authentication, Approval, Signed DUA" [26].

As expected, all of the licenses in the sample contained attributes regarding the privacy and protection of sensitive data, whether it is personally identifiable information (PII) or proprietary information. The level of specificity for these protections varied drastically, but the most common attributes pertaining specifically to protecting sensitive information were adherence to federal/state/international data protection laws and regulations (61.5%), as well as explicitly prohibiting direct or indirect re-identification of data subjects (61.5%). This makes sense, considering that presumably all stakeholders would want to avoid the potential legal repercussions of violating privacy laws, particularly in the event that data subjects are re-identified. The results here will help in developing our framework to support privacy, and ensure data integrity. Advances by Barth, et al. [27], in which they developed a framework to incorporate legislation found in HIPPA, COPPA, and GBLA, and support reasoning about the transmission of personal information, may further inform our research in this area.

Although many of the licenses examined were from academic institutions, they all identified attributes related to privacy. Academia, industry, and government averaged an almost identical number of attribute occurrences related to privacy and security concerns (Academia had an average of 5.45 attributes in this group, Industry: 5.71, Government: 5). Close to a third (27%) of the agreement sample specifically involved industry, with 15.4% involving government. Although we are continuing to build our sample base, the sample used was sufficient for this initial study, and is already informing our prototype system design. Specifically, research team members have started to develop a prototype that will interconnect with DataHub, and the results presented above have helped us to determine which facets can more easily be automated. This determination has helped in more clearly identifying areas of greater priority for automation and implementation (e.g., automating the removal of PII categories, as well as aspects of agreement access and termination). The results have also been important for understanding where our system must, instead, support opportunity for textual phrases, either accessible via a dropdown menu, or through the flexibility to generate desired statements for the parties pursuing the agreement. This mixed approach is common across many data systems, from library serials control [28] to data repositories, such as the Morpho system [29], for ecological data. Automated controlled attributes, as well as open text options, will be features in our system, supporting data sharing agreements, permissions, and licensing.

8 Conclusion

Data sharing of sensitive and private information introduces a set of challenges, and requires the development of most robust agreements, far different than with open data, where data sharing is established with an open license. The research presented in this paper is part of a larger effort to expedite the process of developing data sharing agreements. The research focused on metadata aspects that can help with the automatic generation of agreements to support data sharing in these more restrictive environments. A content analysis examining a sample of 26 data sharing agreements was conducted. Key findings were:

- 6 high-level categories
- 15 mid-level attributes, and over 90 lower-level specific attributes, which can help to inform the development of automatically-generated data sharing agreements
- Observations that showed a prevalence of particular privacy and data handling attributes over others

The results have already proved useful in taking steps to help develop a prototype system. Research team members have already taken steps to automate the removal of personal identification information, specify controlled access for particular researchers to specific tables/cells of data, and execute termination of access to some or all of the dataset at the end of the agreement. In addition to aiding the development of the data sharing platform, this paper also shares our initial methods, which may help other researchers pursuing similar work. While the results presented in this research have helped with our next steps, we recognize the sample limitations, and intend to address this challenge by developing a process that will allow to obtain a more representative sample of data sharing agreements.

Next steps include developing and analyzing a larger sample of data sharing agreements, to confirm our initial findings and gain a more comprehensive understanding of stakeholder data sharing requirements, particularly when privacy, sensitive information, and other restrictions are involved. Other next steps include minting key phrases that associate with our metadata categories — specifically, the mid- and lower-level attributes — that would be inserted into data sharing agreements. Longer-term goals will include user review of the metadata attributes, and testing the prototype system being developed by other key members.

Data may hold the solutions to addressing many of society's grand challenges. To this end, researchers need to pursue steps to improve data sharing across all environments, including those with sensitive/private/restricted information. The research presented here is a strong effort toward addressing the current data sharing challenges, and our next steps forward will further contribute to metadata and data sharing research initiatives in the future.

Acknowledgements. We acknowledge the support of the National Science Foundation/IIS/BD Spokes/Award #1636788; and thank Sam Maddden (MIT), Carsten Binnig (TU Darmstadt), and Tim Kraska (Brown University), and other individuals who provided us with data sharing agreements.

References

1. Janssen, M., Charalabidis, Y., Zuiderwijk, A.: Benefits, adoption barriers and myths of open data and open government. Inf. Syst. Manage. **29**(4), 258–268 (2012)
2. McGuire, A.L., Oliver, J.M., Slashinski, M.J., Graves, J.L., Wang, T., Kelly, P.A., Fisher, W., Lau, C.C., Goss, J., Okcu, M., Treadwell-Deering, D.: To share or not to share: a randomized trial of consent for data sharing in genome research. Genet. Med. Off. J. Am. Coll. Med. Genet. **13**(11), 948–955 (2011)
3. Pencarrick Hertzman, C., Meagher, N., McGrail, K.M.: Privacy by design at population data BC: a case study describing the technical, administrative, and physical controls for privacy-sensitive secondary use of personal information for research in the public interest. J. Am. Med. Inform. Assoc. **20**(1), 25–28 (2012)
4. Gleason, C.J., Hamdan, A.N.: Crossing the (watershed) divide: satellite data and the changing politics of international river basins. Geogr. J. **183**(1), 2–15 (2017)
5. Metadata Research Center: A Licensing Model and Ecosystem for Data Sharing (2017). http://cci.drexel.edu/mrc/projects/a-licensing-model-and-ecosystem-for-data-sharing/
6. Northeast Big Data Innovation Hub (2017). http://nebigdatahub.org/
7. Datahub: What is datahub? (2016). https://datahub.csail.mit.edu/www/
8. Creative Commons: Licensing types (2017). https://creativecommons.org/share-your-work/licensing-types-examples/
9. The National Archives (n.d.): Open government license for public sector information. http://nationalarchives.gov.uk/doc/open-government-licence/version/3/. Accessed 1 July 2017
10. Open Data Institute (n.d.): What is open data? https://theodi.org/what-is-open-data. Accessed 1 July 2017
11. Dietrich, D., Gray, J., McNamara, T., Poikola, A., Pollock, P., Tait, J., Zijlstra, T., et al.: Open data handbook (2009). http://opendatahandbook.org. Accessed 15 June 2017
12. CC0. (n.d.). https://creativecommons.org/share-your-work/public-domain/cc0/. Accessed 1 July 2017
13. Greenbaum, D., Sboner, A., Mu, X., Gerstein, M.: Genomics and privacy: Implications of the new reality of closed data for the field. PLoS Comput. Biol. **7**(12), e1002278 (2011). https://doi.org/10.1371/journal.pcbi.1002278
14. Segall, L.: Ashley Madison: Life after the hack. CNN Tech (2017). http://money.cnn.com/mostly-human/click-swipe-cheat/
15. Kwon, D.: Google's DeepMind, UK's NHS criticized for sharing data. The Scientist (2017). http://www.the-scientist.com/?articles.view/articleNo/49812/title/Google-s-DeepMind–UK-s-NHS-Criticized-for-Sharing-Data/
16. Kaplan, B.: How should health data be used? Camb. Q. Healthc. Ethics CQ Int. J. Healthc. Ethics Committees **25**(2), 312 (2016)
17. Dryad Digital Repository (2017). http://datadryad.org/
18. Liu, X., Li, X., Motiwalla, L., Li, W., Zheng, H., Franklin, P.D.: Preserving patient privacy when sharing same-disease data. J. Data Inf. Qual. **7**(4), 17 (2016). https://doi.org/10.1145/2956554
19. El Emam, K., et al.: De-identification methods for open health data: the case of the heritage health prize claims dataset. J. Med. Internet Res. **14**(1), e33 (2012)
20. Raymond, E.: The cathedral and the bazaar. Philos. Technol. **12**(3), 23 (1999). https://monoskop.org/File:Raymond_Eric_S_The_Cathedral_and_the_Bazaar_rev_ed.pdf

21. Atkins, D.E., National Science Foundation (U.S.): Blue-ribbon advisory panel on cyberinfrastructure. Revolutionizing Science and Engineering Through Cyberinfrastructure: Report of the National Science Foundation Blue-Ribbon Advisory Panel on Cyberinfrastructure (2003)
22. Hey, T., Trefethen, A.: The Data deluge: an e-science perspective. In: Berman, F., Fox, G., Hey, T. (eds.) Grid Computing: Making the Global Infrastructure a Reality, pp. 809–824. Wiley, Chichester (2003). https://doi.org/10.1002/0470867167.ch36
23. Hey, T., Tansley, S., Tolle, K.: The Fourth Paradigm: Data-Intensive Scientific Research. Microsoft Research, Redmond, WA (2009)
24. Greenberg, J., Grabus, S., Hudson, F., Kraska, T., Madden, S., Bastón, R.: The Northeast Big Data Hub: "Enabling Seamless Data Sharing in Industry and Academia" Workshop. The Northeast Big Data Innovation Hub, Philadelphia (2016). https://doi.org/10.17918/D8159V
25. Zhang, Y., Wildemuth, B.M.: Qualitative analysis of content, applications of social research methods to questions in information and library science. Google Scholar, pp. 308–319 (2005)
26. Crosas, M.: The DataTags system: sharing sensitive data with confidence. In: RDA 8th Plenary, Denver Colorado, 16 September 2016 (2016). https://scholar.harvard.edu/mercecrosas/presentations/datatags-system-sharing-sensitive-data-confidence
27. Barth, A., Datta, A., Mitchell, J.C., Nissenbaum, H.: Privacy and contextual integrity: framework and applications. In: 2006 IEEE Symposium on Security and Privacy, 15-pp. IEEE, May 2006
28. Blake, K., Collins, M.: Controlling chaos: management of electronic journal holdings in an academic library environment. Serials Rev. 36(4), 242–250 (2010)
29. Higgins, D., Berkley, C., Jones, M.B.: Managing heterogeneous ecological data using morpho. In: The 14th International Conference on Scientific and Statistical Database Management, pp. 69–76 (2002). https://doi.org/10.1109/SSDM.2002.1029707

Track on Digital Humanities and Digital Curation (DHC)

Battle Without FAIR and Easy Data in Digital Humanities

An Empirical Research on the Challenges of Open Data and APIs for the James Cook Dynamic Journal

Go Sugimoto[✉]

Austrian Centre for Digital Humanities, Austrian Academy of Sciences, Vienna, Austria
Go.Sugimoto@oeaw.ac.at

Abstract. There are theoretical and technical challenges for Digital Humanities scholars to develop and use Application Programming Interfaces (APIs). Whilst data owning culture in our institutional settings seems to hinder truly interdisciplinary research, the emergence of Linked Open Data implies the increasing opportunities of distributed-data research. This article is based on an API application to address those issues in the context of Open Data. James Cook Dynamic Journal was created to assist users to study the Cook's journal, integrating various sets of APIs which facilitate full-text search, Named Entity Recognition, and map views. The development revealed some critical issues of data federation and processing automation. The standardization of data structure and the development of user-friendly GUI tools would significantly increase the value of APIs. Taking recent initiatives into account, the paper also proposes "Easy Data" to liberate Open Data for a wider spectrum of users outside the programmer community.

Keywords: API · Digital Humanities · James Cook · Open Data · FAIR principles · Easy Data

1 Open Data and API in Digital Humanities

"Open" has been the term of a decade in the time of digital research. Most researchers are occupied with Open Data, Open Science, Open Source, and Open Access. In many ways, the open movement is driven by the fact that everything has been too closed until recently, be it the balance sheets of public institutions, or the scientific data of publicly-funded projects on climate change. Tax payers have the right to ask for transparency and data sharing. Consequently, the exponential expansion of Big Data contributes to the "web democracy", and vise versa. Likewise, data repository managers in scientific institutions have come under growing pressure to open their data. In Digital Humanities (DH), the advocacies of Open Data and Access have had substantial impact over the last years. As a consequence, Application Programming Interfaces (APIs) are often chosen as a part of Open Data policies and Data Management Plans. In fact, it is nowadays possible to easily access a wide range of data remotely and useful spin-off services and mobile apps are developed. The Executive Director of the Digital Public Library of America (DPLA) Cohen [2] rightly addressed

© Springer International Publishing AG 2017
E. Garoufallou et al. (Eds.): MTSR 2017, CCIS 755, pp. 315–326, 2017.
https://doi.org/10.1007/978-3-319-70863-8_30

the long-term values of APIs for DH. On the other hand, more recently the Findable, Accessible, Interoperable, and Re-usable (FAIR) principles are proposed in the broader field of e-Science, which aim to "more easily discover, access, interoperable and sensibly re-use, with proper citation, the vast quantities of information"[1] both for machines and humans.

This article will explore an empirical application of APIs from a DH point of view. The first part consists of a theoretical background for the rationale of this research to outline the issue of data owning culture and the trend of Open Data to be thought about in the near future. The second part presents the technical details of the API experiment. It does not investigate the latest and the most innovative technologies of APIs for technicians, but rather it highlights the experience of using APIs and their pros and cons thorough the eyes of a novice software developer. Taking the recent viral phenomenon of the FAIR principles into account, the author comes up with a set of recommendations to improve the APIs environments within DH. In addition, the paper points out how important it is to remove the current barriers of Open Data to pave the way for true data liberation through "data revolution" and proposes "Easy Data".

2 Research Without Data

2.1 Data Owning Culture

One of the objectives of this paper is to examine how to build a useful service without owning data in DH research. Although there are DH departments and centers, until now, it seems that many fields of DH are still exercised in a traditional domain-specific and institutional style, simply because "modern" researchers tend to belong to scientific institutions split into specific domains. They create or acquire data as a part of their professional fieldwork or desktop studies, be it an archaeological excavation, 3D scanning of a painting, or a socio-political survey. Therefore, the generated data becomes the property of the institutions.[2] In short, researchers are usually employees and they own data in the realm of their institutions. Alternatively, they at least might have easy access to data due to collaborations and partnerships between institutions and data suppliers. Indeed, the Austrian Centre for Digital Humanities (ACDH)[3], for example, collaborates with many domain-specific institutes.

This situation can be sketched in the form of a DH matrix (Fig. 1). The above-mentioned researchers fall into the first category: data providers and research institutions. They work in a museum, a library, archives, or a university to carry out their research, and they are the data owners as well as the users. They might also develop services for the data. For instance, Maegaard et al. [4] describe researchers as not only consumers but also providers in the context of stakeholders of CLARIN[4], a linguistic

---

[1] https://www.force11.org/group/fairgroup/fairprinciples accessed 2017-07-05.
[2] This convention is probably not a result of individual preference, but a consequence of a social system which, more or less, forces individual researchers to do so.
[3] https://www.oeaw.ac.at/acdh/acdh-home accessed 2017-07-05.
[4] https://www.clarin.eu accessed 2017-07-05.

research infrastructure. Historically institutions and researchers incline toward data owning culture, which does not only hinder Open Data and Open Access, but also lead to empirical research without third-party verifications. As opposed to natural sciences which rely more on experiments and mathematics, the reproducibility of their research has been extremely limited. To rectify this environment, new initiatives such as the FAIR principles [11] have recently emerged to foster the publication of data and documentation of research processes.

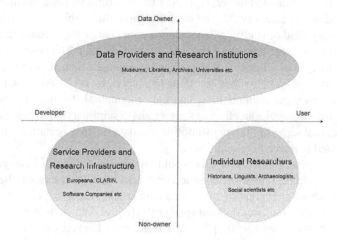

Fig. 1. Digital Humanities researchers and institutions in relation to the data owning culture

The second category is classified as service providers, especially research infrastructures as well as software vendors, in the area of DH. For example, Europeana[5], DARIAH[6], and CLARIN are the principle actors in Europe who develop technical services for others, without owning data[7]. They may have employees who are also heavy users of their own services, but, in that case, they often simultaneously belong to the first category (e.g. a university researcher in the CLARIN consortium), or other employees such as software developers whose work does not primarily focus on humanities research. Obviously the categories are not static. For instance, the respondents of a survey of tool developers in DH [9] are diverse and may represent a mix of the first and second category. The ACDH would primarily be classified as the second category, delivering consulting, hardware, and software services, but may as well belong to the first category, because the data is deposited to its repository by the first category institutions. The third category is individual researchers such as art historians, linguists, anthropologists, and political scientists who explore research topics, using existing data and tools. Thus, they are more independent from the resources they study. They can be

---

[5] http://www.europeana.eu accessed 2017-07-05.
[6] http://www.dariah.eu accessed 2017-07-05.
[7] A strict definition of the term "ownership" should not be argued in this context. Here, it merely means that their main jobs are to aggregate data from partners and develop services and infrastructures. They may own metadata and additional resources.

institutionally affiliated researchers, but also more independent hobby or semi-professional researchers. Their characteristics are defined by no ownership and no development. They use data and services offered by data providers and/or service providers for their research purposes.

2.2 Frontline of Interdisciplinary and Distributed-Data Research

There are some questions to answer, regarding the institutional isolation and data fragmentation of the first category: "Is the data-owning culture able to promote DH as a cross-disciplinary field of study?", "Is the data created under this circumstance considerate enough to facilitate the use of data in different domains?" These questions also apply to the struggle of CLARIN of the second category, which seeks to enable more interdisciplinary research, so that the data and services of CLARIN can be more frequently used by other communities than only the natural language experts. Unless individual institutions make an effort to start a trans-disciplinary DH research and open up data for external serendipitous consumption, the data use may remain confined within domain-affiliated research communities.

The author foresees that a new DH would emerge from the third category. In the near future, it would become more common or even a norm for the researchers to carry out their research without creating or owning data at all in the name of web-Science or Open Science. Even if one uses own data primarily, hybrid data –to interconnect internal and external data– is a beneficial option at a time when Linked Open Data is gaining momentum. The researchers could find new ways of analysis and interpretation, by mixing different types of data they had not considered. As a matter of fact, the more interdisciplinary a research becomes, the more likely it borrows data externally. This is the starting point of this article, contributing to this discourse, because the developed application uses data only from external APIs of different disciplines. It is hoped that it uncovers the advantages and disadvantages of "distributed data research".

3 Experiment of James Cook Dynamic Journal

This section illustrates the background and development of a simple API application as a case study, focusing on the resources of James Cook (1728–1779). He was chosen, because he is a subject of interest for a wide spectrum of science and history, therefore, there is a big potential for interdisciplinary research in DH.

James Cook is renowned for his epic journeys to the Pacific. They were not only the important historical moments of navigation, but also scientific missions. He was accompanied by leading scientists of his time. Most notably Joseph Banks and Daniel Solander were the two prominent figures who collected biological samples of animals and plants. Their research advanced the understanding of fauna and flora in the regions previously unknown to the Europeans. The recordings of natural wonders by Banks and Solander are preserved in various natural and cultural heritage institutions across the globe which are not easily accessible. It can be expected that the various aspects and layers of Cook's journeys would be able to trigger unexpected research.

3.1 Federated APIs

The James Cook Dynamic Journal (JCDJ) was developed to provide a new way of exploring a journal by James Cook. It integrates The Open Library API[8], Google Maps API[9], Dandelion API[10], and DBpedia[11]. The Open Library has a new full-text search API, however a bit of work-around was necessary. Not all resources of the library are accessible via the API and it is not trivial to identify parameters to access a resource[12].

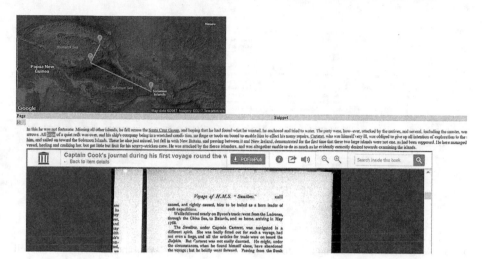

Fig. 2. A result block containing a consolidated map (route), snippet, and book viewer, followed Named Entity Recognition (Fig. 3).

The starting page of the JCDJ is nothing more than a search box. The user makes a full-text query on "Captain Cook's journal during his first voyage round the world made in H.M. Bark "Endeavour", 1768–71 [microform]"[13]. The search result page is divided into a block of information per search result (Fig. 2). Each result consists of: (1) a snippet of texts with search terms highlighted in blue, (2) a book viewer displaying the page on which the snippet and the search terms appear, (3) a table which shows named entities and their descriptions per row, (4) a consolidated map with all identified locations plotted. The snippet also includes hyperlinks to the named entities of Wikipedia, if the Dandelion API detects them there. In general, the JCDJ is meant to be a reading aid especially when unfamiliar technical terms appear in the snippet. For this reason, the author calls the service "Dynamic Journal" as it contains a lot of automatically generated

---

8 https://openlibrary.org/developers/api last accessed 2017-07-05.

9 https://developers.google.com/maps/documentation/embed last accessed 2017-07-05.

10 https://dandelion.eu/docs/api/datatxt/nex/v1 last accessed 2017-07-05.

11 http://wiki.dbpedia.org/ last accessed 2017-07-05.

12 A support person stated that the lack of resources is the main reason for incapability of delivering a stable public service. (Jake Johnson. Personal communication. 2016-02-16).

13 https://archive.org/details/cihm_14800 last accessed 2017-07-05.

links. The page preview is merely an embedded iframe which is created based on a page number, however, it is convenient, because the user can check the search results in context. Due to the lack of API functionalities, it is technically not feasible to provide the highlight function in the embedded preview, which the Open Library offers in its own web interface. The following table displays (a) types of recognized entities, (b) confidence level of the entity (zero to one), description, thumbnail, and location on a map. Thumbnails and maps are subject to availabilities (Fig. 3).

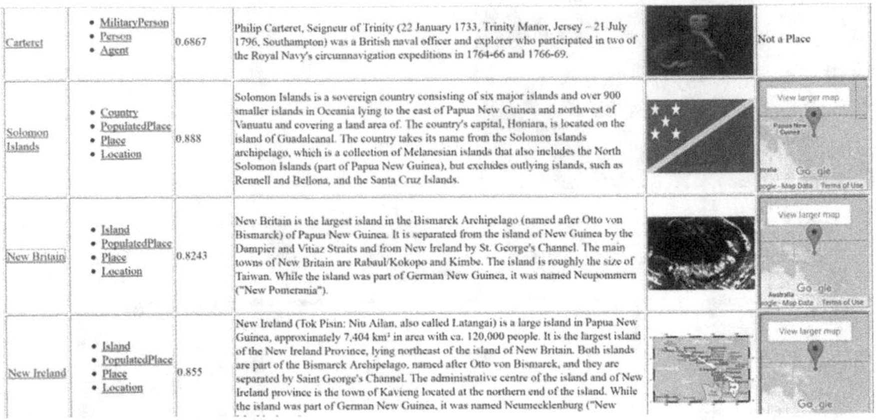

Carteret	• MilitaryPerson • Person • Agent	0.6867	Philip Carteret, Seigneur of Trinity (22 January 1733, Trinity Manor, Jersey – 21 July 1796, Southampton) was a British naval officer and explorer who participated in two of the Royal Navy's circumnavigation expeditions in 1764-66 and 1766-69.		Not a Place
Solomon Islands	• Country • PopulatedPlace • Place • Location	0.888	Solomon Islands is a sovereign country consisting of six major islands and over 900 smaller islands in Oceania lying to the east of Papua New Guinea and northwest of Vanuatu and covering a land area of. The country's capital, Honiara, is located on the island of Guadalcanal. The country takes its name from the Solomon Islands archipelago, which is a collection of Melanesian islands that also includes the North Solomon Islands (part of Papua New Guinea), but excludes outlying islands, such as Rennell and Bellona, and the Santa Cruz Islands.		View larger map
New Britain	• Island • PopulatedPlace • Place • Location	0.8243	New Britain is the largest island in the Bismarck Archipelago (named after Otto von Bismarck) of Papua New Guinea. It is separated from the island of New Guinea by the Dampier and Vitiaz Straits and from New Ireland by St. George's Channel. The main towns of New Britain are Rabaul/Kokopo and Kimbe. The island is roughly the size of Taiwan. While the island was part of German New Guinea, it was named Neupommern ("New Pomerania").		View larger map
New Ireland	• Island • PopulatedPlace • Place • Location	0.855	New Ireland (Tok Pisin: Niu Ailan, also called Latangai) is a large island in Papua New Guinea, approximately 7,404 km² in area with ca. 120,000 people. It is the largest island of the New Ireland Province, lying northeast of the island of New Britain. Both islands are part of the Bismarck Archipelago, named after Otto von Bismarck, and they are separated by Saint George's Channel. The administrative centre of the island and of New Ireland province is the town of Kavieng located at the northern end of the island. While the island was part of German New Guinea, it was named Neumecklenburg ("New		View larger map

Fig. 3. A result table containing recognized named entities, displaying their information as well as thumbnails and maps.

It might seem relatively simple to implement such a table, but there is quite some data processing behind the scenes. The normalization of data values is frequently required in order to display data in a meaningful and user-friendly manner. For example, JSON Array was converted to bullet points in the type column, while map creation involves several steps. Firstly, the PHP code reads all the recognized named entities and, only when the type of the entity is a place, a data processing is initiated. The geographical coordinates are fetched by a second API call to DBpedia. After some data normalization, the Google Maps API can show the point of location on a map. Finally, all coordinates of recognized places are consolidated into one map and lines are drawn between them. The initial idea was that the map would be able to trace the route of the Cook's journeys. Although the routes of his three journeys are already academically known, the attempt of this experiment is to partially automate the process of displaying them. However, the route tracing is limited to a snippet, and the places in it are not only the points of the voyage, but also any places mentioned in completely different contexts. Nonetheless, the approach of this project proved that Named Entity Recognition would be helpful for automatically detecting the place names and plotting them on a map for different research purposes. It is especially effective if the entire journal, instead of query snippets, is processed in full-text. Errors can also happen due to entity recognition failures and missing and/or wrong data.

Despite the difficulties, the project is interesting with regards to methodology and the code of the JCDJ could be easily re-applied to other similar projects. For instance, it is already being adopted for "Voices from the Orient" (1884) by George Burnfield[14], "A voyage round the world" (1789) by William Beresford and George Dixon[15], and "The Hittites" (1890) by John Campbell[16]. In these examples, due to their lesser popularity, it is more likely that many places and travel routes have yet been examined, which might bring some new insights into humanities research. In addition, it becomes clear that the approach of this paper is suited not only for natural history but also for any research employing full-text processing. It should also be noted that The Open Library/Internet Archive publishes large amounts of freely accessible resources and has a significant potential for DH.

Admittedly, the JCDJ is not a serious technical solution. There is clearly a slow performance due to the real-time data access. In addition, the project depends on too many free APIs and the code may not be optimized. However, the emphasis of this experiment is to demonstrate the possibility of APIs integration with full-text and relevant information, without owning data at all, which is rather rare in DH.

3.2 Storytelling of Interdisciplinary Natural History

In the course of the development, the author searched for a wide spectrum of data on the web. Hence the first prototype was a simple platform where the user can query several APIs, including, among others, Atlas of Living Australia[17], Europeana, Biodiversity Heritage Library[18], and Encyclopedia of Life[19]. Apart from the same problems of data handling explained earlier, this step was successful in accessing the knowledge of versatile interdisciplinary resources. This is an echo of the statement of Cohen [2], describing the value of APIs as their unexpected use by the unexpected users.

However, it turned out that the prototype focused too much on query and dataset. That is to say that each piece of data has its value and is somehow connected to the others, but the users have to examine and interpret the retuned data in order to understand the meaning. It is data, but not yet information and knowledge. In other words, it does not tell stories about the subject. In addition, as many APIs on the web are resource-discovery query services, there is a gap between structured metadata and (often unstructured) source data that the metadata describes. This is exactly what services like Europeana have been struggling with. This phenomenon seems to prevent the users from contextualizing the connected datasets and formulating old and new knowledge in a human-interpretable way[20].

---

[14] https://archive.org/details/cihm_00341 accessed 2017-07-05.
[15] https://archive.org/details/cihm_27968 accessed 2017-07-05.
[16] https://archive.org/details/cihm_08523 accessed 2017-07-05.
[17] http://www.ala.org.au accessed 2017-07-05.
[18] http://www.biodiversitylibrary.org accessed 2017-07-05.
[19] http://eol.org accessed 2017-07-05.
[20] It could also be argued that this is a consequence of the "database-zation" of the web, chiefly driven by the idea of Semantic Web as the web of data.

In this regard, the JCDJ is an attempt to connect the two sides of the resources. Although it is always human users to interpret the aggregated data, the reading aids such as Wikipedia and route maps would significantly increase the level of storytelling, transforming pieces of fragmented data into contextual information. This is important especially when multi-disciplinary data is presented. Despite the criticism of being too generic, in the JCDJ project, Wikipedia is the answer for the users who are not familiar with the terminology outside their own area of expertise.

Another obvious concern is that the JCDJ is built upon preselected resources. It is still not completely satisfactory in this respect, because new discovery may be less likely than searching information on the entire web. In addition, there are more fundamental theoretical and technical questions how to search and identify distributed data (i.e. resource discovery), connect them more seamlessly on demand (i.e. resource connectivity), and create a story (i.e. information and knowledge formulation). Indeed, some of these questions are also articulated by the FAIR principles [11]. They tap into the needs for "machine actionability" for research data, which enables both humans and machines to discover and explore data more automatically and efficiently according to the user needs. Nevertheless, some of the solutions derived from experiences in this project are discussed below.

4   Technical Discovery of the API Journey

This section gives the summary of technical experiences discussed in the previous sections. In particular it outlines the challenges encountered in connection to the global discussions of API implementations and web services [7] as well as Open Data, in order to raise the issue of API applications in DH. The most notable points are listed below:

- Data structure varies considerably
- Real time multiple calls result in slow performance
- Many APIs use API keys which need to be manually requested
- Time consuming data normalization and decoding hampers the automatic processing

These discoveries are not something new. Richardson et al. [8] describe the characteristics of APIs very well. However, the actual use case of the JCDJ can be of substantial help to concretely specify future resolutions to address the technical issues mentioned in the FAIR principles. The first point is one of the most challenging tasks of the development. Even if the author is an experienced data analyst, it is not easy to analyze the data structure of an API. Ranging from the analysis of the data schema/model used for the interpretation of JSON serialization, domain knowledge as well as technical skills are required to "decode" the data. The problem is further multiplied by a number of APIs (and their domains) used. This is what makes interdisciplinary study more difficult, in fact. Not much can be done about the slow performance, as the application entirely depends on the external APIs, but in terms of practicality, it is not a trivial problem for data re-users. Both technological progress and financial investment are needed to enable truly useful distributed research. The issues of API keys are tricky, because the service providers need a certain level of security and trust. However, their use actually contradicts the philosophy of Open Data as there are services such as DBpedia which do not require them. The problem of data normalization is, for example, caused by different string separators for POST method. Typical separators are + and − and such a small difference requires the developers to normalize the data to make it compatible.

As Bülthoff and Maleshkova stated [1], the degree of human interaction is not at all neglectable. From an administrative human intervention of API key registration to a data normalization and curation, development with APIs is in fact time-consuming. Verborgh [10] harshly criticized the complexity and misuse of APIs, presenting critical issues in the DPLA and Europeana[21]. There were some counter-arguments, but it is somewhat ironical and contradictory to the theoretical goal of APIs that a lot of human interference is necessary, despite APIs being engineered for machine automation. In conclusion, Verborgh suggested not to ask APIs, because that will lead to the implementation of thousands of APIs that he thinks wrong. In addition, he sticks with HTTP content nego-tiation to provide various possibilities of machine-access such as JSON, ousting the need of (extra) APIs. Whether his opinion is favored or not, it is true that currently many APIs useful for DH may not offer an optimal access and data reuse environment. In contrast, DBpedia is implemented in a user friendly manner, offering staggering twelve formats of access for each resource and it does not require an API key. In addition, the URI can be effortlessly inferred by the human readable version of Wikipedia[22].

Not surprisingly, two popular web movements, Open Data and Web APIs, pose a controversial question to the data owners [3]. Colpaert analyzed types of data re-users, motivations of the data owners, and methods of data dissemination. Unlike Verborgh, he distinguished the Open Data to keep data highly available (data publishing) from Web APIs to serve data for a specific use case (data service), and suggested the approach of Open Data first and Web APIs second to satisfy different types of data re-users.

Versioning could become another factor of pain in the long run, although it has not influenced the JCDJ so far. On the websites of Europeana and Biodiversity Heritage Library, the API version changes are described in their documentation areas, implying the possibility of regular or irregular updates. Third party applications break easily if no regular maintenance is planned. Although updates are necessary in all computer systems, the nature of software dependencies for data and system integration (perhaps also for the broader context of software reusability and modularity) is destined for increasing overheads.

5 Data Democracy and Easy Data

5.1 Building User-Friendly APIs

While this article examined the negative aspects of APIs, there are certainly various ways to improve them. The last section is a little attempt to close the paper with some possible solutions. Hopefully, the author can find a clue to answer how DH can contribute to on-going discussions and the future of Open Data, and, at the same time,

---

[21] Note that DPLA and Europeana seem to support content negotiation, but API services remain.
[22] http://wiki.dbpedia.org/services-resources/datasets/data-set-39 accessed 2017-07-05.

benefit from it. Firstly, based on the lessons learned in the former sections, what the author suggests for the DH community is two-fold:

- Standardization of APIs (especially core data structure)
- User friendly GUI tool to use APIs more efficiently

The former concerns the theoretical framework of the data interoperability, whereas the latter is a technical solution to handle the result of the former. In both cases, it seems that a lack of technical coordination on API dissemination causes a lot of redundancies. This problem is, however, relatively simple to resolve, as long as DH implementers can share a common understanding and vision. If the APIs are standardized, technical problems could be minimized. It would become unnecessary to spend hours on analyzing the data structures/schemas and data types (e.g. JSON array, object, or string) of the third parties that the developers are not familiar with, and to change the data formats and encodings, as well as to clean data (e.g. problems concerning the separator for HTTP POST method, BASE64 encoding, format of geo-coordinates, etc.).

There are several players on the web who attempt to address this issue including JSON Schema[23] and API Blueprint[24]. Both specify a way of API documentation. In particular, Swagger[25] and OpenAPI[26] based on JSON Schema have been rapidly deployed in the APIs community over the last years. This framework is also related to the second point of the GUI tool (see below). In DH, Europeana API console was recently renovated with Swagger. As JSON Schema is still under development, there is room for improvement. For instance, APIs metadata could use the element names from a widely-used schema such as Dublin Core and DCAT[27] rather than proprietary ones. In addition, the metadata can specify if it is a data discovery API or datasets access API.

On the other hand, the competition among industry-standard creators always has advantages and disadvantages. The obvious downside is that APIs are documented using several standards, thus, "data mapping" would be necessary for interoperability, unless a de-facto standard is set. Nevertheless, if standardized API documentation became more popular, DH data would become more interoperable and reusable, suitable for automatic processing and data integration.

The GUI tool is especially targeted for non-developers to browse and organize data from APIs. For example, currently quite some efforts have to be sought to easily view and manipulate JSON. The tool should be able to visualize it in a standard web browser. Typical functions would be to detect the API parameters based on the data standardization above, thus being able to query, display, filter, sort, paginate data, depending on the API's specifications. The above-mentioned Swagger is equipped with some of such functionalities with a modern interface. However, this tool is not oriented toward data analysts, but software developers. What the author suggests is a client side tool which can also deals with multiple APIs. Desirably it could, for instance, map or unite different API datasets, if a foreign key can be specified. Other helpful functionalities include the

[23] http://json-schema.org accessed 2017-07-05.
[24] https://apiblueprint.org accessed 2017-07-05.
[25] https://swagger.io accessed 2017-07-05.
[26] https://github.com/OAI/OpenAPI-Specification accessed 2017-07-05.
[27] https://www.w3.org/TR/vocab-dcat accessed 2017-07-05.

possibility to search and identify APIs from the whole web. In fact, there are known API discovery websites[28], although many are manually curated. Instead APIs.io[29] and APIs.json[30] are among the initiatives to define high-level API metadata and an attempt to automatically index APIs. This would be a model for the proposed GUI tool if combined with a Swagger-like software and interface.

5.2   Data Liberation and Easy Data

In addition to the needs for user-friendly APIs, the author recognizes that there is still a high barrier for novice technicians to use Open Data via APIs in general. If Open Data is meant to be used by as many users as possible, as Murdock and Allen hinted [5], it is of crucial importance to make it as easily usable as possible for users. Currently, a lot of Open Data projects seem to be tailored for skilled developers and programming-savvy researchers who can write a code. This seems to be especially the case in DH, where many humanists may still not have competence in coding. There are also numerous debates about the programming skills of Digital Humanists [6]. In this respect, APIs and Open Data have not yet sufficiently achieved their goals to engage with the majority of the audience who would like to use data on their own.

In the author's opinion, it is not desirable to split user targets by different access methods. It is a popular opinion that web interfaces aim for non-technical users and APIs are for developers and machine access. But, APIs and web interfaces quite often do not offer the same service. For example, users cannot compare different datasets from different websites/domains by using a web interface, while APIs can as the JCDJ demonstrated. If APIs are claimed to be advantageous to offer more flexibility, equal accessibility and lower threshold for adaptation should be more carefully considered. It is mostly developers who generate APIs (if they are on the data provider side) and use APIs (if they are on the data consumer side), but it is data experts or curators who identify and examine the data to be used for their (research) purposes. Although the number of humanist programmers may be increasing and the territory of the two sides is becoming vague, this "digital divide" needs to be amended in general. APIs are neither a difficult concept nor technology, but, they seem to pose some psychological hurdle for non-technical people to work on. In addition, technical people do not seem to be particularly keen on sharing the technology with beginners, by providing easy tools and documentations. This is technology owning culture. If the right training is provided, everybody should be able to use them in the way they do with word processing or spreadsheet software.

In conclusion, Open Data needs a universal design. We should aim for the true liberation of data, a "Data Revolution", so that all types of people can use Open Data regardless of their level of technical knowledge and expertise. The envisioned result of the data revolution is to publish what the author would like to call "Easy Data". Going back to the background of this paper in the sections one and two, one may have realized by

---

[28] http://nordicapis.com/api-discovery-15-ways-to-find-apis accessed 2017-07-05.
[29] http://apis.io accessed 2017-07-05.
[30] http://apisjson.org accessed 2017-07-05.

now that the move from the first and second category (data and technology owners) to the third category ((re)users), and the blending of data ownership (Fig. 1) –the consequence of Easy Data– resonates with the true principles of Open Data initiatives as web democratization. This democracy would also call for more self-sufficient and independent research practices, which may liberate researchers from conventional institutional research approaches. As stated earlier, the FAIR principles have been recently discussed and promoted, but the next step: "battle for Easy Data in DH" has also begun and we will see what the future holds.

References

1. Bülthoff, F., Maleshkova, M.: RESTful or RESTless – current state of today's top web APIs. In: Presutti, V., Blomqvist, E., Troncy, R., Sack, H., Papadakis, I., Tordai, A. (eds.) ESWC 2014. LNCS, vol. 8798, pp. 64–74. Springer, Cham (2014). https://doi.org/10.1007/978-3-319-11955-7_6. Accessed 5 July 2017
2. Cohen, D.: Do APIs have a place in the digital humanities? (2005). http://www.dancohen.org/2005/11/21/do-apis-have-a-place-in-the-digital-humanities/. Accessed 5 July 2017
3. Colpaert, P.: Publishing Data for Maximized Reuse. SALAD@ESWC (2014). https://www.semanticscholar.org/paper/Publishing-Data-for-Maximized-Reuse-Colpaert/60abcbfc31437202e81b06cfed391974b294f09a. Accessed 5 July 2017
4. Maegaard, B., Van Uytvanck, D., Krauwer, S.: D5.4 CLARIN value proposition (2016). https://office.clarin.eu/v/CE-2016-0847-CLARINPLUS-D5_4.pdf. Accessed 5 July 2017
5. Murdock, J., Allen, C.: InPhO for all: why APIs matter. J. Chic. Colloq. Digit. Hum. Comput. Sci. 1–6 (2011). https://letterpress.uchicago.edu/index.php/jdhcs/article/view/88. Accessed 5 July 2017
6. O'Sullivan, J., Jakacki, D., Galvin, M.: Programming in the digital humanities. Digit. Sch. Hum. **30** (suppl_1), i142–i147 (2015). https://academic.oup.com/dsh/article/30/suppl_1/i142/364055/Programming-in-the-Digital-Humanities. Accessed 5 July 2017
7. Renzel, D., Schlebusch, P., Klamma, R.: Today's top "RESTful" services and why they are not RESTful. In: Wang, X.S., Cruz, I., Delis, A., Huang, G. (eds.) WISE 2012. LNCS, vol. 7651, pp. 354–367. Springer, Heidelberg (2012). https://doi.org/10.1007/978-3-642-35063-4_26. Accessed 5 July 2017
8. Richardson, L., Amundsen, M., Ruby, S.: RESTful Web APIs. O'Reilly Media Inc., Sebastopol (2013)
9. Schreibman, S., Hanlon, A.M.: Determining value for digital humanities tools: report on a survey of tool developers. Digit. Hum. Q. **4**(2) (2010). http://digitalhumanities.org/dhq/vol/4/2/000083/000083.html. Accessed 5 July 2017
10. Verborgh, R.: The lie of the API (2013). https://ruben.verborgh.org/blog/2013/11/29/the-lie-of-the-api/. Accessed 5 July 2017
11. Wilkinson, M.D., et al.: The FAIR Guiding Principles for scientific data management and stewardship. Sci. Data **3**, 160018 (2016). http://dx.doi.org/10.1038/sdata.2016.18. Accessed 5 July 2017

Enrichment of Accessible LD and Visualization for Humanities: MPOC Model and Prototype

Alicia Lara-Clares[✉], Ana Garcia-Serrano, and Covadonga Rodrigo

ETSI Informática, Universidad Nacional de Educación a Distancia – UNED, Madrid, Spain
{alara,agarcia,covadonga}@lsi.uned.es

Abstract. In this paper, it is presented how to enrich available linked data to facilitate the work of experts in the Musacces project (http://www.musacces.es/). First step has been implemented in the current version of a prototype MPOC1, that allows the access and visualization of information related with the Spanish Prado Museum (the target of the project). Main aim of the project is to work with semantic technologies in two ways: the management of available data from different resources creating in a first step a "local repository" for research purposes. The implemented functionalities are based on a crawler that extracts all the available metadata from an artwork and its artist, and on an enrichment component allowing the collaboration of the experts, in order to access and visualize the information guided by the user.

The second step is going to be the use of a semantic graph that can assist the experts (humanists) not only to create a textual-narrative that explains distinct stages of history but to create a management model that allows interaction with the semantic objects (and its relations) that make up the narration and its presentation modes (textual, sign language, etc.). This way, personalized narratives for certain groups of society can be created by the experts and being visualized from different points of view (storylines, maps, events lists...) as well as different presentation to the public, taking their abilities into consideration.

Keywords: Museum · Digital curation · Linked data · Narratives · Semantic graph

1 Introduction

In Digital Humanities, Digital Curation is the active and disciplined management of digital information over its entire cycle. The first purpose in this paper is to find a new creative way to handle semantic technologies, giving experts (humanists) the tools needed to manage the available information, create narratives to different users through a semantic graph as result.

According to Saeed, "semantics is the study of meaning communicated through language" [1]. A "semantic network" represents interconnected concepts [2] as in the case of Museo del Prado (MP) Spanish Museum, where these concepts and relations represents most artworks, artists, exhibitions and activities of the museum. With this

© Springer International Publishing AG 2017
E. Garoufallou et al. (Eds.): MTSR 2017, CCIS 755, pp. 327–332, 2017.
https://doi.org/10.1007/978-3-319-70863-8_31

information, it is possible to bring the public closer to art, by establishing new ways to model the concepts and their relationships and create adaptive narratives.

The work presented in this paper is framed in the Musacces project (http://www.musacces.es/), and includes a description of the LD extraction related task, and the first version of the prototype MPOC1 (http://catedra.lsi.uned.es/metadata/), that allows the access and visualization of information related with the museum. We are going to show how semantic technologies related with Linked Data, allow the integration and discovery of new information and knowledge by allowing the use of information by experts and further users.

The main antecedent of this work is the project DECIPHER [3] developed in 2012 based on the Curate [4] ontology to describe the stories of the museums in which the relation between plots (such as the cause and effect relation) can be expressed as events. Our work at the Musacces project is even more ambitious than the aforementioned in that it intends to give meaning to narratives by using a semantic graph (which starts with the data linked to artworks and authors) improved by the experts. This graph can be expressed as a knowledge graph with events, histories, characters, artworks and references. Also in [13, 18] can be shown previous experiences of some of the authors in the Digital Humanities domain contributing to organization models and linked data.

In the rest of the paper it is included a global view of the project task related with narrative modeling, and the description of the developed MPOC1 prototype.

2   A Proposal for Narrative Modeling

The term "narratology" was coined by Tzetan Tdorov in 1969 in his book "Grammaire du Décaméron" [5]. It refers to the study of narratives and their structure, as well as the way in which the structure has an effect in our perception of narratives. Narratology is a branch of Structuralism, which studies the nature of history rather than by parts, and of Semiotics and Semiology, which analyses communicative signs between societies and their behavior.

The Museo del Prado (https://www.museodelprado.es/) or Europeana [6] are two institutions that are very active in the open data world. This allows the research reusing the data stored in their webs. These web pages are visited by the software applications (crawlers) that crawl the web to import (copy and store) and index the information contained in them.

However, for the narrative to be interesting and to provoke a feeling of expectation in visitors, it is not only necessary to have the structured data and its relationships, but also to provide new information to eventually build a story/tale in which, for example, characters are identified and how they play a role in the stories is described. This is done by answering questions such as 'how does the artwork get to the museum?' or 'in which historical context is the story set in? Answers to these questions are very diverse and they can be combined in different ways. But… how can these answers be discovered? And how can they be articulated automatically?

To answer the first question a small workshop was organized between the experts (humanists) and technological partners (UNED) of the project. Before to make a proposal to answer the second question, we have been working in the conceptual model we want to use as the basis for a useful and accessible implementation of the goal.

In this work, we understand that events are facts that occurs in a time and/or space. The history is the union, sorted chronologically, of all the events. A plot is an unordered subset of events. The narrative form is the way that the information is presented (textual, sign language, video, audio, etc.). A narrative is a plot with a narrative form. Therefore, a narrative is the process to give a sense to, in principle, independent elements from the plot by presenting it in a narrative form selected. For example, a narrative can be explaining the life of the Spanish Infanta Margaret Theresa through the artworks in which she appears, and the temporal events (e.g. wars and reigns) that occurs when she lives; and presenting it in audio format as well as in a web page.

The available information through the metadata obtained with the MPOC1 prototype and the one created by the experts and their relationships are added to the MPOC local repository, in order to support the generation of semantic graphs like the one in Fig. 1.

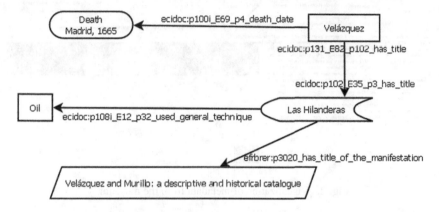

Fig. 1. Example of a semantic graph shown in the cited project workshop.

In order to show the experts the availability of information extracted from available web resources the MPOC1 prototype was available for them.

3   MPOC1: A Web-Based Prototype

The current Museo del Prado web is very complete and information is organized according to its own ontology [7]. This ontology has different standards and vocabularies that model all the information: CIDOC-CRM [8] model artworks, authors, exhibitions and activities; FRBR [9] models bibliographic records; SIOC [10] models the social contents, etc.

The standard CIDOC Conceptual Reference Model (CRM), provides definitions and structure to describe the concepts and relationships used in cultural heritage. Thanks to this, it was possible to access all the information as is explained in the following.

The web-based system of the museum integrates the metadata available from its semantic model as well as the data in JSON-LD format [11]. This format is a useful one to serialize Linked Data. This makes indexing easier to search engines and improves the search results.

In the project, in the first step of the research, it was needed to create a "local repository" of the metadata, and give that this information is currently available in the webpage, the Google Tool "Structured Data Testing Tool" [12] was used, to extract the metadata and relate it with its meaning.

Regarding content information, the related metadata is provided by the museum web page. For example, Fig. 2 shows the CIDOC property "ecidoc:p102_E35_p3_has_title" corresponding to the title of the artwork can be seen.

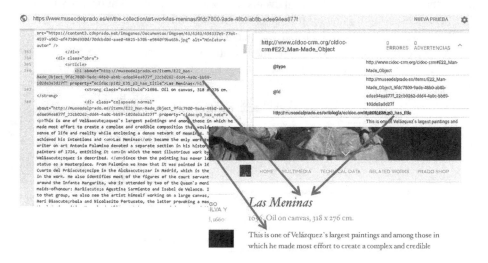

Fig. 2. Visualization of metadata from the museum.

MPOC1 prototype, create trough "on a fly" consults (posted by the experts) the so-called MPOC local repository maintaining metadata and structure and will allow the addition, within the "narrative" under construction, predefined objects such as characters (real and fictitious), events of the plot, the museum's artworks (and its associated metadata) and external references (e.g. Youtube or the press). Next step is the creation of narratives and its visualization with some degree of adaptation to different users (a second main goal of the project is to take into account users with special needs) (Fig. 3).

At present, MPOC1 (http://catedra.lsi.uned.es/metadata/) allows the search and visualization of artworks and their associated metadata and their modification. Besides, new artworks can be added from the museum's webpage on a fly.

Finally, some technical details about MPOC1: web application developed with the framework Laravel 5.4 [14]. To define the format and the composition of the Web pages, Bootstrap [15] was used. For DOM interactive events, jQuery libraries were used and Datatables [16] were used for the creation of dynamic tables using Ajax calls to the server, to get an efficient and fast system. The PHP SimpleHTMLDom [17] library was also used for the implementation of the crawler.

Fig. 3. Main MPOC1 webpage

The interactive prototype is obtained by using these technologies and by leveraging the possibilities offered by the HTML5 language (access password has to be requested).

4   Discussion

The aim of this work is the design of a model and its implementation to create narratives by using a semantic graph created from the information extracted from the "Museo del Prado" web site and enriching this information with the collaboration of experts, in order to bring the artworks and their context to the public, including which has special needs.

Some of the questions given in this track are addressed in this paper, starting with the information available in the web that uses metadata and using semantic technologies to create new ways to the management and access of the information.

Right now, the achieved result is the automatic extraction of the information available in the web of the museum by using different standards, implemented in MPOC1 as the first prototype. In the future, MPOC2 will implement a complete narrative model that allow experts to semi-automatically create narratives by using semantic graphs and finding the needed concepts. For example, the system could recommend some artworks to an expert that is creating a narrative when selecting an event in the same time period or location were object have been created.

Acknowledgements. This work is funded by the Spanish projects Musacces (S2015/HUM3494) and VEMODALEN (TIN2015-71785-R).

References

1. Saeed, J.I.: Introducing Linguistics: Semantics, 4th edn. Wiley-Blackwell, Hoboken (2015)
2. Simmons, R.F.: Semantic Networks: Their Computation and Use for Understanding English Sentences (1973)
3. DECIPHER Project|IMMA BLOG. https://immablog.org/2014/01/13/decipher-project/
4. Mulholland, P., Wolff, A., Collins, T.: Curate and storyspace: an ontology and web-based environment for describing curatorial narratives. In: Simperl, E., Cimiano, P., Polleres, A., Corcho, O., Presutti, V. (eds.) ESWC 2012. LNCS, vol. 7295, pp. 748–762. Springer, Heidelberg (2012). https://doi.org/10.1007/978-3-642-30284-8_57
5. Todorov, T.: Grammaire du "Décaméron": par Tzvetan Todorov. Mouton, Paris (1969)
6. Europeana Collections. http://www.europeana.eu/portal/es
7. Modelo Ontológico - Museo Nacional del Prado. https://www.museodelprado.es/modelo-semantico-digital/modelo-ontologico
8. Doerr, M., Ore, C.-E., Stead, S.: The CIDOC conceptual reference model: a new standard for knowledge sharing. In: Tutorials, Posters, Panels and Industrial Contributions at the 26th Internation Conference on Conceptual Modeling, vol. 83, pp. 51–56. Australian Computer Society, Inc., Darlinghurst, Australia, Australia (2007)
9. Doerr, M., LeBoeuf, P.: Modelling intellectual processes: the FRBR - CRM harmonization. In: Thanos, C., Borri, F., Candela, L. (eds.) DELOS 2007. LNCS, vol. 4877, pp. 114–123. Springer, Heidelberg (2007). https://doi.org/10.1007/978-3-540-77088-6_11
10. Berrueta, D., Brickley, D., Decker, S., Fernández, S., Görn, C., Harth, A., Heath, T., Idehen, T., Kjernsmo, K., Miles, A., et al.: SIOC core ontology specification. W3C Member Submission 12 June 2007. World Wide Web Consort (2007)
11. World Wide Web Consortium: JSON-LD 1.0: a JSON-based serialization for linked data (2014)
12. Herramienta de pruebas de datos estructurados. https://search.google.com/structured-data/testing-tool/u/0/
13. Castellanos, A., García-Serrano, A., Cigarrán, J.: Concept-based organization for semi-automatic knowledge inference in digital humanities: modelling and visualization. In: Proceedings of the 10th Conference of the International Society for Knowledge Organization (2015). https://www.researchgate.net/publication/291102972_Concept-based_Organization_for_semi-automatic_Knowledge_Inference_in_Digital_Humanities_Modelling_and_Visualization
14. Laravel 5.4. https://laravel.com/docs/5.4
15. Bootstrap Framework. http://getbootstrap.com/
16. Datatables. https://datatables.net/
17. Simple HTML DOM Parser. http://simplehtmldom.sourceforge.net/
18. Garcia-Serrano, A., Castellanos, A.: Modelling, access and visualization in the DIMH spanish project. In: Cámara, A. (ed.) Draughtsman Engineers Serving the Spanish Monarchy in the Sixteenth to Eighteenth Centuries, Fundación Juanelo Turriano, pp. 383–404 (2016). ISBN: 978-84-942695-8-5. http://juaneloturriano.oaistore.es/opac/ficha.php?informatico=00000233MO&idpag=1884503562&codopac=OPJUA

Author Index

Printed in the United States
By Bookmasters

Printed in the United States
By Bookmasters